Dear Beatle People
The Story of the Beatles North American Fan Club

Author:	Sara Schmidt
Designer/Illustrator:	Eric Cash
Editor:	Janet Davis
Layout:	Amy Hughes
Cover Illustration:	Eric Cash

Published by
Texas Book Publishers Association
www.texasbookpublishers.org
Houston Texas

DEAR PEOPLE BEATLE

The Story Of The Beatles North American Fan Club

AUTHOR: SARA SCHMIDT
DESIGNER/ILLUSTRATOR: ERIC CASH
EDITOR: JANET DAVIS
LAYOUT: AMY HUGHES
COVER ILLUSTRATION: ERIC CASH

TEXAS Book Publishers
Houston, Texas
WWW.TEXASBOOKPUBLISHERS.ORG

Copyright © 2022, Sara Schmidt.
Dear Beatle People

First Edition Published 2023

Library of Congress Control Number: 2023932435

Hardback ISBN: 978-1-946182-25-8
Soft Cover ISBN: 978-1-946182-26-5
ePub ISBN: 978-1-946182-27-2

The Beatles are copyright Apple Corps. Ltd., London, England. This book is not endorsed or authorized by The Beatles, Apple, nor any of their representatives. It is solely the author's work both in researching and editing.

All rights reserved. No part of this book may be used or reproduced in any manner whatsoever without written permission except in the case of brief quotations embodied in critical articles and reviews.

Where possible, we have endeavored to track down the copyright owner of every photograph used in this book. However, the proliferation of Beatles images across thousands of websites on the Internet can make it impossible to determine who the owner of a specific image is. If you are the owner of a photograph used in this book, and can prove ownership, we will be happy to credit you in future editions.

Author: Sara Schmidt
Designer/Illustrator: Eric Cash
Editor: Janet Davis
Layout: Amy Hughes
Cover Illustration: Eric Cash

Published by the Texas Book Publishers Association, Houston Texas
www.texasbookpublishers.org

Dedication:

In memory of Paul Shawn Inman.

He always encouraged me to follow my dreams and write books about the Beatles.

I did it, Shawn. I finished the book about the fan clubs.

Acknowledgements:

Much love and thanks go out to everyone who helped with this book. Richard Adler, Julie Alleva, Jamie Alonzo, Arma Andon, Jennifer Appel, Jeff Augsburger, Sandi Bellack, Elaine McAfee Bender, Eric Cash, Mary Cockram, Axel Corinth, Terry Crain, Andrew Croft, Kay Crow, Ivor Davis, Janet Davis, Marti Edwards, Dee Elias, Barb Fenick, Robyn Flans, Lori Freckleton, Patti Gallo, Rick Glover, Richard Goldman, Chuck Gunderson, Leslie Healy, Amy Hughes, Jo Ann Jaacks, Judy Johnson, Katie Jones, Kathleeen Kaiser, Richard Keen, Jude Southerland Kessler, Ida Langsam, Mark Lewisohn, Shery Liscio, Liverpool Central Library, Andy Mackey, Joanne Maggio, Joann Maloney, Pat Mancuso, Judy Matheson, JoAnne McCormack, Jude Milne, Victoria Moran, Mark Naboshek, New York Public Library, David Persails, Sam Priem, Pat Rainer, Jim Ramsburg, Linda S. Reincke-Woods, The Rock and Roll Hall of Fame Library and Archives, Rockaway Records, Rob Rodriguez, Joanne Russo, Coral Schmidt, David Shepard, Pat Simmons, Carrie Mae Snapp, Jay Spangler, Jean Steinert, Anita Thornton, Vivek Tiwary, Joseph A. Tunzi, Frank Visco, Laura Wishinsky, Patricia Woodcock.

In memory of those Beatles fan club officers and members we have lost: Fred Arnold, Lizzie Bravo, Kathy Burns, Karen Commarato, JoAnn DiFillippe, Cindi Gonzales, Dave Hull, Sandi Morse, Vikki Paradiso, Patti "Gripweed" Randall, Rusty Rhan, Evy Salas, Betty Shepard, Tommy Sullivan, Carol Webber, Pam Williams, and Bernice Young.

The writings and other items they left behind were helpful and beneficial.

Contents

Foreword 9

Introduction 11

Chapter 1 – Make Us Real Famous 15

Chapter 2 – The Fan Club People 29

Chapter 3 – Doing Something Nice
            and Having Fun in the Process 91

Chapter 4 – Growing and Maturing Fans 127

Chapter 5 – A New Sound and Movement 159

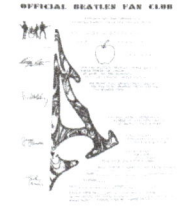

Chapter 6 – You Say You Want A Revolution? 193

Chapter 7 – Fan Facts and Fan Fiction 241

Chapter 8 – The Autumn for Fan Clubs 273

Chapter 9 – Dear ~~Beatle~~ People 303

Bibliography 333

OBFC Photos & Checklists 338

About the Author

Sara Schmidt is a second generation Beatles fan from Alton, Illinois. She is the author of the book *Happiness is Seeing the Beatles: Beatlemania in St. Louis*, and a contributing writer for *A is for Apple* (volumes 2 & 3). Her writing has been included in several Beatles books, magazines, and online articles.

Sara has spoken about the Beatles at conventions, libraries, and museums around the United States.

Since 2009, she has run the acclaimed website Meet the Beatles...For Real. Sara is an elementary school reading teacher who loves The Beatles, Disney pin trading, and traveling.

Author Sara Schmidt

The author and her mom Coral with Ringo Starr as he looks at Sara's first book: Happiness is Seeing The Beatles.

Foreword

Amid the din and perpetual motion of The Beatles arriving in the USA in the 1960s, the excitement, the unending city-to-city tours, the concerts, the press, the everlasting photographs... we (the fans) were also there. In fact, you might say that the Beatlemaniac fans were as much a part of the whole story as The Beatles themselves. The fans were part of the phenomena! We lined the streets to wave, lined the gates and rafters at the airports, made posters and signs to wave at their concerts, stood in front of hotels just trying to get one glimpse of our beloved Beatles. It was imperative that we showed The Beatles, the press, and the whole world just how much we loved and supported them.

I am **Patti Gallo-Stenman**, a member of the Three Beatle Babes. We are three original Sixties fans who banded together to tell the world about fandom. We were actually born out of a panel discussion moderated by the very talented and professional Sara Schmidt. The subject was Beatles Fan Clubs, which Sara was researching for this book. The Beatle Babes: Marti, Pat, and I were all presidents of Beatle-related fan clubs in the mid Sixties. Sara brought the panel to life. She is an incredible scholar of Beatleology, and now has authored this well-documented and important piece of Beatles history. I was a devout 14-year-old fan who kept a Sixties diary and scrapbooks, wrote a teenage column for a Philadelphia newspaper, co-founded The Victor Spinetti Fan Club, and later became a journalist. My story is told in my book, published by Cynren Press in 2018, *Diary of a Beatlemaniac: A Fab Insider's Look at The Beatles Era*.

I am **Pat Kinzer Mancuso**, a member of the Three Beatle Babes, a retired secretary of thirty-eight years and a retired travel agent specializing in Disney Parks. At age 17 (1964) I started The George Harrison Fan Club, which grew to 1000+ members and was advertised in *Teen Screen* magazine the next year. And thanks to George's mother asking him to sign our fan club charter, we became The Official George

Harrison Fan Club by June of 1966. Ours was the only club to be authorized by a solo Beatle. I rewrote the charter, went to visit George in person and asked him to sign it again on August 6, 1968 at his home in Esher. In 2005, I wrote a book about the entire experience titled *Do You Want to Know a Secret? The Story of the Official George Harrison Fan Club*. The sequel to this book, titled *Do You Promise Not to Tell?* was published in 2021.

I am **Marti Edwards**, a member of the amazing Three Beatle Babes, a retired teacher and artist. However, at age 15 (1963) I helped start and was president of The Chicagoland Beatle People Fan Club. Many life skills were learned while operating a large fan club of 1000+ members. Our club was eventually able to present an honorary plaque to The Beatles at their September 5, 1964, Chicago press conference. I shared my story in my book *16 in '64: The Beatles & The Baby Boomers*. Today, my mirror reflects the face of an old fan, but still an ardent fan. However, if I close my eyes and listen to all those wonderful and familiar Beatle songs, I am transformed back in time and into that young girl that was so impressed and captivated by The Beatles. We found and loved The Beatles and in doing so we also found ourselves.

Sara Schmidt took on the incredible and daunting task of writing a book about all the various fan clubs and how they operated. We wondered why she would want to do this, especially in light of the fact that she was a second generation Beatles Fan and therefore did not live through it. The research alone took her several years. However, after meeting Sara at the Chicago Fest for Beatles Fans and talking with her, we realized that if anyone could do the job, it was Sara. Sara has an old soul and probably knows more about The Beatles than many first-generation fans.

    We Beatle Babes have excitedly followed Sara's literary journey and we were honored to be interviewed by her for this book. She has also coordinated some of our Zoom and podcast presentations as The Three Beatle Babes. We are thankful for her friendship and hard work, and wish her the best. We know that you will also delight in her amazing research and this book, *Dear Beatle People: The Story of the North American Beatles Fan Clubs*.

    We Love You Sara... Yeah! Yeah! Yeah!

The Three Beatle Babes

Introduction

Individuals known as fans have been around for as long as there have been authors, actors, singers, and other performers for people to admire. Fans are a group of people that show devotion toward an artist. They often band together and have their own fashion, language, and customs. The main focus has always been to see or even meet the object of their desire. In 1842, British author Charles Dickens paid a visit to the United States. Thousands of fans tried to meet him.

When motion pictures became popular, fans of the actors began to get together and read movie magazines such as *Photoplay* or *Modern Screen*. The fans who read these magazines were typically teenage girls. They would cut out photos and talk about their favorite silent film stars, especially Rudolph Valentino.

Movie magazines and motion picture studios learned about the fans and began to form fan clubs for teenagers to join. These clubs offered glossy photos and membership cards while promoting the movie stars' latest films. Soon the fan clubs began to target younger viewers. Two of the largest fan clubs in the 1930s were for Mickey Mouse and Shirley Temple.

The 1940s saw a surge in fan clubs for not just movie actors but also singers. Teenage girls known as "bobby soxers" fell for many big bands and crooners. The largest fan club at this time was for Frank Sinatra. There were two types of clubs fans could join: official and independent. The official clubs were run with the artists' knowledge and participation. Teenagers themselves started the independent fan clubs. They would write newsletters, organize activities to do together, and trade glossy photographs with one another.

Both rock and roll music and television became important parts of teenage life in the 1950s. Buddy Holly, Ricky Nelson, Chuck Berry, Fabian, *American Bandstand*, and Annette Funicello all had clubs full of devoted fans. None of those compared to the clubs for the King of Rock and Roll, Elvis Presley. In the United States, clubs for Elvis began to form in 1956. Elvis' manager, Colonel Tom Parker,

Elvis Presley.

saw the independent fan clubs as a great marketing strategy and initially encouraged their creation. As a result, Elvis club officers were sent information about upcoming albums, concerts, and movies, and told to spread the word. This strategy helped Elvis' records to sell out all around the United States. A 16-year-old, Kay Wheeler, started the first and largest Elvis Presley Fan Club. Membership grew to 60,000 teenage fans. Kay received thousands of letters a week. Because she was the president of his fan club, she was able to meet Elvis seven times.

Elvis was not only popular in the United States but also in Britain. The Official Elvis Presley Fan Club of Great Britain and the Commonwealth was founded in 1957. Members received photographs, a membership card, a badge, and a bi-monthly newsletter. The original founders ran the club until 1961.

While they were not known to be members of the Elvis fan club, John Lennon, Paul McCartney, George Harrison, and Ringo Starr were big fans of the King of Rock and Roll. Elvis' music significantly influenced the four guys in Liverpool, England and the music they were making.

The Beatles (John, Paul, George, and Pete Best) were playing lunchtime

One of the first Beatles fan club membership cards. Roberta "Bobby" Brown was the club's secretary.

shows at the Cavern Club in Liverpool regularly in 1961. At that time, they had a large following of fans. One of those fans was a young man named Bernie Boyle. Bernie mentioned to the Cavern Club's compere, Bob Wooler, that the group should have a fan club. Bob introduced Bernie to two girls, Maureen and Jennifer, who had the same idea. The first Beatles fan club was formed in September 1961 with Bernie as president. As The Beatles became more popular, the club membership grew. Soon it became too much for the original officers to handle.

Paul McCartney knew that having a fan club was important, so he asked a girl named Bobby Brown to take over the club. Bobby worked closely with The Beatles' new manager, Brian Epstein, to relaunch the fan club. Brian realized that the fans were The Beatles' driving force and wanted them to have a professional-looking club. He never expected the dues collected for club membership to yield a profit. He was even willing to absorb any losses from the club because he valued the fans' support.

By 1962, Bobby had a serious boyfriend and was no longer interested in running the club. She had a friend, Freda Kelly, who had been helping her. Freda was happy to take over. Freda became the official fan club secretary at a very exciting time. Ringo had just replaced Pete as the drummer and The Beatles had released their first single, *Love Me Do*. More people became interested in joining the fan club, so Freda moved the headquarters from her home to Brian's office.

The fan club remained there until Beatlemania took over Britain in 1963. The club moved to London later that year, but Freda chose to stay in Liverpool and became the fan club secretary for her hometown. The club had its own office in London and branches with club secretaries around the country. The Official Beatles Fan Club was well organized and professional, just as Brian wanted.

Chapter 1 — Make Us Real Famous

At the beginning of 1963, The Beatles were starting to make waves throughout England. Freda Kelly, from The Beatles' hometown of Liverpool, ran their first fan club, which had been established two years earlier.

At this time, they were almost completely unknown in North America, but a few North American girls had heard their music and liked the different sound. These early fans became pioneers in The Beatles' North American fan clubs that would soon be starting there.

Kathie: The First Beatles Fan in the United States

One of the earliest Beatles listeners was Kathie Sexton from San Diego, California. When she was 13 years old, Kathie wrote to some of the people listed in *Teen Screen* magazine's pen pal section. She began corresponding with a few boys in England, and traded records with them through the mail. She would send them the popular surf records from California, and they would send her the latest English hits. In late 1962, Kathie received her first Beatles single, *Love Me Do*. Instantly liking it, she eagerly read newspaper clippings and other information about the lads that her English pen pals had enclosed. Kathie was intrigued by it all, and became one of the first Beatles fans in the United States.

"At that time, I was head of the dance committee in my junior high," Kathie recalls. "So I took the record and played it for the kids, and the kids actually liked to dance to it."

One day in the spring of 1963, Kathie was sick and didn't go to school. She was listening to the Top 40 station KDEO on her Emerson radio when the disc jockey announced that he was going to play a song from a weird group popular in England. They had a strange, buggy name. "I said, 'Well, you're an idiot,'" Kathie remembered. "I didn't know who this guy was, so I called him up and told him that what he said was all wrong. I told him, 'They are a huge group in England. They're up-and-coming. They're really cute. Their music is very popular. Their name is a tribute to Buddy Holly and the Crickets.' And he goes 'How do you know all this?' I said, 'Well, I have all these newspaper articles and their records because I have English pen pals.' He invited me out to the radio station. I was 15 years old. I took a box of clippings that had been sent to me, the records, and he played them, and the afternoon disc jockey interviewed me. Before I left, he told me to let him know if I hear anything more about The Beatles."

Kathie continued to hear more about The Beatles from her pen pals. As she started high school in the fall, she did not think much about her day at the radio station. Then came November 1963, when The Beatles' new album *With The Beatles* was released. Kathie's neighbor was a secretary at the station, and she told Kathie's mother that Kathie should call the program director. Kathie's mom took her back to the station, and Kathie spent the day telling the program director, Glen, about The Beatles and other British groups.

Afterward, Glen said she had a good radio voice and asked if she would like to be the station's high school representative, which involved taping a show that would air once a week. Kathie and her mom were both excited about this new opportunity, and worked out a schedule. Glen also told her that she should start a chapter of The Beatles fan club, and gave her a phone number to call in New York. The people there would tell her how to do it.

In November, when Kathie called New York, they told her that she would have to join the Los Angeles chapter of the fan club. Kathie tried to explain that San Diego was over 100 miles from Los Angeles, and most San Diego radios couldn't even get the L.A. radio stations. Her reasoning was ignored, and Kathie

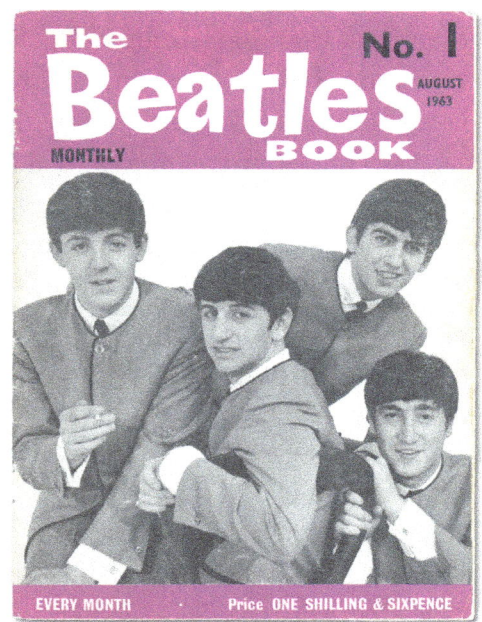

The Beatles Book Monthly, Issue No. 1. August 1963.

decided to give up on her idea for a San Diego chapter, but her local radio station was still promoting a Beatles fan club, and Kathie was listed as its head. Girls were starting to mail her dollar bills to join up.

"I had enough money, and I told my parents, 'I'm calling London. I'll call Brian Epstein's office, and I'm getting a Beatles fan club — an official one,'" Kathie says, still remembering her determination. "I called, and I talked to a girl named Maureen Payne. I had to call her a couple of times, and finally, in December, she issued me the 11th charter of the National Beatles Fan Club. It took off from there." The name Kathie gave to her new Beatles fan club was The Yeah Beatles Fan Club.

Early Beatlemania in Canada

The Beatles had also impressed a girl named Jody Fine, who lived in what was then Canada's largest city, Montreal. In the spring of 1963, Jody and her friend Valerie Jaffe had seen a photo of The Beatles in a British newspaper. Because she liked their looks, Jody wrote a letter to the boys. "I guess they took a special interest because I was about the first person to write them from North America," Jody told the *Montreal Gazette* in 1964. On an impulse Jody decided to start the club, and was thrilled when she received a photo of The Beatles with a special handwritten thank you from John Lennon. "Make us real famous," it said. "So we can come visit you." By June, the Canadian branch of The Official Beatles Fan Club was listed in the summer newsletter with Valerie as the contact person.

At the beginning, The Official Beatles Fan Club in London didn't give Jody much material. She got a negative of a Beatles photograph, and used it to develop prints for new club members. She obtained members through an ad she placed in the newspaper and *The Beatles Book Monthly* magazine. The magazine had been operating in the U.K. since August of 1963.

In 1963, Trudy Medcalf of Toronto, Ontario spent her summer with relatives in England. She was 13, but her cousins were slightly older. These cousins adored The Beatles, and Trudy watched the group on television. When the family went on a holiday to the seaside town of Margate, Trudy got to see The Beatles in concert, and she became a full-fledged Beatlemaniac herself. At a different relative's house, she spotted an article in a newspaper about starting a Beatles fan club. "I didn't have a lot to do," Trudy recalls. "So I wrote to the address of The Beatles fan club in London. I told them that I wanted to start a fan club in Canada and told them I was 17 because I thought that was old enough to start a fan club. About two months later, I heard back from them. They said, 'Sure, you can start a fan club.' They didn't say anything else. I had never even been in a fan club. I didn't even know what running a fan club was all about."

Trudy decided to see if she could get help from a local radio station. She went to the station CHUM in Toronto, and ended up going on air to talk about the fan club. She gave out her home address and phone number. Soon letters and telephone calls came pouring in from teenagers hungry for any information about The Beatles. These teens asked for the boys' names, which one sang on each song, their favorite colors, and other basic things. Trudy also started receiving letters from fans who saw her address in The Official Beatles Fan Club magazine, *The Beatles Book Monthly*. By November, there were 300 members of The Official Beatles Canadian Fan Club. Trudy's neighbor Dawne Hester came on board as the club's vice president to help with the incoming mail. Two years later, this club became the largest Beatles fan club outside of England, with 90,000 members.

At the start, Trudy tried to answer each letter by hand. Things quickly got too big for the two 14-year-olds to handle, and CHUM got involved. "I went in to

CHUM," Trudy recalled. "And they had drop-down bins that held letters, and each bin had 5,000 letters. He pulled two of these bins, so 10,000 letters from fans."

For a cost of 25 cents, each member received a membership card and a newsletter written by Trudy. The membership cards, made by CHUM, had The Beatles Fan Club on the front, and a Dezo Hoffman Beatles photograph on the back. The newsletters were four pages long. "I wrote these newsletters, and it

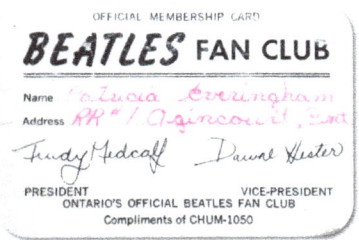

Above: CHUM 1050 AM Ontario Official Beatles Fan Club card, front and back.
Patricia Woodcock collection

Left: Ontario's Official Beatles Fan Club creator Trudy Medcalf's, response to Beatles fan Taya who wrote in asking for information.
Andrew Croft collection

was quite wonderful because CHUM never changed anything," said Trudy. "They printed them up, and they had a distributing company that sent them out. People would send 25 cents to The Official Canadian Beatles Fan Club in care of CHUM." Trudy was getting Beatles information frequently from the fan club in London. She was also corresponding with The Beatles' press officer, Tony Barrow. Barrow helped supply Trudy with Beatles photographs from the U.K. Club and NEMS so she could give them to club members.

THE OFFICIAL ONTARIO BEATLES FAN CLUB

TRUDY MEDCALF
President

DAWNE HESTER
Vice-President

Mailing address: CHUM Radio, Toronto 7

VOLUME 1   FEBRUARY, 1964

MEET TORONTO'S OFFICIAL BEATLE PEOPLE!

TRUDY MEDCALF ... is 14 years old, was born in Luton, Bedfordshire,
President of England. She attends Midland Avenue Secondary
Beatle's Fan School and is in Grade 10. Trudy's hobbies include
Club for playing drums, writing poetry, looking through mus-
Ontario. eums and of course, The Beatles. When she completes
her schooling, Trudy would like to be a comedy
script writer for TV. Her favorite colors are
bright red and pink (not together!). Trudy's favorite foods are tea and Chinese food.

DAWNE HESTER ... is 14, was born in London, England. She also at-
Vice-President tends Midland Avenue Secondary School where she is
in Grade 9. Dawne is one of the original organi-
zers of the Beatle Fan Club in Ontario along with
Trudy Medcalf. Dawne's hobbies include playing
guitar, writing poetry and stories and the Beatles.
She would like to be a foreign correspondent for a
newspaper when she completes her schooling. Dawne's
favorite colors are Beatle Black and hazel (the
color of Paul McCartney's eyes!). Her favorite
foods are roast beef and Yorkshire pudding (what
else?).

A LETTER FROM TRUDY MEDCALF, President, Official Beatles Fan Club for
Ontario.

Dear Beatle People:

First, I want to express my sincere thanks for all the wonderful
cards and letters you have sent me saying how much you enjoy the
Beatles many records and the Paunch and Trudy programs on CHUM.

The past months have been very exciting ones for the Beatles and myself here in Toronto because the fellows have continually held down
the top spots on the CHUM CHART and I have had the opportunity to
make many new friends through my appearances on CHUM.

It would be impossible for me to answer all the letters I have received here at the radio station, and the office which CHUM has so
kindly made available for me, is piled high with bags of mail. My
only way to thank all of you is by printing this letter in the Official Beatle Fan Club Letter, and on behalf of myself and the
Beatles may I once again say THANK YOU.

Front page of the first issue of The Official Ontario Beatles Fan Club newsletter. February 1964.

CHAPTER 1 – MAKE US REAL FAMOUS

The Official Canadian Beatles Fan Club introduction letter. Biographies of The Beatles as a group and individuals prepared by Jody Fine of Montreal, Quebec, Canada in early 1964. Jody would meet The Beatles on stage at the band's September 8, 1964 appearance in Montreal. Andrew Croft collection

Because Trudy had the most up-to-date Beatles information, in December, CHUM asked her to do a radio show. "On Fridays, a taxi would come and pick me up at my high school and take me to the CHUM station. We would tape a week's worth of half-hour shows. After I would tape each night, a technician would go in and edit the three or four songs that went into the right slots."

The First Official Beatles Fan Club in the United States

Please Please Me U.K. LP released March, 1963.

Two American sisters attending boarding school in England served as catalysts for the first official Beatles fan club in the United States. In early 1963, Carol and Jenny Condit left their home in Mountain Lakes, New Jersey and began attending the same school their British mother had attended, The Convent of the Sacred Heart, located in Hove on Britain's southeast coast. The 16-year-old and her 13-year-old sister were allowed to play pop music on the weekends, so on the girls' trips to Brighton they bought The Beatles' *Love Me Do* single, followed by their *Please Please Me* album. "We listened to it nonstop and read everything on The Beatles we could find," Carol remembered.

That summer, Carol's best friend from home, Karen Commarato, visited for two months. As soon as Karen arrived, Carol wanted her to hear The Beatles: "Carol said to me, 'You've got to hear this new group that's popular over here.' She played me a Beatles record. I loved it immediately. It was a new sound. I loved the music, and I was a Beatles fan after one play. It hit me. It was happy music." When the first issue of *The Beatles Book Monthly* came out in August, the girls pored over the magazine, with Carol claiming John as her favorite and Karen liking George. There they found information about The Official Beatles Fan Club. The two friends came up with the idea of having an American branch of the club. The first step was to call the fan office, which had recently moved from Liverpool to London. This task was given to Carol's little sister, Jenny, who went into a phone booth to place the call. "I remember being forced on the phone at 14 years old saying 'We're Beatles fans. We're American, and we want to start a fan club for The Beatles in America.' They said, 'Well, come on over and talk about it.'"

Carol recalls making the trip to Monmouth Street in London to the fan club office. "Can you imagine how intimidated we would have been to go to an office above a sex shop? It was just a stairway to some little offices jam-packed with photos on the wall of The Beatles, Gerry and the Pacemakers, everyone. We talked to a young woman and told her, 'We're American. We're big fans of The Beatles, we've got friends in America who want to run the American fan club,' and they kind of glommed on to us."

The location of the Beatles Fan Club in London (2017).

Meanwhile, Karen had returned to New Jersey and was trying to recruit an American Beatles fan base. She had bought the *Please Please Me* album in England, and as her senior year of high school started that September, she shared the music with her classmates. Both boys and girls gathered at Karen's aunts' house after school to listen to The Beatles. They liked the new sound. In October, Karen and her friends sent a barrage of postcards to WABC radio station, asking them to play Beatles music. They were thrilled when they heard *She Loves You* one Saturday morning.

The Beatles manager, Brian Epstein, 1963.

NEMS business card, 1963.

At the end of 1963, Karen got a letter from Carol, who wrote that The Beatles were soon coming to America, and the London office wanted to know if Karen would be the U.S. address for the club. "Shortly thereafter, a carton arrived from London with different color sheets with a bio of each Beatle, and an autographed photograph, and also a Beatles blanket," said Karen.

Back in England, the Condit sisters also received a box from the London office. "They provided us with enormous stacks of photos of The Beatles, some of them conveniently pre-autographed," said Jenny. "They started to divert mail to us, the American mail. It started coming by the mail-sack. And for some period of time, at least we dealt with it. People would send money. The deal was, they sent money, and in return, they got a picture, a newsletter, and whatever." The sisters were receiving the mail from Americans that the London office had not answered. As Carol explained: "The office was sitting on mail from the U.S. which they'd not dealt with yet, and we got it. There was a mailbag full of letters. Many American kids were coming to Europe between high school and college – maybe they'd been writing."

Jenny and Carol worked on answering the first big batch of American letters, and then those became Karen's job. One of the sisters' duties was to forge The Beatles' autographs on photos, and they got good at it. Answering for The Beatles was exciting, but it was a surreal experience, as Jenny

Beatles U.K. Fan Club welcome letter. Early 1963.

CHAPTER 1–MAKE US REAL FAMOUS

THE Beatles

In the annals of British show business 1963 has already gone down as The Year Of The Beatles. In 1964 it seems totally certain that the group will consolidate its position as an internationally renowned theatre, television, recording and film attraction. The Beatles have already visited Sweden for a series of quite phenomenal concert appearances. Immediately after their Christmas/New Year season at London's Finsbury Park Astoria they will open for three weeks at the Olympia in Paris. Three days after their final performance in Paris The Beatles will fly to New York to top the bill of no less than three coast-to-coast productions of The Ed Sullivan television show. Two of these appearances will be live transmissions on consecutive Sunday evenings and the third will be filmed for screening a little later on. Towards the end of February The Beatles enter a completely new phase of their history-making career when they begin work on their first major film for United Artists with that distinguished playwright Alun Owen writing the screenplay script.

The list of 1963 triumphs and achievements notched up by The Beatles reads in the form of a series of record-splintering 'firsts' which are unprecedented.

At one time in November there were three EP discs by the group in the Top Twenty when the million-selling August-released single "She Loves You" made its dramatic return to the Number One chart spot after several weeks of sinking and rising around the second, third and fourth positions. Even this was not to be the sum total of the group's fantastic domination of the Autumn hit parade for The Beatles' fifth single, "I Want To Hold Your Hand", came flashing in from nowhere to top the charts at the end of November and the LP album "With The Beatles" came scuttling into the half-million sales bracket normally reserved for the nation's fastest-selling singles.

Before November? The three singles, "Please, Please Me", "From Me To You" and "She Loves You", had been chart-toppers of exceptional strength. The group's first LP album had held its absolute monarchy over the microgroove best-sellers for over six months. The "Twist And Shout" EP was the first release of its kind to penetrate the hit parade and set itself high up amongst the contemporary Top Five singles. A long awaited top-of-the-bill debut on television's "Sunday Night At The London Palladium" in October came less than 72 hours before the announcement that The Beatles had accepted an invitation to appear in the 1963 Royal Variety Performance at the Prince of Wales Theatre, London, on Monday 4 November.

Now an old year is rounded off and a fresh one begun during the group's appearance in "The Beatles Christmas Show". Only a fortnight before the first pre-London presentation of this show B.B.C. Television celebrated Saturday 7 December as a sort of national small-screen Beatles day by televising a special edition of "Juke Box Jury" together with a half-hour stage performance which were screened on the same evening after being filmed at the Liverpool Empire during a Northern Area Convention of The Official Beatles Fan Club.

So far as Britain's record-collecting public are concerned The Beatles may be said to have been born on Friday 5 October 1962 - the day when Parlophone Records released that first "Love Me Do" single. But the amazing story of these four highly individual young personalities goes back much further than that.

JOHN WINSTON LENNON was born on 9 October 1940. His life began in the Liverpool suburb of Woolton and he went to school at Dovedale Primary and Quarrybank Grammar School before becoming a student at Liverpool College of Art.

RINGO STARR was born Richard Starkey on 7 July 1940. A resident of Dingle, he was educated at St. Silas' School, Dingle Vale Secondary Modern and Riversdale Technical College.

JAMES PAUL McCARTNEY was born on 18 June 1942. His home is in the Allerton area of Liverpool and he was one grade ahead of George Harrison at Liverpool Institute.

GEORGE HARRISON was born on 25 February 1943. This youngest Beatle lives at Speke and attended the same junior school as John Lennon before following his grammar school studies at the Institute.

The embryonic musical development of these four boys can be traced back to 1955 when John was instrumental in the setting up of The Quarrymen Skiffle Group which operated with moderate success at local youth clubs in the Woolton area.

Paul came on the Quarrymen scene shortly afterwards, having been introduced to John via a mutual friend. George, meantime, had established himself as a leading light of an even more youthful schoolboy group known as The Rebels.

According to indisputable legend George met John on the top deck of a Corporation bus; one hour and one audition later he joined The Quarrymen although, in 1958, he was still at school and his appearances with the skiffle unit were far from regular. In the months which followed the demand for skiffle shrank at an alarming rate. Elsewhere in towns and cities all over Britain redundant groups pitched their guitars into dustbins and turned to other hobbies.

Sara Schmidt collection

Front of letter sent out to Beatles Fan Club members in the United States from Karen Commarato. Early 1964.

For some reason Merseyside groups were not discouraged to the same extent and it was from the dying skiffle boom that the Mersey Beat drew its first breath. The Quarrymen ceased to exist but John, Paul and George met for frequent front-room practice sessions using stacks of American rhythm and blues records as the basic starting-point for their improvised music-making. As Johnny And The Moondogs they made a brief 'come-back' by entering and winning a Carroll Levis contest.

In 1960, turning down a number of other proposed group names (including Long John And The Silver Men) the boys went off to Scotland as 'The Silver Beatles' to accompany a local vocalist, Johnny Gentle, on tour. That summer, deputising for another Mersey Beat combo, they were asked to make their first trip to Hamburg. They left in August with bassman Stu Sutcliffe and drummer Pete Best augmenting the original trio.

If anything taught these boys to withstand the abnormal onslaught of the hard work they were to find in 1963 it was those strenuous weeks in Germany at the Kaiserkellar and Top Ten clubs. Hamburg also left the boys with concrete memories in the form of more professional equipment. The days when two or three of them would plug their secondhand guitars into a single over-worked amplifier were over.

Between December 1960 and the end of the following year many, many encouraging and disappointing experiences sent forward and set back the group which had now become known to thousands of Merseysiders as The Beatles. There is space here to recall only one 1961 landmark - the one which was to alter the entire course of The Beatles' future. This was the meeting of Brian Epstein and The Beatles in Liverpool's subterranean cellar of beat, The Cavern.

There can be no doubt that the revolutionarily rhythmic music of The Beatles paved the way for the 1963 record industry boom which has been pigeon-holed under that over-simplified classification of 'The Mersey Beat Craze'. It is equally true to say that Brian Epstein was the brilliant young man responsible for transferring The Beatles from local to national supremacy. He signed the group shortly before the announcement of the 1961 popularity poll conducted by the North West's Mersey Beat publication. The Beatles were the outright winners of the 1961 and 1962 poll.

Many milestones have to be bypassed in a brief commentary of this nature. There is not space to chronicle in any detail the period when John, Paul and George plucked out the frenzied musical setting for a stripper in Liverpool's Chinatown quarter. Nor to make more than passing mention of the busy build-up which Brian Epstein gave his freshly-signed quartet of stars throughout 1962. Nor to describe the long months of hard work put in by The Beatles and their manager before the ultimate release of "Love Me Do" on record. Incidentally, drummer Ringo Starr joined The Beatles as Pete Best's replacement in the middle of all this bustling pre-disc activity a few months before the signing of a Parlophone contract.

The more recent chapters of The Beatles' unique story have been unfolded under the glare of the public spotlight. They have been followed with zealous avidity by millions of teen 'n' twenties record fans to whose enormous number a fair quantity of mums 'n' dads generation Beatle People have been added in the later half of 1963. The Official Beatles Fan Club now boasts a membership larger than that of any other British artist in pop music history. Advance record sales of half a million copies have seldom been accumulated before but are now almost commonplace so far as The Beatles are concerned. On the recent November/December stage tour every theatre box office clocked up new records - not a single spare seat stayed empty at any one of the more-than-seventy performances given by The Beatles in towns and cities all over the country.

The Christmas Show seen at this theatre tonight stars one of the most versatile, most ingenious and most popular vocal/instrumental teams ever to perform here. This production forms a thoroughly worthy climax to The Year Of The Beatles, a magnificent culmination which must make another lasting landmark in the group's successful career whatever new glories come the way of this fabulous foursome in the first months of 1964.

Reprinted from the Programme of "The Beatles Christmas Show" held at the Finsbury Park Astoria, London, December 1963 - January 1964.

Back of letter sent out to Beatles Fan Club members in the United States from Karen Commarato. Early 1964.

explained: "Here I was, a 14-year-old reading the mail of many other 14-year-olds proposing marriage to Ringo Starr."

The mail was slow coming into Karen's house at first. After short clips of the Fab 4 ran on a few news programs in November and December, letters began to trickle in to Karen's home address. She didn't realize that this was just a small preview of the volume of mail her fan club would soon experience.

Beatles (U.S.A.) Ltd. Begins

In the spring of 1963, Debbie Gendler, a 13-year-old Beatles fan living in the New York City area, was fortunate enough to get a copy of the *Please Please Me* album straight from England. With the record came an advertisement telling readers: "If you love The Beatles, join the fan club." It included the club's address. In late May, Debbie wrote a letter saying that she wanted to join the club. She did not hear back from the fan club, but she remained a loyal fan throughout that summer.

In late October, The Beatles' manager, Brian Epstein, responded to Debbie's fan mail request with a Western Union telegram. He said he was coming to New York City to arrange for The Beatles' upcoming appearances in America. He wanted to meet with fans and explore the possibilities of working together. Listed in the telegram was a New York City phone number, which Debbie's mother called. It led to the law office of Walter Hofer.

Hofer was a young business and music lawyer who had met Epstein through Dick James, The Beatles' London music publisher. Hofer became instrumental in

The Official Beatles Fan Club card. 1964.

establishing Epstein in the United States. He held a party at his home in honor of Epstein and invited many top American music executives to network with the Liverpool manager. Hofer was also one of the key figures in negotiations between The Beatles and *The Ed Sullivan Show*. Epstein developed a good working friendship with Hofer and his wife Sondra, hiring the American to be the NEMS New York attorney. Epstein knew the importance of a Beatles fan club. He'd been key in developing The Official Beatles Fan Club in the U.K., along with Freda Kelly. Hofer agreed to use a small room in his office suite as the center for the fan club in the United States.

When Debbie's mom called, she learned that Epstein and Hofer would like to meet with her daughter on November 11, 1963. Because that was Veterans Day, a U.S. holiday, Debbie did not have school. Her father drove her into the city to find out exactly what these two men wanted.

"I don't think they were expecting someone quite 13 years old," said Debbie. "I walked into the room, and Walter Hofer was there, a tiny man with a slight German accent. Brian was standing there with another man who also had a British accent. My first thought of Brian was that he was so elegant. I remember his glistening cuff links. They were so bright and sparkling. He greeted us nicely, asked me a little bit about myself. He looked at me and said 'I'm looking for someone to organize fans and run the fan club and get involved in organizing because fans are so important to The Beatles' success.'" Being so young, Debbie had to turn down the offer because she had high school and college ahead of her. The entire meeting lasted only 15 minutes, but Debbie was impressed by Epstein's professionalism. "He thanked me for coming. He was really very nice with my Dad. Everyone shook hands and were very, very civil."

Before she left, the secretary at the front desk stopped Debbie. At Walter Hofer's request the secretary wrote down Debbie's phone number. Hofer had a feeling that the fan club might need her help at some point. As 1963 was ending, Hofer had no idea just how much help he was going to need by the end of 1964.

Chapter 2 — The Fan Club People

As 1964 began, teenagers across the United States experienced the first wave of Beatlemania. The Beatles' U.S. record label, Capitol Records, contacted many AM radio stations about starting Beatles fan clubs to promote the group's upcoming arrival. As Chicago disc jockey Clark Webber explained, this promotion was beneficial for both the radio stations and The Beatles. "Radio and The Beatles were a perfect marriage because both used the other so effectively.

We were into it because we recognized it was a massive infusion into a very sick body [that] had become stagnant, and it desperately needed that excitement. Capitol Records desperately needed that hit. We both got on the bandwagon of massive teenage hysteria and exploited it."

Capitol Records and AM Radio Stations

Capitol Records got things rolling at the start of the New Year by sending disc jockeys pin-back buttons that said, "Be A BEATLE Booster!" The first radio station that joined with Capitol Records in starting a fan club was "America's first Top 40 radio station," WTIX in New Orleans, Louisiana. The membership cards were printed *"Beattle Fan Club"* on the front, with the band's name misspelled. Initially, the name was also misspelled on the Vee-Jay Records 45 single of *Please Please Me*.

Beatles buttons given to radio disc jockeys. Jeff Augsburger collection

Other stations started Beatles fan clubs and joined forces with Capitol Records. WLS in Chicago claimed to be the first Beatles fan club in America. Disc jockey Art Roberts said, "I had the first Beatles fan club way before they ever came to this country. I started Beatles fan club number one. We had maybe 150 members. But then when they hit, it was kind of neat to know that those few were very proud of the fact that they belonged to the Chicago Beatles Fan Club number one." Art Roberts and Ron Riley got a photograph made of The Beatles and a photograph of themselves. With Capitol Records' assistance, 25,000 photos were made and sent out to fans in the Chicago area. A fan club membership card was also printed with The Beatles' single *I Want to Hold Your Hand* and their LP *Meet The Beatles* listed as being "on Capitol Records" on the back of the card.

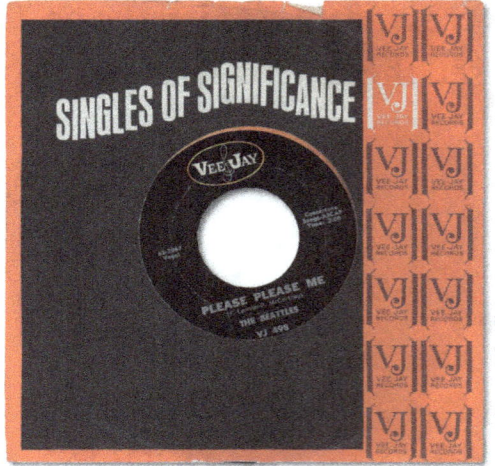

Vee-Jay Records "Please Please Me" single with the misspelling of "The Beattles" on the label.

Another AM station that started a club was WSAI in Cincinnati. Dusty Rhodes was the disc jockey who started it. "I was on the air and said, 'Let's form the first Beatles fan club' and wham! It was like the dam had burst. Mail started coming in, and we had to hire secretaries to handle requests. We called Capitol Records and asked them to print us The Beatles Boosters cards. It was overwhelming."

Not all radio stations jumped on the Capitol Records fan club bandwagon. Some places started clubs separately from Capitol Records. On January 10, 1964, WABC in New York City announced the Scott Muni Beatles Fan Club. Disc jockey Scott Muni offered fans a membership card free of charge if they each sent a self addressed, stamped envelope to the station. In two weeks, he was receiving from two to three thousand pieces of mail each day about the fan club.

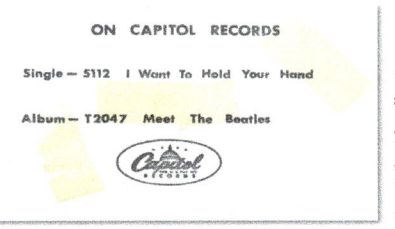

Front and back of the Beatles Fan Club membership cards for Chicago's WLS radio station.

On January 18, DJ Dick Moreland of KRLA in Los Angeles recommended that a fellow disc jockey, Dave Hull, start The Official Beatles Fan Club of Southern California and be its president. At the start Hull thought The Beatles looked too scruffy and would never make it, but after some discussion, Hull was convinced that it was going to be the right decision. "I told Dick (Moreland) that was great, but that I not only wanted to be president – I wanted to be vice president, secretary, treasurer, and sergeant-in-arms!" By the beginning of February, KRLA was officially known as "the original Beatles station in L.A." KRLA printed out numbered membership cards and sent them to fans. A fan club member won Beatles prizes if her membership number was announced on the air. Between January and June 1964, over half a million fan club cards were mailed out to Beatles fans in the Los Angeles area.

AM radio stations helped establish and promote fan clubs in many American cities, including New York, Chicago, Los Angeles, New Orleans, Cincinnati, Miami, and some

Fan Club membership card for Beatles Fan Club of Southern California from Los Angeles' KRLA radio station.

smaller areas. The stage had been set for the next wave of Beatlemania: the Fab Four's arrival on American soil.

They've Arrived!

The New York radio stations used their power to make The Beatles' U.S. arrival into a historic event. February 7, 1964 was dubbed "B-day." Radio stations WINS, WABC, and WMCA gave moment-by-moment updates on the current

Left: Beatles fans in Miami wave to the Beatles. Right: Beatles wave to New York fans.

whereabouts of the Pan Am airliner carrying The Beatles. Stations aired the news that The Beatles would be arriving on Pan Am Flight 101 at 1:20 PM. Nicky Byrne, the head of The Beatles' merchandising company Seltaeb, arranged a bus ride to John F. Kennedy Airport for fan club members. Club members each also got a free Beatles T-shirt to wear while welcoming the band to the United States. The bus held only a small fraction of the 3,000 teenagers, who stood and screamed as the airplane rolled onto the tarmac. After it stopped, John, Paul, George, and Ringo descended the stairs.

WABC DJ and Beatles fan club founder Scott Muni was there that day. In 1989, he recalled what happened after the boys got off the plane: "They ushered The Beatles into this little room, and shut the door. And then they had the press conference. The Liverpudlian charm and wit illuminated the first meeting between the press and The Beatles. They had this keen sense of humor, and it proved the perfect foil to some of the questions the assembled media threw at them. The press quickly became unwilling straight men for these four comedians. In all fairness, I don't think anyone assembled really knew what was taking place. But at least the radio people didn't ask dumb questions."

WINS had Murray the K, who called himself "The Fifth Beatle." WMCA started telling listeners that it was "32 Beatle degrees outside." Scott Muni later recalled: "That day our station went from WABC to W-A-Beatles-C. The management of the station was a little hesitant about that nickname. It took a while for them to OK the fact that we would devote a lot of time and energy to The Beatles and their music."

The Beatles arrived at the Plaza Hotel to find it besieged by fans, who kept vigil the entire time The Beatles were in New York City. One fan who stood outside the hotel on those chilly winter days was 12-year-old Linda: "They came to the window. We were screaming and screaming. Just screaming and singing: 'We love The Beatles!' I was dying for anything from them. I just wanted to touch them, and say hello to Paul."

The Beatles performed on *The Ed Sullivan Show* on February 9, 1964. Seventy-three million American viewers tuned in to see the group that, up until then, they had only heard on the radio. Fans who had joined a fan club through a local radio station were familiar with the music, but seeing them moving on their screens for the first time allowed them to pick their favorite Beatle. Girls took photos of their

The day the world changed forever: The Beatles on The Ed Sullivan Show. February 9, 1964.

television screens. All over the country they screamed, cried, and swooned. Many future fan club members later pinpointed seeing The Beatles on *The Ed Sullivan Show* as the moment they fell in love with the Fab 4.

One girl who became an instant fan that night was Sherry. She had never heard The Beatles until she tuned in to *The Ed Sullivan Show*. She said, "I screamed! The experience was highly exciting. There was this band inciting mobs of kids into frenzies, and I wanted to be part of that." Another fan, Marti Whitman Edwards, who had been a fan of The Beatles' music since 1963, vividly remembers seeing The Beatles on television. "I was sitting on the floor with my legs crossed, watching *The Ed Sullivan Show*. My mom was sitting in the chair next to me, and I said to her, 'I am going to meet The Beatles.'"

The Monday after *The Ed Sullivan Show*, huge numbers of independent Beatles fan clubs began in the United States. Pre-teen and teenage girls were wild about the four boys with the long hair. They talked on the playground and in school hallways. "Everyone was asking, 'Did you see The Beatles on *"Ed Sullivan"*?'" recalled Pam Williams. "We were all talking about how wonderful they were and how cute they were…we were very excited!" Many fans came together, or called one another, verbally starting clubs. They vowed they would love John, Paul, George, or Ringo, or all of them together. "There was a group at my high school that loved The Beatles. We decided to start a fan club, and so that is how The Chicagoland Beatle People Fan Club started," said Marti.

These brand new Beatlemaniacs promised to meet and listen to Beatles records. They often read each other's magazines to learn what happened with the group. Right away they began writing fan letters to The Beatles. Two groups of people were handling all of these letters, as well as those written before the boys arrived in the country.

Fan Mail

The first was NEMS New York attorney Walter Hofer. Brian Epstein summoned Hofer, saying that they needed him right away to help with something significant. "He gave me the job of dealing with all The Beatles' fan mail. I put my usual messenger service to work on it. Later on, I got this call from the manager, 'Mister, I'm 77 years old! There are 37 sacks of mail here.'" Realizing there were many more fan letters than he had anticipated, Hofer decided to make changes. "We set up a special department in another hotel to deal with it," he later said. "One of the letters they opened had come from Lyndon B. Johnson. Another was from the manager of the Plaza. 'When are you guys going to settle your check?' it said."

The other pair that helped with fan mail was two fans from The Official Canadian Beatles Fan Club. Club president Trudy Medcalf received a notice from NEMS in early 1964 stating that she and another club member were welcome to meet The Beatles during their time in New York City in February. Trudy informed CHUM radio of the notice, and they agreed to pay for Trudy and her father as well as

Trudy Medcalf and Dawne Hester help with the fan mail at the Plaza Hotel, while George Harrison is on the telephone.

club vice president Dawne Hester to fly from Toronto to New York City and stay at a hotel near the Plaza. CHUM wanted Trudy to call in to the station and tell the listeners all about her experience. They thought paying her to go to New York would be great publicity for their station.

It took three days to get into the Plaza. Even though Trudy had an official letter of introduction, the police guarding the Plaza refused to let the Canadian fans inside. On the day after *The Ed Sullivan Show*, Trudy's dad had an idea. "My Dad thought we should get our suitcases, and pull up in front of the hotel in a cab. He would walk up to the desk, and I would go around to the house phone. So Dawne and I made the call, and someone with The Beatles came down and got us."

At that time, there was no organized fan club in the United States. It was important for The Beatles to meet with fan club members. "That's because they had this ethic about people who were included with their fan clubs," said Trudy, "Not everyday fans, but people who'd taken on the challenge of trying to run one. And there wasn't another fan club in North America at the time." The boys knew some fan club representatives would be arriving, so their press agent, Brian Somerville, arranged for one of the rooms on the 12th floor of the Plaza to be designated to hold fan mail that had arrived during The Beatles' stay. The plan was for Trudy and Dawne to sort the fan mail and meet the boys. Trudy recalls, "No one asked us to do that. We got in and stayed in one of the bedrooms. People were coming and going. Every now and then, one of The Beatles would come in and talk to us." The famed Beatles' photographer Dezo Hoffman was there and took photographs of the girls with the stacks of mail, alongside The Beatles. Trudy wrote in a 1964 newsletter, "The next hours were spent chatting with the boys and helping them with the mountains of fan mail. Paul sat flinging elastic bands at people, while George danced. John made funnies constantly, and good ole Ringo was his ever-silent self. We found them to be just as gear as possible."

The most memorable moment happened after they arrived. "John came in and said, 'Oh, you're the fan club people?'" remembered Trudy, "And I said, 'yes.' He got down on his hands and knees, and he was bowing."

While Trudy and Dawne spent the afternoon in the mail room, The Beatles held a series of press conferences for writers and newspaper reporters, and then for disc jockeys, radio, and television reporters. The Beatles took a brief break to freshen up in their suite before going down to the hotel's Baroque Room, where they hosted a cocktail party for one hundred and fifty disc jockeys, press agents, and pretty girls.

Trudy and Dawne helped get The Beatles to the party. "There was a cocktail reception happening in the hotel, so we went into the hallway, and about 11 of us got into a circle. The Beatles got into the middle, and we shuffled down the hall to one of the elevators. Then we all shuffled off to the room where the cocktail party was."

The girls were only able to stay at the party for a short while before they had to leave to catch the returning plane to Toronto. At the party, they met Ray McFall, the man who owned the Cavern Club in Liverpool. He made Trudy and Dawne official Cavern Club members and encouraged them to come to Liverpool.

Meanwhile, the guests at the party mingled with one another and posed for photos with The Beatles. Some disc jockeys couldn't resist having a one-on-one (or as the newspaper reported, "thrust microphones") with The Beatles.

One radio station was the WPTR Good Guys from Albany, New York. WPTR was a 50,000-watt radio station with a large listening base. They wanted anything Beatles. They had a Beatles fan club and promised Beatles contests, latest news, and information along with a blitz of Beatles music.

Program director Jim Ramsburg was at the reception with a microphone in hand. He recorded each of The Beatles individually, stating that each was a WPTR Good Guy. Ramsburg phoned Frank Visco, the station's continuity director, and told him the good news. Visco got to work and made a promo for a contest. For this contest, one of the disc jockeys would call a Beatles fan club member at random, and she would have to guess which Beatle would say that he was a WPTR Good Guy. If she guessed which of the four was played, she would win a Beatles record or other Beatles prize.

When Ramsburg got back to the station, he played back the tapes for Visco, and they heard: "I'm Paul McCartney, and I'm a WPTR Good Guy, too." "I'm George Harrison of The Beatles, and I'm a WPTR Good Guy, too." "I'm Ringo Starr, and I'm a WPTR Good Guy, too." Then there was complete silence. John Lennon's message had not been recorded. The station had already played the promising promo messages from all four Beatles. Not having John's message could be detrimental to the station. Visco took the microphone and tried his hand at doing a Beatles imitation. "Of course, The Beatles had Liverpudlian accents, which I had never heard before, so I tried to copy the strange accent as I said, 'I'm John Lennon of The Beatles, and I'm a PTR Good Guy also.' I said 'also' because it sounded more British to me." Visco's Lennon imitation was mixed with some background noise to sound like a party was going on, and the contest went on without anyone learning the truth.

One of the girls at the cocktail party was 22-year-old Carol Webber. Carol worked in the publicity department of a record company in New York. One of the men she worked for took her to meet The Beatles at the Plaza Hotel. Carol had many inside scoops on The Beatles because she had seen them several times in New York City, and she'd attended both the Carnegie Hall and Washington Coliseum concerts. Carol's inside information made her a favorite writer for new fan club newsletters. The Beatles West Coast Fan Club newsletter, The Beatles Booster, she told members all about her thoughts on each Beatle: "They are down to earth, warm, friendly, mannerly, polite and sincere fellows." Fans loved reading that. Carol started her own Beatles fan club The Official Beatles Headquarters and remained active in the club for many years.

Because of a snowstorm, The Beatles could not fly to Washington, D.C., where they were scheduled to perform their first full concert in the United States. Two thousand fans packed Washington's Union Station to see them arrive by train on February 11. The police would not allow the screaming girls to get close to the platform. As the cops were pushing back one girl, her friend declared "You can't throw her out. She's the president of The Beatles Fan Club." That fan club president, Pam Johnson, and two other fans were the only ones allowed on the platform. They were chosen to hold a large banner that said: "WWD Welcomes The Beatles." Pam rode in a limousine to the Washington Coliseum with John Lennon's wife Cynthia and George Harrison's sister, Louise Harrison Caldwell. She had the opportunity that all fan club presidents dream about: she got to meet The Beatles. "Paul remembered having met me at Union Station when I met him again at the Coliseum. Paul seemed genuinely warm and enthusiastic when he asked me, 'Are you REALLY president of a Beatles fan club?' George told me to keep up the good work."

Before they had time to meet with anyone, The Beatles were interviewed by the first American disc jockey to play *I Want to Hold Your Hand*, Carroll James. During the interview, James asked Ringo how many rings he owned. Ringo said that he had 2,761 rings. James asked where fans could send rings to Ringo. Ringo said they could send them to The Official Beatles Fan Club in London at 13 Monmouth Street. He also added, "Make sure they're gold. I only wear gold." Ringo was just joking, but he gave American fans something desirable: The Official Beatles Fan Club address. It wasn't long before North American fans started to contact The Official Beatles Fan Club in London, wanting to know how to join and get involved. By the time The Beatles left America and went back home, Beatlemania had taken over the continent.

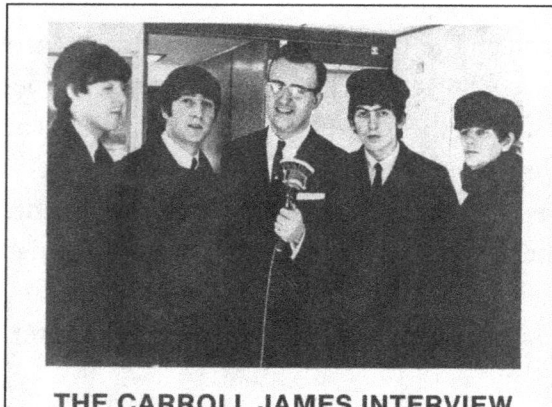

The Carroll James Interview With The Beatles *record and sleeve.*

Beatles Fans' Letters Invade New Jersey

Karen Commarato in Mountain Lakes, New Jersey was still the only fan who had an official Beatles fan club in the United States. At the start of the year, The Beatles appeared in a short clip on *The Jack Paar Show*. Karen put an ad in a few of the local newspapers about the club. Letters from fans increased after that, but *The Ed Sullivan Show* was the big game-changer.

"I was getting 700 letters a day," Karen recalled. "I had kids from school – girls come over every day, open the mail, sort it into three categories. If they wanted to join the club, we sent them an application form. If they were writing personally to The Beatles, we forwarded the letters to London. If they were seeking information, we tried to help them." In February and March of 1964, four girls and two boys spent at least six hours every day after school dealing with Beatles fan mail. While the teenagers opened and stuffed envelopes, Karen's two aunts printed informational letters about The Beatles. They cranked these out by hand on a copy machine. Karen and her friends discovered that most fans who wrote liked Ringo best, and that everyone wanted to thank The Beatles for coming to America.

It was a lot for a group of teenagers and two elderly aunts to do out of their home. Karen was looking to the future. She would start college that fall, and didn't want to continue leading the fan club. "I was relieved when, in April, I heard that the fan club was being taken over by an office in New York. My motivation had been achieved. My feeling was, 'If I like them this much, and my friends like them this much, then they'll be popular.' But we never imagined how big it would become."

The Official Beatles Fan Club

With more American fan mail arriving at the fan club in London, the need for an organized club in the United States was becoming urgent. The head of The Official Beatles Fan Club, Mary Cockram (also known as Anne Collingham), said, "The volume of U.S. fan mail increased enormously, and we were overwhelmed. What an impossible task we were faced with. I'm afraid many letters would not have been answered." An official U.S. fan club had been in the works since the end of 1963. With the fan club in London swamped with American letters, putting the U.S. club into working order became a top priority.

The fan club's headquarters were in a small room in Walter Hofer's office, suite 224. West 57th Street in New York City was the secret address. On March 18, 1964, a press release appeared in U.S. newspapers announcing: "An official Beatles Fan Club has now been established in the United States." It named Miss Marjorie Minshull as the fan club's director. For a dues payment of $2, fan club members would receive an official membership card, an official Beatles book, a quarterly newsletter, and other items. They just had to send their money to a Radio City post office box. This official U.S. fan club was called Beatles (U.S.A.) Ltd. Word of its existence spread through newspapers, magazines, and anything else a Beatles fan might read.

One of the first fans to volunteer at the fan club was Debbie Gendler. "Walter Hofer called me, and I started at the fan club in March 1964, when I just turned 14. I would go to Walter's office where he started the fan club with professional people working there – older people – meaning they were in their 20s and early 30s."

The Official Beatles Fan Club in the U.K. was run by a woman known as "Anne Collingham." Tony Barrow, The Beatles' press manager, came up with the idea to use a pseudonym for the head of the fan club to help screen phone calls. If someone called asking for "Anne," they knew it was most likely a fan and not an urgent call. Various names were given for the woman that ran the United States fan club: Feather Schwartz and Lynn Hargrave were names people signed on letters and Beatles fan club materials. However, the real director of the club was an efficient Black woman named Bernice Young.

This Beatles Fan Club advertisement hung in record shops around the country. 1964.

As Debbie explained, "There was a woman who had many names. Tony Barrow, The Beatles' PR guy, loved to have different names for everyone. Bernice stayed for several years and ran the fan club out of Walter Hofer's supply closet in his law office."

In 1964, Bernice Elizabeth Young was a 33-year-old professional writer and advertiser. She had been one of the first six Black students accepted into Vassar College in 1949. When Walter Hofer interviewed

Bernice to be the national director of the fan club, he knew right away that she had the skills and abilities necessary for the position. He contacted Brian Epstein in England and told him that he had found the perfect candidate for the job, but he wanted to let him know that she was a Negro and asked if that would be a problem. Brian responded that her race was definitely not an issue and so Bernice was hired for the job.

On June 19, 1964, the television game show *To Tell the Truth* broadcast an episode where three 20-something white women all claimed to be the National Director of Beatles (U.S.A.) Ltd., Feather Schwartz. The three contestants were asked a series of questions by a panel of four judges who would ironically decide who the "real" Feather Schwartz indeed was. Her job involved authorizing the charters for local fan clubs, editing a Beatles newsletter, and conducting interviews with disc jockeys across the country. The judges asked a variety of questions. The point was for "Feather" to stump them as they determined which contestant she was.

One of the most interesting questions came from Orson Bean. He asked if Feather's mother was an Indian and how she got her name. Contestant Number One truthfully answered, "Feather just happened." The brunette, who was the "real" Feather Schwartz, got two of the judges' votes. One judge asked why she'd started the fan club. "I didn't start it," she explained, "It was organized by the attorney of The Beatles. It was under his supervision – it still is." The contestants won $500 and a carton of Winston cigarettes.

"Feather's" time with the fan club was short-lived. The December 1964 issue of *Cosmo* magazine referred to her as "the ex-secretary of The Beatles fan club of America."

By July 5, 1964, Beatles (U.S.A.) Ltd.'s pay-off was reported to be the most successful in the history of show business. It cost $2 to join, and the club already had 50,000 members. However, the club was not making a profit. The Director of Brian Epstein's company, NEMS, Geoffrey Ellis, conjectured, "I doubt if the fan club made any sort of profit, but the membership fees helped to cover expenses."

Beatles (U.S.A.) Ltd. book. 1964.

With Love, From You To Me...

Does Paul McCartney park his car outside the gates of his house? Does he drive a yellow car? I hope he has a yellow Mercedes. Does he call the police when girls are outside of his house?

Mindy

Editor: We believe Paul McCartney is currently driving a large bus around London. If you go to his house and get arrested, please do not call us. We don't have bail money.

∽

Hi Dear Beatle People, I've been a long time subscriber and an even longer Beatles fan. I just wanted to say that I am very grateful for this magazine and for all the hard work you put in to it. There are a few good Beatles magazines out there, but this is without a doubt my favorite. As a lifelong fan of the Beatles my love for them has never waned, so being able to come here and see photos and read stories from like-minded people is always a joy.

Tony

Editor: Thank you Tony for the kind words. Your letter has been chosen as the "best letter of the month." You will be receiving a year's supply of Turtle Wax. Congratulations.

∽

Do you think Ringo would sign an autograph on a pineapple?

Pattie T.

Editor: No, but we think he will sign a papaya.

IT APPEARS JOHN HAS DYED HIS HAIR A LIGHTER SHADE!! WHO IS HE TRYING TO LOOK LIKE?

Pam

Editor: We believe he is trying to look like Jayne Mansfield.

∽

I went to the Beatles 1st concert at Shea. I just turned 17. I was in the nosebleed section, very annoyed at the screaming girls. So, I wiled away the time "people watching" and who was sitting 2 rows in front of me but John Sebastian and "The Lovin' Spoonful"!

Christine

Editor: We hope that wasn't just a "Daydream" Christine. We are sure it was an exciting day that "Summer in the City." Hopefully you didn't "Have to Make Up Your Mind" between the Spoonful and The Beatles.

∽

Is Paul ever called Jim or Jimmy by his friends?

Judith

Editor: No. His enemies do not call him by those names either.

Beatles (U.S.A.) Ltd. fan club membership card. 1964.

By the summer of 1964, fan club members were starting to receive their promised fan club items. When a member first joined, she received the official Beatles Book called *Beatles (U.S.A.) Limited*, the same book sold at Beatles concerts during the 1964 North American tour. The cover photo was of The Beatles as seen on the *Meet The Beatles* album cover, only highlighted in purple. It was full of Beatles photographs and some general Beatles information.

Fans also received an official membership card. This card was necessary because fan club members who wanted to order items from the club were required to mail the membership card in with their order. Someone at club headquarters would stamp the card, and it would be returned with the purchased item. What could fans buy from the fan club in 1964? Fifteen different Beatles group photographs, along with one individual photo of each Beatle, for 25 cents each (or five photos for $1).

All members of Beatles (U.S.A.) Ltd. fan club were entitled to a free Beatles fact sheet. To get this double-sided paper, fans had to send their membership cards and a self-addressed stamped envelope to the fan club's P.O. box. The fact sheet gave some general information about The Beatles and their history in Liverpool and Hamburg. The sheet incorrectly stated, "It was in school in 1956 that John, Paul, and George met and formed a Skiffle group." The complete story of how John started The Beatles was not corrected until many years later. The fact sheet gave information on each member that teenage girls would find fascinating, such as: John Lennon likes to eat steak and chips, Paul McCartney likes to wear black polo neck sweaters, George Harrison does not like getting his hair cut, and Ringo Starr's dislikes include Chinese food and Donald Duck.

There was a lot more to being in a fan club than just joining and getting newsletters and fact sheets. Beatlemaniacs wanted to get together with other fans and talk about the boys. Beatles (U.S.A.) Ltd. had a solution for that. If a group had 25 or more members, it could become a chapter of the fan club. Each chapter needed a local president, vice-president, secretary, and treasurer. As soon as there were 25 dues-paying club members, the chapter would receive an exclusive club charter directly from The Beatles. The charter would serve as proof that the chapter was "official and connected to the national fan club."

A letter sent by Marjorie Minshull in May 1964 told

Fan club charter for the "Beat-Isles" chapter of Beatles (U.S.A.) Ltd.

fans, "You must have authorization from us for your chapter." A founder could name her chapter anything she wanted, as long as the title didn't include "Branch of the Official Beatles Fan Club." Her club would always be referred to as a "chapter." The expectation was that all Beatles fan clubs in the United States would join Beatles (U.S.A.) Ltd. There weren't many independently-run fan clubs in the U.K., and those that were in charge assumed the North American counterpart would follow suit.

The chartered clubs were free to organize and do what they wanted in any way they wished. Each club was left entirely open to plan its activities. Clubs could meet whenever they liked, and do whatever they liked at the meeting. Each chapter president would receive an official newsletter full of Beatles information to share with her club.

One of the chartered clubs was the Quad City Beatles Fan Club in Iowa, whose president was Marcia. There were forty-five club members, and they raised money for the John F. Kennedy Memorial Library Fund. The National Beatles Fan Club from Tampa, Florida contacted Alistair Taylor, the general manager of NEMS, in London, and he approved their club. He personally connected them with New York and set them on the path to getting a charter. Every month the club printed a mimeographed newsletter. The one male member of the club, Bill Wilhelm, had the job of promoting club activities. On May 9, they held a dance at the Wellswood Civic Club where all the music was Beatles songs.

In San Diego, California, Kathie Sexton started her fan club, The Yeah Beatles Fan Club, in December 1963 and got charter number 11. She advertised the club during her daily radio show, and it quickly grew. The Yeah Beatles Fan Club was very active, and they did several crazy stunts. At one point, Kathie convinced one fan club member, Becky, to climb out onto the Balboa Park Bridge and claim that she was going to jump if Ringo Starr did not marry her. Following their plan, Kathie talked her down. Of course, these teenagers did not think about the consequences of this stunt, and the police came to take them away. From then on, they stuck with safer events such as getting the newspaper to cover one male fan's conversion from surfer-style hair to a Beatles haircut. His new hairstyle got him suspended from school, and the fan club wanted everyone to know about the injustice.

Unknown to fan club members, Kathie started working for radio, television, and concert promoters to get screaming girls to make noise for various bands who came to play in San Diego. A fan club meeting would often consist of the first 30 members who arrived going to a television show, sitting in the stands, and screaming for the bands. Sometimes this allowed them to meet with other British rock groups such as The Rolling Stones, or British stars with Beatles connections such as Gordon Waller of Peter & Gordon.

However, the thousand-members in The Yeah Beatles Fan Club did much the same thing as other fan clubs. They made Beatles signs and hung them in school corridors, only to find them gone the

Top: Members of The Yeah Beatles Fan Club digging the letter "B" on the hillside. Bottom: Members of The Yeah Beatles Fan Club with Gordon Waller of Peter and Gordan.

next day. Their school principal scolded several members about that. In their area of California, people often carved initials into the brush-covered hills to express support for some cause. Kathie knew of an untouched hill near her house, and club members spent the next two weeks digging out a letter "B" to show their support for The Beatles.

As in any other club, members spent time talking about their favorite Beatle. "I realized that I liked John," said Kathie. "I loved his songs, but he was married. Then I said, 'Why can't I like a married man?'" The fans sitting in Kathie's living room were baffled by her conclusion. "A bunch of them were making posters when I said that and I remember the look on their faces and them saying, 'How can you like a married man?' And I told them that I like his music and I like the way he looks. What is wrong with that? I knew they were confused because they thought I liked him as a boyfriend, but I thought that I liked him as somebody to appreciate. I wasn't thinking of marrying any of them. I just liked their music, their message, and their energy."

The largest chartered Beatles fan club in the United States was in Fort Worth, Texas. Elaine McAfee started a Beatles fan club right after seeing them on television. "I went to junior high school. My three best friends had all watched The Beatles, and we sat down and said, 'Oh my God, we're in love. We need to start a Beatles fan club.'" Elaine was just 14 years old when she and some kids from her school started a fan club. She called it Cheese Forever Club because Paul McCartney said he liked cheese in an interview. It wasn't long until Elaine started to buy various Beatles magazines, where she learned about The Official Beatles Fan Club in London. She decided to take a chance and write to that club to see if the Cheese Forever Club could become part of the bigger official club. "I wrote to NEMS Enterprises, where Brian Epstein had his record store and his family business. They sent me albums that were not available in the United States. So, I already had contact with Epstein's store. I was a shoo-in when it went to the fan club." She got an application, which she promptly filled out. Soon Elaine's club became official, now calling itself The North Texas Chapter of The Beatles Fan Club.

"They made me accountable for all kinds of things and sent us information and photos that other people didn't have," Elaine recalled. At the same time, one of the fan club members' fathers offered to buy the club a basic printing press. They started to put out newsletters with their own articles, and these newsletters made the rounds, attracting more members. "We went from originally ten members to fifty members, to two hundred members to five hundred members, and eventually it was over a thousand members," Elaine said. "By late 1964 and going into 1965, they said it was the largest fan club in the United States."

What got the club going was Elaine's involvement with the local radio station, KFJZ. The disc jockeys would air Beatles news, and Elaine would call them up and tell them what they'd gotten wrong. She had all the facts about what label each single was on and other tidbits that she got directly from England and New York. She called with so many corrections and clarifications that the disc jockeys eventually asked her to come down to the station. They wanted to know how she learned all this stuff.

"I told them I have a local Beatles fan club, and they looked at each other and said, 'Would you read The Beatles news as it comes off the wire after school?' So, I would read The Beatles news, and they liked it so much that the program director asked me to do the regular Beatles news. I was up there every day. I encouraged the listeners to join the fan club and get my newsletter." KFJZ, and disc jockey Mark Stevens, was very good to Elaine, and loved having her at the station. She told the teenagers things they wanted to hear about The Beatles, such as how long their hair was growing and where Paul got his clothes. The station allowed The North Texas Chapter of The Beatles Fan Club to meet in one of their rooms, but the club quickly outgrew it. "We just outgrew everywhere we ended up, and they would rent us space because, for KFJZ radio, it was marketing heaven."

Elaine's club wasn't the only Beatles fan club in Texas. Dallas high school freshmen Yolanda Hernandez and Stephanie Pinter got hooked on The Beatles after watching them on *The Jack Paar Show* and *The Ed Sullivan Show*. Just like many other girls, they desperately wanted to meet The Beatles. Stephanie's mother had read in the paper about Beatles (U.S.A.) Ltd. and told the best friends about the club in New York. She suggested that the girls' best way to meet The Beatles was to form a fan club. They would promote the band and if they succeeded, maybe they'd meet them.

Stephanie's mom advised them to make the club very professional. Stephanie recalled, "We made up stationery, envelopes, bumper stickers, T-shirts, and other items. In the meantime, Yolanda had written off to the fan club in New York for the chapter membership. The long-awaited day came when she called me to come over and see the piece of paper stating 'Beatles Fan Club (U.S.A.), Chapter 24!'"

Independent Clubs

While hundreds of thousands of teenagers joined Beatles (U.S.A.) Ltd. in 1964, not many fan club charters were distributed. There seemed to be a disconnect between the independent clubs that had started in February and the official Beatles (U.S.A.) Ltd. that was trying to get them to join up by May.

Marti Whitman Edwards, who was The Chicagoland Beatle People Fan Club president, tried to make her independent club official: "We had written a letter to the Liverpool fan club and tried to become one of their subsidiaries, but we never heard back from them." Even without Beatles (U.S.A.) Ltd.'s support, during 1964, Marti's club grew to 600 members. They frequently held Beatles rallies. As Marti recalled, "There were about six of us that ran the club. We would tell everyone that we'd be at the park on Saturday morning, and we'd bake cookies and bring banners and share Beatles stories with each other."

While the rallies were fun, Marti still had her mind set on one thing: meeting The Beatles. "I wanted to expand the fan club because I knew it had to be bigger to meet The Beatles," she explained. "So I got the idea to go to WLS radio studios. The DJ was behind a glass window, and you could hold up signs, and he'd read the signs. That was one of the ways to publicize a fan club. We got 600 more members that way and were up to 1,200 members." The Chicagoland Beatle People Fan Club had something that many other fan clubs did not: a newsletter. "I spent a lot of time finding information for our newsletter," said Marti. "It was a little one-page newsletter. You could just fold it, staple it, and put a stamp on it. Most of the news we got out of magazines. We used our own money. Nobody helped us. I babysat to earn money, and the other girls did too. We all chipped in. It was hard once the club got to 1,200, but a lot of members were at our high school so we could pass those out and didn't have to post them."

The Beatles fan club in Reno, Nevada got started after a girl named Linda Schoen thought of it. As she explained to the *Nevada State Journal* in April 1964, she was qualified to create a Beatles club because she "simply has everything there is to have about The Beatles: bubble gum cards, pictures, books, and magazines." Instead of having traditional officer rankings, the head members were named after each Beatle. At their meetings, they listened to records while writing fan letters and reading magazines. Their favorite activity was a unique way of talking: "We can talk funny, you know, Beatle-talk. There is a whole dictionary of it." The club even had a motto: "Happiness is a thing called The Beatles."

Likewise, the Midwest Chapter of The Beatles Fan Club out of Indiana reported that they listened to records at weekly club meetings, discussed Beatles news, talked about The Beatles tours, and recruited new members. This club had a mascot: an English Sheepdog named Ringo. In Salem, Oregon, the Beatles fan club boasted that they had nine Beatles records, thirty Beatles books, over two thousand Beatles bubble gum cards, and three thousand Beatles pictures. As a group, they had chewed twenty-one pieces of Beatles bubble gum just to get the cards. At their weekly Saturday club meetings, a bowl of The Beatles' unofficial candy, jelly beans, was always available. This club would listen to Beatles records while making crafts such as Beatles pictures frames. When asked, one of the members said she liked The Beatles because "their music is great and so are the mop haircuts and their boots."

In the small town of Walnut Ridge, Arkansas, a group of teenagers started a club called The Beatles 4 Forevermore Fan Club. It began when one mother told her daughter that she and her friends started fan clubs for their favorite movie stars. She thought her daughter and her classmates should start a Beatles fan club. As one member, Carrie Mae Snapp, said, "It never occurred to us that there was a national or international fan club that you could associate with."

The fan club met every Saturday night. They had thoughtful conversations about the meanings behind The Beatles' songs. They conversed about why The Beatles were singing, "I wanna hold your hand" instead of "I want to kiss you." This was stuff that Carrie Mae said "was really important to 8th and 9th graders but not necessarily important to the rest of the world." Each fan club meeting would end with a Beatles dance party. "We danced in the living room," Carrie Mae recalled, "You would bring your favorite Beatles album and just dance up a storm."

Being in a small town limited their activities. On Saturday mornings, the club would meet at the Warner Drug Store soda fountain and buy a 10-cent Coca-Cola and a pack of Beatles bubble gum cards. They would sit at the counter trading Beatles cards for about five hours at a time.

This small-town club did have something other clubs did not have: official handmade Beatles sweatshirts. A girl from Louisiana with artistic abilities came to spend time with her grandmother in Walnut Ridge that summer. She painted the club members' favorite Beatle on the front of each sweatshirt and "Beatles 4 Forevermore" on the back. You could get a white or grey sweatshirt. Carrie Mae had one with Paul on the front and wore it every chance she could. "I'd get stopped every place I went, and everybody asked me where I got it because it was so unusual. It was just amazing. My mother had to finally say, 'Carrie Mae, sweatshirts are meant to be worn on a Saturday when you're not doing anything. You shouldn't wear it when we go places.'"

The club that grew to be one of the largest independent clubs of The Beatles' era had humble beginnings. In April 1964, Pat Kinzer, who had previous experience running a fan club for the regular dancers on *American Bandstand*, started the first known fan club for an individual Beatle. "Since George was my favorite," she said, "It was natural that my fan club would be for George and so the George Harrison Fan Club was born." She recruited members from her neighborhood and school. For 40 cents, members got three photographs of George that Pat took off the television, a membership card, lyrics to George's songs, and a fact sheet about George that Pat had compiled from various teen magazines.

Beatles Friends

Some fans fell into a gray area, and considered themselves to be Beatles friends. Beatles friends did not have an organized fan club but they engaged in many of the same activities as fan club members. Typically, four girls would devote themselves to one Beatle each. This way none of the four girls had to share. Lori Freckleton was in a group that wasn't an organized club, but they called themselves

Beatles friends celebrating Lori Freckleton's birthday with Beatles decorations and music.

The Beatles Fan Club. Laurie and her three closest friends started a Beatles group right after seeing The Beatles on *The Ed Sullivan Show*. Lori recalled that eventually the group expanded to 10 girls. "We each had a name," she said. "I was John and my friend was Paul and the whole den. Then we had extras, so we had to have the girlfriends. Of course, innocent as we were, we had to have a Brian Epstein and have a girlfriend for him." This group of young ladies would meet together each day in the school cafeteria and not allow anyone else to sit at their lunch table.

Frequently these girls would have Beatles-themed birthday parties, and invite all of their Beatles friends to celebrate with them. Lori Freckleton celebrated her 13th birthday with all of her friends in the basement of her home. She decorated it in Beatles posters and signs. They listened to Beatles music and had cake to celebrate Lori's birthday. These groups of friends would hang out together in record stores, dime stores, and soda fountains. In these places they bought Beatles items and talked about the band. They were such good friends that the idea of joining a Beatles fan club never crossed their minds.

Bubble Gum Buttons

As soon as The Beatles came to America, Beatles fans started wearing pin-back buttons on their shirts. The Green Duck Company was a button manufacturer whose specialty was producing buttons promoting events and causes. They had made a name for themselves with the famous "I Like Ike" buttons during the 1952 Presidential campaign.

With the newly formed Beatles fan clubs in mind, they made four sets of 7/8″ buttons: black and red, navy and red, blue and black, and orange and black. These had slogans such as "Member Beatles Fan Club," "I'm 4 Beatles," "I Love The Beatles," "I'm a Beatles Booster," and "I'm a Beatle Bug." There were also separate buttons for each Beatle, with his face and name. These buttons were available in bubble gum machines for a penny each. It was fashionable to buy these buttons and wear them to fan club meetings, rallies, and concerts. Fans also

Above: Green Duck 'Member Beatles Fan Club' 7/8" diameter pinback button (actual size), 1964.

Right: Patch for the 'Life Member' of The 'Beatle' Fan Club.'
Sara Schmidt collection

traded among themselves to acquire a full set of buttons. They were popular with fan clubs around the country.

Other manufacturers cashed in on the popularity of Beatles fan clubs. One made a patch for each Beatle, declaring that their wearers had "Lifetime membership" in The Beatles fan club. Other companies made banners fans could hang on the walls wherever their clubs were meeting. Fans did not care if these items were sanctioned by NEMS, Seltaeb, or The Beatles themselves. As long as it had something to do with being in a Beatles fan club, they were buying.

The Beatle Buddies' Club

The Beatle Buddies' Club had an unusual background. Before The Beatles' arrival, Pat Boone was one of the top pop singers in the United States. The songs he recorded were mostly rhythm and blues numbers, and in the decade before The Beatles came, his singles often topped the charts. With his clean-cut image, teenagers across the nation adored Boone. All of that changed drastically after The Beatles' arrival. Boone told the *Kansas City Times* in an October 1964 interview that he had been depressed by The Beatles' fame. "Eighty percent of all records being sold in this country, both albums and singles, are Beatles records," he said. Boone was upset. Not only were his records no longer selling, but he had made two new albums that his record company refused to release because The Beatles were attracting so much attention.

Instead of wallowing in depression, Boone used The Beatles' popularity for his benefit. Boone explained, "The plan was ingenious and, at the same time, simple. The Dutch painter, Leo Jansen, would paint a fine oil portrait of The Beatles, and Boone Enterprises would gain the exclusive right to reproduce it." The painter painted portraits of The Beatles as a group and the four individuals, then made prints suitable for framing. These four-painting sets were marketed as *"The Beatle Buddies' Club* Kit." Each kit came with a membership card in *The Beatle Buddies' Club*. This wasn't an actual fan club; it was a marketing scheme to get fans interested in their product.

The Beatle Buddies' Club kits sold for $1.18 each and were available all around the country. Kits with the group print were also available, but were limited to the 500 that were produced.

Pat Boone was a wise businessman. Before he sold the kits, he met with Nicky Byrne at Seltaeb, who ran all of The Beatles' merchandising. Brian Epstein

The Beatle Buddies' and membership card and application, group portrait by Jansen, and countertop store display with Paul portrait

approved the paintings, and Seltaeb received 15 percent of the sales. The Beatle Buddies' Club was the only "fan club" outside of Beatles (U.S.A.) Ltd. that one of The Beatles' companies approved.

If a fan purchased a The Beatle Buddies' Club kit before August 14, 1964, she had a chance to fly to Las Vegas and see The Beatles in concert. "We had a contest running nationally," said Boone. "With every set of Beatles pictures that we sold, there was a tag, and you kept part of the tag and mailed the other tag in, and there was a drawing. We brought 30 people from all over the country to their concert in Las Vegas." The newspaper ads were very enticing and read: "Several members will be chosen to attend the gala Hollywood Beatles Party as Pat Boone's special guest. You and a parent will visit movie studios, Disneyland and see a Beatles concert... four glorious days, all expenses paid." Boone hoped The Beatles would attend the party he was throwing in Hollywood and meet the contest winners. Seltaeb had told Boone that The Beatles would attend. Still, Brian Epstein gave a firm "no." Boone tried to get Epstein to change his mind, sending a telegram saying, "Your refusal will disappoint millions of American children who might have a minimal chance to see The Beatles in person." He asked for just one hour of The Beatles' time, but his requests were declined.

Boone did meet The Beatles backstage in Las Vegas. "We went back between shows and visited with The Beatles. They had a camera store bring in all kinds of cameras for them to look at, and they were taking pictures. My little girls sat on Ringo's lap and took pictures with Paul and George. They said to me, 'Brian has put our name on a lot of stuff. A lot of it is junk, but we like these pictures. They are very nice, flattering pictures.'"

The contest winners were able to attend the show with Boone. The Beatles seemed oblivious about the contest. Later George Harrison said in *The Beatles Anthology*, "I think the first four rows of that concert were filled up by Pat Boone and his daughters. He seemed to have hundreds of daughters."

Independent Radio Fan Clubs

On February 29, 1964, *Billboard* magazine reported that "stations across the country hyped The Beatles excitement with offers of fan club cards, free records, Beatle contests of all sorts, and a continual push on the Capitol, Swan, and Vee-Jay releases by the group."

It soon became apparent that Capitol Records no longer needed to team up with radio stations to form fan clubs. The Beatles' record sales were outstanding without the help of a fan club. If the radio stations wanted promotional materials for their fan clubs, they were on their own. One such club that started with Capitol Records' initial support, but continued without it, was The Beatles Boosters out of Cincinnati. It was founded by 24-year-old Dusty Rhodes, who was the chief Beatle Bug to his twenty thousand fans in the area. After it ended its relationship with Capitol Records, *Cashbox* called the club, "An active and swinging organization, hard at work at the promotion of North American Beatlemania." Almost immediately Dusty and his new wife found themselves sending out membership cards to two hundred fans a day. Letters arrived from fans declaring love for Paul or wanting to kiss Ringo. Dusty held contests and played Beatles music on WASI AM.

He organized fan club events beyond the radio station. On July 1, there was a Beatles Night at the Cincinnati Reds baseball game. *The Beatles Boosters* members were able to purchase seats together, and before the game, a band played Beatles songs to entertain them. That night all the players on the Reds team became honorary members of *The Beatles Boosters*.

In Los Angeles, Dave Hull, known as "the Hullabalooer," and the president of The Official Beatles Fan Club of Southern California at KRLA, remained head of one of the country's top clubs. Dave would make up rumors, such as that George was giving up the guitar for the trombone, or that Paul was dating Ethel Merman, and then squash those rumors on the air. Fan club members would learn the real stories only after Dave would call George Harrison's parents in Liverpool. George's mother, Louise, was happy to talk.

As Hull explained later, "She told me that she would be more than happy to tell me some private top-secret information, things concerning the boys. She suggested that she could give me addresses, telephone numbers, where they were staying on tour, and even their girlfriends' names." Hull continued his conversations with Louise all through 1964, getting all the inside information. The half-million fan club members could not get enough. "Our listeners went nuts and screamed for more," said Hull. He gave out The Beatles' home addresses, which went over well with the fans, but not with The Beatles. "Brian Epstein and The Beatles themselves wanted to know just who was giving me all their secret information," said Hull. "I never did tell George, his mother was the mouth of the leak."

As if having The Beatles' scoop wasn't enough, Hull also met John and George, and eagerly told listeners all about the experience. The two Beatles had

Murray the 'K' As It Happened Beatles interview disc with sleeve.

been in Hollywood on May 26. They traveled with the important women in their lives to Tahiti for a much-needed holiday, and they spent one day in Hollywood before returning to London. Hull had gotten a tip that they were inside an airplane sitting on the tarmac at the airport. Before being hauled off by security, he was able to sneak onto the plane and talk to John Lennon. Hull's interview aired on KRLA, and was printed in The Beatles West Coast Fan Club newsletter, *The Beatles Booster*. "I became known as 'the fifth Beatle,'" said Hull. "It was a title I was proud of, but it came with royal responsibility."

The man who had already given himself the title of "the fifth Beatle,"

WHOL radio in Allentown, PA with the new president of the station's Beatles fan club.

Murray the K, did not head up a Beatles fan club. His station, WINS in New York, did not have a Beatles fan club at all. The station sent a letter to all the fans who had written in to ask questions about The Beatles. The station wanted a girl to be the president of a newly formed WINS Beatles Fan Club. One of her primary

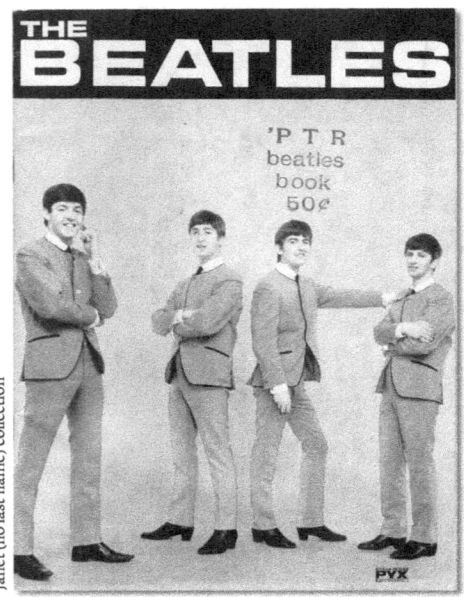

PYX booklet with WPTR stamp.

Janet (no last name) collection

responsibilities would be to sell Beatles buttons and items for WINS. No one was interested, and the WINS Beatles Fan Club never took off, but there was a flourishing *Murray the K fan club*.

Smaller radio stations had successful, if smaller, fan clubs. WHOL in Pennsylvania held a contest for which disc jockey should be the station's Beatles president of their Top Poppers Beatles Fan Club. After a rousing campaign, listeners voted DJ "Frantic Freddie" as the winner. Freddie didn't disappoint. He spoke to The Beatles personally and gave 10 club members tickets to The Beatles concert in Atlantic City, New Jersey.

WJPS in Evansville, Indiana had a Beatles Booster Fan Club. Members got engraved membership certificates, each corner adorned with a picture of one of their disc jockeys wearing a Beatles wig. In the west, seven radio stations joined to form the Intermountain Beatle Fan Club. In San Bernardino, California, The KMEN Chapter of The Beatles Fan Club appointed Wendy Nicholass to be the club president. Beginning in June of 1964, Wendy joined the disc jockey Brian Lord on his show and talked Beatles. She did not meet The Beatles, but she did get to go backstage and meet four other rock stars from England. Her job as president of a Beatles fan club allowed her to meet The Rolling Stones while they were on tour.

WPTR had a leg up on many other stations because they had a directional pattern that shot 50,000 watts north at night, and could be heard as far away as Norway. A British seaman heard WPTR playing his favorite band, The Beatles, and sent the station a Beatles magazine that was not available in the United States as a thank you. Frank Visco said, "Jim Ramsburg asked me to call the publisher listed on the magazine and ask if anyone owned the U.S. rights to the magazine. The rights hadn't been sold, and if we were interested, the publisher said to cable him an offer." The offer was accepted, and the color plates arrived from London. At first, WPTR had a few hundred copies made and started to advertise them on the air. Ramsburg said, "We got the 'Beatle Books,' and the station was flooded with orders in the mail as we caught the first wave of Beatlemania. My job was to stamp the station's call letters on each magazine before it was mailed out." Ramsburg sent offers to rock radio stations around the country and wholesaled the books in each market.

These Top 40 radio stations sold what is now known as the *"PYX Beatles Book"* for $1 each to fan club members. Each station stamped its own call letters on the front of each book. With color photos on the front and back and a color centerfold, as well as detailed information about each Beatle inside, the book became a must-have at Beatles fan club gatherings. Ramsburg was more than pleased with his investment: "In a month we sold over 750,000 copies and indeed made some serious money."

Beatles Fan Club Rallies and Balls

Among the Beatles fan clubs' fun activities were "Beatles rallies." Local radio stations often organized these fan get-togethers. Members of all the fan clubs from one metropolitan area would attend. These rallies often featured contests for the best fan club signs, and a band would play Beatles music.

When The Beatles first came to the United States, they learned about a campaign started by some college boys in Detroit, Michigan called "Stamp Out The Beatles." This campaign was a promotional scheme by W.T. Rabe, a publicist for the University of Detroit. The idea behind the *"Stamp Out The Beatles Society"* was that the boys in Detroit had crew cuts and did not approve of The Beatles' hair. They also did not support The Beatles' music because Detroit was the home of Motown. When asked about this campaign during their first American press conference, Paul McCartney said, "We're bringing out a 'Stamp Out Detroit' campaign." Everyone understood that the controversy was a publicity stunt. Beatles fans in Detroit were extremely concerned that The Beatles thought everyone in their city hated them. They worried that The Beatles might decide to skip Detroit during their upcoming summer tour of North America. CKLW disc jockey Tom Clay started a fan club called the International Beatle Booster Ball Club (the I.B.B.B.). Fans sent Clay $1 and received a membership card. They were entered into a contest where some lucky club members would fly to England and meet The Beatles in person.

In March 1964, Clay held the first International Beatle Booster Ball Club ball at the Coliseum in Detroit. Over 8,000 fans attended. Beatles fans made signs and decorated their cars. One attendee, Valerie Kamm, recalls, "By attending, we

Above left: Photos of Tom Clay displaying a 'Beatle boot' and IBBB club winners meeting The Beatles as shown on the inside of the IBBB record sleeve. Right: IBBB record and front and back of the record sleeve. Top right-hand corner: Membership card for the IBBB Fan Club.

got to listen to great music and demonstrate just how much Detroit truly loved The Beatles. I even made a giant poster with pictures I drew of John, Paul, George, and Ringo to take along." They took photos of the poster, and Clay promised to show these to The Beatles when he was with them a month later. Clay did tell The Beatles about the ball. He was recorded talking to an uninterested John Lennon on a 45 RPM interview disc available for club members for $2. "Everybody came with signs. Some girl had them all over her dress. Pictures of The Beatles were everywhere. They had them on their fingernails."

On April 7, 1964, The Beatles were filming scenes for their first movie, *A Hard Day's Night*, at Twickenham Studios in London. It was there that Clay and his wife, along with the two lucky fan club members, met The Beatles. George Harrison greeted the four Americans. Clay broke the ice, and interviewed each Beatle. The contest winners sat speechless, drinking tea, and watching The Beatles. At one point, the boys sang some of the song, *"It's Alright."* One of the winners, Ellen Deneau, remembers, "They were really goofing around a lot with each other. They were really friendly." They were so friendly that they gave Clay a pair of boots, empty cigarette packets and butts, as well as other miscellaneous items that most people would think were trash. The winners spent three hours with John, Paul,

George, and Ringo. Ellen went home with one of Ringo's rings. She recalls how the meeting ended: "George came back, shook our hands and said, 'It was nice to meet you, and see you in Detroit.'"

Clay now had bragging rights – he had met The Beatles! He took to the air to get more fans to join his International Beatle Booster Ball Club. This time, for $1, fans would receive a picture of The Beatles, a photo of Clay, and something touched by one of The Beatles.

Clay held a second International Beatle Booster Ball Club ball at the Detroit Fair Grounds. Again over 8,000 fans came to show their love for The Beatles. Clay was so excited that he jumped onto the stage and broke a bone in his right hand. Not even a broken bone was going to stop Clay's International Beatle Booster Ball. Clay talked fondly of this event in an interview with his son in 1982: "We had about 15,000 kids there, and it was amazing because even back then, they were restricted by society. The city council passed an ordinance that I could not have a dance in the city. So, I had to tell all the kids that all they could do was come in and sit down and not dance, or otherwise they would have arrested me. Fifteen thousand kids just sat there. I showed them The Beatles boots that Ringo gave me, and I showed them the jacket that George gave me, and all the paraphernalia John and Paul gave me. That was my final shtick. They were screaming and yelling because I said, 'Do we love The Beatles?' They were going, 'Yeah!' They're screaming, right? Then I said, 'Hold it just a minute.' And every one of them stopped. Even then, the power of love — look what it did to those kids. They were so excited that some adult said, 'I love you.'" Clay promised to bring 10 fan club members backstage to meet the band when they came to Detroit in September. This new contest delivered more dollar bills from new club members to Clay's doorstep.

After two successful International Beatle Booster Ball Club balls in Detroit, Clay held another one at the Cleveland Arena in Ohio, where his radio show had a large following. Once again, thousands of teenage girls came dressed in their best Beatles garb and paraded around with signs that declared their undying love for the band. They listened to Beatles music, but the four-hour event's highlight was when Clay shared stories about his recent trip to London to meet The Beatles. One fan, Dee Elias, said, "There was not a band or dancing. Tom played Beatles music and was supposed to show a film of him meeting them personally, but he said the projector was broken. For the next few hours, Tom Clay had us mesmerized as he talked about his trip to meet The Beatles." The pinnacle was when he showed the boot Ringo gave him. He gave out Paul's cigarette butt, John's fountain pen, George's handkerchief, and one of Ringo's rings for door prizes.

After all those public appearances, Clay received 17,000 requests for membership in his International Beatle Booster Ball Club. He quickly discovered that he could not handle the demand. He claimed that he lost some of the applications. Fans were sending him money and not receiving their promised fan club kits. Angry parents began contacting the radio station where Clay worked, CKLW, demanding either a refund or a membership kit.

When they started to investigate Clay, they discovered that he had a background in radio as a con man. In 1959, he'd been fired from WJBK in Detroit when he confessed to taking gifts and money from record companies in exchange for playing records on his program. Then the next year, he lost another disc jockey job for what was called "differences over station policy." Because of all the controversy surrounding his International Beatle Booster Ball Club, CKLW radio fired Clay. His last day on the air was June 19, 1964. Young fans still believed and trusted Clay. They knew he wouldn't let them down, and would even take the 10 fan club members backstage to meet The Beatles in Detroit. But when September came and The Beatles were at Olympia Stadium, Tom Clay was nowhere to be found.

KFWB Beatles Booster Rally newspaper advertisement.

Clay sent out a letter to the International Beatle Booster Ball Club members saying, "Do you honestly believe that I'm a liar…. a cheat … a crook …. A phony? After the hours and hours of trying to get out your I.B.B.B. kits, and messing up terribly because I had never done anything like it before, what reason could I possibly have for promising to take 10 teens with me and not being there? It is because I'm a liar and a cheat?" He went on to say that he never used the kids' money to get rich. In the end, he said he was going back to England in July 1965 and wanted to take two club members with him. All fans had to do was send him $2 to enter the contest.

Besides being entered into the new contest, club members received an interview record titled *Remember, We Don't Like Them We Love Them*. When Beatles (U.S.A.) Ltd. learned about the record and fan club, they were not pleased. Walter Hofer sent Clay a cease and desist letter that told him to stop selling his interview record, which would put an end to the International Beatle Booster Ball Club. Clay ignored the lawyers' demands, and continued to sell the album. Both sides corresponded, but neither Clay nor Hofer would back down.

After hearing of Clay's successful International Beatle Booster Ball Club balls, KFWB radio in Hollywood decided to cash in on the concept and held "The Beatles Booster Rally." On May 22, 1964, more than two hundred Beatles fans camped out overnight outside Wallach's Music City Show to purchase the 98 cent tickets to the rally. While in line, the fans cheered, sang, and danced. Meanwhile, one fan, Linda Ackerman, walked up and down the queue of mostly independent fan club members with a sign that read, "Join now – National Beatles Fan Club of America." The fans made themselves comfortable on the sidewalk in sleeping bags they'd brought with them. A local pizza parlor stopped by to deliver a midnight pizza to the Beatlemaniacs.

With 50,000 tickets available, and after much advertising and fanfare, The Beatles Booster Rally was held at Los Angeles Memorial Stadium on May 27, 1964. Seventeen hundred Beatles fans, almost all in their teens, celebrated their love for the Fab 4. One of the events at this rally was for the best fan club presentation. The fan club members dressed in Beatles clothing, and carried signs declaring their club's devotion to John, Paul, George, and Ringo. One club that was represented was The Beatles West Coast Fan Club. This chartered club's president was a girl named Ping Tom, whose mother made her a Beatles-styled collarless jacket specifically for the rally. Two attendees, Paula and Mickey, were not involved in a fan club, but when they saw Ping's banner advertising her club's newsletter, *The Beatles Booster*, it sparked an idea in Paula's head. The girls called themselves the Beatles Booster Fan Club and made a scroll that said at the top, "To show our true devotion to you." Their goal was to gather 10,000 signatures supporting their efforts to meet The Beatles. They got a few friends to help them go around to the markets and bus stops, asking everyone they met to sign the scroll. By the time they were finished, it was about five inches thick. The girls were successful in getting it to The Beatles. Eventually they met the boys.

Besides the sign parade for Beatles fan clubs, The Beatles Booster Rally held a variety of contests, including a Beatles sound-alike contest where local

FAN CLUB SING-ALONG

Can't Find My Glove
(sung to the tune Can't Buy Me Love)

Can't find my glove, oh!
Glove oh
Can't find my glove, oh!

I'll buy you a diamond ring my friend
If you help me with my plight
I'll get you anything my friend
"Cause I'm just not feelin' right
And I don't care too much for Mommy
Mommy can't find my glove

I'll give you all I've got to give
If you say you'll help me to
Find the glove I've lost today
Cause sadly now I don't have two
And I don't care too much for Mommy
Mommy can't find my glove

Can't find my glove oh!
Even though I need it so
Can't find my glove
No, no, no, no!

Say that you'll help me find my things
And I'll be satisfied
Tell me that you have the kind of thing
That Mommy just can't find
I don't care too much for Mommy
Mommy can't find my glove
Owww

Can't find my glove, oh
Even though I need it so
Can't find my glove, oh
No, no, no, no!

Say that you'll help me find my things
And I'll be satisfied
Tell me that you have the kind of thing
That Mommy just can't find
And I dont care too much for Mommy
Mommy can't find my glove

Can't find my glove, oh
Glove, oh
Can't find me love, oh
Oh

When I Was Four
(sung to the tune The Night Before)

We sold our good pies, ah, when I was four
Mud was in your eyes, ah, when I was four
Now today I find you have changed your mind
Treat me like you did when I was four

Were you selling pies, ah, when I was four?
Was I so unwise, ah, when I was four?
When I held your ear you were so sincere
Treat me like you did when I was four

last bite is the bite I will remember you by
When I think of things we did,
it makes me want to cry

We sold our good pies, ah, when I was four
Mud was in your eyes, ah, when I was four
Now today I find you have changed your mind
Treat me like you did when I was four

When I held your ear you were so sincere
Treat me like you did when I was four

Last bite is the bite I will remember you by
When I think of things we did
it makes me want to cry

Were you selling pies, ah, when I was four?
Was I so unwise, ah, when I was four?
When I held your ear you were so sincere
Treat me like you did when I was four
When I was four

I've Just Cleaned My Face
(sung to the tune I've Just Seen A Face)

I've just cleaned my face
I can't forget the time or place
Where it got wet
It is just the one for me
And I want all the world to see
It's wet mm-mm-mm-mm-mm

Had it been another day
I might have looked another way
And I'd have never been aware
But as it is I'll clean it more
Tonight, di-di-di-di'n'di

Paul n' yes I'm fallin'
And she keeps callin'
Me Flanagan

I have never known
The like of this, I've been alone
And I have missed spots
That were out of sight
But other soaps were never quite
Like this, di-di-di-di'ndi

Paul n' yes I'm fallin'
And she keeps callin'
Me Flanagan

Paul n' yes I'm fallin'
And she keeps callin'
Me Flanagan

Iv'e just cleaned my face
I can't forget the time or place
Where it got wet
It's just the one for me
And I want all the world to see
It's wet, mm-mm-mm-di-di-di

Paul n' yes I'm fallin'
And she keeps callin'
Me Flanagan

Oh, Paul n' yes, I am fallin'
And she keeps callin'
Me Flanagan

♡ do you want ringo to be your man?

♡ is george the one for you?

♡ are you a john girl?

♡ is paul your boy?

take the quiz

Which BEATLE is meant to be your top gear guy?

1. How do your friends describe you?
   a. Smart and witty
   b. Cute and kind
   c. Quiet and mysterious
   d. Sweet and Funny

2. What is your favorite color?
   a. Green
   b. Blue
   c. Black
   d. Red

3. When you go out on a date, where do you like to go?
   a. A poetry reading
   b. A nice restaurant
   c. The cinema
   d. Dancing at a nightclub

4. What is your favorite subject in school?
   a. Art
   b. Literature
   c. Science
   d. Music

5. Which of the following would you like a boy to say to you?
   a. "I wanna hold your hand"
   b. "P.S. I love you."
   c. "Do you want to know a secret?"
   d. "I wanna be your man."

A.

If you chose mostly A: John - You are a John girl because you like to be with a boy that is interested in the arts. You like spending your time with a romantic guy who is smart but doesn't take himself too seriously.

If you chose mostly B: Paul - Paul is your guy because you like a boy that is both good-looking and nice. He enjoys spending time with you at a fancy restaurant and writing you love letters.

If you chose mostly C: George - If you are a girl that is devoted to George, you like to have a little mystery in your relationship. You prefer to be with a boy that is thoughtful and quiet instead of someone that is always the life of the party.

If you chose mostly D: Ringo - The Beatles' drummer is your man. You like to be with someone who keeps you laughing and enjoys having fun, especially out on the dance floor. He also enjoys spending time with you listening to your favorite records.

bands sang Beatles songs. The winner was a band called the "Inland Empire Beatles."

The fans had a great time, but Coliseum manager Bill Nicholas did not. He told the *Los Angeles Times*, "They jumped up and down on the seats. They gave our new seats a rough time. We're going to have to reset the springs." Nicholas continued that it was more than just the seats that were hurt: "One officer was bitten on the hand eight times by a bunch of delirious dames." In the end, it was decided they would not have any more Beatles rallies. It was too expensive.

Other radio station fan clubs had Beatles balls and rallies. KQV Beatles Fan Club in Pittsburgh, headed by disc jockey Chuck Brinkman, had a special guest speaker when George Harrison's sister Louise Harrison Caldwell came to the KQV Beatles Ball. Some individual fan clubs held Beatles rallies, including California's San Mateo County Beatles Fan Club, which had one on August 8, 1964. Topics of discussion included the opening of The Beatles' movie, plans for their upcoming airport arrival, and fan club business. Club president Liane Hoolsema told fans to, "Bring your signs, lunch, voice, and manners. We want this to be the greatest rally yet."

Ringo Stops By San Francisco

Ringo surrounded by fan club members and press at the San Francisco Airport. June 12, 1964.

The Beatles were scheduled to begin their first world tour on June 4, 1964, when Ringo Starr was stricken with a severe case of tonsillitis. Following doctor's orders, the drummer had to recover in the hospital. Because it was too late to cancel the tour, a stand-in drummer, Jimmie Nicol, was given the job. John, Paul, George, and Jimmie traveled to Holland, Hong Kong, and Australia while Ringo remained in London.

On June 11, Ringo was given a clean bill of health and was released from the hospital. He needed to get to Australia as quickly as possible to join his bandmates. A route through San Francisco, where he would change planes, would get Ringo back with The Beatles 24 hours faster than any other flight plan.

Ringo was about to leave with Brian Epstein when the drummer realized he'd forgotten his passport. Though Brian sent someone to Ringo's house to retrieve it, it would not arrive before the plane took off. Ringo was able to receive special clearance to travel without a passport because, "After all, a Beatle's a Beatle all over the world, isn't he?" The document was put on the next flight and reunited with Ringo before leaving San Francisco.

The San Francisco International Airport was trying to send teenagers looking for Ringo on detours all day long. They told fans he would go straight from the plane to a private lounge, and would not speak to anyone, but the newspaper also gave Ringo's schedule. He would arrive at 5:30 PM on Pan Am Flight 121 and enter at the South Terminal Gate 71 or 72. This information was like gold to his fans.

San Francisco had several large, active fan clubs. Once the fan clubs learned the flight information, they organized themselves into groups. They got to the airport and gathered in the Pan Am plane loading area. Their "We love Ringo" signs made them obvious. One fan club president brought a megaphone, and led the crowd of 800 fans in chants of "Beatles I love you," and "Yeah! Yeah! Yeah!" Forty sheriff deputies hoped that they wouldn't face a riot once the famous drummer finally arrived.

The big moment happened at 7:40 PM. Ringo wore a collarless black suit, black boots, and a white and lavender striped shirt. He was ushered into a lounge where the press was waiting for him, along with two San Francisco-area fan club presidents. One was Maurie Brigham of *The San Francisco Beatles Fan Club*. She gave Ringo a wrapped present that he held but did not get to open. Five days after this extraordinary meeting, Maurie wrote a letter to the editor of *The Times* (San Mateo, California) describing it: "I walked into the press room. I could hear him talking but couldn't see him. Suddenly I was being introduced to him. He held both of my hands. I wandered around, still finding it hard to believe that I talked and held hands with Ringo Starr!" The president from the other club gave Ringo a large stuffed koala bear. You can see Ringo with the bear in photographs of him arriving in Australia.

Other fan club members weren't so lucky. They had to rely on the help of reporters and police to deliver their gifts. One passionate fan told a television reporter, "He's so cute! My girlfriend and me, Judy, gave him a present and they took it to him, a surfer shirt. And we wrote on the card that it was the latest fad in California."

One of the press reporters asked Ringo if he'd like to see his fans, and he said he would. Ringo and Brian Epstein went out into the Pan Am lounge to greet the 800 Beatles fans, most of whom were there with their fan clubs. The hysterical fans were screaming, waving, and trying to climb over one another to get close to the Beatle. Ringo waved to the crowd, then stood on top of a table to be seen better. Ringo tried to "shush" everyone by putting his finger up to his lips, but the screams just got louder. As Ringo left for his connecting flight, he heard girls screaming, "Ringo, I love you!" As they chased Ringo down the hallway, one girl yelled: "Ringo, tell George I love him!"

Ringo For President

In the summer of 1964, fans across the United States formed an unexpected club. 1964 was an election year. Democrat Lyndon B. Johnson and Republican Barry Goldwater were hitting the campaign trail, and their supporters were backing them with the usual barrage of signs, buttons, and T-shirts. So Beatles fans began their own grassroots campaign for their ideal choice: Ringo Starr.

The Ringo for President campaign began on July 7 in San Francisco during a protest against Barry Goldwater. Twelve teenage girls from the The Beatles Fan Club of San Francisco stood one block away from the rally holding signs that declared "Ringo for President." It did not matter that none of the picketers were old enough to vote. The group took a break only to sing "Happy Birthday" to Ringo, who was celebrating his 24th that same day.

This new club gathered again on July 13 when the Republican National Convention was in San Francisco. Adults laughed when they saw the group of 100 teenage girls (with a few boys) marching through the hotel lobby and into the street carrying signs bearing slogans like "Go Bingo with Ringo" and "Ringo is the Most from Coast to Coast." The march was led by the president of The Beatles Fan Club of San Francisco, Helena Rand. Through a bullhorn she told the marchers to move in an orderly fashion, reminding them to act as if Ringo was watching them. The marchers ended up at Union Square, where others were marching to support Barry Goldwater or Governor Scranton.

News reporters found the group to be a funny addition to the day's typically dull news story. They interviewed some of the fans, putting them in newspapers and on television. One fan told a reporter, "If Ringo were in the White House, I'd get to do the frug there, too, and not just that Luci. It ought to be more democratic. Why should that Johnson kid have a monopoly?" When asked where Ringo stood on defoliation, a supporter said, "If that's the stuff they put in water to keep kids from getting holes in their teeth, we're for it."

Elaine McAfee and The North Texas Chapter of The Beatles Fan Club show they support Ringo For President while waiting to buy tickets to A Hard Day's Night.

After seeing the The Beatles Fan Club of San Francisco support Ringo for President, fan clubs around the United States joined the cause. Two fan club members from Cleveland were inspired. Lynette Powell and Sharon German worked with radio station KYC, planning a thousand fans' march from the radio station to the Public Square. A group from Detroit chartered a bus to join in. Each participant was given an armband, poster, and badges that said, "Ringo for President." In Mansfield, Ohio, five members of fan clubs took to the streets with "Vote for Ringo" signs. They carried the signs to Cleveland for the rally there.

In Fort Worth, Texas, while waiting to buy tickets for *A Hard Day's Night*, Elaine McAfee from The North Texas Chapter of The Beatles Fan Club led one hundred fan club members in a "Ringo for President" demonstration. They held homemade signs. The local newspaper said, "If the voting power of the young fans only matched their enthusiasm, Goldwater might have cause to worry."

One fan club formed the offshoot Kingsport Association for Ringo for President Club (or KARPC) from Kingsport, Tennessee. This 30-member group worked all summer to give Ringo the publicity he needed. Founding member Carolyn Dockery said, "I think Ringo is better looking than all the other

Presidential nominees. I'm just crazy about Ringo." The club made signs and paraded around town with them. They looked forward to having Ringo in the White House because "we'll have Beatle furniture, Beatle wallpaper and Beatle music." The parents of KARPC members encouraged the girls. The club president's mother told a reporter what many parents were thinking: "It's keeping them busy, and they're having a ball making posters and listening to Beatle music." In other words, the kids were keeping out of trouble and not bothering their parents for the whole summer.

The campaign had commercial appeal as well. On August 8, 1964, a group known as The Young World Singers released a novelty 45 single titled *Ringo for President*. It only went to number 132 on the U.S. charts. One record shop, The Ritz, sponsored a Ringo for President Rally. On a Saturday morning, fans were able to get membership cards and hear a live band.

Some adults did not quite understand that this was all in fun. One woman wrote an editorial that said, "[These fans] are very immature, and the very thought is utterly ridiculous!" She went on to write, "Perhaps they aren't familiar with the actual basic qualifications for being President." To this, the KARPC president responded, "She should really understand that this isn't really serious business and that one would be daft to really vote for Ringo in the upcoming election (not that we wouldn't like for them to, but you understand the circumstances)."

Ringo Starr and the other Beatles were in on the joke. During a San Francisco press conference, Ringo was asked what he thought of the campaign. He said he thought it was marvelous. When asked about who would be in his cabinet, George Harrison volunteered to be the door while John Lennon wanted to be the cupboard.

Johnson won the election by a landslide over Goldwater. However, a few unknown people wrote in "Ringo Starr," much to the delight of Beatles fans around the nation.

A Hard Day's Night

In August of 1964, the first major Beatles event of the summer occurred. The Beatles' first motion picture, *A Hard Day's Night*, was released in theaters. Beatles fan club members were excited to share the moment of seeing The Beatles on the big screen. Many clubs went together. The club's size didn't matter; The Beatles movie was showing in cities both large and small.

CHAPTER 2 – THE FAN CLUB PEOPLE

A Hard Day's Night newspaper ad and Beatles movie ticket promotional item.

Most cities in the United States and Canada started selling advance tickets in the middle of July. In many towns The Beatles' new film was the event of the summer. The advance ticket buyers lined up outside the theaters making the movie into news. Disc jockeys were on hand to sell tickets. They broadcast live from the sites, held contests, and gave away albums and movie tickets. The DJ from one radio station told the waiting fans he was making an international phone call to speak to The Beatles about the film. What fans actually heard was an open-ended recording that was part of the station's information kit promoting the movie. The disc jockey asked scripted questions, and someone back at the station played the record with The Beatles' answers.

Every fan got a ticket bearing a photograph of The Beatles, and an identification tag that read, "I've got my Beatles movie ticket – have you?" Tickets sold quickly. In Toronto, fans bought three thousand tickets in ninety minutes, while New York City took only four and a half hours to sell out all of their theaters. In Pittsburgh, members of *The Beatles Crackers* radio fan club had the privilege of moving to the front of the ticket line.

United Artists wanted to bring a lot of publicity to the New York premiere of *A Hard Day's Night*. It was scheduled for August 11 at the Beacon Theatre in Times Square. As one area president, Debbie Gendler, recollected in 1994, "They decided to send the New York metropolitan fan club presidents a telegram asking the presidents to please get their fan club members to the premiere the night before. They would have police officers there, serve us hot chocolate and donuts, and we'd be secure. We would camp on the sidewalk overnight, waiting to see the movie. Of course, I had to do that, and I remember begging my parents to please let me do this and showing them the telegram and telling them how safe we'd be. It was incredibly exciting just to be there with everyone else. All the fans. It was terrific!"

Fan clubs came from all over with signs to show their love for The Beatles. Signs included "Beatles 4 Ever," "The Beatles are Gear," "Ringo is a Starr," and one politically-minded fan had a sign saying, "Not the Elephant, Not the Donkey, but The Beatles." One fan club arrived in a decorated school bus with a large banner on the front, declaring "It'll be a Hard Day's Night if Ringo Doesn't get Elected."

Many girls were wearing buttons declaring "I love Paul" or "I love The Beatles." They spent the night and early morning hours singing Beatles songs and reading magazines, as they made new friends. When the police arrived with the film reels, the screams were so loud; you would have thought The Beatles themselves were delivering the reels. While none of The Beatles were at the New York premiere, there were a few celebrities in the crowd. Milton Berle was there as well as one of the movie's co-stars, Norman Rossington. The actor, who played the part of "Norm," the road manager, was besieged by girls. They wanted to kiss and touch him

Milton Berle and Beatles fans show off their movie tickets at the New York City premiere of A Hard Day's Night.

just because he had been with The Beatles. The 2,000-seat theater was sold out for all three screenings. One fan observed that for the first 10 minutes of the movie, there was one continual scream. She also noted, "Whenever anyone in the film made an unkind remark about Ringo, they were greeted with boos and hisses." By the end of the movie, she had succumbed like everyone else. "The whole audience joined in with clapping, screaming, and singing. I could scarcely hear The Beatles at all, but it just didn't matter. It was like being at an actual show."

In another part of New York, eight members of Chapter IX of Beatles (U.S.A.) Ltd. were waiting in line to see the 7 PM showing of *A Hard Day's Night*, at the Asher Theater. They all wore handmade name tags in the shape of The Beatles' heads. A teenage reporter from *The New Yorker* was there to speak to fans and observe what was going on. The members informed him of what their fan club had been doing: "Cheryl and Chris wrote a 300-page novel about The Beatles." The reporter noted that many of the fans were holding signs and singing "We Love You Beatles." One moment brought drama when a girl came to the line waving a flag that boldly read "Up with The Rolling Stones, Down with The Beatles." The entire queue of Beatlemaniacs started to chant "Down with The Stones." Cheryl from Chapter IX of Beatles (U.S.A.) Ltd. stepped forward and yelled: "A Rolling Stone gathers nothing!" All The Beatles fans laughed and cheered, and the one fan of The Rolling Stones left.

During the film, kids screamed during the songs but were quiet during the dialogue. Afterward, the reporter met up with Chapter IX of Beatles (U.S.A.) Ltd.'s president, Carol, to get her reaction to The Beatles' movie. "The movie was good," she said. "It showed that The Beatles weren't phonies."

This kind of scene was playing out across the United States and Canada. In Davenport, Iowa, members of the chartered Quad City Beatles Fan Club spent the early morning hours of August 12 camped out in front of the RKO Orpheum in sleeping bags. They were determined to be first inside the theater because a rival club had already beat them to the box office for tickets. Members spent their time reading magazines and a special Beatles scrapbook. They had their transistor radios handy to hear the summer's hottest songs.

In Calgary, Alberta, 1,300 fans set up camp, many arriving as early as 5 AM. The movie wasn't showing until 8 PM. The local newspaper's reviewer wrote, "Take 1,300 youngsters yelling once every minute, and you have pandemonium. Add at least four fainting or swooning spells, and the result is chaos."

Above: Elaine McAfee leads The North Texas Chapter of The Beatles Fan Club in singing "I Want To Hold Your Hand" before seeing A Hard Day's Night.

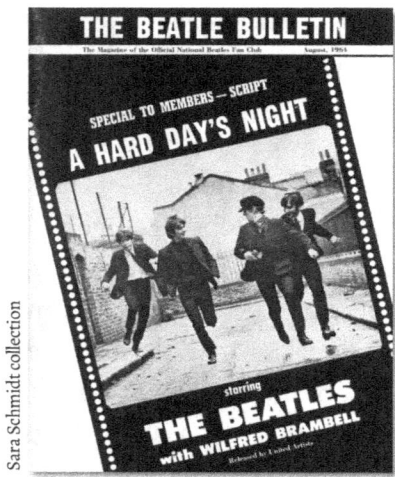

The full script of A Hard Day's Night *included in the August 1964 Beatle Bulletin.*

In Houston, Elaine McAfee and The North Texas Chapter of The Beatles Fan Club stood outside a local theater and led the club in singing *I Want to Hold Your Hand*. In Queens, New York, fan club president Leslie Samuels was not going to miss the film's premiere. "I spent the whole weekend watching it at least seventeen times with a bunch of girls. Of course, we screamed the entire time." Some of the fan clubs took the movie very seriously. The Ralston Avenue Branch of the School 91 Beatles Fan Club in Indianapolis charged a 25 cent fine to each club member who did not attend the movie premiere without a proper excuse.

In early August 1964, Beatles (U.S.A.) Ltd. mailed out their first *Beatle Bulletin* newsletter. More than just a newsletter, it included the full script for *A Hard Day's Night*. The bulletin was a pleasant surprise for those who had joined Beatles (U.S.A.) Ltd. Fans would use the script to act out scenes from the movie during fan club meetings. Janis Stover recalls, "I was a member of The Beatles fan club, and I received a copy of the movie script from it. By the time I saw the movie, three of us had memorized parts of the script, and after seeing the movie three or four times, we had memorized it."

Fans Protest

The month before The Beatles returned to the United States for their 1964 North American tour, fan clubs began plotting ways to meet them in person. One popular method was to meet the mayor of the city and talk to him about The Beatles. The earliest such meeting was held in March of 1964 when members of The Yeah Beatles Fan Club in San Diego demonstrated peacefully in front of City Hall with signs and a written request for The Beatles to perform in San Diego.

"I was talking to one of the guys at the *San Diego Union*," recalls The Yeah Beatles Fan Club president Kathie Sexton. "He said that I should make the mayor a member of the fan club and go up to his office. I never dreamed of doing that. But I led a protest march through downtown and ended up getting to meet the mayor and making him a member, and we ended up on the front page of the newspaper. We were lucky it was a slow news day."

The Beatles Fan Club of San Francisco marched to City Hall on August 10. They carried "Ringo for President"

The Yeah Beatles Fan Club with the San Diego mayor.

The Beatles Fan Club of San Francisco jumps into the fountain at City Hall.

signs, and asked to talk to the mayor. They wanted a key to the city to present to The Beatles when the band got to San Francisco on the 19th. At City Hall, fan club president Helena Rand learned that the mayor was on vacation. The city's Public Director was all out of cardboard keys.

To protest, Helena led the club members into the Civic Center fountain. One member, Darlene Fagley, told the newspaper, "We told him that we'd do something drastic."

Beatles Bobbies International Incorporated

Beatles Bobbies International Incorporated membership card.

In the summer of 1964, a new group of dedicated Beatles fans organized themselves for a different mission. They wanted to give real help to The Beatles, the police, and the fans by attempting to ensure safety at concerts, airport arrivals, and outside of hotels. This group went by various names, including Teen Screen's Beatle Guardian Angels, Beatles Safety Patrol, and Fantastic Fans. However, the best-known group was Beatles Bobbies International Incorporated.

The first group of Beatles Bobbies International Incorporated was formed in Baltimore, Maryland, and by September, there were two hundred and fifty active members. Beatles Bobbies clubs popped up all over the country, in San Francisco, New York City, Miami, and Dallas. They were organized just like any other Beatles fan club, with a president and regular meetings. Each Beatles Bobbie signed a pledge to keep her composure around The Beatles while encouraging other fans to do likewise. Each member had a membership card and wore an armband emblazoned with "BBII."

During the 1964 Beatles North American tour, Beatles Bobbies International Incorporated were out in full force. They led crowds in singing "We Love You Beatles." Singing helped fans remain calm. The Bobbies discouraged concertgoers from standing on chairs, barring the view of others. The police didn't know what to think of the girls. Baltimore's president, Jo Kandalis, said, "The police were skeptical, and although they could not stop us from trying to help, they would not give us the authority to do so either. It was most important that they realize we were truly trying to help."

The Philadelphia group put a notice in a local paper stating that anyone acting disorderly would be arrested, and anyone throwing eggs or rotten fruit would be removed from the theater. Fans in Dallas, Texas were especially concerned about The Beatles' safety. It had only been 10 months since President Kennedy was assassinated in their town. Dell Perry, from Beatles (U.S.A.), Chapter 56, asked fans not to pull The Beatles' hair or rip their clothes. She reminded everyone, "Don't you just know what would happen to Dallas if a Beatle was hurt in our city."

Beatles Bobbies in San Francisco meet to discuss how they will keep Beatles fans 'orderly and happy.'

Touring the U.S.A.

At the tour's first stop in San Francisco, area Beatles fan club members wanted to show the rest of the country how to welcome the world's best band. On August 14, Helena Rand and three other officers from The Beatles Fan Club of San Francisco met with the manager of the Hilton Hotel, where The Beatles would be staying. The manager wanted to ensure the safety of The Beatles, and that of the hotel. The fans promised that the

Members of various fan clubs in the San Francisco area get ready to greet The Beatles at the airport.

girls surrounding the hotel would act civilized. Helena explained to a reporter, "We have formed the Bobbies. They'll try to keep the kids orderly and happy."

In exchange, the fan club was allowed to set up an informational table in the Hilton lobby. On August 19, the girls arrived at 4 AM and began setting up. They put up a large banner that read: "The San Francisco Beatles Fan Club says San Francisco will Twist and Shout now that The Beatles are Here." Another flag said, "San Francisco says Hello to Cynthia Lennon." On the table were Beatles photographs and information on how to become a club member. Two members, Kathy and Pam, had made a 150-pound "Beatles beetle" out of scraps of cloth at a cost of $400. They displayed it in the lobby. When the *San Francisco Chronicle* asked why they were there, Helena answered, "The Beatles have talent, sex appeal, personality, wit, and hair."

Meanwhile, at San Francisco International Airport, a 25-square-foot wooden platform was built near the main terminal, with a five-foot fence surrounding it. This area was called "Beatleville." When The Beatles arrived, they were to stand on the platform and greet the fans, who would be standing behind the fence. Beatles Bobbies International Incorporated were there in their white shirts, red jackets, and "BBII" armbands. They were ready to keep Beatles fans orderly. "We were just keeping the kids back," said a 15-year-old Bobbie named Rita. At one point, the police told the large group of fans to move back from the

The Beatles on display for less than one minute in "Beatleville" as Beatles fan club members from the Beatles Bobbies International Incorporated, San Francisco, Oakland, East Bay, and Peninsula fan clubs surround them.

fence. The Beatles Fan Club of San Francisco's Bobbies then tried to take charge, telling the Oakland, Peninsula, and East Bay clubs that they needed to move back. A screaming match started.

The most vocal club was The East Bay Beatles Fan Club. They argued with The Beatles Fan Club of San Francisco about who loved The Beatles the most. One San Francisco member said, "It's not that we're critical of the East Bay members. It's that we feel we love [The Beatles] more." Terry Plumb, from East Bay, answered, "Not true. We have four presidents. The San Francisco club only has one." The yelling and screaming got so out of hand that the police announced that everyone would have to leave if the fighting did not stop. Desperate to see The Beatles, the girls calmed down, but anger and excitement still fueled them as the plane landed.

The four Beatles descended the stairs. The fans lost control and began pushing on the fence surrounding the platform. The Beatles made it to the platform, and Paul McCartney began to speak into the microphone. Fearing for The Beatles' safety, the police corralled them into a limousine in less than a minute. As they did this, the fans knocked down the fence. When asked about what happened, John Lennon said, "There's no doubt about it, a crowd like those we just encountered would tear us limb from limb if we were not surrounded by a large police guard." This was The Beatles' last announced airport appearance.

In January 1964, Cheryl Stewart, Sharman Weston, and Sharon Wallinger formed The Seattle Beatles Fan Club. Seven months later, on August 21, they found themselves sitting in front of The Beatles during the Seattle press conference. Cheryl asked a question, and the fan club president enthusiastically reported, "They were just wonderful! Just as I'd pictured them!" Vice president Sharon was just as enthusiastic when she said, "I love them! Ringo held my hand!" A witness to this event didn't think Ringo was as excited: "One girl held Ringo's hand. Someone called to him to leave. He said, 'Sorry, luv, I've got to go.' She wouldn't let him go. 'Luv, I've got to go.' She still wouldn't go. 'Luv, LET ME GO!'"

The three girls collected The Beatles' cigarette butts from the ashtrays on the press table. They would show these to their fellow fan club members.

The Beatles gave a press conference at the Cinnamon Cinder, a teenage club in Los Angeles, on August 24. Many adolescent girls were present, including several fan club officers. Directly after the press conference, John Lennon was presented with some gold records. One of the fan clubs gave Paul and George a

Ringo at the press conference in Los Angeles on August 23, 1964, with the key to the city presented to him by fan club members.

special scrapbook, and another presented Ringo with a giant key to California. Paul left the presentations holding a bouquet of roses from yet another area fan club president.

Not every fan club president was as lucky. San Diego Fan Club president Cathy Owens had two trophies she wanted to give to The Beatles. The eighty-member club had saved money to buy Ringo an award for being the world's greatest drummer. They also had one for the entire group for bringing joy to the fan club members. The broken-hearted Cathy told the *Herald Examiner*, "Everyone was so proud because I was going to make a presentation. They all counted on me. Now I've let them down." She hoped the fan club members would be understanding and know that she had tried. "Paul knew I was there," she continued. "But they kept pushing him away."

When The Beatles came to Cincinnati on August 27, Dusty Rhodes did not disappoint the members of The Beatles Booster Club. The disc jockey held a contest that allowed seven fan club members to briefly meet The Beatles backstage. "It was very secretive," said Joyce Cunningham, one of the winners. "We went through a door under some of the seating into a very crowded, somewhat small room, and all of a sudden space opened up in front of me, and I could see John, Paul, George, and Ringo sitting at a table not more than a few feet away." Each of the fan club winners shook each Beatle's hand and spoke to them for a short moment. "Someone had given Ringo a drawing," Cunningham recalled. "When he stood up to unroll it, I was able to reach out and touch his hair. I remember the other Beatles watching and chuckling."

Membership in the fan club had its advantages. When The Beatles performed in Philadelphia, one girl was lying face down in front of the stage while the fabs sang. The police told her to move back to her seat. She refused and said to them that she was the president of the National Beatles Fan Club, and the police left her alone for the rest of the show.

Linda McMillan and Ethel Mako, fan club officers from Hammond, Indiana, went on a mission to legally meet their idols when The Beatles came to Indianapolis on September 3. The girls asked the mayor of Hammond for the city's key to present to The Beatles, but he refused because it wasn't educational. Undiscouraged, the girls went to the next town over, East Chicago. That mayor thought it was a great idea. They had a gold key with "To The Beatles, East Chicago, Indiana 9-64" engraved on it. On the day of the Indianapolis show, Linda and Ethel had the police escort them to The Beatles' press conference. Besides giving the boys the key, Ethel gave flowers to Paul and Linda gave a bouquet to George. They also asked for permission to charge the sixty fan club members' dues as donations to the John F. Kennedy Memorial Library Fund. After the meeting, the girls were speechless. All Linda could say was, "It was the biggest thrill of my life."

Chicago, Illinois had numerous fan clubs, and all of them desperately wanted to meet The Beatles on their stop there on September 5. Twin sisters Cindy and Cathy Strohacker ran the Chicago Beatle Fan Society (CBFS) and hoped to present The Beatles with the keys to Chicago. The mayor told them, "We have no knowledge of The Beatles other than what we have read in the papers. The Beatles will be one more group of entertainers coming to Chicago, and their status will be that of all entertainers who are interested in nothing more than that they will have a bunch of customers at the box office." It was discouraging, but they did not give up: "Now we're going to try to give The Beatles a scrapbook we've made of all their press clippings. We'd give anything if only we could meet them." They were able to get their club's badges sent to The Beatles. Ringo wore his pinned to his suit throughout the press conference.

The Wheaton Community Beatles Society had baked the guys a sizeable beetle-shaped cake. The C-Beatle Fans promised not to scream if they could meet them. Sue Meirseonne from the The Official Chicago Beatles Fan Club said it best: "If there's any way that we can meet The Beatles, we'll find it."

Marti Whitman Edwards and her club, The Chicagoland Beatle People Fan Club, had been trying since July to find a way to meet The Beatles. She wanted to present them with a plaque that read, "To Four Great Guys Who With Warm Smiles

Marti Edwards presenting The Beatles with a plaque from The Chicagoland Beatle People Fan Club. September 5, 1964.

and Fun Loving Ways Have Earned This Plaque of Recognition of Outstanding Worldwide Musical Achievement. From Your Loving Fans, The Chicagoland Beatle People." After several disappointments, three of the fan club members were allowed into the press conference, thanks to Marti's father and Derek Taylor. Before the conference began, the fan club girls presented the plaque. It was all a blur to Marti, but she remembers, "First John and Ringo read it, then John turned around and handed it to George. George read it and handed it to Paul." One of the girls, Jan McFadden, said that shortly afterward she could not feel anything. She was numb. John then slapped her lightly on the arm and asked, "You feel that, don't you?" Jan was disappointed that he did not leave a bruise on her arm. The dazed girls then posed for photos with The Beatles. The Chicagoland Beatle People Fan Club had accomplished the goal that many others in their area had not achieved.

By the time The Beatles arrived in Toronto, Ontario, The Official Canadian Beatles Fan Club had grown to become the largest club outside of the United Kingdom. President Trudy Medcalf had become a minor celebrity due to her job at CHUM radio, and her appearance on Canadian television's version of *To Tell the Truth*. On the day The Beatles came to town, Trudy was sitting in the CHUM radio booth at a public appearance. She was signing autographs. A messenger told her she would welcome The Beatles to Toronto and give a little speech. Trudy had already planned to attend the conference, but now she had to come up with a statement.

Trudy attended the first concert of the night and then went to the press conference. She'd had a special outfit made for the event: all pink and red, including a pink leather hat and pink gloves. "I had on a pair of culottes," Trudy recalled, "You know, pants cut to look like a skirt. Paul started playing with the fabric and said, 'Are these pants, luv? I really like them.' I almost died on the spot." When it was time to welcome The Beatles, Trudy said, "We love you all very much." Trudy will never forget what happened next: "Paul put his hand on my shoulder and looked right in my eyes and said, 'Oh you don't – do you?'" Trudy's photograph with The Beatles was printed on the CHUM radio survey, much to Canadian fan club members' delight and envy.

The mayor of Tampa, Florida, Nick Nuccio, had a controversy on his hands. He wanted to present the keys to Tampa to The Beatles when the tour brought them to Jacksonville, Florida on September 11. He'd gotten a set of keys made with "John, Paul, George, and Ringo" engraved on them. Three girls had written to the mayor, asking him if they could be the city's ambassadors and present the gift to The Beatles. Nuccio agreed. A local fan club from Tampa, The One and Only National Beatles Fan Club, had already made Nuccio an honorary club member earlier that summer. So the club's officers were extremely angered when he did not ask them to be Beatles ambassadors. He chose three random girls instead. His own eight-year-old granddaughter had been heartbroken when her grandpa didn't pick her. In the end, the mayor apologized to the fan club and said, "I want you all to go to Jacksonville as my representatives."

1050 CHUM Radio Station Top 30 chart (cover shown). September 7, 1964.

Not all club members were able to meet The Beatles. Even those who made elaborate plans found themselves heartbroken at the end of the night. One such fan was Marcia Edelston, the president of The Beatles Fan Club Unlimited. A local disc jockey had promised Marcia that he would get her into the press conference when The Beatles came to Baltimore on September 14. She had a plaque she wanted to give Ringo. It read "To The Beatles with luv." She went to the door where she was to meet the disc jockey, but instead was met by a policeman who refused her entry. Clutching the plaque, she stood at the door through the entire conference, hoping her moment would come. When the press conference was over, people poured out. Marcia dropped the plaque, and the engraved metal shield broke off. Marcia left in tears that night. Not only had she failed to meet The Beatles, but she also felt she had disappointed her fan club members.

One group of fans did meet The Beatles that night. Jo Kandalis, president of Beatles Bobbies International Incorporated, along with two other officers, Ellen and Vicki, met the lads at the Holiday Inn after the show. Jo had become friendly with one of the reporters traveling with The Beatles, Bess Coleman, and it was through her that the Bobbies were allowed into The Beatles' suite. They were first introduced to Paul and George. The girls gave them a copy of the "Beatles Bobbies pledge," which Paul read aloud. George was interested in their mission. Vicki said, "He was a good listener to what we said about Beatles Bobbies Inc. although I do think he was a bit confused." They were offered cigarettes by Paul, which they kindly refused. The three girls then went into the bedroom where Ringo and John watched television and laughed at a commercial for Fab laundry detergent. A woman was doing her laundry in a wedding dress, while she explained how the detergent made her clothes "wedding white."

The two Beatles were in good moods and were happy to talk to the three fans about *A Hard Day's Night*. John even sang a little bit of the song and did a little dance. After about 15 minutes, Derek Taylor said that it was time for Jo, Ellen, and Vicki to leave. Getting to meet all four Beatles made their work for Beatles Bobbies International Incorporated worth the effort.

Initially, The Beatles were not supposed to perform in Kansas City, Missouri. However, Charles O. Finley, owner of the Kansas City Athletics baseball team, persisted in badgering Epstein with money. He was able to get The Beatles for a Kansas City performance on September 17. When Finley returned home on August 28, the *Leabets*, a fifty-six-member chartered fan club, greeted him at the airport with a hero's welcome. The club's president, Tina Mitchell, and several club members were there. Fan club member Victoria Moran recalled, "We had a plaque and a box of Annaclairs, specialty chocolates from the Price Candy Company. Mr. Finley liked publicity, so he got the press there." After giving him the gifts, the girls got in a cab and cheered their hero.

Victoria used that encounter to her advantage when The Beatles gave their press conference in Kansas City. She had gotten a press card from *Teen Life* magazine. These were generic press cards that the magazine would sell to anyone who paid them $1. Usually, a teen magazine press card did not get a fan into a Beatles press conference. However, Victoria took things to the next level. She contacted the editor of *Teen Life* and ended up with an official invitation signed by The Beatles' press officer, Derek Taylor.

When she arrived at the hotel for the conference, a police officer would not allow her to go up to the press room. She then noticed Charles O. Finley walking by with a *Playboy* bunny on his arm. She went up to him, explained her predicament, and reminded him that she had been with the fan club that welcomed him at the airport. He pitied the teenager and gave her his open arm, telling her, "Just don't say anything."

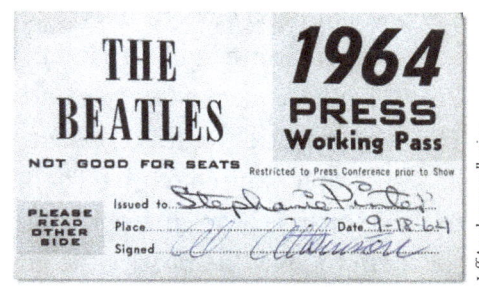

Beatles Fan Club (U.S.A.), Chapter 24 in Dallas fan club president Stephanie Pinter's press pass.

"He didn't have to tell me that because once I saw The Beatles, once I was eight feet from The Beatles, I couldn't have spoken if my life depended on it," Victoria said later. "It was the most extraordinary time and feeling, getting to listen to them with their banter, and everything was funny, witty, and clever. When it was all over, and they were gone, I went up to the table and took one of Paul McCartney's cigarette butts. Then I met up with Tina and others from the fan club, and we went to the concert. We had front-row seats. I didn't think I'd scream – I mean, I was just in the room with The Beatles – but with the first chord, I was on my feet screaming like everybody else."

Like all fan clubs that met The Beatles, Beatles Fan Club (U.S.A.), Chapter 24 out of Dallas, Texas laid the groundwork to meet the boys months before they arrived on September 18. Co-presidents Stephanie Pinter and Yolanda Hernandez

Above: Dallas area fan club members meeting The Beatles.
Right: Signatures obtained by Stephanie Pinter at the Cabana Motor Hotel of Dallas.

learned that The Beatles' favorite color was black. They decided the boys would like black Stetson cowboy hats to represent the Lone Star State. They also had an oversized cigarette lighter that had been engraved, "To the Fab Four – Jolly John, Pretty Paul, Gorgeous George, and Ringo-a-ding Ringo – Dallas Fan Club #24." They wrote a letter to Brian Epstein on fan club stationery, letting him know they had gifts they wanted to give The Beatles when they performed in Dallas. Much to their surprise, Epstein wrote back telling the girls that he'd try to arrange a way for them to give The Beatles the gifts. Beatles Fan Club (U.S.A.), Chapter 24 was so happy to receive the letter that they had a large cake made with a marzipan photo of The Beatles on top. They served the cake at a fan club meeting, but none of the members wanted to eat The Beatles' photo. The club's work did not stop with the letter. They made their intentions known to disc jockeys, newspaper and television reporters, police officers, and staffers at the Cabana Hotel. In an unusual move, they befriended their rivals, Beatles (U.S.A.), Chapter 56. The clubs worked together to make sure all concert-goers were going to be safe. They held a press conference at the Preston State Bank, spreading the word on safety.

With Epstein's letter in hand, Stephanie and Yolanda went to the Cabana Hotel on the day of The Beatles' arrival. A staffer let the girls inside, and while waiting in the lobby, they saw a member of Beatles (U.S.A.), Chapter 56, Marie. Marie had taken a hotel room directly below The Beatles' suite. Once the girls knew The Beatles were in the building, Stephanie, Yolanda, and Marie took the service elevator up one floor. Luck was on their side; just as a policeman started telling them to leave, a hotel staff member recognized Stephanie and Yolanda and allowed all three girls into the corridor. Ultimately, they got into The Beatles' suite. Once inside, they were allowed to mingle with The Beatles. The girls were shocked by their luck, but they held their composure. When approaching her favorite, Paul, Stephanie recalled, "I extended my hand to introduce myself, and he took my hand to acknowledge the handshake and introduced himself to me in a Texas accent. He did a great job, too."

Stephanie also made a point of talking to Brian Epstein, who wanted to know about the gifts for the boys. She told him that she had five black Stetson cowboy hats, one for each of The Beatles, and one for him as well.

The Beatles had received beige cowboy hats when they arrived in Dallas but did not like them. When Epstein mentioned them, John "picked up a beige Stetson from the table and threw it across the room, saying 'You mean this hat, Eppie?'" Brian immediately announced, "The girls have some black Stetsons for you, John." This announcement caught Paul's attention. He asked, "You have black hats?"

Stephanie told him that the girls knew black was his favorite color. Paul chuckled and informed her that blue was actually his favorite color, but he'd love a black hat. The co-presidents were invited to the Dallas press conference to present The Beatles with the black cowboy hats. Epstein suggested that Stephanie get The Beatles' autographs, and he got a sheet of hotel paper. All four Beatles plus Epstein signed. Derek Taylor then took two photographs of the three girls with The Beatles, with Ringo's Polaroid camera. As Taylor took photos, George asked the girls their ages, and they truthfully told him they were 15 and 16. To this, George responded, "Brian, we have illegals in the room!" It was a joke, but the party was ending. It was time for the fan club members to leave. When it was all said and done, they had spent two incredible hours with their idols.

Later that evening, at the press conference, Stephanie and Yolanda got to see The Beatles again, and gave them the cowboy hats. The boys loved these hats and put them on right away. A few days later, they were photographed wearing the hats while they went horseback riding.

The co-presidents of Beatles (U.S.A.), Chapter 56, Dell Perry and Suzie Chapman, were also at the conference. Like Beatles Fan Club (U.S.A.), Chapter 24, they also had Texas-themed gifts for the boys. Their presents were engraved belt buckles and leather Western belts with The Beatles' names stitched on them. The Beatles loved the belts as much as the hats. They also wore these on horseback rides. Dallas was the last stop of the main tour, with just one benefit concert left. Throughout the tour The Beatles remained grateful to the fan clubs across North America.

Their next stop took them to a small town to change airplanes. The Beatles were going to the Reed Pigman Ranch in southern Missouri for a day of relaxation. They landed at the airport in Walnut Ridge, Arkansas, and moved from their touring American Flyers Electra to a small Cessna that took them to the ranch. Only a few boys saw them when they arrived that night, but it was not long until the members of The Beatles 4 Forevermore Fan Club learned the unbelievable news. Many of the members gathered at the airport. They were in awe of The Beatles' airplane. Carrie Mae Snapp said, "We sang Beatles songs and made up stories. We picked cigarette butts off the tarmac in case they had Beatles DNA." A few of the girls then noticed an emergency door that was open a crack, and soon all three found themselves standing on the wing of The Beatles' airplane. The smallest girl got inside and grabbed three small pillows from the seats.

The next morning, Carrie Mae returned to the airport with hopes of seeing The Beatles. Not all of the fan club members could come because it was Sunday.

Their parents would not allow them to miss church. About 50 fans did get to the Walnut Ridge airport. A small white airplane with teal trim landed, and John Lennon got out.

"He was wearing a black suit," Carrie Mae remembers. "He walked by and went straight up the airplane steps." Next out was Ringo Starr in a blue suit, and he followed John. A red (Chevrolet) Suburban was parked three feet from Carrie Mae, and much to her shock, Paul McCartney got out, followed by George Harrison. "He hesitated, and my Dad said, 'Touch him, Carrie Mae! Touch him!' and I reached out and touched George's elbow. He laughed and grinned and then went on up the steps." Once The Beatles were on the airplane, the fans saw Paul and John waving to them. Carrie Mae recalls, "Every girl there will say that Paul looked at her, but they are not right because he made eye contact with just me. I know that for a fact. We never saw them after that, but it was wonderful."

George Harrison as Carrie Mae Snapp saw him at the airport in Walnut Ridge, Arkansas.

Fan Club Growth

Although The Beatles were back home in England by the end of September, North America's love for them continued to grow. More fans joined the various fan clubs, and membership increased. The Beatles' American concerts were still the topic of many club meetings. Members who had met them were happy to share their stories, and fans were buying and trading photos, both candid and professional. At meetings, fans read letters from pen pals from around the country.

The Beatles 4 Forevermore Fan Club in Arkansas still reveled in the joys of having had The Beatles in their town. Founding member Mary had connections with the mayor's office, and got a Xerox copy of The Beatles' autographs from the mayor's daughter. "Boy, did we look at that like it was a holy relic," Carrie Mae recalled. "Everybody came around just looking at it and saying: 'Ooh, look how he makes his "e"' and 'Look at George Harrison's signature. He doesn't say much, but he sure knows how to write.'" Suddenly all of the members changed how they signed their names to look a little more like The Beatles. "For years, I curved the 'e' in my name when I'd write 'Carrie Mae' to look the way George's did," Carrie Mae continued "I remember that it was a big to-do, and everyone told their story because some of us were out there at the airport when The Beatles were there. Myself, Scott, and Mary were out there. It was so amazing that we talked about it forever."

While the fan clubs were growing, some fan club presidents discovered they had taken on a bigger job than they could handle. Future Grammy Award winning country music singer Rosanne Cash was running a Beatles fan club from her home. "I was only about 10 years old," she said. "I organized a system to connect pen pals so kids could write to each other about their favorite Beatle. Ultimately the mail volume overwhelmed me, and I let it go."

The Victor Spinetti Fan Club

In September, a group of friends in the Philadelphia area learned that Victor Spinetti was rehearsing the play *Oh! What a Lovely War*. As Beatlemaniacs, they knew Victor Spinetti played the part of the television director in *A Hard Day's Night*. Longing to talk to anyone who knew The Beatles, one of the girls, Patti Gallo, wrote Victor a letter at his hotel. Much to her surprise, he wrote back. After hearing from him and discovering how kind Victor was, Patti and her friends went to the rehearsals at Forrest Theatre: "After school, we went there and met him. We would just hang out. He was so gracious to us fans. He would bring us all back to his dressing room, and he'd talk about The Beatles and his interactions with them during *A Hard Day's Night*."

Norman Rossington, John Lennon, Paul McCartney, Victor Spinetti, and John Junkin in a scene from A Hard Day's Night.

The group of four fans returned to see the play and talk to Victor several times. When the production moved to Broadway, the girls in Philadelphia decided to start The Victor Spinetti Fan Club. Patti explained, "He was just so gentle, sweet, and nice. We just wanted to do something special for him." The four girls became co-presidents, secretary, and treasurer. They recruited members by asking classmates at their all-girls Catholic high school to join. One hundred fans paid their 20 cent dues to become members. While the club was for Victor, this Beatles co-star shared the spotlight with the boys.

Working at Beatles (U.S.A.) Ltd.

Bernice Young had some Beatles fans help with the overwhelming and never-ending task of answering fan letters. The New York office of the fan club had a secret address known only to a few teenagers. Since March, Debbie Gendler had been volunteering at the office and helped even more once school let out for the summer. "I didn't go to camp in the summer of 1964," Debbie recalls. "I had Beatles work to do. So I spent that whole summer in New York staying at my grandmother's apartment, going to the fan club."

By September, two more girls joined the front lines at Beatles (U.S.A.) Ltd. Best friends Susan Friedman and Pam Barlow tried to meet The Beatles when they performed at a charity event in New York City. Pam's father had work connections with Walter Hofer's office. He gave his daughter the secret address in hopes that the girls could meet The Beatles through the fan club.

When the girls arrived unannounced, Bernice was surprised to have visitors, but she gladly showed them around the small club headquarters. The two 17-year-olds commented on how they wished they could work there, and Bernice hired them on the spot. They worked four hours every day after school, and all day on Saturday. Their primary duty was to sort the mail. This was not easy with a stack of letters three feet high, but they loved working at the fan club and had a lot of fun. They were always pulling pranks and playing jokes on visitors. When Tony Barrow, the publicity officer who headed the U.K. fan club, went into the office, the girls did not know who he was. They talked him into putting his hands over his head while saying "U-R-G-E bulb" (You are a GE bulb). Barrow thought it was funny, and took a quick liking to the teenagers.

Pam and Susan met many influential people in The Beatles' inner circle, including Cilla Black, Gerry Marsden, Tommy Quickly, and most importantly, the manager himself, Brian Epstein. Epstein adored the two girls and their silly behavior. "Brian was just so nice and really seemed to be amused by us both," remembers Susan.

The Anti-Beatles Association

Members of The Beatles-Haters Association try to break up a Beatles rally in San Francisco.

The Beatles Fan Club of San Francisco remained very active. One hundred fifty members gathered in Union Square and held a "Bring Back The Beatles" rally. They made signs and had a parade. The day's highlight was "show and tell" items collected from The Beatles' hotel suites after they had left. These included a glass, an ashtray, and a Do Not Disturb sign. A group of 10 boys, known as The Beatles-Haters Association, interrupted the rally. They were carrying signs with anti-Beatles slogans and an American flag. They threw tomatoes at The Beatles fans and booed their singing. They tried to trample on fans' signs but the boys were vastly outnumbered, and the girls destroyed their signs instead. The boys made a hasty retreat carrying only their flag.

Beatles Birthdays

The four most important days of the year for any Beatles fan club were The Beatles' birthdays. These were a great reason to get together and celebrate, even if the birthday boy was far away. *The Beatles Fan Club of Salem* had a ritual: they lit candles and sang a special Beatles birthday song of their own creation on any Beatle birthday.

For many years, Beatles Fan Club (U.S.A.), Chapter 24 out of Dallas held a fan club party on each of The Beatles' special days. Before the big day, members spent hours planning these parties. Not only did they have a club meeting during the party, but they also used the party to raise money for charities.

On Ringo's 24th birthday, nine members of the Mesa High Beatles Fan Club had a slumber party. Before the party, the club had written a letter to the Beatles (U.S.A.) Ltd. fan club office in New York to let them know about the upcoming celebration, and they included the phone number. At 5:30 AM, the phone rang. It was an international long-distance call, and the caller was Ringo Starr. The nine excited girls shared the three phones in the house. As they all tried to wish Ringo a happy birthday, he couldn't understand what they were saying. He said, "I'm going to have to go. I can't understand a word of this conversation. Cheerio, and goodbye."

On October 9, John Lennon turned 24, and fan clubs celebrated in a big way. In Oregon, the East Salem Chapter of The Beatles (U.S.A.) Ltd. served a giant cake for its 23 attending members. In South Dakota, the Sioux Falls Chapter made an oversized birthday card signed not just by club members, but any Beatles fan in the area. The club shipped the card to John through the London Fan Club.

The Beatle Boosters sponsored a Beatles hop in the high school gym on the Friday night of John's birthday. The disc jockey played only Beatles records. The star of the night was a three-year-old who gave an adorable Beatles impression, including a guitar and a Beatles wig.

The club that outdid them all was the California Beatles Bombers. This club threw a Beatles rally in San Mateo Central Park on John's birthday. The rally's theme was "Little Ole London." Giant replicas of Big Ben and the London Bridge decorated the area, and the members got birthday cake and tea. Fans signed what they called "the world's largest birthday card," and sent it to John.

Christmas Celebrations

Newspaper advertisement for the Christmas re-release of A Hard Day's Night.

As 1964 ended, Beatles fans wanted to celebrate the holidays with the Fab 4. They topped their Christmas trees with photos of Ringo Starr, planned parties, and prepared gifts to send to their favorite foursome.

That Christmas season, *A Hard Day's Night* was re-released. In Wisconsin, the Bugs Over The Beatles rented a local movie theater and held their club's Christmas party there, watching the movie together. The club sent Christmas messages to The Beatles on Christmas tree-shaped ornaments. The Beatles West Coast Fan Club led by Ping Tom made a special scrapbook of memories of 1964. They sent it, along with notes to their favorite Beatles, to the fan club office in London.

Seasons Greetings from The Beatles

The Beatles had a present for the members of the official Beatles (U.S.A.) Ltd. In 1963, The Beatles' press officer, Tony Barrow, noticed the many fan letters arriving, and the difficulty in answering them promptly. He thought if The Beatles recorded a message and sent it on a flexi-disc to all paid fan club members, it would satisfy those fans who'd never gotten responses.

The 1963 *Beatles Fan Club Christmas Record* was a success. Fans loved hearing The Beatles being their classic funny selves. Barrow wrote the script, but The Beatles made it their own. It was so popular that The Beatles recorded a second Christmas record in 1964. However, the American fans did not get the new recording; instead they received the 1963 message retitled *Season's Greetings from the Beatles*. The Official Beatles Fan Club members in the U.K. got a flexi-disc in a record sleeve. The Americans were given a seven-inch square trifold cardboard package with the phonograph record in the middle.

Allied Creative Services in New York manufactured these gifts. Many fans didn't notice that the recording was a year old, a fact disguised by the inclusion of recent photographs of The Beatles in the recording studio, and a professional studio shot of the boys on the tri-fold. Also included was the latest issue of *The Beatle Bulletin*, signed by Lynn Hargrave and Bernice Young. This bulletin informed club members that The Beatles could not greet everyone personally, so they were sending their greetings to fans "in their very own voices" on the

Season's Greetings From The Beatles *Christmas message was sent to Beatles (U.S.A) Ltd members at the end of 1964.*

record. It went on to tell readers about The Beatles' autumn tour of the U.K., and the Christmas shows they were scheduled to give in London. It also said that The Beatles were set to make their new movie in February. It would be a "comedy thriller." There was a note that the club was working on matching U.K. fan club members with American members as pen pals, but they had so many girls in the U.S. that wanted pen pals, they ran out of names in the U.K.

The instructions in the bulletin made playing the recording sound easy. "Simply punch out the center dot," it read. "Place the newsletter on your record player, set it for 33 1/3 RPM, and sit back and enjoy your holiday greeting from The Beatles." The truth was more complex. "They were a pain to play," recalled fan club member Wally Podrazik. "They would slip on the turntable mat when you put your record player's tonearm on them, requiring a quarter or some other light object to give them enough weight to stay put." Once the fans got the hang of listening to the record, they enjoyed it and laughed at the jokes repeatedly with fellow fan club members.

During the holidays, Susan Friedman, Pam Barlow, and the other teenage volunteers at the Beatles (U.S.A.) Ltd. fan club headquarters in New York City weren't forgotten. Each girl received a Christmas card and a gold pendant personally inscribed with the words, "With luv Brian and The Beatles." This cherished gift is something they refused to take off.

1964 had been a wild and successful year for The Beatles. Their fan clubs in the United States were just getting started, but The Beatles' popularity was at an all-time high. The fan clubs were set to make 1965 an even better year for the Fab 4 and their fans.

As 1964 turned into 1965, the momentum of The Beatles' fan clubs continued across North America. By January, stories of Beatles Bobbies International Incorporated in Baltimore, and meetings with John, Paul, George, and Ringo during the summer tour, had spread everywhere. New Beatles Bobbies International Incorporated clubs started to appear. Many fans hoped to have the same luck when The Beatles returned in the summer of 1965.

Chapter 3 — Doing Something Nice and Having Fun in the Process

Beatlemania was alive and well the year after The Beatles invaded North America, however the girls in the Beatles fan clubs around the continent were tired of being only known for screaming. 1965 was the year they set out to show that there were not just boy-crazed fans, but desired to help out each other and others in their communities.

Beatles Bobbies International Incorporated New Chapters

Two fans in Fort Lauderdale, Florida started the Florida branch of the Beatles Bobbies International Incorporated. They'd heard a rumor that the boys would be returning to Southern Florida in August. President Pat Froster declared the club aimed to "calm down the kids if they threatened a riot around hotels and places around where The Beatles were playing." On a windy January 17, forty fans showed up at an outdoor shopping mall to learn about the club, and join in a rousing chorus of "We Love You Beatles." By the second meeting on January 23, over one hundred Beatles lovers came. There were so many fans that Pat ran out of membership cards. The group drank Coca-Cola and joined in a guitar-led Beatles sing-along. They all recited the Beatles Bobbies International Incorporated pledge, and formed committees to help keep The Beatles and their fans safe.

Members of the Beatles Bobbies International Incorporated's Boston branch had pledged that they would not rush the stage and would only throw confetti at The Beatles during their concerts. Each member had to be at least 16 or have written permission from their parents to join the club. They prepared for the summer tour by offering their services to Herman's Hermits and other concerts that came through Boston. If The Beatles did not return to Boston, the club was prepared to take a bus to New York City to help the Bobbies there. Above all, they wanted to prove that Massachusetts had the most devoted Beatles fans.

Not all Beatles Bobbies International Incorporated were happy clubs. Five members of the Philadelphia club met with the mayor in January. They discussed how the city could save thousands of dollars if he allowed the Bobbies to help the police control the fans the next time The Beatles came to town. The mayor swiftly rejected the girls' proposal, informing them that the police would handle things and proposing that maybe The Beatles' next visit could "be postponed for a long, long time."

Back of the membership card for the Tennessee chapter of the Beatles Bobbies International Incorporated. 1965.

Fan Club Fun

Meanwhile, the large clubs, both chartered and independent, returned to business as usual after the holidays. The junior chartered club, Children of Little Liverpool, held a "Bring Back The Beatles" rally on January 30 at the San Rafael Courthouse. Fifty members were present. The rally had two purposes: first, to collect

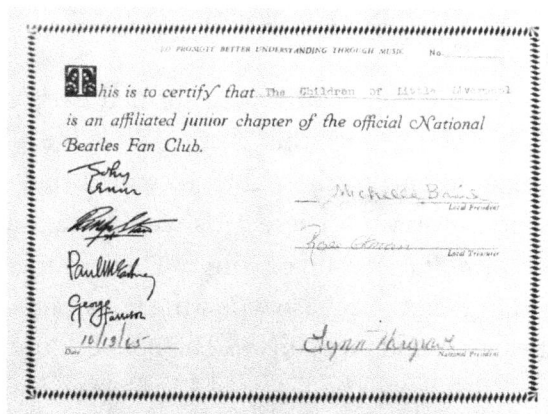

Junior Charter for the Children of Little Liverpool Chapter of the Beatles (U.S.A.) Ltd.

signatures on two petitions, one to Queen Elizabeth II declaring The Beatles should receive knighthoods, and a second to Brian Epstein asking The Beatles to return to California. The second purpose was fun. Though a band was ready to perform, the guitar players couldn't find an extension cord for the amplifiers. So the only performer was a drummer who wore a ski mask and dark glasses. He went by the name "the bouncing pebble" and said that was meant as an insult to The Rolling Stones. As with all Beatles rallies, there were signs with Beatles photos and messages like "The Beatles are Gear." An informal poll measuring scream quantity and volume determined Paul to be the most popular Beatle.

In West Virginia, sixty members of The Charleston Beatles Fan Club screamed and sighed during a showing of *The Making of 'A Hard Day's Night.'* One cold night in January, the club met in the cellar of a record shop owned by a man known to all as "Mr. T." Fan club officers had already decorated the cellar with Beatles signs, posters, and photos. Things warmed

Beatles fan club members in Denver volunteer to mail out fan club materials. 1965.

up once they got a projector and hung a bed sheet on the wall as a screen. Fans sat on the floor.

A few new clubs were formed early in 1965. One in Minneapolis started each meeting with this pledge: "I pledge allegiance to The Beatles of Liverpool, England, and to the public to which they sing. Four lads, over us, our motto Beatles Forever." These girls would make Beatles scrapbooks while discussing who was cuter: Paul or Ringo. Their primary objective was to raise money for a group ticket purchase when the boys came to Minneapolis. There were rumors the city would be a stop on The Beatles' summer tour.

Pat Kinzer had started The George Harrison Fan Club in her neighborhood in 1964, but in 1965 things went to the next level. In the fall, Pat had sent an ad for her club to *Teen Screen* magazine. Each month this magazine printed the names of fan clubs readers could join. Pat had no idea how that one little ad would change her life: "In February 1965, I came home from school to find that I had letters from about 20 people wanting to join my fan club."

Though Pat was excited to have new George fans join the club, the work quickly overwhelmed her. "I received over a thousand letters in a very short time from all over the world, all containing 40 cents and three 5-cent stamps," Pat recalls. While this was the point where many other fan club presidents called it quits, Pat enlisted her parents' and friends' help.

Pat was only 16, and did not have help from any radio station. She ran The George Harrison Fan Club by herself out of her parents' home in Pennsylvania. It was two months before she could send fan club kits to the thousand new members of The George Harrison Fan Club. "At the end of April, I put out my first newsletter and started selling pictures," she said. That's when The George Harrison Fan Club went from a fun activity to a full-time commitment. Whether she knew it or not, Pat was the perfect George fan to take on the challenge.

Wedded Bliss For Ringo and Maureen

Beatle business came to a standstill on February 11, 1965, when Ringo Starr married his girlfriend, Maureen Cox. Ringo's marriage was a shock to many fans. They hadn't been sure if Ringo and Maureen were dating or if Maureen was just Ringo's secretary. Even those who believed Maureen and Ringo were a couple were shocked. There hadn't been any reports of an engagement. As the Owensboro Beatles Fan Club president told the *Messenger-Inquirer*, "He could have warned us." The *Chicago American* newspaper contacted two of the most significant Beatles fan clubs in the area to break the news and get a reaction. When she heard the news, The Official Chicago Beatles Fan Club president, Barbara Rossi, was at a loss and began to cry. Through her tears, she said, "Oh my God, what will the fans say? I'll have to put out a special bulletin for the members. They'll cry all over the nation." Sue Meiresonne said that she would spread the news to members via phone chain and follow that with a telegram to national headquarters. They could tell her what to do next. Finally she asked the reporter, "Do you think that his music will be affected now that he's married?"

Ringo and Maureen Starkey on their honeymoon.

Beatles Fan Club (U.S.A.), Chapter 24, in Dallas, held an emergency meeting to discuss the marriage. President Stephanie Pinter seemed to still be in shock. "We had heard rumors before, but I guess this time it's true," she said through tears. Co-president Yolanda Hernandez had a more positive outlook, "Everyone is really happy for him, and we wish him the best of luck. We're glad it was Maureen."

Many fan clubs mourned by wearing black clothing or black armbands to school in the days following the wedding. It wasn't long before fan club members accepted that Ringo and Maureen's love and marriage wouldn't change Ringo or The Beatles. Carol Esque from the Washington D.C. Beatles Forever Club said, "All true Beatlemaniacs wish Ringo and Maureen all the happiness in the whole world. If you really like The Beatles, you won't let another Beatle marriage ruin their popularity." Most fans did not mind. George and Paul were still on the market. "Teens should be happy and hope that Maureen will make him a good wife," said another Beatles Forever club member. "After all, there are still two fab Beatles who are unwed."

Victor Spinetti and the Making of *Help!*

George and Victor Spinetti on the set of Help!

Soon after Ringo's wedding, The Beatles left for the Bahamas to begin filming their second motion picture, *Help!* When the plane to the Bahamas stopped to refuel in New York City, everyone stayed on board during the brief layover. An immigration officer boarded the plane, asking if Victor Spinetti would come to the door. A chapter of his fan club was waiting to see him. The Beatles were shocked that Victor had a fan club. The actor appeared, and his Philadelphia fan club members stood cheering. He waved and received their gifts.

John Lennon said, "Eh, Vic, y'know we're really impressed with your fan club. Do you think we could join?" Victor contacted Patti Gallo and Diane, co-presidents of his Philadelphia fan club, and John, Paul, George, Ringo, and Brian all received green membership cards for The Victor Spinetti Fan Club in America. Victor presented the cards to them after a day of filming. The Beatles were happy to be members of Victor's fan club, and the members of the club were thrilled to have The Beatles as honorary members.

Victor sent unique gifts from the Bahamas to his fan club. The first was an à la carte menu from their flight to the Bahamas. On the menu, he wrote, "For all in Philly, Love Victor Spinetti. We are working on "Beatles Two." See back page for autographs from the four lads." On the back of the menu were their autographs. Two were in pencil, and two were in ink. John Lennon signed "John ala Lennon" on the à la carte menu. As if that weren't enough, Victor also sent two blue candles from George's 22nd birthday cake, John's cigarette butt, and a baby blue plastic cocktail stirrer Paul had used in a nightclub in Nassau. These trinkets of appreciation were given to the fan club officers, with the cocktail stirrer being broken in half for the two girls who liked Paul the most.

Victor loved the girls in his fan club, and appreciated all they did for him. Patti's 16th birthday was approaching quickly, and her mother wanted to make it unique. She contacted Victor, who by this time was in the Swiss Alps with The Beatles, and asked him if he'd do something to help Patti celebrate. Wanting to make his fan club president's 16th birthday unforgettable, he asked for something from her favorite Beatle.

On Patti's birthday, she received a postcard with a picture of the snowy Swiss Alps on it. The other side read, "Happy Birthday, Love." It was signed by Paul McCartney. Not long after, Victor sent her a lock of Paul's hair. "Every night for a year and a half, that lock of Paul's hair went under my pillow," Patti recalled with a smile.

Fan Clubs Become More Involved

The fan clubs' focus had always been to celebrate the music and the fans' love for John, Paul, George, and Ringo, but in 1965 the emphasis shifted. While still celebrating their love for The Beatles and their music, the girls — and a few boys — in the clubs began putting their energy into helping their local communities. "Our fan club does more than people think. We do useful things too," explained the president of The Beatles (Southern) Ltd. chapter out of Jackson, Mississippi. The 150 members sponsored a fashion show to help raise money for the children's ward of the local hospital. The club also cleaned up the litter in the town so they could "Keep Jackson Beatleful."

Another club raising funds for a children's hospital was the Bugs Over The Beatles in Wisconsin. On January 24, 1965, this official chapter

Bugs Over The Beatles Fan Club in Wisconsin holds a bake sale for charity.

held a musical benefit show. Club members lip-synced to Beatles songs, sang original songs, and acted out scenes from *A Hard Day's Night*. The band Elray and the Nightbeats performed. With a donation from Beatles (U.S.A.) Ltd., they provided door prizes. Marian Dauer, the club president, said, "We want the public to stop thinking of Beatles fans as screaming, crying maniacs, and come to know us as we are: a group that has more in common than just liking The Beatles. We're just ordinary people who want to do something nice and have fun in the process."

Chartered and independent clubs raised money for good causes. Proceeds from their car washes, bake sales, and dances helped the John F. Kennedy Memorial Library Fund in Wallington, New Jersey, the March of Dimes, and Teens Against Cancer (in memory of Paul McCartney's mother, who died of breast cancer when Paul was a boy).

This change didn't go unnoticed. In the spring of 1965, a reporter from *Datebook* magazine visited the Beatles (U.S.A.) Ltd.'s headquarters in New York City and spoke to Sue Friedman and Pam Barlow, two of the teenage workers. Responding to a question about the contents of the mail, Sue said, "More and more of the kids in the club are collecting money for charities by washing cars, cake sales, and variety shows." Pam added, "There has been a big change in the character of the fans writing in. They're not so involved in just hollering anymore. They're more involved in community activities and other responsible things."

Fan club members didn't realize it, but they were developing essential skills they would use as they entered the adult world. One such fan who began her writing career due to the work she did for a Beatles fan club was Jo Ann Jaacks from Connecticut. This inspiring writer was a member of The Enfield Beatle Fan Club. Jo Ann began a Beatles newsletter called *Beatles Unlimited*. Not only did she write for the newsletter, she also encouraged other club members to contribute poems and articles.

Jo Ann scored an interview with a disc jockey who had traveled with The Beatles. In explaining why she started the newsletter, Jo Ann said, "I started thinking about how I liked to write and how The Beatles are a never-ending source of the material." She received permission to use the typewriters and mimeograph machine at her high school, and received extra credit in English class for her efforts. To help spread the word, Jo Ann sent information about *Beatles Unlimited* to friends, teen magazines, and Beatles (U.S.A.) Ltd. This caused some problems. As Jo Ann remembers, "I originally used the word 'Beatles' in the masthead and received a cease and desist letter from an attorney representing the group. So, I changed the masthead to 'four mop tops' since true fans would instantly recognize that image." This newsletter was the first instance of a fan club member receiving a legal letter from The Beatles' attorney, but it would not be the last.

Another fan club that regularly sent out newsletters was The Victor Spinetti

Fan Club. Their newsletters highlighted Victor's acting career. They received information from Victor's British fan club, and from Victor himself. He spoke with co-president Diane in trans-Atlantic telephone conversations. Much of the newsletter was about The Beatles. Co-president Patti Gallo recalled, "The main focus was The Beatles, and Victor knew it, and he loved it."

Sometimes a fan club would learn of injustice with one of their own, and take action. In Toronto, Ontario, a 15-year-old boy named Wayne was forced to get his Beatles haircut trimmed. Wayne had been growing his Beatles-styled mop top ever since he first saw a photo of The Beatles 18 months earlier. The long hair made his principal so angry that the man took matters into his own hands. With Wayne yelling in protest, two teachers held him down in a chair while the principal sheared off his bangs. Wayne was so angry that he brought the ordeal to the attention of the local press.

Members of The Official Canadian Beatles Fan Club were outraged. They started a letter-writing campaign to the school board. A spokesperson from the fan club said, "The principal's action represents a terrible infringement on personal individualism and liberty."

Not only did the uproar cause an investigation by the school board, but it also got the attention of Ontario's Secondary Schools Special Teachers' Disciplinary Committee. The committee determined that the principal was not within his rights to cut the boy's hair. However, they acknowledged that he was just trying to make sure the students were neat — a requirement of his job. He had to pay for Wayne to get a professional, first-class haircut. Wayne was not pleased but was willing to drop the matter.

A fan club member holding the Beatles book obtained from Beatles (U.S.A.) Ltd.

Beatles (U.S.A.) Ltd.

Even when The Beatles weren't touring, Beatles (U.S.A.) Ltd. received 6,000 letters a week. Their youngest member was one-and-a-half, and the oldest was 74. Ninety percent of fan club members were girls, and just 10 percent were boys. Whenever a letter was addressed to the club in New York City, it went through a mail service. The mail service took out club membership fees and dues. Dues were still $2 for the year, and new members received the same materials others had gotten the previous year, including the 1964 Beatles (U.S.A.) Ltd. tour book.

The rest of the fan mail went to the Beatles (U.S.A.) Ltd. office, where the girls who worked there, or one of the young volunteers such as Leslie Samuels, sorted it. Leslie recalls, "I worked hard. I stuffed envelopes. I did whatever was needed to do." The club received personal communications to any Beatle, requests for club charters, photos sales, *A Hard Day's Night* script sales, free fact sheet requests, information about concert tickets, pen pal requests, and complaints. The club also received many gifts meant for John, Paul, George, and Ringo. Presents included

Beatles (U.S.A.) Ltd. members could buy this set of four Beatles photo album booklets in May 1965.

rings for Ringo, artwork, guitar picks, four-leaf clovers, ID bracelets, diapers for Ringo's soon-to-be-born child, wedding bands, pillowcases, shirts, combs, and keys. Headquarters claimed that all letters sent to the fan club were opened and answered. This might have been the goal, but it was not happening. During busy seasons (when The Beatles were touring or had released a new album), the club sometimes received over 10,000 letters a week. The girls couldn't keep up, so the stacks of unopened letters grew. It was often six weeks or more before a fan got a response or an ordered item. Fans got frustrated and wrote to find out what was taking so long. Of course, this added to the mass of letters, slowing down the process even more.

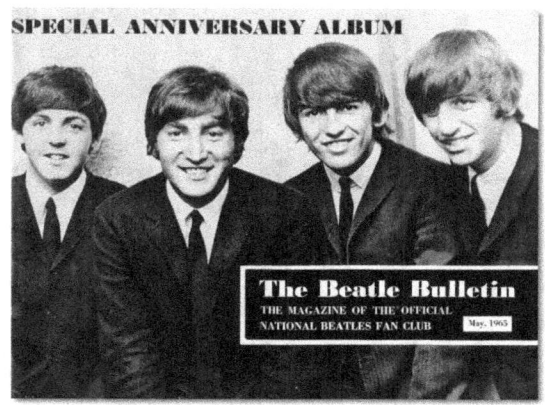

Fans thought they might get a quicker response from The Official Beatles Fan Club in London, but all United States mail that arrived at the London office was mailed right back to the New York office.

With so many letters, lost mail was inevitable. The Official Beatles Headquarters president Carol Webber had the required 25

The Beatle Bulletin, May 1965, which included one of four Beatle "roulette" drawings.

paid members and should have received a charter, but her members hadn't even received their membership kits. Carol reached out to Bernice Young. Bernice apologized for the mistake, obtained the members' names and addresses, and reprocessed their packages. She wrote to Carol, "This time, we hope they get their kits." Bernice knew there was no guarantee.

Carol received her charter, and she and the other one hundred and thirty seven U.S. chapter presidents also got exclusive rewards for all their hard work. In May of 1965, all Beatles (U.S.A.) Ltd. presidents received a set of four Beatles photo albums. There was one booklet for each Beatle. Each booklet included seven new full-page pictures. The presidents could show these booklets to fan

Top: Photograph fans received when they became members of the Brian Epstein Fan Club. Above: Brian Epstein Fan Club card.

club members at meetings. All the girls loved to see the latest photos of their favorite Beatle. Members could purchase their booklets for 35 cents each or all four for $1.25. These booklets were well made, and an ideal item for Beatles fan club members.

In July, chapter presidents received another letter from Bernice Young. She informed the girls that Brian Epstein had arranged with Capitol Records to send all presidents any future Beatles record release free of charge. She stated, "This is another way which The Beatles and their management have selected to say 'thank you' for all your fine work on their behalf."

All members of Beatles (U.S.A.) Ltd. received the annual *Beatle Bulletin* in May. The 1965 bulletin was called "The Special Anniversary Issue." The book was full of new Beatles photographs and covered everything that happened to The Beatles in 1964, and up to that point in 1965. The book also had pictures of The Beatles in their upcoming movie, *Help!* The bulletin included what they called "Beatles Roulette." Inside the back cover was a pen-and-ink sketch of one of The Beatles drawn by William Foge. Photos of John, Paul, George, or Ringo were randomly distributed. If you did not receive your favorite, you were encouraged to trade with a fellow club member, or purchase a print of the drawing from the club for 25 cents.

A month later, members received another newsletter that included the itinerary for the upcoming North American tour and four pages of Beatles photos.

Beatles (U.S.A.) Ltd. ran not only The Beatles' national fan club but also the fan club for The Beatles' manager, Brian Epstein. The December 1964 *Beatle Bulletin* announced that joining the Brian Epstein Fan Club would be free for all members of Beatles (U.S.A.) Ltd. The club started because many members thought there should be a tribute to the man who brought The Beatles to the world. Brian was a mysterious, handsome, older man that Beatles fans admired. Some girls, especially those who were a little older, were devoted to the band's 30-year-old bachelor manager.

Those who joined the club received a membership card, an 8″ x 10″ glossy photograph of Brian, and a fact sheet. The fact sheet gave basic information about Brian, how he met The Beatles, and got them a recording contract. It also covered Brian's management of other groups, stating that he was proud that he did not use any false images to promote his acts. The fact sheet finished with the fact that Brian had brown hair and green eyes.

There was not a lot to the Brian Epstein Fan Club. The only thing it offered after the initial membership kit was a 3″ x 5″ glossy photo of Brian. This offer was free to all Brian Epstein Fan Club members as long as fans included a self-addressed stamped envelope and their membership card.

One of Brian's employees, Geoffrey Ellis, who saw Brian get mobbed by autograph-seeking teenagers, wasn't sure what to make of his boss' sudden fame. "I found somewhat to my surprise that there was also a 'Brian Epstein Fan Club.' He was a popular figure among teenage fans and indeed, good looking as he was, and the manager of The Beatles, it was hardly surprising that his own publicity in the pop world had resulted in his own fan club. This rather modest outfit both amused him and fed his vanity."

Nat Weiss

For all of 1964 and part of 1965, the headquarters of Beatles (U.S.A.) Ltd. was located in Walter Hofer's office. Hofer's focus had changed significantly since the fan club began. He was now deep into litigation over The Beatles' merchandising venture, Seltaeb. Brian Epstein needed a new lawyer to represent NEMS in the United States. Luckily, he already knew the perfect person.

Brian had met New York divorce attorney Nat Weiss at a party in 1964 when they were introduced to each other by another British rock group manager, Larry Parnes. The two hit it off

Nat Weiss enjoying the rewards of Beatlemania in his apartment.

and eventually became best friends. Nat introduced Brian to the mid-1960s New York gay scene, which was like nothing Brian had ever experienced. Homosexuality was still illegal in Great Britain then, so Brian enjoyed the clubs and bars he went to with Nat. As their friendship grew, Brian asked Nat to join NEMS as an attorney.

One of the areas Nat dealt with was Beatles (U.S.A.) Ltd. Bernice and the others packed everything in Walter Hofer's small space, and moved into Nat's suite at 1501 Broadway in Times Square. This was also known as the Paramount Building. In the 1920s, it had housed the popular and elaborate Paramount Theatre, showing motion pictures. As film patronage declined, by 1964 the building had changed hands. The new owners were more interested in offices than movies.

Weiss was the right man for NEMS. He had integrity and kindness. Musician Lon Van Eaton remembers, "Nat was a sweet man. He was smart, soft-spoken, and a bit overweight. He had a very understated facial expression, almost a British-type reserve." Richard Adler agreed. "Nat Weiss was a sweetheart. He was always so nice to me." Brian and Nat became business partners, and worked together to sign new groups. Once they made an offer to promoter Sid Bernstein for the contract of The Young Rascals. As they met, Bernstein seemed to think seriously about signing the band over to Brian. Brian took a quick break to the men's room.

Adler recalls, "When Brian was out of the room, Nat told Sid to hold on to the Rascals because they were going to be big. Sid was very thankful to Nat for his kindness. Nat could have taken advantage of Sid but chose not to. Brian never found out that it was Nat that killed the deal." Nat kept a dutiful eye on Beatles (U.S.A.) Ltd. and assisted whenever he was needed. He was more than The Beatles' lawyer; he was part of The Beatles' family.

Louise Harrison Caldwell

Beatles fans knew it was almost impossible to get close to John, Paul, George, or Ringo, so many fans reached out to the next best thing: a Beatle family member.

The most accessible family member for American fans to talk to was George Harrison's sister, Louise Harrison Caldwell. Louise and her husband had left England due to her husband's job, and by the time The Beatles came to the United States, her family was living in Benton, Illinois. It was a small town 100 miles southeast of St. Louis,

Signed Louise Harrison Caldwell promo card from her fan club.

CHAPTER 3–DOING SOMETHING NICE AND HAVING FUN IN THE PROCESS 105

Missouri. Soon fans discovered Louise's home address and telephone number. They were pleased that she would speak to them and answer their letters. The vice-president of the Kansas City Chapter of The Beatles Fan Club interviewed Louise for *The Kansas City Times*. Louise was very candid about the six days she spent with The Beatles when they first arrived in America. Later she gave interviews to The Beatles Fan Club in Arnold, Pennsylvania, gave her blessing to The Chicagoland Beatle People Fan Club, and became an honorary member of numerous clubs across the United States and Canada.

Soon Louise was bombarded with one hundred and fifty letters a day. She never learned how to type, so it was difficult for her to keep up with all the mail. Most fans did not include a self-addressed stamped envelope. Stamps and stationery became costly.

Illustrated Louise Harrison Caldwell membership card.

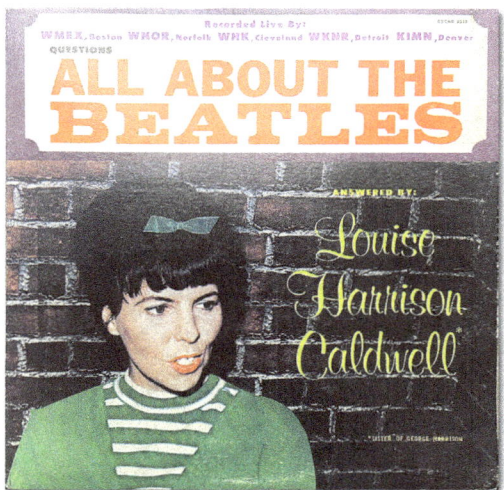

Louise Harrison Caldwell's All About The Beatles album cover front and back, with photo album offer insert card.

WNOR Radio Norfolk, Virginia, newspaper advertisement.

Louise started broadcasting her insider Beatles news on the radio. Her new job was reporting. Her radio spot was called "Louise's Beatle Minute." This provided her with enough money to cover her answers to all the fan letters. She also made enough to hire a secretary.

Joyce Kirsch was a 19-year-old Beatles fan from Alton, Illinois. She had tried to get The Beatles to perform in St. Louis in 1964. When that was unsuccessful, Joyce made national news by asking a Congressman's help in getting tickets to see The Beatles in Indianapolis. Louise got to know Joyce through fan letters, and the two women became fast friends. Joyce became a live-in secretary. She was paid $30 a week plus room and board. She was excellent at typing and shorthand. By January 1965, with Joyce Kirsch as National Director, The Louise Harrison Caldwell Fan Club was formed. In the first newsletter, Louise stated, "The main purpose of this club is to help me keep The Beatle fans correctly informed about the boys." For 50 cents a year, fans received an autographed photograph of Louise, a newsletter every other month, fact sheets about Louise and The Beatles, plus a membership card.

The Louise Harrison Caldwell Fan Club was an independent club, unaffiliated with Beatles (U.S.A.) Ltd. It was very efficient and well-organized. Each branch had its own president. Louise would send information and supplements to the newsletters to the branch presidents. They would pass the info along to club members. By May, the club had 4,000 members and was still growing. Louise was pleased and told the *Indianapolis News*, "I just try to keep up to date on the boys. Having fan clubs organized is an easy way to write to all of the kids."

The fans trusted Louise to give them the scoop on The Beatles, and she did not disappoint. When she returned from the Bahamas, where The Beatles were making their new film *Help!*, she gave a brief synopsis without telling too much of the plot. Fans could not get enough from the sister of a Beatle.

Louise frequently made appearances around the United States, meeting members of her fan club along the way. Radio stations airing "Louise's Beatle Minute" would have her host events, such as dances, autograph sessions, and talks. While these were open to the public, fan club members were encouraged to attend. No other fan club offered the chance to talk to a Beatle's relative. Fans reveled in this opportunity.

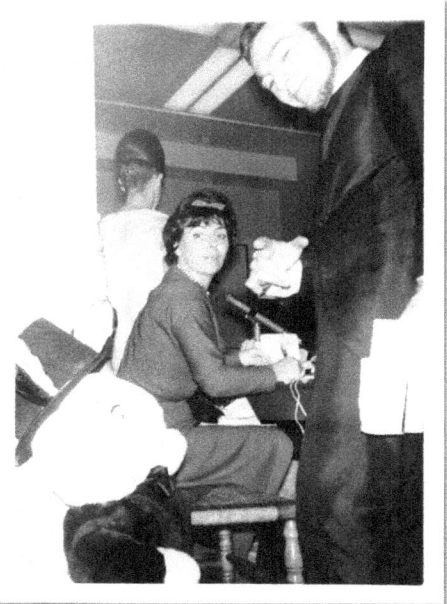

Louise promoting her fan club in St. Louis, with KXOK disc jockey Johnny Rabbitt.

On May 30, 1965, the Indianapolis branch of the club, which boasted two hundred and fifty members, had an open house at the home of the president, Georgeanna Lewis. The guest of honor was Mrs. Louise Harrison Caldwell herself. She was there to answer questions. Fan club members came dressed in Beatles sweatshirts, with cameras and autograph books in hand. They crowded into the Lewis family living room, mesmerized by everything Louise had to say. After the event, Georgeanna said, "Louise is awfully nice and sweet. We can get the truth about the boys from her."

Louise conducted a few press conferences where fans asked the questions. The sessions in Boston and Cleveland were recorded and made into an album called *All About The Beatles*. Five thousand records were pressed, and it was released on June 2. Fan club members could purchase a copy for $3, with 25 cents going back into the club. Members had to act fast because Louise received a cease and desist letter from Brian Epstein's legal team. Anything not sanctioned by Brian could not have the name "Beatles" in the title, so all album sales were halted.

Even worse news followed. In September, Louise's radio segments were canceled, and the funds to keep the fan club began running out. Club dues went up to $1 a year, and Joyce Kirsch agreed to stay onboard with payment of room and board only. Louise reported, "Many of our members who are also members of Beatles (U.S.A.) Ltd. have told us that our club is more interesting." She did not want to disband a flourishing club, so she did everything she could to keep it going.

Mr. and Mrs. Harrison with Pattie, George, and an American fan, Patty Juliono.

Mrs. Louise Harrison

George's sister wasn't the only Beatle family member who got letters from fan club members. George's mother, also named Louise, quickly became a friend and pen pal to many American fans. Fan club newsletters and meetings appeared to be more official when a member could quote directly from a letter written by Mrs. Harrison. She always had news of her son and his friends, and what they were doing in England. She frequently gave out her home address in Liverpool to American disc jockeys and newspapers. Mrs. Harrison sent a handwritten reply to any fan who included an international stamp coupon. She even encouraged fans to come to the Harrison home if they ever traveled to the United Kingdom. Mrs. Harrison became a friend to Beatles fan clubs, and that friendship grew through the years.

A Summer Song

By the summer of 1965, the fan clubs were ready to have some fun. While still involved in community service, they also held a few more light-hearted events. The Official Salt Lake Beatles Fan Club threw a party in July. The theme was "Great

Britain," and the party site was decorated with giant cutouts of British bobbies and crepe paper with the Union Jack flag. There was authentic British food, and dessert was a sheet cake with a giant British flag. In an area made to resemble Liverpool's Cavern Club, a band called The Keymen performed. Fifty-three club members — including two boys — had fun dancing to the music.

Ringo said his favorite color was red, so to celebrate his July 7 birthday, The Beatle Backers of America had a red birthday cake, red soft drinks, and red jelly beans. They signed a 15-foot scroll they hoped to give to Ringo when The Beatles came to Chicago later in the summer. The Beatles Crackers threw a

Girls in California enjoying their Beatles albums—with A Hard Day's Night *currently spinning on the turntable.*

beach party to celebrate Ringo's birthday. The party had Ringo pictures and cake with red icing. Another group, The Idty Bugs Club, gathered at a park on the big day. They spread dirt from Liverpool on the ground. One member had bottled air from when The Beatles performed the previous summer. After wishing Ringo a happy birthday, the "Beatle air" was released into the summer breeze.

Help!

For the second summer in a row, The Beatles released a new movie. And just like the previous summer, fan clubs gathered to see The Beatles on the big screen, only this time they were in color.

Help! premiered in the United States at the Woods

The Beatles—in full color— in their second motion picture, Help!

Theatre in Chicago, Illinois, on August 11, 1965. Fans, including many from fan clubs in and around the Windy City, spent hours in line, waiting to enter the theater for the first showing. In that first week, *Help!* at the Woods Theatre made a record-breaking $42,000. After the premiere of *Help!* there was a slow release across North America until August 25.

In St. Petersburg, Florida, the line at the box office stretched around the block. One boy told the *St. Petersburg Independent*, "You have to see a Beatles movie three times. You have to sit next to the projector to hear anything." Several girls came carrying copies of the Beatles (U.S.A.) Ltd. fan club book. One yelled, "I like Ringo! He's adorable," as she pushed her way through the crowd to get a front row seat.

In St. Louis, members of The Louise Harrison Caldwell Fan Club began screaming as soon as the pre-show cartoons ended. They were able to contain themselves during the dialogue, although there was plenty of laughter. As soon as a Beatles song began to play, the screaming started again.

In New York State, four hundred and fifty fans lined up to see *Help!* The wait didn't faze them. As one fan said, "it's fun to wait when you're waiting for The Beatles." To help pass the time, the local fan club held an informal poll of the fans in the line. They discovered that a boy named Dennis had read the most books about The Beatles, and only one person had a pet named after a Beatle (a parakeet named George). The most times seeing *A Hard Day's Night* was

Help! movie newspaper advertisement.

Fans in Chicago line up to see *Help!* at the Woods Theatre.

12. The best Beatles encounter was by a mother who saw The Beatles in a car while at a red light in Atlantic City, and the most Beatles pictures were 6,402.

Fans in Windsor, Ontario started arriving at 5:30 AM for the 12:45 PM showing of *Help!* Reporters were surprised to find both boys and girls waiting to see The Beatles' new movie. One boy said, "Why not? Boys like The Beatles, too." Ringo was still the crowd favorite, with one girl calling him a "loveable little doll." Most fans planned to make a day at the Vanity Theatre by watching the film at least three times.

On August 23, the The Official Beatles Fan Club of Southern California, sponsored by Dave Hull at KRLA, hosted a star-studded Los Angeles premiere of the movie for five hundred club members at the famed Cathay Circle Theatre. Those who could not get tickets had to wait until the next day. The Glendale Senior Citizen Beatles Fan Club was in the audience. They seemed to enjoy themselves as much as teenagers.

Right before the premiere of *Help!*, The Victor Spinetti Fan Club received an extraordinary gift from Victor. It was the oversized, fuzzy V-neck sweater he wore in *A Hard Day's Night*. That sweater was part of the dialogue in one of the scenes, so it

Victor Spinetti in the fuzzy sweater he gave to his fan club in Philadelphia.

was well known to Beatles fans. During the opening of *Help!* in Philadelphia, co-president Diane wore the sweater in 90-degree summer heat. "We had little cards that said, 'Join our Victor Spinetti Fan Club,' and we put pieces of fuzz from the sweater taped on it. We went up and down the line with the sweater trying to promote the club," recalls the other co-president Patti Gallo.

After seeing *Help!*, the club was proud of the great job Victor did acting as the mad scientist. They decided to send him a telegram to congratulate him. When they got to the Western Union office, they learned that there was a charge for each word. Not having much money, they knew they had to have the perfect word to send to Victor in London. "'Mary Poppins' had just come out," Patti recalled, "We wrote to Victor 'supercalifragilisticexpialidocious.' The longest word we could spell. It was so funny, but he appreciated it."

Two fan clubs used the publicity of the new movie to help their community. The Bay Area Beatles Fan Club in San Francisco teamed up with the Anti-Litter Committee and held a rally outside of the theater where *Help!* was showing. A large banner read, "The Beatles Join in Helping the City of San Francisco Keep the Streets Clean." Club members marched around with signs that said, "Help! Sweep Up Litter" and "Beatle fans should Help!" They carried brooms and swept up litter in the street.

In the summer of 1965, New York City was experiencing a water shortage. There, Beatles (U.S.A.) Ltd. and United Artists joined forces to get the Goodyear Blimp featured in The Beatles' new film to fly over New York City bearing the message, "Help! Save Water."

After the film was shown, *The Newark Star-Ledger* gave *Help!* a less than favorable review, stating that it may be too "far out" for original fans. In response The Beatles Boosters of New Jersey wrote a letter to the editor. "We speak for many when we say that The Beatles could make a movie just sitting still and looking to the camera for an hour and a half and still be a hit."

In May, Beatles fans became concerned that the group might not be allowed to return to the United States. There was a dispute between the British Musicians' Union and the American Federation of Music. The two unions were at odds about the huge number of British groups filling up the United States hit charts and touring the country. Due to this British Invasion, some American musicians were no longer working. One solution was a proposal that a musician on either side of the Atlantic would travel and play only in their home countries. Knowing this would be news to Beatles fans, the Associated Press reached out to The Official Chicago Beatles Fan Club for a response. One member, Isabella, said, "All the kids will go out of their minds when they hear about the ban." The only thing member Margaret was able to say was, "Oh! Ye Gods! Unfair!" The girls didn't need to worry. The dispute was settled before the 1965 North American Beatles tour began.

Back In The U.S.A.

The 1965 Beatles (U.S.A.) Ltd. book was on sale for $1 at each stop on tour. The fan club book had new photos of the band, both group shots and individual Beatles. This tour book was the only Beatles merchandise officially sold. The Beatles contract stated, "No other merchandise, including but not limited to photographs, dolls, pins, games, program books, and any other novelty merchandise, is to be sold at this engagement." Any fan could buy the program at the concert, even if the fan wasn't a club member. Fans used the program books to write the setlist. During the concert many fans turned to a page picturing their favorite Beatle, and held it high. Those in Beatles (U.S.A.) Ltd. knew that they could always get another through the club in New York if something happened to their book.

A fan with a Beatles (U.S.A.) Ltd. book during the 1965 North American tour.

On August 13, 1965, The Beatles arrived back on North American soil. Fan club members were beyond ready for their return. The 1965 tour was shorter than the previous year's, but The Beatles were performing in larger venues this time.

The Beatles take to the field heading towards the stage for their monumental Shea Stadium performance, August 15, 1965 in front of 55,000 fans.

New York City was the first stop, and Beatles (U.S.A.) Ltd. wanted to reward the girls who had been working at the fan club office. They asked Debbie Gendler to be the first teenager to welcome The Beatles to America. She first went to the press conference at the Warwick Hotel, where she sat by disc jockey Cousin Brucie. "I did have my camera with me, my little Brownie Instamatic," she remembered. "I had a cartridge in there for 12 pictures, and I took all 12 pictures." After the press conference, there was a party at The Beatles' suite. Once Debbie arrived, she welcomed The Beatles, while Cousin Brucie was talking to the boys. They had ordered sandwiches from Stage Deli, and were waiting for the food to arrive. "Paul was incredibly gracious and friendly," Debbie said. Before she left the party, she told them, "It's been so wonderful actually to get to meet you." Beatles road manager Neil Aspinall walked back downstairs with her, and before they parted he handed her a copy of John Lennon's newest book, signed by John.

A fan showing off the sign she made for The Beatles concert in Chicago. August 20, 1965.

Two girls who worked at the fan club office after school each day, Sue Friedman and Pam Barlow, got to spend some time with John, Paul, George, and Ringo in their hotel suite. The Beatles talked to the girls about the pranks they liked to play on the staff. Paul suggested a game of Scrabble. Always one to make up new words, John won by bringing up words no one had ever heard.

On August 15, The Beatles gave an unforgettable performance at Shea Stadium in New York City. Among the audience of 55,000 Beatlemaniacs were a few members of the George Harrison Fan Club. The girls were all dressed in identical empire-waist dresses with flowers on top and corduroy on the bottom. They joined in with the other crying and screaming fans. From the stadium's third level, these fans had to use binoculars to see The Beatles.

Someone who had a much better view of the concert was a *Brooklyn Times* reporter, Jim Dezego. Dezego stood on the right side of the stage, and took some fantastic photographs of The Beatles. At the press conference at the Warwick, Dezego had become acquainted with fan club director Bernice Young. Dezego promised to send Bernice a set of photographs. In exchange, Bernice made Dezego's daughters, Margaret and Mary Ann, honorary members of Beatles (U.S.A.) Ltd.

One member of The True Beatles Club wrote to her local newspaper a few days after the concert. "Never in my whole life have I witnessed anything so wonderful or touching as that night," she wrote. She told how everyone was screaming to show their support of The Beatles. "It's been two days since the concert," she finished the letter, "I cry just at the mention of their name or sound of their voice."

The Beatles had one stop in Canada on the 1965 North American Tour where they gave a pair of concerts in Toronto. Two fans from Nova Scotia traveled a thousand miles to see the Fab 4 in person. When asked why they made such a long trip, they said, "Once you get Beatlemania, you can't do without it. I hope I never lose it." A few fans from The Mansfield Fan Club came to Toronto as well. They said it felt as if The Beatles were performing just for them, and not for 20,000 other fans. One girl described the concert like this: "John made all sorts of crazy motions, Paul was just smiling and winking, George was ducking wads of paper. Ringo? He was pounding away at the drums like always."

On August 18, The Beatles moved along to Atlanta, Georgia, where four fan club members from Newark, Ohio, had a big surprise for them. For nine months, Gail Richardson, Karen Forrer, Nancy Haas, and Susie Pittman had been making life-sized dolls of The Beatles. Using foam rubber, wood, and sheets, each girl made her favorite Beatle. The Beatles gave a typical press conference where they were "courteous, witty, and extremely obliging to the press." Press officer Tony Barrow called the fan club members forward, and the girls presented each Beatle with his likeness. Photographers snapped pictures, and The Beatles left for their dressing room. The girls said that the boys were "delighted with them." Someone took photographs showing the guys goofing off with the dolls, so they must have enjoyed their unusual gift.

The Atlanta concert was one The Beatles remembered as being one of their best because of the excellent sound system. Six girls from The Official Atlanta Beatle Fan Club will never forget their experience after the concert. They had climbed onto

Phunny Fotos

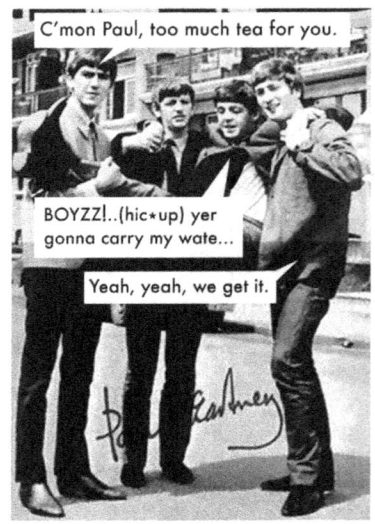

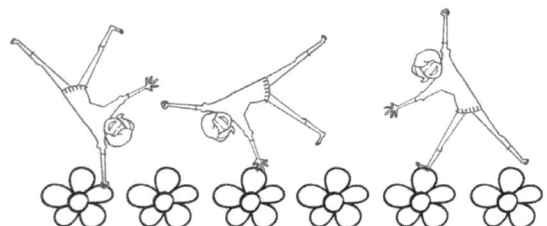

the field and begged the cops to allow them to stand on The Beatles' stage before it was dismantled. The police pitied the girls, and soon they were standing on the stage. Two of the girls climbed up onto Ringo's drum platform, where they hugged each other and cried. Those fans had a lot to share at their next fan club meeting.

After Atlanta, the tour stopped in Houston, Texas. One of the local clubs had made a giant paper chain. They tore off one link from the chain each day until it was August 19 — concert day.

Elaine models a Mary Quant dress, similar to the one she wore when she met The Beatles.

Elaine McAfee's club, The North Texas Chapter of The Beatles Fan Club, had grown to be the largest chapter of Beatles (U.S.A.) Ltd. in 1965. To reward Elaine for her hard work, Beatles (U.S.A.) Ltd. gave her a free concert ticket and the opportunity to meet The Beatles when they arrived. Elaine went to the airport with special gifts for John, Paul, George, and Ringo. "I had a cowboy shirt for each of them," she recalled. "I got their sizes, color preferences, and style. Ringo had a traditional Western with pearl button snaps." She was standing in a line, ready for her big moment, when chaos broke out on the tarmac. Fans broke through the barricades and rushed to the airplane.

Elaine was caught in the insanity. "They ran all over everybody, and I got out of the way because I saw it coming," she remembers. "I did my best to get out of the way, but I dropped the boxes and got my elbow scratched." The girls made it to the airplane, climbing onto the wings, trying to see the boys through the windows. Later John told the *Chicago Sun-Times*, "Houston was the worst. That was the nearest thing to death. Those kids were even all over the airplane, smoking on the wing." The Beatles were trapped inside the aircraft. Eventually, a large catering truck had to come and get them off the plane to safety.

Meanwhile, Elaine figured she had lost her chance to meet The Beatles. Then she learned that the meet-and-greet was moved to the terminal inside the airport. She stood wearing a badge identifying her as being with KFJZ and the fan club. She held the four boxes that had gotten trampled in the stampede, and waited for her moment to meet John, Paul, George, and Ringo. After finding out that she couldn't take a camera with her and various other rules, Elaine entered the room where they were.

"Oh my gosh! I got to meet each one of them and gave them a shirt," she recalled later. "For the most part, they were shaken up, having just had the stampede of girls hanging off the wing. Nobody was really in a good mood, but they smiled at me." Each

The Beatles performing in Houston on August 19, 1965. Elaine McAfee is somewhere in the front row.

of the guys thanked Elaine for the cowboy shirts. Ringo was the one who most appreciated the gift. He thanked her several times. John and George were quiet, but Paul was very upbeat. "Paul talked to me for the longest time. I told him, 'You're my favorite Beatle,' and he smiled. He said, 'Wait a minute, you are our fan club leader? Thank you. Thank you so much.'" He then asked her age and about the work she did at the radio station. "He asked so many questions. He was just so personable. I talked to him way longer than I was supposed to." The line of press behind her was telling her to move along. Paul asked her to stay longer, so she went out into a hallway and waited to go back.

A man she didn't recognize asked her if she was with the fan club, and took her back where she found Paul and John leaning against a wall. When John spotted Elaine in her Mary Quant miniskirt, he gave her a look, then whispered something into Paul's ear that made Paul look embarrassed and frown. Elaine thinks she heard John whisper "jailbait." While John was laughing, Paul said, "John, this is our fan club leader." John said, "Oh, we're supposed to say thank you very much to our fan club leaders." Elaine acknowledged the thanks and reminded John that she had brought the cowboy shirts. John said "Ta" to her.

Paul and Elaine chatted about the concert, and he told her that he would look for her in the audience. Paul was surprised that she was only 15, and had accomplished so much. He told her that she didn't behave like a typical fan. After they'd talked for a while, one of the other Beatles came over and told Paul they were going to eat and needed to leave. "Paul said, 'Well, come here and give me a hug.' So, I went over and hugged him and felt 'Oh my God!' and then I got a kiss on the cheek. He kissed me on the cheek and said, 'You are absolutely gorgeous. Thank you for all you do.'" Paul then said he'd get in contact with her through the fan club to thank her. When she reminded him that her name was Elaine McAfee, Paul says, "Oh, you're a 'Mac,' and I'm a 'Mac.' I'll remember you." While still on cloud nine, Elaine went to the concert. The fan club had given her seats in the front, on the same side as Paul. Everyone was standing on their chairs. During the song *All My Loving*, Paul noticed her and gave her a wink. Everyone around Elaine was amazed that Paul acknowledged her. It has all remained a pleasant memory for her.

Another fan club member said this about the Houston concert: "The show was unbelievable and there aren't enough adjectives created to describe it, so I won't even try. You can only experience a Beatles concert to understand it. You can only be under the spell of The Beatles to know."

In Chicago, there was a new president of The Chicagoland Beatle People Fan Club. Marti Whitman Edwards was still involved in the club, but a girl named Barb Tibert had taken over the reins and wanted to meet The Beatles just as Marti had the previous year. With Marti's help, they made a 20" x 40" pop art Beatles collage to give to The Beatles on August 20. Sadly, Barb did not have Marti's good luck. "She got a letter saying they were not allowing anybody to present anything, and only certain press people could get in to see them," recalled Marti. That didn't stop the Beatlemaniac from trying. Unfortunately, Barb could not talk her way past the strict security, and did not meet The Beatles.

August 21, 1965 was an exciting day for twenty-five members of The Mod Mockers Club from Sioux Falls, South Dakota. These fans had spent the year washing cars, babysitting, and picking up pop bottles to save money to see The Beatles in Minneapolis, Minnesota. They had earned enough money to be able to ride a bus to the show.

The Mod Mockers Club bought their tickets early, but promoter Ray Colihan expected more from the other fan clubs. He could not understand why ticket sales in Minneapolis were slow. "The local Beatles Fan Club says it has three hundred members. So how many tickets did its members order? Exactly fifty-two," Colihan lamented to *Variety*.

The fans who made it to the Minneapolis show enjoyed every moment. Soon-to-be fan club president Kathy Burns said, "There they were. Right there. All four of them. Right in front of us, all of them waving and Paul swinging his guitar like a baseball bat. Yeah, it was the best. They only played forty minutes, but it was still the best." The same cannot be said for the city's authorities. The *Minneapolis Star* reported that The Beatles and their entourage were "the worst." The article quotes a police officer saying, "Most of them seem to have no idea of proper behavior." According to the story, the entourage lured girls from the sidewalk and into the hotel. Paul McCartney was said to have been in his room with a 21-year-old woman who claimed to be a Beatles fan club president. Paul was threatened with jail time if the female did not leave.

This report naturally angered the fans, and Tari Tarbell, president of The Liverpool Luv's, wrote a letter to the editor to give them a piece of her mind. "I belong to an organization of Beatles Fan Clubs. These clubs have a lot of members, and the members have parents who I'm sure some must take your paper, but that could change if you keep telling lies about The Beatles all the time."

Members of The Montana Beatles Fan Club had high hopes of attending The Beatles' press conference when they arrived for the Portland, Oregon, show on August 22. Sadly for them, press passes they obtained from a teen magazine were not enough to get them in. However, two girls from The Seattle Beatles Limited Club were allowed inside and reported what they saw in the *Seattle Daily Times*. Paul told how the plane's engine was smoking when they landed in Portland. "Beatles, women, and children first!" he declared. They witnessed George Harrison get

The Beatles hold a press conference at the Capitol Records Tower, Los Angeles. August 29, 1965.

angry at a reporter who asked if he was going to marry his girlfriend, Pattie Boyd. When George realized the woman asking the question was from the magazine that printed that rumor, he spouted out, "Tell your editor that he publishes a lot of rubbish!" They said Ringo wore a red and white surfer's shirt, and was quiet.

The Portland concerts were described as "loud but orderly." The Seattle girls heard one Beatle say, "This is the most orderly crowd we've seen on our American tour."

The Montana Beatles Fan Club girls were not among the orderly. Sitting just 20 feet from the stage, they experienced full-blown Beatlemania. "There is no way to describe how you feel when George, Paul, John, and Ringo run on stage. If you're a loyal Beatles fan, you get a warm, happy feeling inside, and you just don't sit still and keep quiet. You simply have to express your emotions by screaming eeee!"

Before the tour, press officer Tony Barrow contacted one of the promoters in Los Angeles, Louis Robin, and told him, "A certain amount of discussion has taken place with the New York headquarters of The Beatles Fan Club." With the club's help, he had prepared a list of modifications for Robin to look over. As a result, Robin wrote to Beatles (U.S.A.) Ltd., and Bernice Young sent him a list of the twenty official chapters and twenty-seven junior chapters active in the state of California. With this information, Robin contacted representatives from the chapters in the Los Angeles area. On August 29, during a press conference at the Capitol Records Tower, girls from one of the area clubs presented The Beatles with a handmade bug.

Two days later, The Beatles performed at the Hollywood Bowl. There, a local reporter sneaked behind Ringo and snipped a bit of his hair. He gave the hair to two girls who were fan club members, Jackie and Nancy. Jackie publicly thanked the reporter, "You'll never know what that small strand of hair will mean to me for the rest of my life."

The last concert of the tour was on August 31 at the Cow Palace in San Francisco, California. Among those in the crowd were members of The Bijou Chapter of The Beatles Fan Club. Before one of the girls left home, her father told her and her friends that they must behave in a "reasonably civilized manner." Fans failed to heed that advice, and a full-blown riot broke out. As soon as The Beatles came onto the stage, the girls surged forward, trapping Julie Stewart, wife of one of the singers in the Kingston Trio, and five months pregnant at the time. As Julie's friend Joan Reynolds explained, "She was getting badly kicked. We were scared for her. We almost died protecting her. All the girls were screaming various Beatle names. We were screaming Paul's name.

The Beatles arriving in San Francisco—last North American concert of 1965—to a throng of reporters.

We sounded like these girls. We just wanted to get Julie out of there." While this was happening in the front row, fans were getting onto the stage while The Beatles were performing. One girl got Paul in a bear hug, and another had to be pulled off John. One police officer got knocked out by a thrown Coke bottle.

Paul somehow heard Julie's friends cry for help, and stopped the show. The house lights came on, and Paul pleaded for the fans to calm down, saying, "Things are getting dangerous." Much to Joan's relief, this was enough for the crowd to stop pushing and allow Julie to move out of danger: "How this happened amazed us, and we were totally grateful that Paul stopped the show." However, the fans did not stop the rioting. One boy climbed to the top of the twenty-foot fence behind The Beatles. He rolled over the top, slid down, jumped onto the stage, and snatched John's cap off his head. The boy then dove into the crowd, injuring five girls.

Mal Evans helps a girl from the stage during the pandemonium of the Cow Palace concert, August 31, 1965.

After the fence was fixed, the evening show started an hour late. The audience was warned to curb their behavior, but this time it was even worse. Fans started throwing chairs. *San Francisco Chronicle* critic Ralph Gleason wrote: "The girls continued to push and shove and scream and dash on stage. In the end, after the boys scampered off, the bodies lay on the stage like the aftermath of a battle."

As news spread about the events in San Francisco, fans began to worry. Though Paul McCartney said, "We kind of like it. The commotion doesn't bother us anymore," it didn't change the fact that people got hurt. Beatles Bobbies International Incorporated broke up after the 1965 tour. They had done their best to keep The Beatles and their fans safe, but the teenage Bobbies could not compete with hurled bottles and chairs. Around this time several of the San Francisco fan clubs disbanded. No one knew for sure if the Cow Palace concert was the reason, but it did not help.

A Lull In Activity

Once the tour's excitement ended and girls went home to tell their stories, life was quiet for the first time in twenty months for Beatles fans across the continent. Some fan clubs disbanded and others stopped meeting regularly. The Beatles were busy in the recording studio, and there wasn't any news coming out of the Beatles (U.S.A.) Ltd. headquarters. There was not much to talk about.

This lull in activity led many people to speculate that the bubble had burst on The Beatles, and perhaps their popularity was over. *The Arkansas Democrat's* teenage reporter talked to a variety of teens about the supposed decline of The Beatles. The consensus seemed to be that it wasn't that The Beatles weren't good, but so much more music was coming out of England that was just as good. Others called the boys "snobs" and "ridiculous looking." One boy said that without a new gimmick, their popularity would fade soon. Their long hair wasn't enough anymore. Fans of the band were quick to respond that The Beatles would never die because their music is "the type of sound that you never get tired of." One fan declared, "As long as there are teenagers, there always will be The Beatles."

Some fan clubs were disbanding, but others were just starting. One such club was The Greenfield Chapter of The National Beatles Fan Club from Massachusetts. This club — which called its members "Beatle Budgies" — had fourteen members, including two boys. It began as a club on Paul McCartney's birthday, June 18, and the club received a Junior Charter certificate from Beatles (U.S.A.) Ltd. This club considered itself to be a "fun" club that met every two weeks after school. They planned a Christmas party, and sold candy to raise money for a club trip to New York City. All of the members of the club had seen The Beatles in Boston and New York City. They enjoyed talking about their experiences, while collecting Beatles magazines and photos. When asked if The Beatles were losing popularity, club president Roberta Hampton said, "The shock has gotten over, but they're still very popular."

After seeing the band in concert in Minneapolis in August, Kathy Burns was filled with The Beatles' spirit, and soon after the show, she decided to start a Beatles fan club. "I decided I wanted my club to be dependable, global, and that I would be hands-on with the members. And I wanted it to be different. How to be different? I wasn't just a Beatles fan, but a huge John Lennon fan, and I wanted to incorporate that fact," Kathy recalled. The fan club bug had bitten Kathy, but it took until 1966 before her club got off the ground.

Rubber Soul

The Beatles' *Rubber Soul* album.

The Beatles' album *Rubber Soul* was released just in time for the Christmas holidays. Fans of The Beatles were anxious for this new album, and they were not disappointed. After nine days on the market, it topped one million sales. *Rubber Soul* received critical acclaim from reviewers who had not taken The Beatles seriously up until then. Fan club members were quick to write to the papers to praise this new album. One girl wrote to the *Ottawa Journal*, "This is the first set The Beatles have ever done in which I loved every song, and that's the truth." The president of The Beatles Fan Club of Louisiana, said, "This new album is the mostest. I mean it. Never have The Beatles had such a really fab album. And take it from me, it is just too great for words."

Broken Christmas Promise

The members of Beatles (U.S.A.) Ltd. were anxious to receive their Beatles Christmas message album just as they had the previous year. In 1965, many fans had joined to receive this members-only perk. Much to their shock, the fans did not receive a record. Instead, the members received a postcard saying: "Season's Greetings," with a recent photo of the boys. They weren't even looking at the camera. And where was the Christmas record they'd been promised?

Fan club members wrote to their pen pals in England. They quickly learned that the British fans had received a flexi disc. A rumor spread contending that the U.S. club had the record, but was not releasing it to the American fans. In

1966, Beatles (U.S.A.) Ltd. announced that London hadn't sent the tapes in time to have the records ready by Christmas. This was true. The Beatles recorded the album in November, so getting the 1965 album pressed and packaged for the holiday would have been challenging. But American fans had never gotten the 1964 message. They would have been happy to receive a record with the previous year's message instead of a postcard. Fans wrote nasty letters to the club, demanding a copy of The Beatles' Christmas record.

When that did not work, the fans tried to rely on their pen pal friends in England to purchase a copy for them from the U.K. Fan Club. U.K. fans were informed that The Official Beatles Fan Club could not supply additional copies for fan club members to give to family or friends.

The Season's Greetings postcard Beatles (U.S.A.) Ltd. members received instead of a Christmas record in 1965.

The loss of the Christmas record was upsetting. Beatles (U.S.A.) Ltd.'s $2 membership fees were due at the beginning of 1966. Many members wondered if it was worth it. As 1966 opened, more fans began thinking about organizing a totally independent club.

GEORGE HARRISON

JOHN LENNON

PAUL McCARTNEY

RINGO STARR

Chapter 4 — Growing And Maturing Fans

Though Beatles fans were disappointed with Beatles (U.S.A.) Ltd., their devotion to John, Paul, George, and Ringo was still as intense as ever. The band's Christmas release, *Rubber Soul*, remained in the Top 10 for the first seven weeks of the new year. Over the previous two years their fans had matured. Some of the mania had dissipated.

Disc jockey Scott Burton, from WDGY in Minneapolis, told the *Star Tribune*, "The initial shock wave is gone, but The Beatles are going as well as ever, maybe better."

Presidents of several fan clubs agreed. Sue Delmont, from the 100-member McLesh Clan, stated, "We're not as nutty as we were, but we're still loyal to them above any other." Mary Lou Koenig, of the eighty-member chartered club Seltaeb Sect, agreed. "Now we appreciate them more as real people, not as idols. We admire them as musicians."

The Beatles were attracting more than just teenagers. Many adults enjoyed their music. At the age of 31, Mrs. Keith Houston was one of the older members of The Official Beatles Fan Club. Through the club, Mrs. Houston obtained twenty-two pen pals from six different countries. Her perspective was, "In the hearts of the true and loyal fans, The Beatles are still on top."

In January, many fan clubs were still going strong. In Helena, Montana, a fan named Karen Holt was begging her parents to allow her to start her own Beatles fan club. She pleaded with them, saying, "We're all decent, law-abiding kids who want to have some fun for a change. We plan to help charities and to show the world there is such a thing as a good teenager."

Other clubs were setting out to help others in honor of The Beatles. The Active Beatles Club of Detroit sponsored a 13-year-old American Indian girl through the Save the Children Foundation. They raised money by selling 2-cent Tootsie Pops for 5 cents. The money went towards the girl's clothing, shoes, and school supplies. Fan club president Phyllis Bergsman said, "We worked hard and accomplished something, and we never want to hear it said that Beatles or Beatlemaniacs are bad ever again." She went on to say, "Beatlemaniacs do other things besides screaming and listening to Beatles records."

A club in Jackson, Mississippi held a fashion show to benefit the Heart Fund of Hinds County. Club members wore London fashions provided by a local boutique.

Only One Bachelor Beatle Left

The first major news in The Beatles world in 1966 was the marriage of George Harrison and Pattie Boyd on January 21. The couple had met on the set of *A Hard Day's Night* two years earlier, and had been honest about their relationship from the start. Fans knew George and Pattie were going to wed eventually, but no one knew when. Many fans were devastated, just as they had been when Ringo had married the year before. The media reported that one of the area secretaries of The Official Beatles Fan Club in the U.K. had resigned from her position after hearing about the wedding. It was just too much for her.

George Harrison and Pattie Boyd on their honeymoon.

In the United States, Pat Kinzer of the George Harrison Fan Club was equally troubled. "I dressed in black and wouldn't talk to anybody all day," she recalled. "My shorthand teacher even made a point of looking at me and saying, 'Ahh, what happened, did he marry someone else?'" Pat's feelings changed that night when she saw footage of the couple's wedding on television. It was apparent they were in love, and George's new bride made him happy. Pat accepted Pattie Boyd as part of the Harrison family and reported news about her to the fan club.

One club in Michigan, The Screamies, was not unhappy about the marriage, but was upset by their local newspaper's lack of coverage of the wedding. The same newspaper had reported when John Lennon had gotten his driver's license a few months earlier. The fan club sent an angry letter to the editor, stating "Does it hurt to be kind to teenagers once? It seems to me that a wedding is more important than getting a driver's license." Newspaper coverage was essential to fan clubs because many of them kept a club scrapbook. George Harrison's wedding was big news, and a clipping from the newspaper would have been essential for a perfect club scrapbook.

Nonexistent Correspondence

By March of 1966, members of Beatles (U.S.A.) Ltd. needed to send their $2 dues payment to the New York office. Members hadn't heard anything from the club since the disappointing Christmas postcard in December. Correspondence with the New York office had become almost nonexistent for many. Joyce Kenn, president of The Beatles Fan Club of Baltimore, was confused about the expectations of her chartered club. "We get no answer from New York when we write and ask if we should pay dues for another year," she said. "We paid $2 for one year, but that has expired. We wonder if they extended the price to include another year." Likewise, Kathy Burns, who had been a member of Beatles (U.S.A.) Ltd., did not renew her membership in 1966. She recalled, "Though they gave away a lot of worthwhile souvenirs over the years, they were remarkably unreliable, and it might be a year or better between connections." Beatles (U.S.A.) Ltd. members also complained that they sent payments for items to the office in New York, and never received the items or a refund. Because they were required to submit their fan club membership cards with their orders, they had no proof that they were paid members. Letters written to the central office went unanswered. It wasn't that national director, Bernice Young, and her teenage staff were deliberately trying to rip off American Beatles fans. The fan club was extremely understaffed and was in over their heads with the mail. They were doing the best they could with a limited staff, but it just wasn't enough for the many fan club members throughout the country.

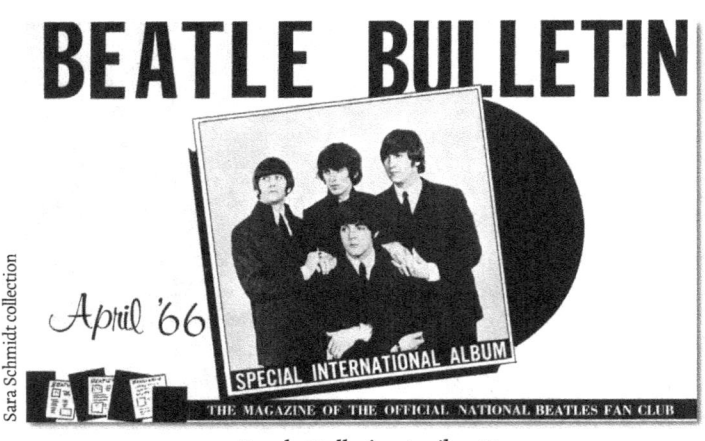
Beatle Bulletin. *April 1966.*

In April, Beatles (U.S.A.) Ltd. released its annual *Beatle Bulletin* magazine to all current paid members. This bulletin was called the "Special International Album." It featured photos of The Beatles in their hotel room in Barcelona during the 1965 European Tour. Bernice wrote a letter in the magazine congratulating The Active Beatles Club of Detroit for raising funds to sponsor a child, as well as the Renton Chapter for sponsoring a boy from Japan. She encouraged all of the other chapters to keep doing good deeds with their clubs.

Beatles (U.S.A.) Ltd. did not have any new items for sale. The same 15 assorted photos from 1964's film *A Hard Day's Night* remained available for 25 cents each. These same photos were sold in 1965. The hardback *Help!* book was marked down from $1 to 85 cents for fan club members. The Beatles photo albums and Beatles roulette drawings were still available for sale, but none of the items sold showed The Beatles in 1966, and the magazine did not have any information about upcoming concerts or recording sessions.

Fan Clubs Ending

Beatles (U.S.A.) Ltd. wasn't the only fan club losing members. The Beatles weren't in the public eye as much in the spring of 1966. For the first time since Beatlemania hit America, the boys weren't making a movie, and though they had a new single, *Paperback Writer*, AM radio stations no longer played their music non-stop.

The Beatles Fan Club of Baltimore was down to thirty-nine members that spring. At one point, they had been one hundred members strong. Membership plummeted after Ringo and George's weddings. The club hadn't met since January, and no meetings were planned. When asked, president Joyce Kenn simply stated, "There's nothing to talk about."

In Philadelphia, The Victor Spinetti Fan Club was also ending. By 1966 the girls who had run it were high school seniors, and they were parting ways. Co-president Patti Gallo recalled, "All the girls were busy. They were going to hairdressing school – you know, planning to go to college or into the workforce. It was sad. We still loved Victor and still were in touch with him, but the fan club had dissolved."

Louise Harrison Caldwell also had to end her fan club. Since her radio show had been canceled, Louise struggled to keep The Louise Harrison Caldwell Fan Club operating. She had hoped to get new members and more money by appearing on *The Tonight Show* with Johnny Carson. Unfortunately, her bid to be on the talk show failed, and Louise had to let her secretary go. George's older sister struggled to keep the club going by herself but ended it in August. She was sad to see her club stop. "I would have liked to do more, but I'm sure you all understand," she wrote in her last letter to members. "At least I know I did my best and did not treat you like so many 'clubs' in the magazines."

"BEATLES & ME"
A thrilling story of one fan's exciting and unique meeting with -THE BEATLES!

My father worked for American Airlines, the airline that The Beatles always chartered for their American tours. I found out that he and his friend were in charge of setting up security arrangements for the Beatles at the airport.

For two years, I bugged my Dad to tell me when The Beatles would arrive or leave the next time they came to Cleveland. The Friday before they were due to appear at the Cleveland Stadium, two penciled notes were on the floor under my door when I got up. One of them said, "I have some info on your 4 friends if you will be free at 2 p.m. Monday. Let me know. Dad."

After arriving at the airport Monday, I went to my dad's office because I wanted to stash my books. After all, you can't meet the Beatles holding SCHOOL books. I had my camera and a nifty purse, the kind that doesn't close at the top. I loved it because it held so much swell junk.

Dad took me down to the gate where the chartered plane was waiting. They were loading equipment and food on – everything but The Beatles. Dad told me that the plan was that the plane would arrive at the end of the runway about 10 minutes before the bus containing The Beatles would arrive from their downtown hotel. The moment the plane stopped, I was to get off. I would be permitted to stand at the end of the ramp and watch them go up the stairs.

Dad took me on the plane and planted me toward the back. I busily took pictures of guitar cases and Ringo's drum kit through the window. Then I talked to a stewardess who said she'd been to The Beatles party at the Sheraton Hotel the night before. I wasn't sure how much time had passed. The only thing on my mind right then was my contact lens, which had just started ripping my eye apart. I forgot all about the Beatles and airports and plans. I found my mirror and began poking and prodding my eye, tearing like mad. I finally got it shoved down to where it belonged, but just to make sure, I covered my other eye and looked straight ahead to see if my vision was blurry or clear. The reality of where I really was slammed me right in the face because right there before my watering eyeball was John Lennon, walking down the aisle of the plane straight toward me.

I'd like to put into words what my first thoughts were right at that moment, but I couldn't tell you. My mind and intelligent conversation froze, as did my whole body. Paul was right behind him, wearing a blinding yellow jacket. Sitting there stunned, staring in utter disbelief, I'm sure it was just gibberish if I said anything at all. John was the only one who said anything to me, "Ah, you wear contacts, too!?" Brilliant opening;

why couldn't I give him a brilliant answer, like saying, "YEAH!" Nope, I just continued to gape. Sensing nothing clever would come out of my mouth, John, followed by the others, continued to the rear of the plane on the opposite side of where I was.

John and Ringo were in the very last seats. Paul and George were in front of them. I was so petrified by this time that I couldn't even look back there, much less go up and ask something original like "Can I have your autograph" or "Do you know I have all your records?" But here I was with the golden opportunity to talk, and I was blowing the whole deal.

Suddenly the spell broke. I asked if I "could take just one picture, please, I'll hurry, just one?" "No," the stewardess said, the plane was about to take off, and I was to leave immediately. I must've looked totally crushed because right then, a voice that was distinctly Paul said, "Oh, let her take a picture. What harm can it do?" Before anyone could say otherwise, I whizzed around and snapped the shutter. By that time, my main objective was to get off the plane without looking any more like an idiot.

I grabbed my purse, which had been sitting on the seat, but I grabbed the wrong end in my rush.

The contents of my purse flew all over the floor of the plane. I don't think I have ever felt so embarrassed in my life. It made such a racket that they would have HAD to hear it and probably looked. All they saw, I'm sure, was a blur of flying arms scrammed all this junk back into a small purse.

I then proceeded to WAIL off the plane, steamrolling anyone in my path. Brian Epstein was the only face that really struck home in my gallop. I roared out of the plane, down the ramp, and up to my father, half scared that he'd be really mad. I didn't get out of the plane right away and already mortified, realizing I'd made a complete fool of myself in front of The Beatles and hadn't even talked to them once. Yet knowing that if I had to do it all over again, probably the same thing would happen. -- **Patricia Simmons**

For more stories of fans that met The Beatles, go to www.meetthebeatlesforreal.com

Independent Fan Clubs Take Off

While some Beatles fan clubs were ending, others were starting. These new clubs were independent of Beatles (U.S.A.) Ltd. They were not local so there were no club meetings. Instead, they did everything through the mail. Throughout the United States and Canada, members relied on these clubs to keep up with the new friends they were making and with Beatles news.

One of these new clubs was The Cyn Lennon Beatle Club run by president Kathy Burns. Kathy and her friends were frustrated with Beatles (U.S.A.) Ltd. and wanted to do something different. A club for the wife of John Lennon was just the thing. "At the time, Cynthia Lennon was still a bit of an enigma," recalled Kathy. "I didn't know a great deal about her, but I did like her, and I found that a lot of people agreed. So, the decision was made. It would be a Beatles fan club, but also integrating Cyn as much as we possibly could. That would be different from any other Beatles Fan Club I was aware of. The first thing to do was to write and ask for Cyn's permission. And so I did."

The dues for the club were 10 cents a month. Members received a newsletter every other month, a membership card, photographs, and an information sheet about Mrs. Lennon.

Cynthia Lennon writes well-wishes to the founder of The Cyn Lennon Beatle Club.

The first newsletter was published in February. The first members were Beatles fans from Minnesota, where Kathy lived. She asked the local radio station to mention the club on-air, and more fans joined. Her next move was to write a letter to *Datebook* magazine, praising them for an article they'd run. In the letter she included information about how to join the club. After reading *Datebook* many girls joined, so Kathy then sent the fan club information to *16* and *Tiger Beat*. By August, The Cyn Lennon Beatle Club had 100 members with more joining every day. One of the club's first efforts was to have each member buy greeting cards, not only for The Beatles' birthdays but also for each of the wives' birthdays. They sent these cards to Kathy, who then mailed them to the homes of The Beatles in England. Kathy also collected greeting cards to send to Cynthia on August 23, John and Cynthia's fourth wedding anniversary. On tour in North America, John was not home to celebrate. Kathy felt that Cynthia would need to be cheered up on that special day without her husband. She hoped cards from her fan club would do the trick.

Early on, the club began selling photographs of The Beatles and their wives. Kathy purchased Louise Harrison Caldwell's remaining pictures that Louise had been selling through her now defunct fan club. Kathy sold them to members to cover the cost of printing the newsletters.

More than anything else, Kathy wanted to have the support of Cynthia Lennon herself. Finally, she received a letter from Weybridge in England. "I opened the envelope carefully and out fell a postcard-sized photograph," recalled Kathy. "On the front was a black and white photo of The Beatles and on the flip side was handwritten: 'Best of luck with your Cyn Lennon Club, luv Cynthia, and Julian Lennon.'" Kathy was thrilled to have heard directly from Cynthia and sent a copy of the card to every club member.

The George Harrison Fan Club also began communicating exclusively through the mail. Pat Kinzer sent the first newsletter, *The Harrison Herald*, in May 1966. Fans got the latest news about not just George, but also the other Beatles. That first issue was not her best effort. As Pat remembered, "It was done on a terrible mimeograph machine, and was very poor quality."

Information about the George Harrison Fan Club.

The most exciting part of the newsletter was a column written by Mrs. Harrison. This column was a unique feature that set the George Harrison Fan Club apart from the others. Club members were encouraged to send questions to Pat, the club's president, who would pass them along to George's mother to answer in her column. Mrs. Harrison loved Pat and fully supported the fan club for her son. Pat worked hard to make the George Harrison Fan Club into a professional club, independent of Beatles (U.S.A.) Ltd. in New York. She typed up a Fan Club Charter and sent it to Mrs. Harrison, asking if she would ask George to sign it the next time he came to visit his family. Mrs. Harrison always answered the club's letters, and this time wasn't any different. "I got it back in the mail," Pat said. "Where I left a spot for George to sign, he just signed his name, 'George,' and nothing else. That was okay with me."

Lace Chu Lu from New Jersey was the president of The International Beatles Fan Club. She started the club in 1964 with just 10 local fans, but she began to get more members through the mail after putting announcements in several teen magazines. By 1966, the club was run entirely through the mail, and new members joined from the United States, Mexico, and England. She said that the three hundred club members were all just regular teenagers, both boys and girls. These teenagers paid $1.50 to join the club. In return, they received a pennant with the club name on it, a jacket emblem with the initials IBFC, a membership card, a Beatles slang dictionary, a record list, and a biography. As

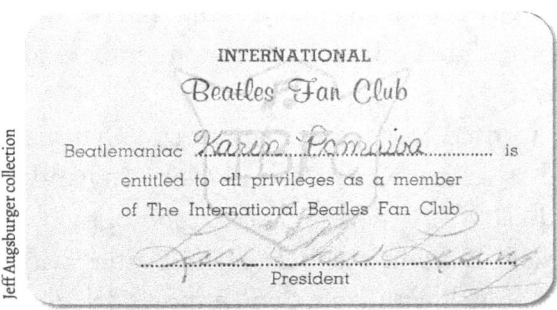

I.B.F.C. membership card. 1966.

I.B.F.C. pennant. 1966. (Jeff Augsburger collection)

the only officer of the club, Lace typed and mimeographed all of the written material. Newsletters went out once every other month, or whenever Lace saved enough money from her allowance to mail an issue. She got the club's patches and pennants made professionally.

Lace encouraged club members to become pen pals with one another. She said she was having fun with the club because "I like to learn about different countries and cities and make new friends." She also encouraged club members who lived near one another to meet up at Beatles concerts, as she and three club members had done before the previous summer's Shea Stadium concert. Lace's main goal in starting the club was to meet The Beatles. "I intend to meet them someday," she stated, "even if I have to go to England!"

One thing stood in her way. The International Beatles Fan Club was independent. Nat Weiss, representing Beatles (U.S.A.) Ltd., demanded that her club get a charter. He wanted her and each of the club's members to pay the $2 dues to join Beatles (U.S.A.) Ltd. The lawyer also asked her to give the New York office her entire membership list. He warned that if she did not follow these demands, she would be blacklisted in Beatles circles. Lace refused to join Beatles (U.S.A.) Ltd. She was happy running The International Beatles Fan Club on her own. She never experienced any repercussions for not answering their demands.

One club that worked to get a charter from Beatles (U.S.A.) Ltd. was the Boss Beatles Fan Club in San Diego. This club had initially been The Yeah Beatles Fan Club run by Kathie Sexton. When Kathie was ready to end the club, she gave everything to Cindi Gonzales. Cindi worked hard to get the charter with Beatles (U.S.A.) Ltd. updated. She corresponded with Bernice Young to work things out so she could officially take over. Cindi teamed up with a local radio station, KGB, to help with the club's cost. She asked members to pay the $1 dues. Each member received a membership card, a fact sheet with copies of each Beatle's autograph, an 8″ x 10″ photo of the group, and a bi-monthly newsletter.

Cindi had members from all around the United States, but most were from California. She was able to order tickets for the club to see The Beatles in concert in San Francisco. Cindi and a few others from the Boss Beatles Fan Club saw The Beatles in Los Angeles, and even tried to get a glimpse of them at the private mansion they rented while in L.A. The Boss Beatles Fan Club was one of a few growing fan clubs in the country.

4463 51st Street
San Diego,
California
92115
February 6, 1966

Miss Bernice Young
BEATLES (U.S.A.) LTD.
PO Box 505, Radio City Station
New York, New York 10019

Dear Bernice:

    We are writing this letttes for several reqsons. There are a few problems that have developeed with the 'Yeah' Beatles fan club Chapter #61 in San Diego. We are applying for a new charter or another official charter for Chapter #61. The reason for this is that Marlou Formanek and Cindi Gonzales, forner director, have been given this club by Kathleen Sexton, former president, for complete reorganization and leadership by them. A signed statement by Kathie relinquishing all authority and possession of the club to Cindi and Marlou has been enclosed. We were not able to enclose the old charter as Kathie lost it about a year ago. She applied for a new charter but did not receive one. We have already started reorganizing the club and we would thoroughly appreciate all information concerning Beatles (U.S.A.) Ltd. for this reorganization, Could you please enclose a list of the Beatles (U.S?A.) Ltd. membees in the San Diego area as we would like to compare them with our list for reference to those who have not rejoined. Thank you very much.

                            Yours Sincerely,

                            Cindi Gonzales
                            Marlou Formanek
                            co-directors

*Letter sent to Bernice Young
from the officers of the Boss Beatles Fan Club.*

A False Start

The Beatles' most infamous photograph was taken on March 25, 1966. Robert Whitaker took the photo as the four Beatles, dressed in white butcher smocks, posed covered with slabs of meat and baby doll parts. As Whitaker explained, "It was entirely my idea. I had this dream one night about The Beatles being ripped to bits by all the young girls when they came out of a stadium. And then I thought about Moses coming down from Mount Sinai carrying the Ten Commandments. He came upon people worshipping a golden calf, and people were worshipping The Beatles like gods."

John Lennon understood what Whitaker was doing and appreciated the surreal photos. John decided the butcher photo would be the perfect cover for The Beatles' summer Capitol Records release in the United States, *Yesterday and Today*. Brian Epstein did not like the photograph and had some serious concerns about what it could do for The Beatles' image. However, Brian could not change John's mind, so he had no choice but to support and defend The Beatles' decision on the album's cover photo.

By May, Capitol Records approved the cover, and pressed 750,000 copies. Distributors, disc jockeys, newspaper and magazine reviewers, and chapter

The Beatles' Yesterday And Today *album, Capitol (S)T-2553, released June 15, 1966.*

presidents of Beatles (U.S.A.) Ltd. got advance copies, but Capitol Records was bombarded with angry telephone calls as soon as the albums were shipped out.

Recipients said the photo was bizarre, grisly, grotesque, or even cannibalistic. Some of the distributors refused to sell it, and demanded a new cover. Capitol Records saw they had a problem. Without a new album cover, they could lose a lot of money. They immediately recalled the released copies of *Yesterday and Today*, and told distributors to return the album.

Capitol Records manager Ron Tepper sent a letter to those who had received the advance copies. Tepper explained that the original album cover was going to be discarded. He explained the decision by quoting Capitol Records' President Alan Livingston: "The original cover, created in England, was intended as 'pop art satire.' The cover design is subject to misinterpretation. For this reason, and to avoid any possible controversy or undeserved harm to The Beatles' image or reputation, Capitol (Records) has chosen to withdraw the LP and substitute a more generally acceptable design."

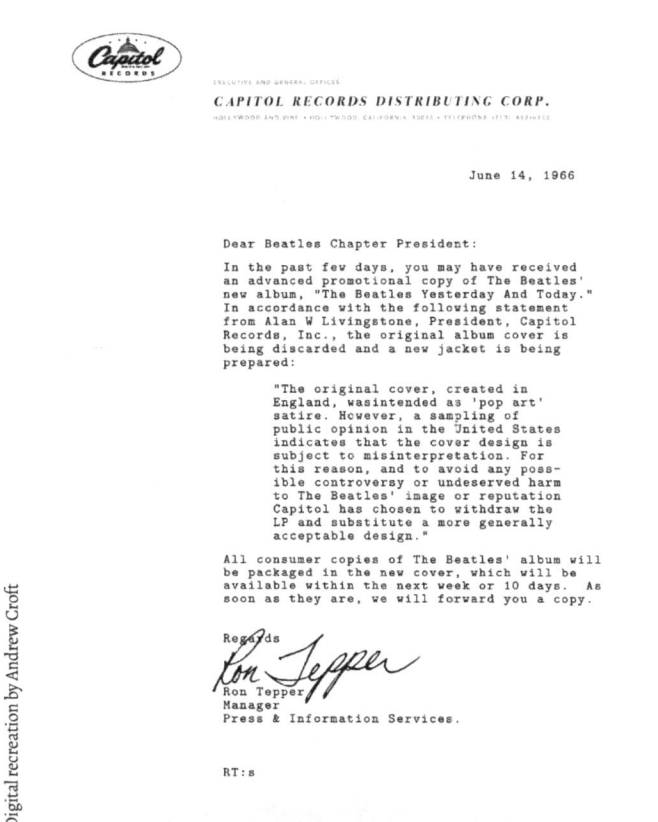

Recall letter sent to Beatles (U.S.A.) Ltd. chapter presidents from Ron Tepper at Capitol Records. June 14, 1966.

Tepper promised to send the album with the new cover within 10 days. Disc jockeys, reviewers, and fan club presidents all received the same letter, with one exception in the content. The disc jockeys and reviewers were told to return the album, cash on delivery, to Capitol Records on Tower and Vine Streets in Hollywood. Perhaps Tepper knew it would be impossible for a fan club president to return a Beatles album because the paragraph asking for the LP to be returned was not in the fan club letter.

The album was recalled, and over the course of a weekend, Capitol Records employees at all Capitol Records pressing plants systematically opened the sealed albums, removed the disc and inner sleeve and the covers were pasted over with the more acceptable 'trunk' cover. The open edge was trimmed slightly, the albums reinserted and the paste-over covers were sealed and shipped out again.

In the spring of 1966, there were fewer than 100 chartered fan clubs in the United States. Many clubs no longer met the membership requirements or did not have their dues paid for the year. Without an active charter from Beatles (U.S.A.) Ltd., the fan club presidents would not have received the complimentary album. There is no way to know precisely how many 'butcher' cover albums of *Yesterday and Today* were sent to club presidents. Those lucky fans who received a copy had a piece of Beatles history.

Banning The Beatles

The controversy over the 'butcher' cover was minor compared to the one that erupted just before The Beatles' 1966 North American tour.

Beatles memorabilia thrown into a fire in Florida. August 1966.

On July 29, 1966, the September 1966 issue of *Datebook* magazine went on sale. *Datebook* was known to be a little more progressive than other teenage magazines. Besides reporting on The Beatles and other favorites, they published articles about drug use and sex. The September issue featured Paul McCartney on the cover. It was subtitled "The Shout-Out Issue." It had thought-provoking quotes from cultural icons such as Paul, Bob Dylan, and Timothy Leary. What got the most attention was John Lennon's remark: "I don't know which will go first — rock and roll or Christianity!" This quote was part of an extensive interview John had given to Maureen Cleave at his home in 1965. In March 1966, her article had appeared in the *London Evening Standard*. John's comments didn't raise any concerns then, but when *Datebook* published John's words in America, people were filled with rage. The part that burned people the most came later in the interview, when John said: "We're more popular than Jesus now."

The following day Tommy Charles, the WAQY radio disc jockey in Birmingham, Alabama, was looking for fresh news. He'd heard about John's claim from a coworker. Charles got on the air, and started venting his outrage at the band. He announced that WAQY would no longer play The Beatles' music. A UPI reporter, Al Benn, heard about The Beatles ban in Birmingham and thought it was a good story. He wired it to New York City, and the word spread through many newspapers around the country, including *The New York Times*. Once the match was lit, the fire was hard to contain. Twenty-one other radio stations banned The Beatles. Some radio station-sponsored fan clubs, such as the 1,500-member KEAN club in Texas, disbanded.

Some adults felt so strongly that they supported an end to all Beatles fan clubs. A man named T.J. Lee wrote an open letter to Beatles fans stating: "If you, or any official of a so-called 'Beatle Club' has any doubt that this bunch of mopheads are not dirty, rude, profane, vulgar, irreverent, pornographic, uncouth, smutty, anti-Christ, anti-Christian, agnostic, atheist, then you should read *Rhythm, Riots & Revolution*, a book by Dr. David A. Noebel."

A group of boys known as The Ban The Beatles Club formed an anti-Beatles group. They went to various radio stations in the southern United States, and worked with any who were sympathetic to find a way to stop The Beatles from touring the country. One member named Warren stated why he felt it was necessary to ban The Beatles: "I believe this was the most deplorable statement anyone could make no matter how rich they are or how popular they think they are."

As if banning The Beatles was not enough, radio stations and church groups started organizing Beatles burnings. They encouraged people to bring their Beatles records, magazines, buttons, photos, and other memorabilia to large bonfire sites. The first of these public burnings was in Starke, Florida. Three hundred teenagers watched as their Beatles records and mementos went up in flames.

The most massive Beatles burning took place on August 12. A Texas radio station, KLUE, sponsored it. Sobbing members

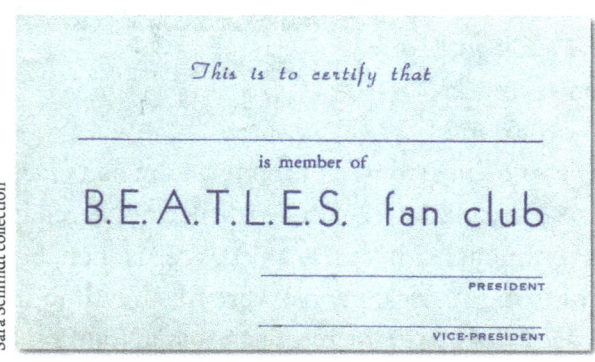

Membership card for the fan club in support of John Lennon.

of the local Beatles Fan Club called the station, saying they would bring all of their Beatles items collected over the past two and a half years, and contribute them to the fire. It took place in front of the KLUE station. Fifteen hundred people watched as records, magazines, sheet music, and photos turned to ash. Some booed as teenagers came forward to burn their items, while others would have preferred to burn The Beatles themselves. The day after KLUE's Beatles burning, there was a freak accident. Some loyal Beatles fans were amused when the station was struck by lightning, knocking the manager temporarily unconscious, and halting the station's broadcast.

All of this disturbed Beatles fan club members. The Trenton Area Chapter 159 of Beatles (U.S.A.) Ltd. called all of the fan club members to see if they were unified. They held an emergency meeting to discuss the furor. All 35 members stood together in support of John's right to say whatever he wanted, even if it was crude. The club also agreed that The Beatles' music was much more important than one of John's random remarks from a year earlier.

Fan clubs gathered to support The Beatles, and to protest The Beatles burnings. At a local church in Delaware, fifty people gathered to burn Beatles records, while a Beatles fan club stood nearby holding up signs that said, "Beatles Forever," "I like The Beatles," and "Freedom of Speech." Fans marched, and sang *Yellow Submarine*, The Beatles' most recent hit song.

Vice president Sharon Liss of Chapter 53 of Beatles (U.S.A.) Ltd. in Philadelphia told the *Daily News* that the media was making an issue of John's statement, not the American people. She brought up the many good things The Beatles had done over the years. "Many people seem to have forgotten that The Beatles did hundreds of charity shows and give several thousands of dollars to charity each year," she said.

The Jesus statement spawned one new Beatles fan club. Two fans, Alice Mang and Denise Longpre, created B.E.A.T.L.E.S. (Bureau of Equality Acknowledging The Lawful Entertainment Standards) on August 11 specifically to show support for John. In two days, the club already had twenty members. Alice had interviewed the boys in Las Vegas and was surprised by how interesting they were. She understood how John talked during an interview. The girls thought Americans were unreasonable. After all, John was talking about England, where more people had seen The Beatles than had attended church. They also felt that the people burning records should have used that energy to help others. The members of the club put together packages for needy children. "We know The Beatles will appreciate this," Alice said. "We cannot get back all the smashed Beatles records and piece them together, but we can do something useful and helpful."

Last Tour Of The Fab Four

Under this dark cloud of anger, The Beatles started their third tour of North America. While some Americans were outraged by what John had said, real fans remained loyal. The president of Chapter 159 of Beatles (U.S.A.) Ltd. said, "The fans, the ones who really count, are still right behind The Beatles with all their support. They always will be."

John, Paul, George, and Ringo quickly learned that their fans still loved them, but many of those fans were growing up. At the first stop on August 12 in Chicago, a 14-year-old fan named Ricki Bluestein said, "I still like The Beatles more than ever, although I no longer belong to the fan clubs." Beatlemania was still in full effect even without an active fan club presence as fans screamed through the concerts. Two girls wore sandwich boards. One said, "I love Paul," and the other, "I love Ringo." On the back of both of the boards, it said, "I'm buggy for The Beatles."

Top: Fans in Philadelphia—two with the Beatles (U.S.A.) Ltd. 1966 book—wait patiently before the August 16, 1966 concert.
Above: Beatles fans—one with the Beatles (U.S.A.) Ltd. 1966 book—scream for their idols at an August 1966 concert.

In Chicago, John apologized for his Jesus comment. Many radio stations accepted the apology and lifted The Beatles ban, but some would not forgive him.

Some fan clubs only existed as a formality. Dee Elias and her best friend, Paulette, lived in a small town near Cleveland. They had heard on WHK radio that the station was sponsoring a Louise Harrison Caldwell talk for officers of chartered fan clubs in the area. The two girls loved The Beatles and wanted to meet George's sister, so they came up with a way to make it happen. "I just started a fan club to be able to meet Louise," Dee recalled. "We had to have so many members, so we faked

I Apologize *(Sterling 8895-6481) record of John Lennon's "apology" recorded at the press conference held prior to the start of their 1966 North American tour in Chicago. August 11, 1966.*

names on the list so that we could qualify as a club." After sending in fifty made-up names, both girls received a fan club charter and membership cards just in time to learn that all area presidents and vice presidents were to come to the station for a meeting. Twenty-five fan club representatives arrived to discover that Louise would be at the Sheraton Hotel on April 12 and would answer their questions. All they had to do was present their membership cards at the hotel entrance.

Dee and Paulette wanted to give Louise a present, so they made a large tea cup from a cardboard box, chicken wire, and papier-mâché. They made a giant tea bag tag that said, "To Louise: You're Our Cup Of Tea!"

After listening to Louise talk about her brother and answer questions from the fan club officers, the girls presented her with the special gift. "She said it was beautiful and very thoughtful of us," Dee said later. "However, it was too big to take on the airplane with her. We were crushed! We told her we understood. We didn't." Dee and Paulette took the giant tea cup back home with them. The girls decided to try to give the gift to The Beatles before the Cleveland concert. Armed with fake press passes, the two made it into the hotel and up to The Beatles' floor before guards stopped them. Paul happened to walk by, and Dee shouted that they had a present for The Beatles. These two fake fan club members ended up being invited into The Beatles' suite. There they met Paul and John, who were happy to keep the giant tea cup.

Cleveland, Ohio remained welcoming towards The Beatles when they played there on August 14. The Cleveland fans loved The Beatles so much that they rushed the stage in the middle of the show. When George began the first notes of *Day Tripper*, hundreds of teenagers left the stands of the stadium and ran onto the field. On their way to the stage they broke through a small fence, and they wound up close to the band. One observer said, "Perhaps one of the concert's highlights was the riot. I thought it was pretty exciting, and I kept wishing some girl would grab one of The Beatles."

Jen Appel, a co-founder of the independent fan club Beatle Fans of the World, Unite!, was part of the action. "I was crushed against the stage and in heaven because I was close enough to touch George's foot. When I reached to touch it, a police officer raised his baton to hit me, but John yelled, 'No, STOP!' at him."

At the start of the riot, The Beatles kept playing. They laughed, and appeared to enjoy the scene. But Jen saw their mood quickly change. "It was frightening to see The Beatles so terrified," she said later. "Ringo looked pale and very frightened."

They had to stop the show. Security escorted The Beatles to the trailer the boys were using as their dressing room. Fans were told that if they would return to their seats, The Beatles would come back. "When the police escorted The Beatles back to the tiny trailer behind the stage, I thought they might be safe," Jen reported. "Then the crazy fans started rocking it back and forth. I saw Paul look out through the window. He looked afraid. When the police got everything under control, it was a great relief. I had not realized that I'd been crying until I got back to my seat, and my brother asked me if I'd been hurt."

In fan club circles, those who made it to the field in Cleveland deserved a badge of honor. They told their stories to pen pals, and these stories made it into fan club newsletters.

On August 16 when The Beatles played Philadelphia, The George Harrison Fan Club was well represented. The officers wore cloth patches embroidered with the club emblem. They also wore matching outfits with the club colors: navy blue and pink. The club purchased a block of tickets for the show so that members could sit together. Before the concert, the club met The Beatles' roadie, Mal Evans. Mal was very kind to the girls, posed for photos, and gave everyone his autograph.

The official emblem of the George Harrison fan club. 1966.

At this show there was a slight change in the fans' response. Instead of just screaming, Beatles fans organized themselves into sections in the stands. Rows of girls yelled "John" or "George" in unison to get one of The Beatles' attention.

Two hundred and seventy fan club members from Rochester, New York traveled four hours by bus to see The Beatles concert in Toronto on August 17. While The Beatles sang, these fans took part in typical Beatlemania. A reporter who'd accompanied them described the fans this way: "They were on their feet screeching, waving, crying, jumping. That was it. Forty minutes of 'Eeeeeee, aaaaaah, oh Paul!'" One boy lowered himself over the balcony, hung onto the stage curtain, and swung himself onto the stage. A girl broke through police lines and tackled Ringo on the drums. The reporter noted, "When John Lennon waved, you could feel the left side of the arena quiver."

Memphis, Tennessee was the one stop John, Paul, George, and Ringo were most concerned about. Memphis had seen Beatles burnings, and the KKK had publicly opposed them. The mayor of Memphis tried to stop the concert, but when August 19 came, the boys were there.

The members of The Beatles Fan Club of Memphis, Tennessee knew the boys would be nervous. They wanted to do something to show the Fab 4 that they still had Memphis fans who loved them. The club members thought it would be funny to present the boys with a dartboard adorned with the mayor's photo. A Memphis city councilman heard about the club's idea. Opposing the mayor's negative attitude, he asked the club if they'd like to present The Beatles with a key to the city. The club members could not believe their good luck. President Pat Rainer remembers, "I went down to his office in City Hall and got the key. I was shocked to see how small it was, like a piece of jewelry you put on a necklace. The club all chipped in and bought a huge

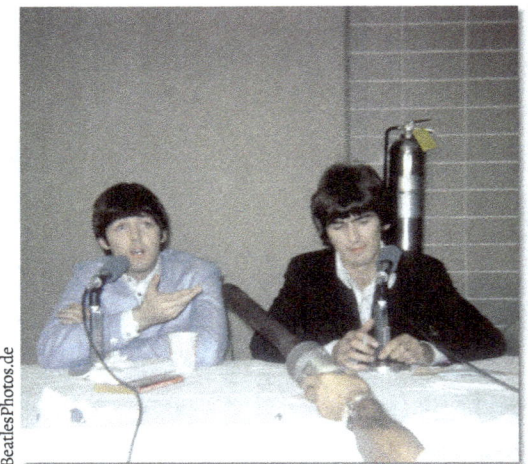 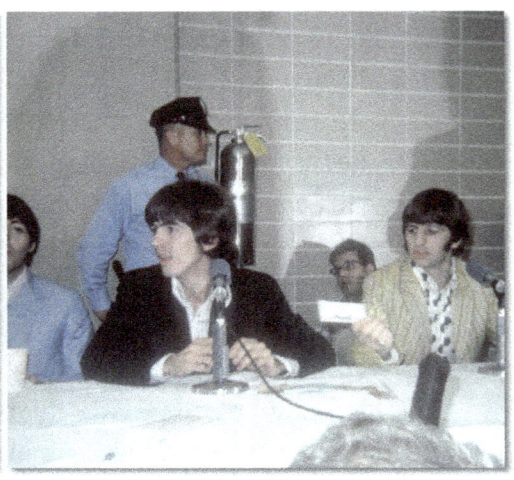

Paul and George, George and Ringo at press conference in Memphis. August 19, 1966.

key and had it engraved and affixed the little key from the city to the big key."

The four club officers attended the afternoon concert together, sitting in the second row. They could not hear any of the music because of the screaming fans.

A press conference followed the first concert. The Beatles Fan Club of Memphis, Tennessee girls had official press passes and were allowed to sit in the front row. The Beatles answered questions from the press, and Pat Rainer waited to be introduced to present the key. As the conference wound down, a disc jockey whispered to Pat that she should give them the key before it was too late. "I got up and walked over to where they were sitting," she recalled later. "At that point, they were standing and getting ready to leave. I wanted to give the key to Paul. I managed to get in front of him, and I held the key and gave it to him. I tried to say something, but I couldn't even talk. I was so totally paralyzed with excitement and the overwhelming nature of the situation. He took the key from me, and then they were hustled out of the room, and that was that."

Pat wanted to make sure they understood they were receiving this key to the city to show that Memphis truly welcomed them, so she followed with a telegram to London. The letter she got back said The Beatles had the key and considered it to be one of their prized possessions.

The Beatles performed an evening concert in Memphis. During the show there was a scary moment when someone in the balcony set off a cherry bomb. Some said The Beatles ducked, but the music didn't stop. Pat was at the evening show, higher up in the stands this time. This time she could hear them. As she recalls it, starting with the cherry bomb incident, "things just kind of kept going. It was weird."

Despite all the adverse events in Memphis, the fans were still crazy about The Beatles. One concertgoer said, "It was unbelievable. We were actually there, and I was staring right at Paul and screaming his name the whole time they were on stage. I was waving my 'I love you, Paul' poster, and I believe he looked right at me."

On the rainy night of August 21, The Beatles performed in St. Louis. The previous night, their concert in Cincinnati had been postponed due to rain. The band played in Cincinnati the next day, then flew to St. Louis for the night concert. Before going on stage, The Beatles kept themselves busy answering fan mail and entertaining visitors from The Beatles Fan Club of St. Louis. This club was run by a woman in her mid-20s named Carol Onion. St. Louis is close to Benton, Illinois, so Carol had become close friends with Louise Harrison Caldwell. The two mothers had a lot in common and traveled to Beatles concerts together. The Beatles Fan Club of St. Louis met at Carol's home, but one of their favorite activities was to go to the St. Louis Hop and dance to Beatles records. Sometimes Carol would bring LPs from England. She'd gotten them from Louise.

Carol's daughter Mary remembers what it was like to grow up in a Beatles fan club house. "There were always girls at the house, and they were always screaming. Also, we were only allowed to listen to The Beatles in the house – absolutely no Elvis."

On the day of the concert, Louise, Carol, and their children went to the dressing room to talk to George. Mary said, "I remember walking down a long hallway and seeing a bunch of men in fedoras and cameras crowded around a door that led to where The Beatles were." As she and the others passed through that door, she saw the man she knew as "Uncle George." "I sat on his lap," she remembers, "Flashbulbs began to go off. I buried my head into his shoulder and asked, 'Uncle George, what is all that light? It hurts my eyes.' He said I was so pretty that everyone wanted to take pictures of me."

Nine members of The Louise Harrison Caldwell Fan Club went to the concert together. They spent the night at president Betty Shepherd's house. The girls watched some films of the boys that Betty had bought through advertisements in the backs of various magazines. The girls were too excited about seeing The Beatles to get much sleep.

The next evening, they got to the stadium in plenty of time. Betty wrote to her pen pal, "We got to our seats about 6:30. I got to see a lot of club members." Once the opening acts started, it began to rain. Many fans used their Beatles (U.S.A.) Ltd. programs as umbrellas. Once the rain let up, the show's producers

The Beatles' rainy concert at Busch Stadium in St. Louis. August 21, 1966.

decided that The Beatles would perform in the middle of the program, rather than at the end. The fan club contingent had great seats, and they could see and hear just about everything. "Our seats were very good," wrote Betty. "With binoculars, we could almost see Paul's capped tooth! The sound system where we were sitting was great. We heard it all; the soft chords of Paul's guitar doing *Yesterday* even came through loud and clear."

As the boys played the rain continued, creating a real safety concern. This heightened when blue sparks flew out of Paul's microphone. Despite the rain, Betty and the rest of her club shared a moment with their favorite, George. "Once when the noise died down between songs, we all hollered, 'George!' real loud, and he heard us, waved and smiled very sweetly. We really loved it."

On August 22, The Beatles held a special press conference at the Warwick Hotel in New York City. One hundred and fifty teenaged Beatle fans were present for the only

A note from Bernice Young about the change in time for the Junior Press Conference in New York City.

CHAPTER 4–GROWING AND MATURING FANS

The Beatles at the Junior Press conference in New York City. August 22, 1966.

Junior Press Conference. Seventy-five of them were fans who'd won a contest held by WMCA radio. The other seventy-five fans were selected from New York area members of Beatles (U.S.A.) Ltd. who had paid their dues. Bernice Young sent press conference invitations to the winners, telling them to pick up their passes at the fan club office. Since the office's exact location had been a well-kept secret, many of the winners did not know where to pick up their passes. They showed up at the Warwick Hotel, using the letter from Bernice to demand entry. Once the guards checked with Bernice, these winners were allowed to go in.

The winners all filed into the Warwick Press Conference Room. It was filled with cameras and lights. With no assigned seats, each girl scrambled to get the perfect spot. They were introduced to Brian Epstein, Neil Aspinall, members of The Cyrkle, and the WMCA Good Guys. At The Beatles' request, only soft drinks were served. Each winner received a gift. As Felice LaMastra recalled, "We were all handed a little gift packet. It contained four individual and professionally taken pictures of The Beatles that were all personally autographed! There were one or two other items as well in the gift envelope."

Many of the fans were screaming. One of the WMCA Good Guys announced, "This is the first time in history The Beatles have come this close to their fans. Let's show them how grown-up we all can be." Conference moderator and disc jockey Gary Stevens also asked for quiet. It wasn't until The Beatles' press officer, Tony Barrow, began hollering that the girls finally calmed down.

It did not last for long. Behind a door, an unmistakable Liverpudlian voice said, "Who's shouting out there?" Paul appeared, shaking his finger jokingly. Felice recalls the moment the Fab Four appeared: "The one hundred and fifty winners went wild with screams when the doors behind the Warwick conference table opened, and The Beatles all appeared. I remember the four of them kind of jumping down a step on to the level of the conference table and then taking their seats. The room went ballistic. Kids were screaming their heads off. It was magical."

The first question was one that everyone needed to know: "Paul, are you going to marry Jane Asher?" "We probably are going to get married," he said, earning a disappointed groan, followed by applause. Many of the questions centered on people The Beatles knew or didn't know. The fans were trying to catch any friends or pen pals in lies: "Do you know Al Perry?" "Do you know Patricia Flater from Cumberland?" "George, do you have a cousin named Maggie?"

Other fans asked more pertinent issues, such as the noise at the start of *Taxman* and the origins of *Eleanor Rigby*. And why were the albums and movies in the U.S. different from those in the U.K.? The strangest question came from a girl holding a leaf. She asked Paul, "Do you recognize this? It's supposed to come from your front lawn." Paul replied, "Sure, I've missed it for months."

Felice decided she would ask John a question. She had read that John had ordered a guitar from her hometown, Hoboken, New Jersey, and wanted to know if it was true. John could not hear her over the others screaming, until Neil Aspinall helped and repeated her query to John. His response was, "No, that's not true. And you shouldn't believe most of what the papers write about us. Most of it is not accurate." But that time the newspaper had been right. At the end of the press conference, Mark Dronge presented John with a Guild Starfire XII electric 12-string guitar. It had been made especially for John by Guild Guitars in Hoboken, New Jersey.

Dronge later described it this way: "As the interview came to an end, I took the guitar out of the case and made my way onto the platform where The Beatles had been sitting behind a long table. George thought the guitar was for him and was annoyed when I passed him and presented the guitar to John, who seemed surprised and delighted."

The Beatles received gifts from the fans, including a big, fuzzy toy spider for Ringo and a tribute book for Paul, but many fans wanted to take home their

"Happy Anniversary John & Cyn" banner behind fans at Shea Stadium. August 23, 1966.

own souvenirs. One girl begged Paul to give her the cigarette right out of his mouth, and he did! Once the boys left, girls raced up to their table and scavenged ashtrays, cigarette butts, table cloths, and anything not nailed down.

The following day The Beatles performed at Shea Stadium. The officers of The George Harrison Fan Club had announced their seat location in the most recent fan club newsletter, so before the concert, many fellow members came to meet them and chat. The George girls made a giant "We love George" sign.

Fans were excited to celebrate John and Cynthia's fourth wedding anniversary. Everyone in the stadium could see a huge "Happy Anniversary John & Cyn" sign. The fan who made that sign said, "It happened to be John and Cyn's anniversary, so I decided to make a banner for them and hang it at the concert. Imagine my dad's reaction when the paint leaked through the sheet, and the message 'Happy 4th Anniversary John & Cynthia' was now on the driveway!" The entire audience joined in singing "Happy anniversary" to the couple.Though there were fewer fans than the previous year, The Beatles behaved as they always did. One concertgoer said, "The funniest thing is during the part where they play a few bars without singing. Paul comes all the way over to the end of the stage and flirts with everyone on our side. All of a sudden, he remembers that he has to get back to the mic to sing and half runs, half skips back to his place."

From there The Beatles traveled across the country to Los Angeles to relax at a rented mansion, but they also held an August 24 press conference, this one at

John, Paul, and Ringo at the press conference at the Capitol Records Tower. August 24, 1966.

Hollywood's Capitol Records Tower. Since The Beatles weren't performing in Texas, the Dallas area Beatles Fan Club (U.S.A.), Chapter 24 officers decided to travel to California to see them. All of the fan club members donated money for gifts. They got branding irons initialed with 'J,' 'P,' 'G,' and 'R.'

Even though they had met The Beatles two years earlier, there was no guarantee they would meet them again, so they appealed to Dick Clark. Officers Yolanda Hernandez and Stephanie Pinter went to his L.A. office wearing black 10-gallon hats. They showed the secretary the photograph of themselves with The Beatles in Dallas. She showed the photo to her boss, and suddenly the girls were telling their Beatles story to Mr. Clark. He agreed to help them get the gifts to The Beatles. "He told us there was a press conference at Capitol Records," Yolanda remembers, "and we should meet him there with the gifts. He would get us seats, and we were to get someone's attention to have the gifts passed off to The Beatles."

Dallas Beatles Fan Club (U.S.A.), Chapter 24 presidents Yolanda Hernandez, Stephanie Pinter, and Debbie Pinter present The Beatles with initialed branding irons.

On the big day, the girls wore matching sleeveless black shirts, patterned skirts, and their cowboy hats. The room was crowded, and they had to stand along a wall. They could barely see The Beatles over all of the reporters, but Yolanda noticed George looking in her direction. "George leaned over to Paul, who then leaned over to John, who leaned over to Ringo, and they all began a private conversation. George then motioned with his forefinger, as if beckoning someone to approach. Stephanie and I looked at each other, and then at him, we then pointed to ourselves, questioning, 'Do you mean us?' and George nodded yes. We quickly ran to the podium, where he helped us up."

George greeted the girls and asked Yolanda if she'd like a sip of the Coca-Cola he'd been drinking. "I eagerly replied, 'yes.' Oh, my lips had touched the Coke bottle that George Harrison's lips had touched." All of the girls received hugs from all of The Beatles, then presented them with the branding irons. The boys were photographed holding them, much to the pleasure of the entire Beatles Fan Club (U.S.A.), Chapter 24.

The Beatles' last stop on the tour happened on August 29 at Candlestick Park in San Francisco, California. The band performed in a cage built on a five-foot elevated platform, surrounded by a six-foot storm fence. Five boys from the centerfield bleachers climbed over a smaller fence and ran toward the stage. A few minutes later, five more did the same thing. The Beatles noticed the commotion, but the police stopped all the boys before they could reach them.

Before the Candlestick Park performance, The Beatles decided they were never going to tour again. The fans didn't know, and fully expected to have another chance to see them again in the coming years. Brian Epstein had told the *Toronto Star*, "The Beatles will be back, most likely the next summer." After the Shea Stadium concert one fan said what everyone in North America was thinking: "They will be back next year. I know that."

Pen Pals

The Beatles left, and a new school year started. Beatles fans needed new ways to talk to like-minded friends. Most of the local clubs had disbanded, so the remaining fans turned to pen pals.

The idea of students in different countries exchanging handwritten letters through the mail had first been raised in 1936. That's when a teacher thought it would be a good way for his students to learn about other countries. By the 1960s some pen pal programs served this educational purpose, but others were just fun ways for teenagers to communicate. Magazines like *16*, *Tiger Beat*, *Datebook*, and *Teen Screen* all offered lists of teenagers who wanted to exchange letters. Many Beatles fans connected through these magazines. One fan, Vicki Schall, recalls, "I found my very first Beatles pen pal through an article in *Teen Set* by a girl who called herself 'Paul Kooch.' She had a free fan club called 'PAUL,' and members were 'Paulists.' PAUL stood for 'Peace And Universal Love.'"

Almost every independent fan club newsletter included a pen pal section. Beatles (U.S.A.) Ltd. provided American fans with addresses of U.K. club members. That's how Jennie Traficenti and Sue Woodruff connected. Jennie recalled, "I was a Beatles fan, so I joined The Beatles fan club. I asked for a pen pal from England. They sent me a name, and I wrote a letter to Sue."

Once fans began writing letters to each other, they started to exchange friendship books. They made these small booklets by stapling paper together and decorating it with drawings and pictures cut from magazines. Each recipient would include her name and address and her favorite Beatle before mailing it to the next pen pal. Many connected through these friendship books.

The focus of most letters was The Beatles. "Full-blown Beatle maniacs we were, and we couldn't get enough of it," Jennie remembered. "We wanted all the information you could get about each one of them." In a time when Beatles news was difficult to obtain, the fans relied on these letters to learn

Beatles pen pals created 'friendship books' to send to each other.

what was happening with the boys. Pen pal circles passed around Beatles photos, newspaper articles, and magazine clippings. The fans used the letters to express their feelings about The Beatles and their music.

Betty Shepherd wrote a letter to her pen pal about her thoughts on the newly released *Revolver* album: "The beginning of '*Taxman*' is great. That's the reason I like the boys so much – they leave stuff in their records, which are mistakes, but are a real addition. My favorites are '*Here, There and Everywhere,*' '*Taxman,*' and '*Yellow Sub.*' One I don't care for is '*Tomorrow Never Knows.*' I think it sounds like Indians attacking a wagon. Maybe it will grow on me..."

Though their main topic was The Beatles, friendships bloomed between the pen pals. According to Vicki Schall: "Besides The Beatles, we also wrote about our lives, school, work, hobbies, and other interests." These fans exchanged birthday and Christmas gifts, and some fortunate pen pals got to call each other long-distance – a rare treat then. The Cyn Lennon Beatle Club president, Kathy Burns, summed up the importance of Beatles friends: "Everyone shared and helped each other and wanted nothing more than to be friends with other Beatles fans because they had something in common."

Aunt Mimi Joins The Club

The fall of 1966 was a busy time for The Cyn Lennon Beatle Club. By October the club was up to two hundred members. Kathy was in desperate need of a $35 printing machine for the monthly newsletters. She asked each member to donate a quarter to keep the club going. The members came through, and the club was saved. With Cynthia's club growing more every day, Kathy appointed a girl from Ohio named Bunny Racey to be vice president. Bunny's responsibility was printing and selling photographs. She found photos of The Beatles in British magazines, made negatives, and sold the prints through the club.

Kathy had Mrs. Louise Harrison, Louise Harrison Caldwell, and Cynthia Lennon as honorary members of The Cyn Lennon Beatle Club. Judy Johnson, president of The John Lennon Fan Club, had gotten the address of John's aunt, Mimi Smith. Judy thought Kathy should reach out to Aunt Mimi and make her an honorary club member.

Mimi, the strict aunt who had raised John like her own son, was a mystery to most fans. She was not as overtly friendly as George Harrison's mother. Regardless, Kathy took the chance and wrote to her, telling Mimi about the

Left: John and his Aunt Mimi. Right: Christmas card sent to Kathy Burns from Mimi 'with much love.'

club, and inviting her to be an honorary member. Much to everyone's surprise, Mimi wrote back. She said she would be pleased to be in the club and wished it all success. She sent this statement about Cynthia, "She's a very nice girl, and I couldn't have wished for John to have a better wife. They are very happy." This letter was the start of a positive relationship between Mimi, Kathy, and The Cyn Lennon Beatle Club. The year ended with club members making a poetry book they sent to The Beatles for Christmas, marking the first year of The Cyn Lennon Beatle Club as a big success.

Everywhere It's Christmas

The four Beatles spent the fall of 1966 apart from one another. John was in Germany and Spain, making the film *How I Won the War*. Paul went on safari in Kenya and worked on the score for the Hayley Mills movie *The Family Way*. George studied the sitar in India, and Ringo was home with his wife and son.

On November 24 at EMI Studios on Abbey Road, the boys got back together for the first time since the San Francisco concert. There they recorded a song John had written in Spain, *Strawberry Fields Forever*. The next day The Beatles met at Dick James Music's basement studio to record their annual Christmas message for their fan club members. It was their fourth Christmas recording, and they wanted to go in a different direction. Paul said, "Ultimately, the final product would contain no greetings and very few references to the holidays."

Pantomime is a Christmas tradition in England. It is a stage performance of many skits that combine music, comedy, and stories. The Beatles enjoyed the comedy of the pantomime. John attended annual holiday pantomimes in Liverpool when he was a child. The Beatles performed live pantomime during their Christmas shows in 1963 and 1964. It was a natural progression for the Christmas message to be a pantomime. *Pantomime: Everywhere It's Christmas* included the title song, which had Paul singing and playing the piano. Producer George Martin had a background in making comedy albums and used his expertise to include some great sound effects. The *Liverpool Echo* reported: "John, Paul, George, and Ringo play twelve different roles. Highlights included John and Paul as 'Podgy the Bear and Jasper,' and

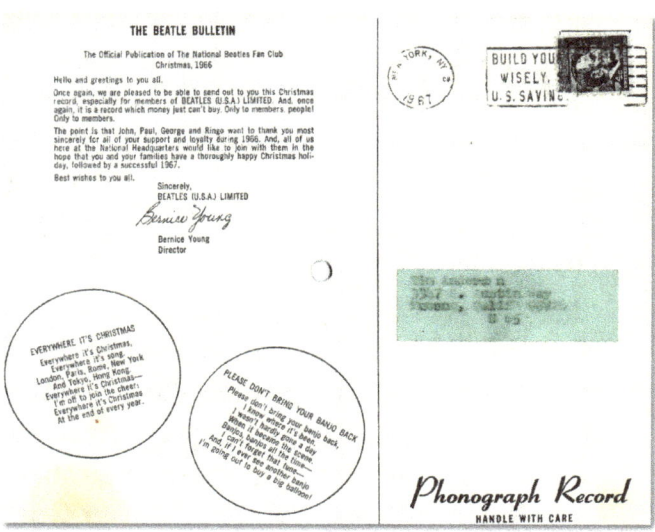

The Beatles' 1966 Season's Greetings message entitled Pantomime: Everywhere It's Christmas *was confusing to some fans.*

George and Ringo as 'elderly Scotsman eating cheese on a Swiss Alps.'" The *Echo* urged fans to join the club to get a copy, saying the record "looks like being a collectors' item from the outset."

The Christmas record was sent to members of Beatles (U.S.A.) Ltd. This disc was only the second Christmas record sent to American fans, and it was the first time they'd heard a current message from the group. However, the American fans still did not get the flexi-disc with a sleeve, like their British counterparts. Instead, American fans received a rectangular 7" x 8½" postcard, with the vinyl record on one side bearing the message "Season's Greetings from The Beatles." The other side had a *Beatle Bulletin*. The bulletin was written and signed by Bernice Young. She wished members a happy Christmas and a prosperous 1967. Also printed on the back were the lyrics to *Everywhere It's Christmas* and *Please Don't Bring Your Banjo Back*. There were no photographs of The Beatles in the record's packaging. Mailed out without an envelope, it displayed the message: 'Phonograph Record: Handle With Care.'

Many fans didn't know what to think of the record. Most Americans weren't familiar with pantomime, but some thought the album was hilarious, especially liking the Podgy and Jasper routine. For most the message was seven minutes of confusion and laughs. Chartered fan club president Debbie Gendler recalls, "A lot of girls in my club, when they got that were unhappy. They thought, 'They're not the same Beatles we always loved.' A lot of them didn't renew."

With *Pantomime: Everywhere It's Christmas*, The Beatles were acting as if they were different people. It is almost as if they were trying to send their fan club members a big hint as to what was to come in 1967.

Chapter 5 — A New Sound and Movement

As 1967 began it felt as if The Beatles' bubble had finally burst. The band had not been heard or seen in five months. Only a handful of Beatles fan clubs existed. Many teenagers no longer loved The Beatles, and pledged their devotion to The Monkees. Plenty of Beatles fans were still scattered throughout North America. They kept in touch through fan club newsletters, pen pal letters, and the occasional long-distance telephone call.

The Beatles At Shea

The fans were all abuzz about the television special, *The Beatles at Shea Stadium*. They crowded around their television sets on January 10, armed with their Instamatic cameras and reel-to-reel tape recorders, ready to relive the excitement of a Beatles concert. For one hour, they watched John, Paul, George, and Ringo perform for 60,000 fans. The film was in color, and showed The Beatles both on and off stage.

Critics felt that the program was passé, just an old relic of pop music history, but fans were thrilled. Bunny Racey, the newly appointed Vice President of The Cyn Lennon Beatle Club wrote in the January newsletter, "Have you all gotten over the shock of seeing The Beatles at Shea Stadium on TV? They really were wonderful."

Breakup Rumors

Just a few days later that joy turned into panic. In an Associated Press story from January 23 Derek Jewell of the *Sunday Times* in London interviewed Paul McCartney. Paul said he had grown a mustache as "part of breaking up The Beatles." Paul went on, "I no longer believe in the image." In UPI's version The Beatles were breaking up because they made too much money. Any additional earnings would go straight to taxes. Paul said they all had grown up. "Now, we're ready to go our own way."

Those weren't the only breakup stories. Brian Epstein told a group of two hundred fans picketing outside his London home that The Beatles' thoughts about their career had been "altered." The Beatles manager was unable to predict what The Beatles were going to do next.

The Beatles movie producer Walter Shenson said, "They won't tour anymore. They are too rich to want to put up with all those hassles. They don't need that kind of misery." He went on to say The Beatles had no plans for a third movie. His last shocking words were, "They don't want to play The Beatles anymore."

What did all this mean? If they were not touring or doing another film, could The Beatles be breaking up? Fans panicked. Fan club president Leslie Samuels in New York got a call from one of the members in Chicago, and almost "had a heart attack" when she had heard that The Beatles had broken up.

Fan club presidents searched for the truth. The head of the Paul McCartney Fan Club, Claudette Cyr, tried to ease members' fears in the January 1967

Beatles (U.S.A.) Limited

P. O. BOX 505, RADIO CITY STATION, NEW YORK, NEW YORK 10019

BEATLES FAN CLUB
OFFICIAL HEADQUARTERS

February 7, 1967

Hello.

Thank you for your letter to The Beatles. They have asked that I reply to you on their behalf.

Under no circumstances will The Beatles be breaking up or separating from their highly popular manager, Brian Epstein. As you may have heard by now, the boys have just signed a brand new nine-year contract for recording with EMI.

The Beatles and Brian Epstein would like to thank you for your continued interest and enthusiasm.

Sincerely,

BEATLES (U. S. A.) LIMITED

Bernice Young
Director

BY/ff

Sara Schmidt collection

Beatles (U.S.A.) Ltd. letter to fans, dated February 7, 1967, stating The Beatles are not breaking up.

newsletter. She had heard from a spokesman for The Beatles in London. He assured her that The Beatles were not breaking up and were "currently writing material for their new film."

Some wrote to Beatles (U.S.A.) Ltd. and got a reply from Bernice Young. She eased members' minds by stating, "Under no circumstances will The Beatles be breaking up or separating from their highly popular manager, Brian Epstein." Others contacted people close to The Beatles. A fan named Kathy heard reassuring news from Mrs. Harrison. "Don't worry," she wrote. "The Beatles are not breaking up. I asked George, and he said, 'We are never, ever breaking up. We will always be a group.'"

Unlike some fans, Leslie Samuels read a copy of the original *Sunday Times* article, and discovered the American papers had taken quotes out of context. Yet when she met Paul during the summer, she let him know just how upsetting the ordeal had been. Paul told her, "Yeah, well, that's 'cause that's all they could think of to say around that time because we weren't doing anything. They couldn't see any shows; they couldn't see us doing concerts. So when they can't see us doing anything very obviously and clearly, they think, 'ahh...they must be breaking up.' They don't understand it, and they'll never understand. They'll never understand how we're never going to break up. The whole thing about us is we're four friends. We don't have to do it. It's not about money. We enjoy it. We like each other."

A New Look and Sound

When the new double-sided single, *Strawberry Fields Forever/Penny Lane*, was released in early February fans realized that The Beatles had not disbanded. As they watched the promotional films on *The Hollywood Palace* television show, fans were shocked to see that all four Beatles had facial hair. Instead of matching suits, they wore colorful jackets and pants. This new look turned many casual fans away from The Beatles. Some fan club members were confused, while others were excited. One group, The United Beatles Fan Club, asked members what they thought of the look. Most of the girls did not like the beards and mustaches. "I definitely don't like it," said one fan. "George looks like some kind of witch." One fan recalled thinking that they looked strange. She hoped the facial hair would go away. Patti Crichton remembers, "I was disappointed in the beards and mustaches, but I loved the colorful clothing."

The Beatles present their new image in their promotional film for Strawberry Fields Forever *with colorful clothing and mustaches.*

Many fans liked that The Beatles showed their individuality and broke away from old stereotypes while still being trendsetters. Bill Martin recalled, "I liked how they changed fashion all over again." Some fans even predicted that other musicians would soon have facial hair and colorful clothing. After all, in 1964 many musicians had started wearing their hair combed down in the front, just like The Beatles.

Their appearance went hand-in-hand with their new music. As one member of The United Beatles Fan Club said, "I think their look matches the new sound and movement in the music." The songs *Strawberry Fields Forever* and *Penny Lane* were different from their previous singles. Katie Jones recalls, "I enjoyed the peppy 'Penny Lane,' but I didn't like or understand the plodding, odd 'Strawberry Fields Forever.'" Katie wasn't alone; other fans thought John's song had a "spooky" sound to it. They said it took them a long time before they understood and appreciated the song. Another member of The United Beatles Fan Club member summed up how the majority of fans felt, "I don't really care if they have beards or what they wear because they're the same people." All of the club members knew The Beatles were working on new material. They would be even more surprised once it was released.

Romeo and Juliet

Jane Asher performing in "Romeo and Juliet" in the United States.

In the meantime fan club members were doing what they enjoyed doing: getting to know those close to The Beatles. Besides the letters from Mrs. Harrison, The Beatles wives, and Mimi Smith, the fans had a new target: Paul's girlfriend, Jane Asher. The lovely red-headed actress came to the United States on a tour of *Romeo and Juliet* with the British theater company, The Old Vic. Jane played Juliet in what was called "a new kind of Shakespeare." Most fan club newsletters printed the tour schedule, encouraging members to see the production and report back. The National Jane Asher Fan Club had reporters in many of the cities on tour. While seeing Jane on the stage was great, the ultimate goal was to meet her. While some of the girls had previously claimed that they hated Miss Asher, when presented with the possibility of meeting Paul McCartney's girlfriend, they suddenly adored her almost as much as they did Paul.

Much to the shock of their parents, Beatles fans throughout the country became instant Shakespeare lovers. Instead of asking for money for Beatles merchandise or concert tickets, they were asking for money to see a live production of *Romeo and Juliet*. Unknowing parents thought their daughters were maturing out of Beatlemania. They were happy to get tickets for these girls.

When Jane arrived in the United States, she refused to talk about Paul McCartney to the press. To deflect reporters, she would say, "The theater is my real love." American reporters did not like that answer, so they continued asking about her famous boyfriend. Not wanting to steal attention from the tour, she said, "I'm in this country as a Shakespearean actress... not just a friend of a Beatle..."

The fans didn't mind. They knew Jane was Paul's girlfriend, so they wanted to see her perform. Fan club members showed up in every city, and though they managed to stay calm through Jane's performance, they lost control when she came out for the curtain call. As she took her bow, fans screamed and flashbulbs popped, often blinding her. One San Francisco fan recalled, "I was thrilled to meet Jane when she arrived at the theater. She was so kind and signed my Old Vic program. The audience was filled with fans who screamed when she took a bow. She had to run to her hotel."

Young actress Judy Matheson was the understudy for Lady Montague, and played some of the background characters. She remembers the mania created by Beatles fans, "There were literally hundreds of screaming fans at the stage door as we approached for the show. One particular evening as we were packing up backstage, ready to move to another town, we were told a couple of fans were found hiding in wardrobe skips."

Not all Beatles fans adored Jane. A few were extremely jealous of her. They thought Jane was acting as if she was too good for a boy from Liverpool. They didn't believe Jane loved Paul. This vocal group wrote to fan club newsletters saying she had to go. They thought she was using his fame to advance her acting career. These anti-Jane fans caused some tense moments. Judy recalls, "On a couple of occasions Jane received death threats, which was very scary for us all, but of course particularly for her."

When the troupe played in Denver, Paul flew from London to be with Jane for her 21st birthday. The fact that one of The Beatles was in the United States went unnoticed by the fan club members. While Jane was playing Juliet on stage, Paul was backstage. The Beatles fans in the audience never even knew he was there. Judy says, "Paul spent most of the time while Jane was on stage in my dressing room as I had much less to do on stage. I have a very strong image in my mind – a memory of Paul sitting with his feet up on the mirrored shelf, very relaxed and chatty."

Independent Fan Clubs Boom

Fans of The Beatles had given up on Beatles (U.S.A.) Ltd., and they turned their attention to independent clubs. In 1967 these boomed. The girls running the clubs worked hard to get Beatles news to their members. They scoured all sorts of magazines and newspapers, corresponded with pen pals worldwide, and got all the latest Beatles news and gossip they could find into these clubs' newsletters. Most were typed and mimeographed. Members spent hours folding, addressing, stamping, and sending them.

Beatles fan clubs sprang up in all regions of the country; females ran them all. Some of the new clubs were the Lennon Luvvers Limited (Maryland), The Fab Four Society (Virginia), Around The Beatles (Michigan), Beatles Birds (California), Beatle Empire (Maryland), The National Jane Asher Fan Club (Iowa), and the Pattie Harrison Fan Club (Nebraska).

In March, 1967 three hundred fans were members of The Cyn Lennon Beatle Club. After the president, Kathy Burns, went on a local radio station to advertise the club, several club members did the same at their local stations. These new members paid 10 cents a month or $1.25 a year. The club had a dog named Paul as its mascot, but when Paul had eight puppies, Kathy changed her name to Paula. She asked club members to help name the new puppies. The club held many contests that year. One of the most popular was the Cynthia drawing contest.

One of the entries for The Cyn Lennon Beatle Club drawing contest.

Kathy continued to correspond with John's Aunt Mimi, but in May, she was able to add another Beatles' insider to her list. Freda Kelly, the Liverpool area secretary who had been with The Beatles fan club since 1962, sent The Cyn Lennon Beatle Club a letter on behalf of Maureen Starkey. The club had sent Ringo's wife a book of poetry, and Freda thanked them. After this, Freda became an honorary member of the fan club, and Kathy corresponded with her from time to time.

When Maureen and Ringo announced they were expecting their second child, Cyn club members wanted to send gifts. By the time the baby, Jason, was born fans had donated so much cash and so many gifts that Kathy decided to give everything to OXFAM children's charity. She gave these things in honor of Jason, sending a card, with good wishes from the club, to the parents.

By the end of 1967, The Cyn Lennon Beatle Club was up to four hundred members and seemed to have a promising future.

"KENWOOD",
CAVENDISH ROAD,
ST. GEORGES HILL,
WEYBRIDGE,
SURREY.

Dear Fans and friends,
   First of all I would like to thank you all for your support and friendship which you have all shown to me by your efforts and enthusiasm in forming a CYN LENNON FAN CLUB.
   I must admit to you all that I'm very honoured and very proud to think I am worth all of your hard work and effort. I'm afraid I have been neglecting you in many ways-- regarding repling toyour letters, information etc, but I do hope you understand that my life is very full and time is very short for me to do all the things I should do and aught to do.
   I willtry very hard in future to find time & to keep in touch with you all. Before I close I would like to wish you all a very happy Christmas I wish you all you wish yourselves, have a marvellous time and lots of fun.
   Love and best wishes,

Cyn Lennon.

John & Julian.

Letter of support from Cyn Lennon to her fan club.

Pat Kinzer kept producing a high-quality newsletter, *The Harrison Herald*, through 1967. News, poetry, and information about George Harrison filled the pages. Other independent clubs patterned themselves after the George Harrison Fan Club.

At the end of 1966, Pat and the club decided to sponsor a child through the Christian Children's Fund. Since George was interested in Indian music and culture, she requested a child from India. In January, she heard back from the charity. They didn't have any children from India available, so the club sponsored a little girl from Thailand named Prapai. Club members were enthusiastic, donations came in, and Pat reported all of it in the newsletters.

That year the club sold T-shirts with a cartoon of George on the front. "George Harrison Fan Club" was printed around the picture. That summer, Pat met for the only time with the two co-vice presidents. They posed for a photo modeling the club shirts.

For a short time Pat's club wasn't the only George fan club. Jeri Glaeser in Maryland started Harrison Huggers Ltd. This club didn't report as much news in its quarterly newsletter, but it made up for that with fun activities. There were contests, like the one for the best George poetry, and George-themed hand-drawn crossword puzzles and word searches.

Judy Johnson took over The John Lennon Fan Club from the previous club president, who gave her names and addresses of past club members. Then Judy was left to run

Pat Kinzer (center) and the officers of the George Harrison Fan Club.

the club. The club newsletter, *Lennon Lyrics*, was full of news and information about John. "I wrote the newsletter myself," Judy recalled. "I created a stencil and then ran copies off on a spirit duplicator in my bedroom. That was tiresome, so I eventually sent the stencil to a printer I found in a magazine and received the printed copies by mail." It was Judy who initially found John's Aunt Mimi's address. She regularly wrote Mimi, who gave her information about John. Mimi was very complimentary about her nephew's fan club. She liked the work Judy was doing.

Much of The John Lennon Fan Club focused on charity work. Instead of sending John a birthday gift in October, the club sent OXFAM children's charity

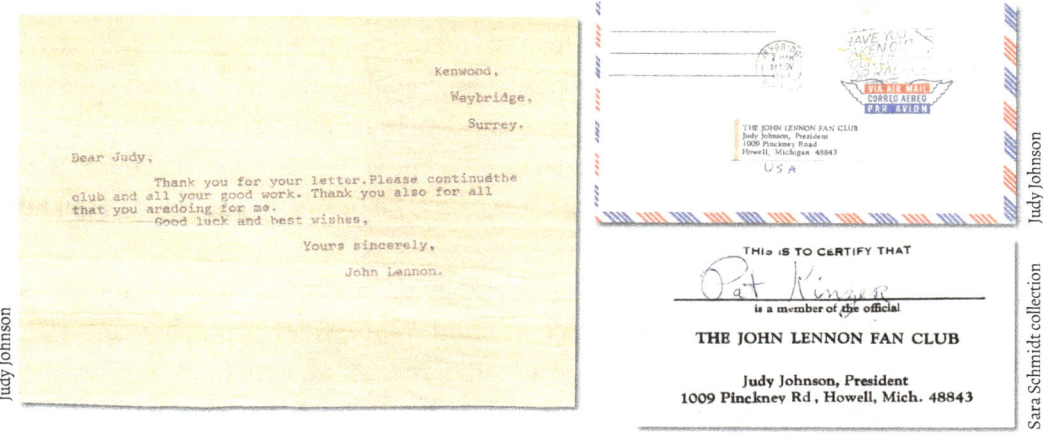

Above: Note to John Lennon Fan Club President Judy Johnson thanking her for her work. Right, top: The postmarked envelope from Weybridge dated Nov. 21, 1967. Right: John Lennon Fan Club membership card.

donations in honor of John's special day. OXFAM was chosen because Mimi told Judy that it was the preferred charity of the Lennon family. John had designed several cards for the organization. All of Judy's hard work paid off. In November, she received a letter postmarked from Weybridge, England. It came from John Lennon, and thanked her for all she had done. He encouraged her to continue her excellent work. "I was disappointed that there was no actual signature!" said Judy. "Still, the letter was authentic, although I doubt John typed it." Most likely, John had his housekeeper, Dot, type the letter. Even without John's signature, the letter was a high point for the fan club.

Much like The John Lennon Fan Club, the Paul McCartney Fan Club got a new president. A California girl named Waynene had started the Paul McCartney Fan Club in 1965. It had two hundred members. Fans in the chartered Big Four Fan Club out of Nashville took their remaining fifteen members and reformed as the Paul McCartney Fan Club for a dollar a year. Claudette Cyr, who had moved to

Florida, was the president. Many fans contributed to this Paul-centered fan club. The club held a Paul-themed trivia contest.

Most of the independent clubs were for the entire band. Beatle Fans of the World, Unite! was one of those clubs. Founders Jen Appel and Sue Kretzmann loved The Beatles. After talking to the George Harrison Fan Club, the two friends from Ohio decided to start their own Beatles fan club. The purpose of the club was to unite all the world's Beatles fans. Jen wrote in the first club newsletter, "We think somehow this feat can be accomplished. You just never know – it may be our daughters who end up finishing the task." They encouraged members to use The Beatles grapevine of friends and pen pals to recruit new members.

The club's newsletters were less formal and full of humor. Jen and Sue created several personas to author their articles. "I loved being able to be creative," said Jen. "But I realized that some of the 'reporters' we invented weren't real and were becoming popular. I felt I needed to let people know they weren't real but much like characters in a book." These characters plus the humor made Beatle Fans of the World, Unite! a favorite club for over one hundred fans.

In 1967 the United Beatles Fan Club run by Kathie Bloesl in Wisconsin was the most organized. One of the problems common to most fan clubs was a lack of member participation. A successful club's members sent in Beatles news, articles, and photos, and wrote reviews and stories. Why hold a contest if no one was likely to enter? Kathie solved this with a point system. Each time a member participated, she would receive points. The number of points depended on her contribution. At the end of each year the club member with the most points won a groovy Beatles prize.

There was also a yearly "Miss UBFC" contest. The winning member became a correspondent, writing a newsletter column for *The Tripper*. She was excused

Left: Beatle Fans of the World, Unite! membership card.
Right: Beatle Fans of the World, Unite! "In case of emergency, please call..." card.

from paying the $1.50 yearly dues. A year spent as fan club royalty wasn't easy. Applicants had to write a five-page paper answering questions such as "What do The Beatles mean to you?" and "What would the world be like without The Beatles?" The bi-monthly newsletter was printed in colorful ink, and was full of Beatles information and opinions from fans. Kathie spent $60 a year of her own money just on printing issues of *The Tripper*.

In 1967, the Boss Beatles Fan Club of San Diego, California broke away from its affiliation with KGB radio. The station was trying to dictate what the president, Cindi Gonzales, could and could not print in her newsletter. Cindi also steered the club away from the Beatles (U.S.A.) Ltd., making it an independent Beatles fan club. She got a donation of a duplicating machine, and printed the newsletters herself. There were one hundred and fifteen fan club members, many from California. Cindi still hosted fan club meetings, and they held a Beatles rally in Los Angeles for all area fans.

Not every independent Beatles fan club was honest and trustworthy. In the summer of 1967 Judy Felgar began advertising her new club, The Beatle People Fan Club. She promised that each dues-paying fan would receive a letter from one of The Beatles. She said that the club had the full support of The Beatles, and they had agreed to send signed letters to the members through Judy.

Many fans, wanting a prized Beatles autograph, paid to become members of The Beatle People Fan Club. Each member received a "Beatle" letter with a few fans getting two. The signatures looked questionable. The fans reached out to some of the larger independent clubs to get to the bottom of things.

Pat Kinzer of the George Harrison Fan Club contacted The Beatles' press officer, Tony Barrow, and Judy Johnson of the John Lennon Fan Club got in touch with John's Aunt, Mimi Smith. Barrow quickly confirmed that Judy's club was unauthorized, and she had no connection to The Beatles. Any signatures obtained through her had to have been forged.

Aunt Mimi had a stern warning for The Beatle People Fan Club. "John has never written letters to a fan through any club. It must be stopped. I suggest you print a warning in the *Lennon Lyrics* saying that John and I emphatically repudiate them. I will also write warning her, and Tony Barrow will follow up. If she continues after that, she will be in serious trouble, especially forging John's signature."

Sgt. Pepper's Lonely Hearts Club Band

The Beatles Sgt. Pepper's Lonely Hearts Club Band *album.*

Sgt. Pepper's Lonely Hearts Club Band was released on June 1, 1967, proving to their fans, and all the world, that they could still make great music. The record grabbed the attention of everyone. It was hailed as the sound of a new era of "sophisticated" Beatles. They had shed their former mop-top, clean-cut image. The LP appealed to a new demographic for The Beatles: young men.

One 18-year-old male said, "The lyrics fit in with our search for meaning in a pretty complex world." Some young people thought the lyrics were like poetry. One reviewer explained, "The Beatles have grown. But they can still satisfy their original audience, the pre-teens who idolize them. And now they can satisfy the older teens and adults."

Many longtime fans pointed out that the changes in The Beatles sound and look should not surprise anyone; they had always set new trends. One fan said, "They set the standards for pop music ridiculously high. Nobody can come close to them." These statements would have seemed impossible three years earlier. Fan club members felt a sense of pride in their early discovery. They had always known The Beatles were the best. Now everyone else agreed. One fan club member told *The Evening Sun*, "They send across the greatest vibrations in the world. If you get up in the morning and put on a Beatles album, you feel pretty good. It's pretty marvelous what they do for you. George did a little masterpiece on his cut. It shows how far he's come with the sitar."

Former president of The Chicagoland Beatle People Fan Club, Marti Whitman Edwards was in college when this album was released. She recalls, "I bought it and thought it was the coolest LP, both artistically and musically. We had a turntable in college, and we all listened in amazement."

But you cannot please everyone. "This album is a big disappointment," one teenaged reviewer wrote. "It seems they've gone too far in search of a psychedelic sound. Most of the cuts sound like a lot of noise. I hope all Beatles fans will give this album a good listening to before buying."

Fans proudly displaying their copy of the album.

Despite this, *Sgt. Pepper's Lonely Hearts Club Band* became the soundtrack of the Summer of Love, and their single, *All You Need Is Love*, became that summer's anthem. The album quickly became part of the culture. In August some UCLA students worked for eight hours, painting a 10′ x 10′ reproduction of the *Sgt. Pepper's* album cover. The man behind the idea, Jeff Grobart, started the painting with two others. When other students saw what he was doing, many stopped and painted. Hundreds of people helped.

Love-in at Griffith Park in Los Angeles. 1967.

When asked why he did it Jeff explained: "When the album came out, I spent three weeks looking at the cover trying to understand it. I decided the only way to understand it was to blow it up and get a better look at it. Now that it's done, I still don't understand it."

During the summer, the phenomenon of "love-ins" began. A love-in consisted of young people, who considered themselves hippies or flower children, getting together and dancing, doing drugs, and spreading a message of peace and love. Often Beatles music accompanied these love-ins.

Four hundred flower children wearing colorful clothing and lots of jewelry gathered in a courtyard on a college campus in Regina, Saskatchewan. Many danced barefoot to the sounds of *Sgt. Pepper* coming from a record player.

At Perris Hill Park in San Bernardino, California, one hundred hippies wearing ponchos and beads played guitars and bongos at a love-in. When the sounds of *Sgt. Pepper* came from a nearby car they all got up and started dancing.

Large love-ins were staged in New York City, and Los Angeles. Thirty-five thousand young people gathered to spread The Beatles' new message, *All You Need Is Love*. The weather was warm, and it was summer vacation. Many hitchhiked to Haight-Ashbury in San Francisco, where they'd heard something was happening. George Harrison was curious to discover what exactly was going on, so he made the trip to California in August.

The fan club grapevine in Los Angeles lit up. They soon learned George would be arriving at the Los Angeles airport. Two hundred fans went to meet him. Pattie got off the plane with George, and security spirited them away, avoiding a mob scene. The only thing the fans had seen was the airplane's descent.

George first saw his friend, Ravi Shankar, perform at the Hollywood Bowl. George then went shopping for colorful clothing and sunglasses shaped like hearts. The next day George, Pattie, her sister Jenny, and Derek Taylor went to San Francisco. There, a man who was playing his guitar handed it to George. As George left the man, about twenty people began to follow him. George had been recognized, sparking a case of Beatlemania. People started crowding around, making George uncomfortable. Derek Taylor began calling George the "The Fab Pied Piper."

George during his trip to San Francisco. August 1967.

Both George and Pattie were disheartened by what they saw in San Francisco. George remarked on the homeless kids who were panhandling to buy drugs. "I don't mind anybody dropping out of anything," said George. "But it's the imposition on somebody else I don't like." Everywhere they turned they saw drop-outs, bums, and mentally disturbed people. "It certainly showed me what's really happening in the drug culture," said George. "It wasn't what I thought... It was like alcoholism, like any addiction."

Sgt. Pepper's Lonely Hearts Club Fan Club

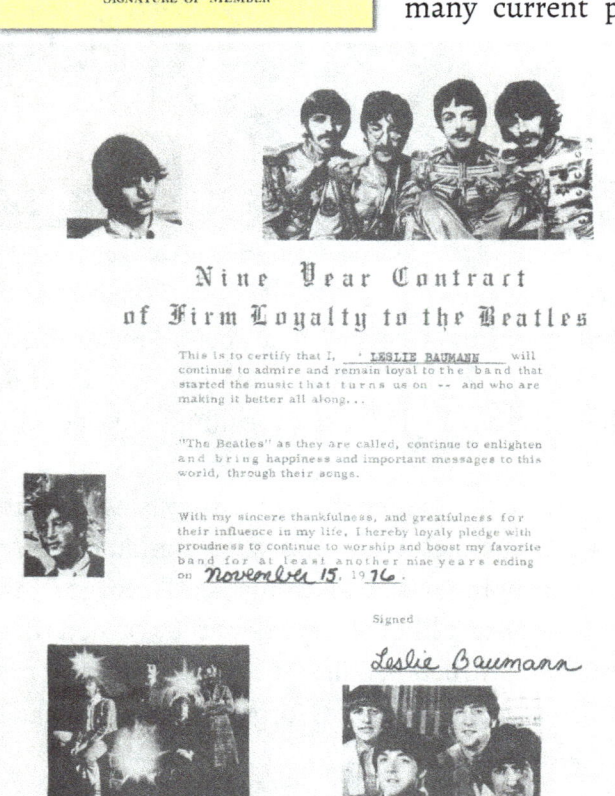

Naturally, an independent fan club began in the fall of 1967 called the Sgt. Pepper's Lonely Hearts Club. Orlando Junco from Tampa, Florida, was the president of this club that was created to please all of The Beatles fans. The bi-monthly newsletter, *Sgt Pepper's Bugle*, gave members up-to-date Beatles' news, many current photographs, pen-pals, and a place to buy and sell. It also contained a "Lonely Hearts" advice column for members to anonymously ask questions about their love lives. All members were expected to sign a nine-year contract of loyalty. In signing the paper, they promised to continue to "worship and boost" their favorite band until 1976.

Sgt. Pepper's Lonely Hearts Club Fan Club envelope (top), membership card (middle), and 9-year contract of "firm loyalty to the Beatles" (bottom).

Kaleidoscope Eyes

The majority of Beatles fan club members were not drug users. The drug culture may have been thriving during the summer of 1967, but drugs were still a scary mystery to many teenage girls.

When The Beatles and Brian Epstein signed a declaration that called for the legalization of marijuana in Britain, many club members were surprised. They'd been in denial about The Beatles' pot use. One club member wrote a letter to Brian Epstein in London

Paul talks about taking LSD at his home on Cavendish Avenue in London. June 18, 1967.

and another to Bernice Young at Beatles (U.S.A.) Ltd. in New York. She wanted to find out if the marijuana rumors were true. She argued that all fans deserved to know the truth.

When newspapers began claiming that one of the songs on *Sgt Pepper's Lonely Hearts Club Band, Lucy in the Sky With Diamonds*, was about LSD, fan club members were quick to defend The Beatles. They wrote letters to editors claiming that The Beatles would never write a song about drugs. After all, hadn't John Lennon told an interviewer he'd written the song about his son Julian's painting of a schoolmate named Lucy? He had, but the media was not convinced. "Readers with doubt about the LSD tie should listen to the words or read them on the album," *The News Journal* wrote. "Lucy is a girl with 'Kaleidoscope Eyes' who drifts through a surrealistic landscape of 'tangerine flowers and marmalade sky."

The Beatles revealed that they used LSD on June 16 in an article in *Life* magazine. In that issue, Paul McCartney stated that he had taken LSD, and it had opened his eyes. Two days later, on his 25th birthday, Paul admitted to an ITN interviewer that he had taken LSD four times. He then blamed the press for deciding to cover the truth that he spoke.

The Beatles' use of LSD was a hot topic in the fan club newsletters. No one quit the club over the band's drug use, but many fans wanted to learn why they were taking it, and expressed concern about The Beatles' health. Bunny Racey,

Vice President of The Cyn Lennon Beatle Club, wrote in the club newsletter, "I have never taken LSD, and I don't feel qualified to give an intelligent answer. I do know it can cause some ill effects, and the fact that it could endanger their health worries me very much." President of the Boss Beatles Fan Club, Cindi Gonzales, wrote, "I really don't think it's my place to give an opinion as I don't know their motive for taking it. I will say it is their lives, and they are mature men who know what they're doing. So I leave my complete trust in their reasoning as they have never let me down before."

Parents were concerned that their daughters would start taking drugs. Harrison Huggers Ltd. club president Jeri Glaeser wrote in *The Harrison Hugger*: "Adults are so worried that their children are going to rush out and take LSD because their favorite Beatle had done so. I think Beatle fans have more sense than that, give us a little credit."

Beatles (U.S.A.) Ltd. fan club members received this colorful Sgt. Pepper *poster with Beatle Bulletin on the back side early in the summer of 1967.*

Beatles (U.S.A.) Ltd. In Shambles

Most of the Beatles fans who paid their 1967 two-dollar dues for Beatles (U.S.A.) Ltd. did so only so they could receive The Beatles Christmas record. By this time, the club was in shambles. Fan mail went unanswered, and orders unfilled. Many independent club members were unhappy. Most felt the U.S. fan club was taking advantage of American teenagers. In March a member of The Cyn Lennon Beatle Club, Judy Vachon, filed official complaints with the Better Business Bureau and the Postal Inspector against the official club. Hundreds of fans signed a petition complaining about how the club was run. Too many kids had sent money and received nothing. They felt that they had been scammed.

Not much was published about Beatles (U.S.A.) Ltd. According to the February issue of *The Beatles Book Monthly*, Canada was without a fan club. The country remained without an official club until July when a new club began in Scarborough, Ontario. It was named The Beatles Canadian Enterprises, and the national secretary was Joan Thompson. Her club had started as a small chapter, but she suddenly had the daunting task of leading Canada's Beatles fans.

Through the first half of 1967 Bernice Young's name was listed as the United States Fan Club Director. *The Beatles Book Monthly* reported that during the summer, Bernice traveled to London and spent time at The Official Beatles Fan Club headquarters. She even had afternoon tea with Cynthia and John Lennon at their home, Kenwood.

Early in the summer, Beatles (U.S.A.) Ltd. members received a pleasant surprise. Each member got a giant "Pepper Poster." The exclusive poster was a colorful display of The Beatles in their Sgt. Pepper suits. The poster claimed to "celebrate the arrival of the one and only *Sgt. Pepper's Lonely Hearts Club Band*," and went on to say, "We hope you'll enjoy it and find a thousand and one uses for your 'Pepper Poster' at home and on the job."

On the back of the poster was the traditional *Beatle Bulletin*. For the first time, Bernice Young did not sign the bulletin, but instead the signature was from someone named Fran Fiorino. The announcement went through the program of *Sgt. Pepper's Lonely Hearts Club Band* song by song. Fran tried to ease fans' concerns about all the unanswered correspondence, writing: "There have been some delays in mailing in some cases, and we are trying to remedy this situation." She asked fans to write the topics of their letters on the outside of their envelopes to help with sorting. Fran said this would guarantee "speedy delivery." But nothing had changed. When a fan sent a letter to the official club in New York City it wasn't likely to receive an answer.

Nonetheless, for the first time in several years, Beatles (U.S.A.) Ltd. offered new Beatles photographs. These showed The Beatles during the making of the promo films for *Strawberry Fields Forever* and *Penny Lane*. Sue Kretzmann from Beatle Fans of the World, Unite! said in a newsletter, "The pix for sale through Beatles (U.S.A.) Ltd. on the back of the Sgt. Pepper poster are fabulous and worth the $1.40."

On July 7, 1967 one of the chartered fan clubs, The M.B.E. (Members of The Beatles Empire), held a Beatles rally to celebrate Ringo's 27th birthday. Club presidents, Rita Angel and Laura Cohen, asked members of the New York City-based club to gather outside the Ed Sullivan Theater. They made a huge birthday card for Ringo, and together they walked to the office of Beatles (U.S.A.) Ltd. at 1501 Broadway to give it to the workers there. While they were at the office, Rita and Laura met the new director of Beatles (U.S.A.) Ltd., Sandi Morse.

A few weeks later, the girls got a call from Sandi. She offered them jobs at the fan club office. They would come in after school and on the weekends and work for $1.43 an hour. Their task was to tackle the mountain of fan mail that had accumulated since 1964. They were specifically looking for cash inside those envelopes. "We didn't find any money," Laura recalled. "But we did get a full set of Beatles trading cards, pictures, articles, and other Beatles items."

Around the same time, Laura and Rita started working at fan club headquarters, so did two young men: Jock McLean and Arma Andon. It was evident that the fan club had gone downhill. "Quite frankly, when I showed up, two people were working there," remembered Arma. "They were not very good, and the mail had piled up." The teenage girls were tackling the old mail, and the two guys were trying their best to handle the mail that was currently pouring in. They were receiving up to three large canvas mailbags full of letters each day. "The mail kept coming and coming," Arma said. "We were just drowning in mail. We did the best we could to keep up with it, but it was just sacks and sack of mail." Arma and Jock found many wild things inside those envelopes, including lady's underwear and nude photographs. Many letters contained the two-dollar dues payment. Every other day, one of the men would make a bank deposit of $15,000 in one-dollar bills and change.

Yet another new employee was Merle Frimark, who had been to both Shea Stadium concerts. She'd discovered the club's secret address of 1501 Broadway, and wanted to see what it looked like inside. "I just walked in," she recalled. "Someone there said to me, 'Are you here to be interviewed?' I said, 'Sure!' As fate would have it, they hired me." Like the others, Merle's first task was to sort through the mail. "There would be sacks and sacks and sacks of mail from the post office," she remembered. "Plus, there were so many thousands and thousands of members that were ordering photos and updates that had to sort out." Still in school, Merle took the subway into Manhattan every day after class, and worked for four hours. Nat Weiss and Sandi Morse saw something special in Merle, and she stayed with the Beatles (U.S.A.) Ltd. for years.

With a new director, and more people working at the Beatles (U.S.A.) Ltd. offices, the only official Beatles fan club started showing improvement. It still had a long way to go, but it was trying to catch up with the standards of proficiency and dedication set by the independent fan clubs.

Fans Travel to London

U.S. and Canadian Beatles Fan Club members had become accustomed to seeing The Beatles in concert each summer. When the band made it clear that they weren't going on tour in 1967, some North American fans decided to see The Beatles in their homeland.

Victoria Moran, who was in the Leabets, and had seen The Beatles at their Kansas City press conference in 1964, traveled to London with her father in April 1967 to audition for drama schools. She had developed a friendship with The Beatles' road manager, Mal Evans, and planned to see him during their trip. Thanks to Mal, the 17-year-old and her father dined almost nightly at the exclusive restaurant, Alvaro's, on the King's Road in Chelsea. Reservations were made through an unlisted number from someone in the know.

Plaque at the Bag O'Nails club in London. (Sara Schmidt)

On the Thursday night of her journey, Mal invited Victoria and her dad to the Bag 'O Nails club, where Paul McCartney would meet his wife, Linda, one month later. "Mal led me through this dark, crowded, smoky room to the very back, and there's Paul McCartney, who was my favorite Beatle," said Victoria. "I couldn't speak. I was just stunned. We were introduced, and Paul said, 'Hello Vicki.' I thought 'If I die right now, I've done it all.'" They sat

Paul at 7 Cavendish Avenue, London.

and chatted while drinking scotch-and-Coke. Paul sang a little ditty including the lyric, "Wish I was not a Beatle because maybe then I could have some fun."

Victoria could not wait to tell the fan club members back home, so as soon as she got back to the hotel, she sent a cablegram to the club president, Tina Mitchell. It merely said, "Met Paul. My God. Met Paul."

Victoria and her dad went back the next night, and she talked to John Lennon. She did not want to bother him but knew she would regret not talking to him. "I went up to him and said, 'I'm a friend of Mal's and here from Kansas City.' He goes, 'Oh, Kansas City, baseball!' He made a little sign like hitting a baseball with a bat." Victoria went back to her seat and was happy when John stopped by to wish her good night at the end of the evening.

Leslie Samuels and her classmate, Donna Stark, signed up for a program to study in Oxford, England, during the summer. The girls were not interested in academics. They wanted to meet The Beatles. On July 12, the girls went to 7 Cavendish Avenue in St. John's Wood. Leslie purchased a small bouquet of flowers at the nearby tube station to give to Paul when she met him. Leslie rang the bell on Paul McCartney's gate and spoke with his housekeeper, Mrs. Mills. Leslie explained that she had a fan club in the United States and wanted to see Paul. The housekeeper said he would be out later. Paul was having electrical work done, and workmen were going in and out of the residence. "I wrote a note and put it inside the bouquet of flowers and handed it to one of the workmen. It said, 'I'm Leslie Samuels, and I am the president of one of The Beatles Fan Clubs in New York, and I got presents from all the kids in my fan club. I want to see Paul. Let me in,'" Leslie recalled. The worker must have gotten the note to Paul because fifteen minutes later, Mrs. Mills appeared at the gate and said to the girls, "He'll see you now." Leslie and Donna followed her through the garage and into Paul's

Left: George's house 'Kinfauns,' in Esher, England. Right: Leslie Samuels poses in front of Kinfauns. 1967.

backyard, where they saw him sitting on a couch-swing. He was wearing white and red striped pants with red socks. It was a warm summer day, and he was not wearing a shirt.

Leslie started giving Paul items from her club members. "I had presents for him. Some of them were stupid little things. Whatever 14, 15, 16-year-old kids want to give Paul McCartney. I was living their dream," said Leslie. While spending time with Paul, they met Paul's sheepdog, Martha, and Paul's newborn kittens. They talked about the *Sgt. Pepper's Lonely Hearts Club Band* album and the song *All You Need is Love*. Paul signed many items for the two girls and some for the club members back in the United States. While Paul was giving autographs, Jane Asher came out and served Cokes to the fans. Before she left, Leslie told Paul, "I've conquered 7 Cavendish."

Leslie Samuels meets Ringo at his house, 'Sunny Heights'. July 1967.

The next day, the duo traveled out to Esher to meet George at his house, Kinfauns. After having a difficult time finding the bungalow, they walked up to the driveway and spotted the psychedelic painted house. George's housekeeper, Margaret, greeted them and went to get George. He appeared from the swimming pool, wearing just swimming trunks and holding a pair of red pants. As with Paul, Leslie had a bag full of things from the fan club to give him. A fan club member had attached a note to one of the photographs they asked George to sign. He read it aloud, and Leslie recorded the interaction. "Leslie, I'm sending you my fave picture of George," he read. "Will you please ask him to put a pen to it or just breathe on it? I'd be happy." Before signing it, George held the photo in his hands and panted on it. Leslie asked George a question from a fan club member: what did he like most about *Sgt. Pepper's Lonely Hearts Club Band*? Leslie recorded his answer: "All, you know. I look at it as a whole thing."

George told Leslie and Donna to inform the fan club members to stop writing him letters and impress on them that he couldn't answer them all. "I either answer all the letters or ignore the letters and carry on being a Beatle," he explained. The girls had a hard time accepting this. "The fan club wants to hear from you," Leslie said to George. "If they don't hear from us, it's nothing to worry about," he replied. "That's why we spend our time writing and singing songs. They can hear us singing, and the message is the answer to all their letters. It's in the album."

The sun had gone down. George wanted to change into clothing, so he invited them to come inside the bungalow. While in the kitchen, they drank orange juice with Pattie and chatted about England. George reappeared in faded blue jeans and a white knit shirt. He offered the fans marshmallows because "rocking horse people eat marshmallow pies." After taking plenty of photographs, the two girls happily left.

In the days that followed, Leslie and Donna met John at his home, Kenwood, and Ringo at his home, Sunny Heights. In order to meet them Leslie explained that she had gifts for them from the fan club members in the United States. She gave all four of The Beatles 'Yellow Submarine' buttons produced by a New York non-violence organization. Leslie remembers with pride, "The Beatles Fan Club made my dreams come true."

New York Area Beatles Fans Activities

The fan clubs back in the United States were still getting together, especially the members who lived in the New York area. For them the summer of 1967 was unusually active and fun. The fan organizing most of these events was JoAnne McCormack, a.k.a. "Johnny." Johnny later recalled, "We'd get together in

Left: Beatles fans attend a rally at Shea Stadium and join in on a sing-along. Right: Beatles fans gather to mark the one year anniversary since their Shea Stadium concert. August 23, 1967.

Manhattan and have Beatles rallies. We'd march around the city singing songs and holding posters."

On a few occasions fans met in Central Park, sit under a shade tree, and sang Beatles' songs. Someone would bring a guitar, and the sing-along would continue throughout the warm summer night.

The most significant event for New York fans that summer came on August 23. It had been exactly one year since The Beatles had performed at Shea Stadium, and it was John and Cynthia's fifth wedding anniversary. More than fifty girls arrived at Gate B of the Shea Stadium parking lot at noon, many arriving on a bus. They had what they called a "Beatle-In."

A local disc jockey promoted the event, but Johnny was the group leader. "I bought a cake from a bakery that said, 'Happy Anniversary John and Cyn,'" she recalled. To celebrate, the Beatlemaniacs dove into the cake. They sang Beatles songs while marching around the Stadium, holding signs that read, "All You Need is Love," "Keep America Beatleful," and "Beatles Forever." In the parking lot, they talked about the boys, and some cried while reminiscing about the previous years' concerts. One of the fans, Sherry Miller, wrote in the *Boss Beatles Fan Club* newsletter, "One boy had brought his guitar, and we sang everything from '*Help!*' to '*With A Little Help From My Friends.*'" They also recited John's poems, and demonstrated their dislike of The Monkees by ripping up magazine photos of the television teen idols.

As baseball fans arrived to see the Mets play the Phillies, the girls began to chant, "Give us The Beatles. We want The Beatles." Johnny had the idea of storming the gates of Shea Stadium. As her friend, Ilona Gabriel, explained, "JoAnne and I decided we were going to sit on second base the exact moment that The Beatles had come on stage. We climbed a twelve-foot fence and a short wall. We were spotted by guards." The guards warned them that even Beatlemaniacs could be arrested if they continued such behavior. Johnny tried to get into the stadium again when a delivery truck drove through the gates. She was sent right back out to the parking lot by the guard. Sherry did a little better. As she later wrote, "We climbed over the gate and made friends with two girls who worked there. We got in and even walked down the same tunnel The Beatles used to go to their dressing room. We then sat in our seats from last year."

The Beatles moment was not forgotten. A *New York Times* reporter wrote, "At 9:15, several fans inside the park heard a long, long screech. It was exactly the minute that The Beatles made their triumphant entry to Shea the year before and outside on the parking lot, not one eye was dry." While it was a successful Beatles rally, there was still a feeling of sadness that The Beatles themselves were not there. As Sherry Miller wrote, "All in all, it was a beautiful day. It didn't take away the sadness, though. When I got home and saw their pictures on my wall, I cried my heart out!"

Giggling Guru

Paul, George, and John listen to the Maharishi in London. August 24, 1967.

The U.S. fans may have been celebrating The Beatles, but the guys themselves were doing some serious soul-searching. George's wife, Pattie, had attended a Transcendental Meditation lecture and could not wait to hear the famous guru, Maharishi Mahesh Yogi, talk when he was in London. George, Paul, and John went to see what it was all about.

Ringo stayed home because Maureen had just given birth to the couple's second child, Jason. The Beatles were intrigued by the Maharishi and wanted to learn more about meditation, so they were invited to come to Bangor, Wales, for a 10-day retreat. On August 25, all four Beatles traveled to Wales, where they stayed in dormitories. They attended a seminar and afterward told the press they were giving up all drugs and living a more natural lifestyle.

Fan club members were curious to learn more about what The Beatles were doing. Many of them wanted to learn about meditation and the Maharishi. The famed yogi released a self-titled LP in 1967, and some fans bought it. One of them reported to Beatle Fans of the World, Unite!, "I didn't think I'd like it, but was very surprised that The Beatles are once again wise in their choice of beautiful people."

On September 26 when the guru appeared on *The Tonight Show* with Johnny Carson, fans tuned in to see for themselves. After watching the Maharishi on the talk show one member wrote that he was "an exceptionally pleasant and intelligent man."

Other fans did not understand meditation, or why The Beatles were so interested in a small Indian man who giggled all the time. However, they thought it was a healthy choice for the boys. As one club member wrote, "I am glad The Beatles have taken up Transcendental Meditation instead of LSD. The meditation can't hurt them."

Farewell To A Gentleman

The Beatles were in Wales, attending the Maharishi's seminar, when the unthinkable happened. Brian Epstein, The Beatles' manager, and friend, unexpectedly passed away. In the footage shown on television the night of his death, The Beatles were shocked and saddened. Members of The Beatles Fan Clubs across America were also devastated. Most young fans had never experienced the death of a loved one, making the news especially hard. Brian was a much-loved part of The Beatles. One member wrote in *The Natch*, "He was so young to die. I never expected him to die. He was like the fifth Beatle." Some girls favored the handsome manager over John, Paul, George, or Ringo. Some of them organized candlelight vigils for Brian. A few clubs had memorial services in place of regular club meetings.

Fans all wanted to do something to honor Brian's memory. Beatle Fans of the World, Unite! collected articles, photos, poems, and other sympathetic accounts of Brian, turning them into a memorial book. Jen Appel made arrangements to

Brian Epstein at Shea Stadium. August 15, 1965.

mail the book to Mrs. Harrison. George's mother would then present the book to Brian's mother, Queenie, and the rest of the Epstein family.

Other clubs shared their grief. "Brian Epstein will always hold a very special place among us," wrote members of the Paul McCartney Fan Club in *The Tripper*. "We will miss him greatly. He was truly a genius and a wonderful man." One of the best comments was printed in *The Natch*: "I was shocked, and I couldn't believe it. Then I felt sorry for The Beatles because I knew they lost a good friend."

How I Won the War

The Beatles had promised to be in a third movie, but two years had passed, and nothing materialized. In the fall of 1966 John tried his acting skills without the other Beatles when he joined the cast of *How I Won the War*. A year later, this war satire came out premiering in the United States in San Francisco on October 18, 1967. Fans were excited to see one of The Beatles back on the big screen, but some had expected the witty John Lennon from *A Hard Day's Night*. Instead, they saw John playing Private Gripweed, a solider who dies. Fans gave it mixed reviews, with independent fan club newsletters working to convince other members to give the film a chance. *Lennon Lyrics* stated, "I saw it twice, and I still can't get over John Lennon. He's absolutely fantastical." Beatle Fans of the World, Unite!

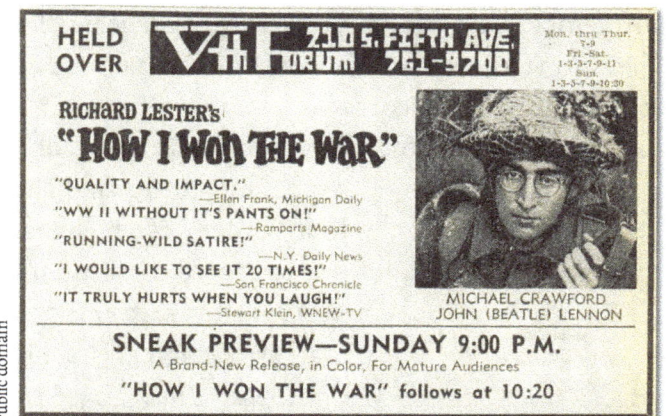

Newspaper advertisement for "How I Won The War" with John Lennon as Gripweed, right.

member Terry said, "John makes the film come alive. Anybody with an open mind would enjoy this nutty film."

Many fans understood the movie was a commentary on war. Young people were protesting the Vietnam war, and *How I Won the War* spoke to them. *Lennon Lyrics* newsletter said, "The film is horrific but truthful. War is a terrible thing, and any film that knocks war is going to be horrific."

Regardless of their views on the movie itself, fans seemed to agree that John was a talented actor, especially in his death scene. They could not wait to see a Beatle in another film.

Christmastime Is Here Again

Christmas was always a significant time for The Beatles and their fans. In 1967, instead of sending Christmas gifts to the boys, the independent clubs decided to do something for charity in The Beatles' name. They raised money, and sent it to charities such as the Strawberry Field Salvation Army in Liverpool and OXFAM. Instead of sending something to Julian Lennon, The John Lennon Fan Club encouraged members to buy toys for needy children who were spending the holidays in the hospital. "Julian will undoubtedly have a warm and beautiful day," Judy Johnson wrote. "But not all children are so fortunate." Clubs sent small gifts to the members for Christmas. A wallet-sized Beatles photo, Beatles-themed labels, and end-of-the-year newsletters were all gifted in 1967.

Of course, the most anticipated Christmas gift was The Beatles Christmas message sent to official fan club members. On Tuesday, November 28, The Beatles gathered to record the disc. They didn't know that this would be the last time all four Beatles would collaborate on a Christmas record.

Earlier that day The Beatles had worked together on a script, with John scribbling it down. The first order of business was to record the Lennon-McCartney-Harrison-Starkey original song, *Christmas Time is Here Again*. John put his coat over some tympani drums, and played them. Paul performed on the piano, George took lead guitar, while Ringo played on his usual drum kit. Mal Evans, George Martin, and actor Victor Spinetti were there too, and joined in. Ringo and Victor tap-danced their way through a number. John worked overtime that night, doing his best to make the record perfect for the fan club members. The session ended at 3 AM, after George Martin recorded *Auld Lang Syne* on the organ.

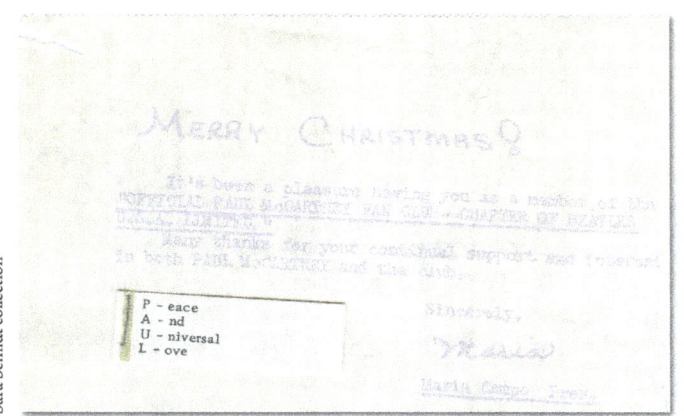

Christmas gift from the Official Paul McCartney Fan Club.

Ringo, John, and his young son Julian designed the sleeve for the flexi disc, but fans in the United States did not get to see it. Instead, they received the record on a 7" x 8½" postcard. The album itself looked identical to the one they'd sent in 1966. All discs were shipped from New York City using third-class mail.

Frances Fiorino and Suz Clark signed *The Beatle Bulletin* on the back of the record. Besides crediting Victor, Mal, and George Martin for their contributions, the Bulletin briefly informed fans of the latest Beatles news. The Beatles had made the film *Magical Mystery Tour* that fall. It was scheduled to appear on television in the United Kingdom, and then, according to the Bulletin, it was "scheduled for release in the U.S.A. shortly after the first of the year." The Bulletin also encouraged fans to purchase the recently released *Magical Mystery Tour* album, then gave a brief rundown of the songs.

Beatles (U.S.A.) Ltd. had a new photo offer, selling ten photos of The Beatles during the *Our World* program. The club was still trying to sort mail properly and reminded club members to make sure they wrote the words "photo orders" on the outside of their envelopes.

Fan response to the 1967 Christmas message was much more positive than it had been the previous year. Fans had learned to expect the unexpected when it came to The Beatles. Some found the chorus to be too repetitious, but overall, liked it. Others loved how it had a psychedelic sound. The overall opinion seemed to be that the fan club Christmas record was worth the price of the dues for the lackluster Beatles (U.S.A.) Ltd.

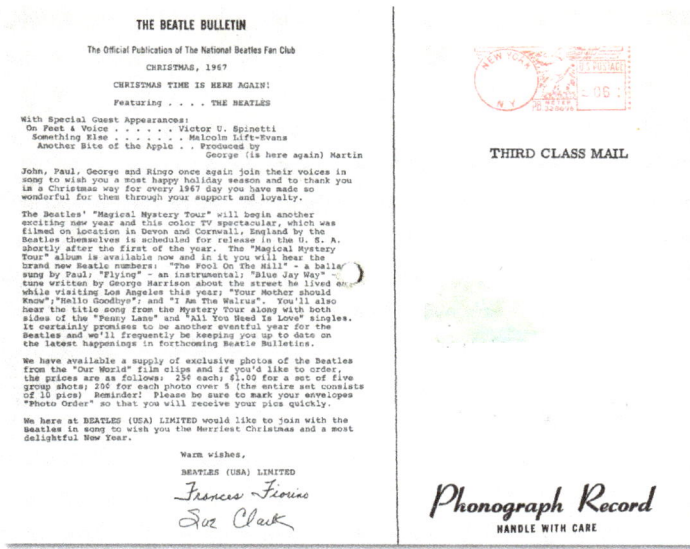

The Beatles' 1967 Season's Greetings message entitled "Christmas Time Is Here Again."

Sgt. Pepper's Lonely Hearts Club — Exclusive Organization for the Beatles
4925 Cresthill, Tampa — OCTOBER 1967 — Editor - Orlando Junco

THE STORY BEHIND SGT. PEPPER; HIS LONELY HEARTS CLUB & BAND

Who is Sgt. Pepper? By now he's in the minds of all Beatle fans... You probably know him as the bandleader of the Beatles' best LP yet (which is really more than just an LP) or as one of John, George, Paul and Ringo's closest friends. But.... How did he come about? Arsk no more ye' groovy fans... For here at last is a complete short writty on the whole thingy!!!!

There once upon a time were four lads from Liverpool (a not so mythical seaport city of England) who called themselves "Beatles". With their guitars and drums they formed a noise... A very nice sound, indeed. The time passed and the four lads were no longer known only in the English city... They had grown (like magic) in every living creature of this earth! (Would ya' believe 80%.)

One day, in the pouring rain, they were strolling down Penny Lane joyfully singing "Good Day Sunshine" when they came across a tall, serious looking, moustached character. "Hello" he said. "Hello" the lads replied. "I'm Sgt. Pepper.... Who art thou?" "Beatles" they replied. "Good" he said, "I've been looking for "Beatles" and "Beatles" I have found!" "Alas" they said "But why?" "Well... It's like this" the Sgt. continued "The original Sgt. Pepper's Band that I taught how to play twenty years ago today has gone out of style... the show must go on, and YOU (working in disguise) can make my band popular again!" "Reely!" they cheered. "Yes", said the Sgt. "But you'll have to sacrifice being "Beatles" for awhile." "What will we be?" the fab four demanded. "Well, we got so lonely when my bands' success died that I started a "Lonely Hearts Club*".... So how about "Sgt. Pepper's.... Lonely Hearts' Club.... Band"?!"

..... And so the Beatles (with moustaches and Sgt. Pepper outfits) joined Billy Shears, Mr. Kite, Lovely Rita, Lucy (who's in the sky with diamonds) and with a little help from their friends and Sgt. Pepper as their bandleader, the show did go on.... And surprisingly enough, the Beatles (with their multi-talents), did bring Sgt. Pepper's Band back in style .... And they hope we have enjoyed the show!!

* The Lonely Hearts' Club of Sgt. Pepper continues as a tradition, but it's members are anything but lonely... the Beatles saved the Day!!

The Bugle Newsletter from the Sgt. Pepper's Lonely Hearts Club.

Chapter 6 — You Say You Want A Revolution?

1968 was a year of turmoil and change in the United States. This was also true for Beatles fan clubs. In 1968 these clubs would go through drastic changes.

On The Road To Rishikesh

When the year began, fan club members were focused on The Beatles' three-month trip to India to learn more about Transcendental Meditation with the Maharishi Mahesh Yogi. The Beatles wanted to study in India to achieve absolute bliss and consciousness. Before the trip a member of The John Lennon Fan Club, Pat Mascaro, wrote to John asking him about it. He replied, saying, "Thank you for your letter. The Maharishi is a yogi, a teacher of the ancient Indian cult of yoga, a means of attaining spiritual awareness. It deals with life – its meaning and the significance and is therefore of the greatest importance. Read *Autobiography of a Yogi* by Paramahansa (pub Rider) if you are interested."

Once all four Beatles were inside the Ashram, busloads of fans from around the globe arrived outside of the barbed wire fence that surrounded the compound. They could not get inside. The Maharishi sometimes came to the gate, and told fans that The Beatles were doing very well.

After two weeks, Ringo and Maureen left India and went back home. They had a 6-month-old and a toddler, so they wanted to get back to their kids. According to Ringo another reason they left early was that: "Maureen and I are a little funny about our food. We don't like spicy things."

Meanwhile, John, Paul, and George were competing to see who could meditate the longest. Paul was the winner with four hours; John came in second with three and a half hours, followed by George with three hours. One fellow

George, John, Cynthia, and Maureen sit across from the Maharishi, far right, in India. 1968.

pupil observed, "The Beatles spent most of the time in their rooms and put aside five hours a day for meditation. They had an audience with his holiness for at least two hours a day. He saw that they ate very well and were equipped with all the comforts of home."

Fan club members only learned Beatles news from India through newspaper articles. They discovered The Beatles were ready to make their third major motion picture. It was to include the Maharishi and would be similar to the *Magical Mystery Tour*, which had not been shown in America. John and the Maharishi took a helicopter ride so John could film scenery for the movie. Paul, John, and George were said to be composing the background music.

In India, the three Beatles could focus on writing music because their attention was concentrated on the moment. They had no contact with their fans, not even the ones waiting by the Ashram's gates. Fan mail wasn't piling up around them.

One fan did manage to get a letter delivered to George. George Harrison Fan Club president, Pat Kinzer, wrote him a letter there because she thought she'd have a better chance of getting a letter back. She was right. On April 1, she received an envelope with "George Harrison, India" and a symbol written on the back. "I didn't think anything of it because I often got letters from fans who doodled George's name on the back of their envelopes," recalled Pat. Once she opened the envelope, it became evident that the letter wasn't from a fan but George himself.

"I got the thrill of my life," she wrote in the *Harrison Herald*. "I got an answer to a letter I wrote to George in India. I'm so happy about it, and I want to share it with everyone."

George started his letter by thanking Pat for all of the things she had done for him. She was happy George approved of the work she'd put into running his fan club. "I feel very pleased because he appreciates what I am doing," Pat wrote to club members. "Now that I know that, I know I'll never give up the club, and I'll work twice as hard on the club to please him." George ended his letter: "Thanks again for everything. Keep smiling and lots of love to you, your family, and all your friends."

Fan clubs during this time had mixed views about The Beatles' activities in India. Judy Johnson, president of The John Lennon Fan Club, encouraged members to read *Autobiography of a Yogi*. "Please give it a try," Judy urged club members in the Lennon Lyrics. "You might be both surprised and elated in what it can mean to you personally."

More and more fan club leaders were wondering if the Maharishi Mahesh Yogi was legitimate. Many believed he was using The Beatles' fame for his own gain. Joyce Kistner, president of The Flying Cow, Ltd., wrote in the club newsletter, "I don't like him for what I know of him. Maharishi is too 'showy' in his tactics of winning converts. In other words—too much publicity." The Pottie Bird Beatle Club had similar feelings as the officers wrote, "We dislike him because he seems so phony, plastic and commercial." The newsletter declared, "We don't think he's that great. But this does not mean that we don't agree with the meditation bit. It is great if it'll help someone to find out what life is all about."

Clubs For Beatles' Wives

As had been true in 1967, new independent clubs were gaining momentum. One such club was called The Flying Cow, Ltd., with Joyce Kistner as its president. The purpose of this club was to honor Maureen Starkey. Serious Beatles fans would recognize the "Flying Cow" as the name of the pub Ringo and Maureen had in their London home, Sunny Heights. The club started in early 1968 with sixty members. The newsletter was full of information on Ringo and Maureen and their two sons Zak and Jason.

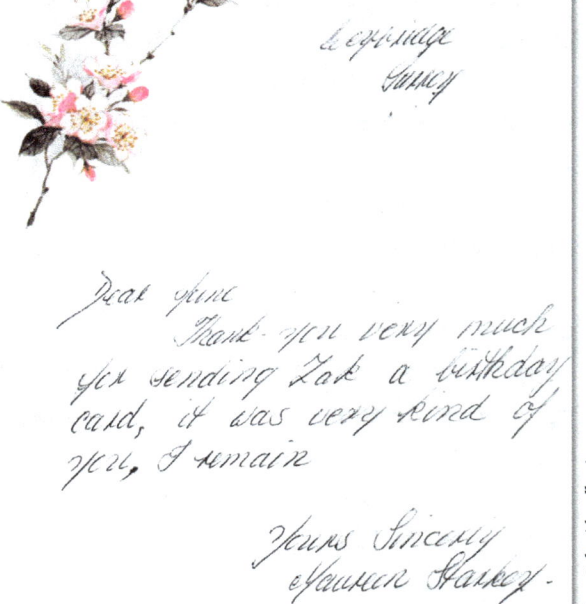

The Pottie Bird Beatle Club membersip card.

Letter from Maureen Starkey thanking a fan club member.

One of the most popular columns gave beauty tips telling girls how to obtain Maureen's mod look. The club held a contest for the best story or poem or image of Maureen. The prize was a beautiful 8″ x 10″ glossy photograph of Mrs. Starkey. Members were encouraged to send gifts to the Starkeys on special occasions such as anniversaries or birthdays. Maureen often sent handwritten thank you notes to fortunate club members.

The Flying Cow, Ltd. officers in the United States were very passionate and outspoken about gun control. They adopted this as the club's cause and encouraged all their members to write and call their Congressmen and sign petitions to make changes in the country's gun laws.

An offshoot of the The Flying Cow, Ltd. was The Pottie Bird Beatle Club. This was a club for Pattie Boyd. The same officers of The Flying Cow, Ltd. ran The Pottie Bird Beatle Club, but with different titles. The president of Pattie's club was Judy Vachon, vice president of Maureen's club. The Pottie Bird Beatle Club began in April, 1968 with twenty-five members. The newsletter focused on Pattie and George as a couple, and featured columns about fashion, and Pattie's career as a model.

Bring Back The Beatles

While The Beatles were studying in India, their U.S. fan clubs joined forces to try to get The Beatles to return and perform. Earl Trout, a disc jockey from Minneapolis, started a campaign. The reported reason that The Beatles had stopped performing live was that the screaming made it impossible for them to hear themselves play. Trout asked fan club members to sign a petition stating they would remain quiet if The Beatles returned. His goal was to have one million signatures. It officially became known as the "Beatles Back Campaign." All of the independent fan clubs participated, passing the petition through their families, workplaces, schools, and communities. Kathy Burns, of The Cyn Lennon Beatle Club, took it to heart. She challenged her 600 club members to send at least twenty-five signatures each. She offered to throw a large fan club meeting/party if The Beatles came to the U.S. to perform. By May, Trout had 700,000 signatures. He said when he had one million he would deliver the petition to John Lennon personally in England.

To fan the flames, concert promoter Sid Bernstein announced he would try to book The Beatles for a single concert in New York City in the spring. When one fan contacted Geoffrey Ellis of NEMS Enterprises, he informed her: "There is no definite information about The Beatles playing New York City in the spring of 1968."

Tony Barrow and others in The Beatles' camp denied that the boys would give any concerts in America or any other country. Nevertheless fan club members never gave up hope.

Beatles (U.S.A.) Ltd.

In 1968 Beatles (U.S.A.) Ltd. made important changes to the official fan club. The American club started the year with 20,000 members, while the British club had a membership of 40,000. The Americans were trying to recruit new members by showing current and former members the improvements they had made. On February 10, 1968 *Rolling Stone Magazine* published an article titled, "Beatles ZAP USA Ltd." The report stated, "The Beatles closed the offices of Beatles (U.S.A) Ltd., their fan club and business offices in this country and fired their American press agent." The brief article explained that The Beatles did not want to conduct business in the United States, so they were moving all their business dealings to London. There was no truth to this story, and fan club director Fran Fiorino spent half of the year debunking the rumor. The story grew into a tall tale that claimed The Beatles were finished with their American fan clubs because they weren't interested in their fans in the States.

Fran wrote to the fans, "The Beatles are very much aware and deeply appreciative of the continued support of their fans." She added, "Beatles U.S.A. Ltd. will continue to function for a long time to come. John, Paul, George, and Ringo continue to remain very much interested in their loyal American fans."

Datebook

One of the first changes that involved the club was when the teen magazine *Datebook* bought the U.S. rights to reprint ten pages of the only magazine approved by The Beatles, *The Beatles Book Monthly*. The magazine had been published each month in England since 1963. Each issue included a one-page letter to fan club members written by the British director of the club. *Datebook* included a letter from the United States fan club director. This letter was a welcome change because it kept club members up to date with The Beatles' news and what was happening with Beatles (U.S.A.) Ltd. After years in the dark, this monthly update was welcome.

CHAPTER 6–YOU SAY YOU WANT A REVOLUTION? 199

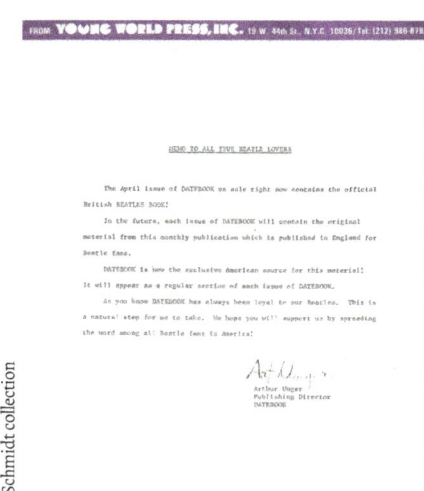

Left: Letter sent to fan clubs about the Beatles Book Monthly *inclusion in* Datebook *magazine. Above: Beatles Book Monthly shelves at Beatle Book Monthly offices. 1968.*

The Official Beatles Fan Club and Datebook flyer insert included with The Beatles' new single
Lady Madonna/The Inner Light *(Capitol 2138) released March 18, 1968.*

Joyce Kistner and Judy Vachon from the independent club The Flying Cow, Ltd. were able to go to the *Datebook* office in New York City and meet with associate editor, Kathy Graham. She told the girls about *Datebook* teaming up with *The Beatles Book Monthly*. Her information excited the two girls, and they made Kathy an honorary club member. "*Datebook* has all kinds of Beatles projects in the works," Judy wrote in her newsletter. "Don't miss an issue!"

The first issue of *Datebook* to include *The Beatles Book Monthly* supplement hit the newsstands in early March. It was *Datebook*'s April issue, and it partially reproduced issue number 54 of *The Beatles Book Monthly* from January. It also had a letter from the fan club director, Fran Fiorino. She wrote, "Along with the latest stories and pics in the *Monthly Book*, the official Beatles Fan Club, Beatles (U.S.A.) Limited, will be reporting on the latest Beatle plans and fan club activities." Each letter included information on how to join Beatles (U.S.A.) Ltd. The Beatles had released a new single, *Lady Madonna/The Inner Light*. The 45 record came with an advertising insert in the picture sleeve telling fans about the latest supplement in *Datebook*. It also offered fans a "new giant-sized full-colour Beatles photo poster" for $2 with each Beatles fan club membership (due before July 31, 1968).

The club knew that many serious Beatles fans had quit Beatles (U.S.A.) Ltd. because they were unhappy with how things were run. Beatles (U.S.A.) Ltd. was trying to win these fans back. They started by becoming friendly with some of the independent clubs, and asking for their help. Judy Vachon from The Flying Cow, Ltd. wrote, "Things are getting better at Beatles (U.S.A.) Ltd. It's under new management, and the new director is a peach." Fran wanted to make things right with any fans who had not received their fan club materials. By early 1968 those who had been official club members since 1964 should have received the following items: Introductory photo album, *A Hard Day's Night* movie script, 1964 Christmas greeting, Souvenir photo album, April 1966 bulletin, 1966 Christmas greeting, *Sgt. Pepper's Lonely Hearts Club Band* poster, and 1967 Christmas greeting. Any longstanding club members who hadn't received any one, or more, of these items could contact Judy, who would let Fran know. Fran would send the fan the missing item if any were still available. If the items were not available, Fran would extend club membership to the member as long as the $2 dues payment was up to date.

Membership Numbers

Another significant change to the Beatles (U.S.A.) Ltd. came at the beginning of March. Each member was given a membership number. Instead of members mailing their precious membership cards into headquarters when they wanted something, fans were instructed to write their new membership number on

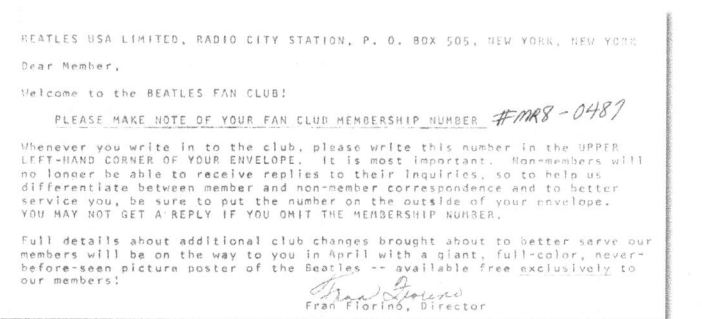 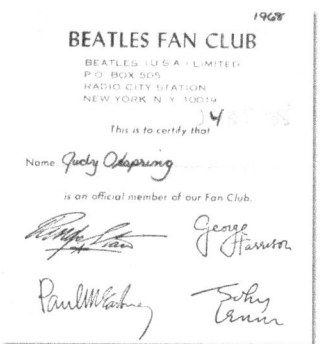

Beatles (U.S.A.) Ltd. notice regarding the new membership numbering system (top) and 1968 fan club membership card (right).

the upper left-hand side of the front of their envelopes. As Fran told members, "We've always received huge quantities of mail from non-members. Due to the fact that we've had to answer thousands of their letters, our members have been experiencing lengthy delays in response." She claimed The Beatles themselves wanted the loyal fan club members to receive special attention, so letters from non-members would no longer receive replies. The new number system was an improvement. Club member Don Wrege wrote in, stating, "I just wanted to comment on how much the letter system has improved since you adopted the number system."

The Independent Fan Clubs Continue

Most of the fans in the independent clubs thought Beatles (U.S.A.) Ltd. would fail to make these improvements permanent. They decided it would be wiser to join forces with one another instead. Robin Gadbury, from Lennon Luvvers Limited, sent an idea to Beatle Fans of the World, Unite!: "I always felt we needed some sort of central club to coordinate all the million and one Beatle Clubs that have come into and gone out of existence," she wrote. "I thought Beatles (U.S.A.) Ltd. ought to have this kind of service, but they don't even manage to keep up with what they are doing." Members all agreed that Beatles fans around America needed to form a strong union. They called themselves "The United Beatle Society." They made a list of all known Beatles club and presidents in the United States and tried to get all the independent clubs to join the union. Like many good ideas, the society started strong but fizzled out after a few months.

Because Beatles fans wanted to travel to London to meet The Beatles, Jamie Sim started the English Bound Beatles Fan's Club. This club allowed participating fans to learn from one another while planning their journeys. In 1968, a Beatlemaniac could fly roundtrip from New York to the U.K. for $300. The English Bound Beatles Fan's Club newsletters were full of great information for soon-to-be travelers. There were articles about riding London's Tube, British food, British words, how to apply for a passport, what to expect when going through customs, how to send a telegram back home, how to use traveler's checks, and how many cigarettes you could take into the U.K.

These newsletters also kept up on London fashion and nightclubs, as well as the most likely spots to find any of The Beatles. Jamie gave out tips on fundraising, and had a large "Swap Shop" where girls could sell their Beatles albums, magazines, and books to finance their London adventures.

In late 1967, a new club made quite an impression in the fan club community, which would continue for years to come. With just forty members, Barb Fenick began Father Lennon's Many Children (FLMC). Based out of Minneapolis, Barb, who was a dedicated Paul girl, wrote articles about The Beatles with humor and honesty. She found material in foreign magazines and reprinted articles overlooked by other clubs. She offered photographs for sale that fans had never seen. This made it apparent that "FLMC" was a different type of Beatles fan club. Barb advertised in teen magazines all around the country, and fans quickly joined. She printed newsletters on the mimeograph machine at her high school, but her resources were strained by May. She began selling more photos to raise money for the club's very own mimeograph machine.

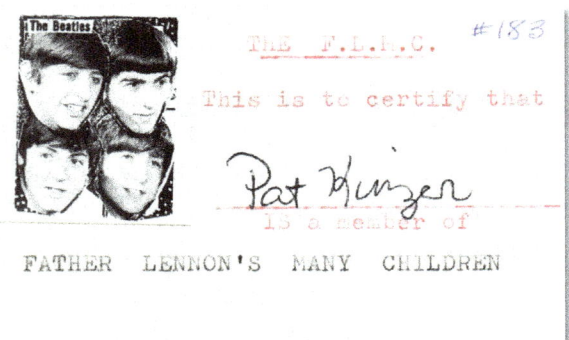

F.L.M.C. membership card, 1968.

The John Lennon Fan Club was changing. President Judy Johnson resigned in March, handing the reins over to a fan named Vikki Paradiso. One of Vikki's first decisions was to change the name of the club newsletter. *Lennon Lyrics* had been the title since 1964. Vikki told club members, "It is cute, but since most of our club members are a little older than so-called teeny boppers, the name of the newsletter should hold a deeper and more, well, John type of significance." The new name was: *Norwegian Wood*.

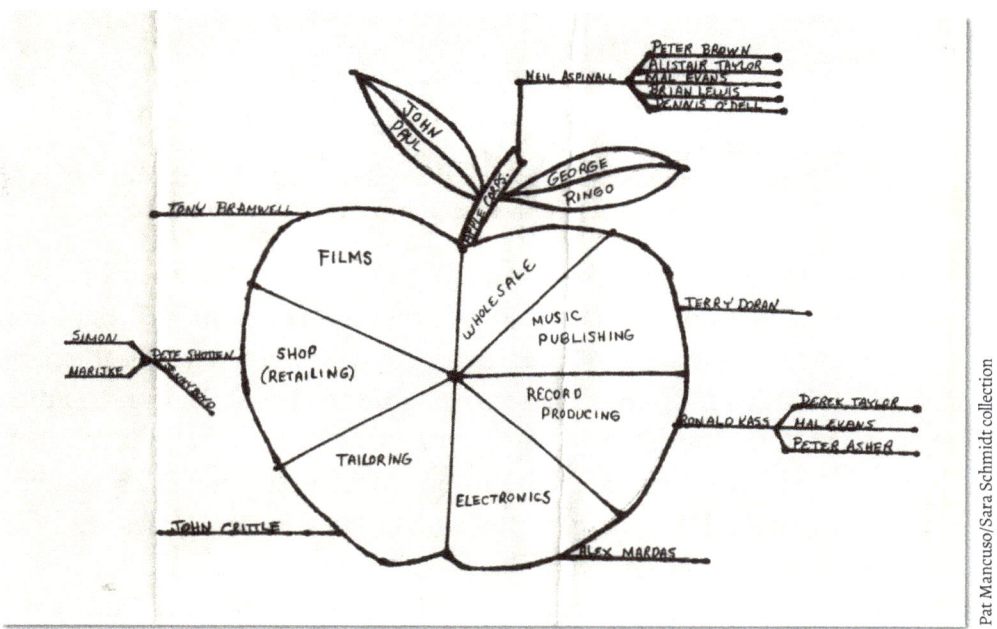

The George Harrison Fan Club's illustration explaining Apple. 1968.

The Big Apple

Once all four Beatles returned from India, the immediate focus was not on recording a new album, but on their company, Apple. On May 11 John and Paul traveled to New York City to publicize their new company. It was the first time since 1966 that more than one Beatle had been in the United States. New York fans hadn't seen The Beatles since the Shea Stadium concert two years earlier. Not only was New York City the home of Beatles (U.S.A.) Ltd., but many active chartered and independent fan clubs were there. The New York fans' love for the boys had never gone away. John and Paul's time in New York was an exciting five days for Beatle fans.

John and Paul introduce Apple to the press at the Americana Hotel, New York. May 14, 1968.

Beatles (U.S.A.) Ltd. employees Arma Andon and Jock McLean had been working for Nat Weiss and the fan club when they were given the task of picking up the famous duo at the airport. It was there that Arma learned that Beatlemania had not died. "We were on the tarmac waiting for the boys to arrive, and there were thousands and thousands of girls. They were on the observation deck above the hangar. I had never heard anything so loud in my entire life. The screaming, the hollering and Paul, he just got it going. He was blowing kisses, and they went ape-shit. Jock and I were given Sharpies, and my job was to make sure that John had a Sharpie to sign autographs, and Jock was in charge of Paul. If they weren't signing photographs for fans, they were signing photographs for all the personnel—the police, the fire, everybody that worked for the airlines. It was a freak show. John Lennon signed every autograph, as many as he could, and so did Paul. It has always impressed me."

Fans followed the motorcade through New York City. Police drove a dummy limo to the St. Regis Hotel with fans close behind, and even more waiting outside the building. However, John and Paul went to Nat Weiss' apartment, fooling hundreds of girls. After John and Paul were inside, Jock and Arma trekked to the St. Regis as Arma recalled, "We showed up at the St. Regis, and everybody thinks we're The Beatles. All we were doing was dropping off luggage, but it was a zoo, and I was a little afraid."

The two Beatles and their entourage were sitting around Nat's apartment, smoking pot and talking about the schedule, when Nat's telephone rang. Two fans, Joanne Rubino and Nina Tornabene, had discovered the guys' true whereabouts. They found Nat's phone number, tried it, and were shocked when John picked up. Joanne recalled, "I spoke to John, and he was so stoned. We were flirting with him basically. Then he handed the phone to Paul, and then Paul asked me for my measurements, it was crazy!"

The next day, the group from England spent time in business meetings, including one on a Chinese junk boat that went around the Statue of Liberty. By the time they arrived back at Nat's apartment, the fan club grapevine had spread the news of John and Paul's arrangements, and crowds of fans were waiting for them outside the building. These included Nina and Joanne. "I made a beeline for John and Nina went to Paul," Joanne said. "She actually gave Paul a Tiny Tim album. John had a cut on his chin, and I said, 'What happened to you?' He said, 'I cut myself shaving.' Probably he was drunk, and he fell down."

John and Paul did use the hotel suite at the St. Regis during their time in New York. There in the suite they conducted many interviews about Apple as thousands of fans waited outside the hotel. Lisa was one of those fans, but she could not stay out there. "My friend and I got away from the crowd. We knew Gucci was connected to the St. Regis Hotel, so we crept through Gucci and right into the St. Regis lobby. We went straight up the stairs to John and Paul's floor. We went right to the suite, where we believed John and Paul were staying. I had the gall to go right up and ring the doorbell. I kept saying, 'Is John there? Is Paul there?'" What Lisa didn't realize was that both Paul and John were standing behind her. "I fell back against the wall, dumbfounded! All I kept thinking was to say something, but I was speechless! Paul's hair was so dark, and John's hair was light. John had on granny glasses and a band-aid on his chin." They were alone and asked if the door in front of them was their room. Lisa found her voice and told them that it was their room. "The next thing I remember, I turned to John and said, 'Oh John, I've come all this way to see you.' Paul was standing there with a very sweet smile. John said kindly but very sarcastically, 'Yeah, and I came all the way from England to see you!'"

By this time, the security guards spotted the two girls. They grabbed them and dragged them down the hall. The entire time the fans were yelling goodbye to John and Paul. They were thrown into the elevator, and then tossed outside with the rest of the fans.

The most crucial interview was the big press conference held in the ballroom of the Americana Hotel. Several fan club members had legitimate press credentials and were more than happy to use them. One such fan was Leslie Samuels, who had met all The Beatles at their homes the previous summer. In 1968 Leslie worked at the *New York Daily News* Washington office. "I heard John and Paul were coming to New York to publicize Apple. It went over the AP wire, and I said to my boss, 'Give me a press pass. I'll pay my own way up there, and I'll get you a story.' And he did! I walked in and sat in the second row. Linda Eastman was sitting in front of me. John and Paul walked in, and they said, 'Hi Leslie.' They remembered me because I was a nice kid. I never hurt them and brought them presents. It was really cool."

Claudia was another fan who was allowed inside. She had brought a camera and a bouquet of daisies. She gave the flowers to Paul, who snipped off one daisy and put it through the buttonhole of his jacket.

Until May 14, fans in New York City had been the only ones to share in the excitement of seeing half The Beatles. Every fan in the country would get to see them on *The Tonight Show* that evening. The news arrived during the morning hours. John and Paul would be appearing on the NBC talk show that night. The phone wires were hot, with fans around the nation calling each other, speculating on what type of appearance it would be. Some thought it would be a clip of *Lady Madonna*, others believed John and Paul had recorded an interview in a hotel room earlier in the week. One hopeful fan thought the two might sing a duet. One fan wrote in *Teen Set*, "A nation full of Beatle fans held its collective breath as, sure enough, just like real people, John and Paul loped from behind the curtain and proceeded to take their place beside Johnny Carson's substitute, Joe Garagiola." John and Paul were on *The Tonight Show* stage in front of a live audience at 30 Rockefeller Center. The interview itself was one of the worst they gave. Garagiola, Johnny Carson's stand-in, was not prepared. He asked strange questions, and kept cutting to commercial breaks.

The addition of a slightly drunk actress, Tallulah Bankhead, who chimed in with equally odd comments, made it one of the worst interviews in Beatles history. Both John and Paul looked uncomfortable, but the fan club members at home did not mind. Several, including Patricia Simmons in Ohio, recorded the audio of the interview on reel-to-reel tape recorders. This was becoming a new trend among pen pals. Trading Beatles' interviews amongst one another was a great way to hear new Beatles content. Fans played these tapes at fan club

Paul and John on The Tonight Show *with Joe Garagiola and Tallulah Bankhead. May 15, 1968.*

meetings and rallies. Another fan took her family's 16-millimeter video camera and recorded the program without sound. Someone synced the audio with the video, and the result circulated through fans and collectors. Since NBC did not keep *The Tonight Show* tapes, the audio and video tapes made by teenage Beatles fans remain the only footage of John and Paul on *The Tonight Show*.

George and Ringo In The Golden State

Not long after John and Paul left the United States, George and Ringo arrived. The two musicians, along with their wives and Mal Evans, landed in California on June 7. They were there so George could film scenes with Ravi Shankar for an upcoming movie called *Raga*. While in California, George, Ringo, and their crew went horseback riding and golfing at Pebble Beach. Ringo and Maureen had a nice dinner at the Luau restaurant in Los Angeles, and George and Ringo were spotted enjoying the nightlife at the Factory and Whiskey a Go-Go nightclubs.

Fans in Los Angeles didn't know they were there. The biggest fan club in the area was the Boss Beatles Fan Club. Member Mar Young was baffled and a little angry that two Beatles came to her town without her knowledge. The restaurant Ringo and Maureen went to, Luau, was in her neighborhood, yet she'd never suspected.

Paul's Dirty Weekend

Luckily, Los Angeles area fans were not disappointed for long. On June 20, Paul made a surprise trip to the west coast city. Capitol Records was holding a convention, and Paul arrived to finalize the deal between Apple Records and Capitol Records.

The Beatle was staying at the Beverly Hills Hotel, and he registered under his real name. Fan Robyn Flans and her three friends thought Paul might come to L.A. to promote Apple as he had in New York City. They decided to call local hotels and see if they could locate him. Once they discovered what hotel he was in, the four 12-year-old girls took the first bus. Robyn was brave enough to call his room. As soon as she heard the voice on the other end, she knew it was Paul. "He told me I had gotten Tony, his assistant, on the line. I knew it was Paul!" she recalled. "And every so often, he'd mess up and say something like, 'I-I mean Paul is going yachting today.' And I'd say, 'Paul, I know it's you...'"

Paul greets fans at the Beverly Hills Hotel. June 23, 1968.

He told Robyn and her friends to come to the bungalow between four and six that evening. To bide their time, the girls went to the hotel coffee shop. From there they spotted Paul and his entourage walking through the hotel lobby. The four fans ran outside, and stared at him. Robyn remembers, "After he got into the car, we went into the ladies' room and screamed! We had just seen our idol and breathed his air."

After an eight-hour wait, the preteens excitedly knocked on the door of Paul's room. Paul answered, wearing his red velvet jacket without anything underneath. The five of them sat on the steps of the bungalow and talked for an unforgettable forty-five minutes. They spoke about the Maharishi, and Paul's feelings about the guru, as well as John's movie, *How I Won the War*. One of the girls, Lesley, had a gift for Paul, a small bean with tiny elephants inside. Robyn recalls, "As she gave it to him, it opened up, and the multitudes of teeny elephants fell onto the pavement. He laughed and hummed while she scurried to retrieve them." They took photos, and Paul said goodbye to each girl, with a kiss. Robyn got a short, sweet kiss on the lips.

Robyn and her friends were part of a growing trend among Beatles fans, especially younger ones. They were no longer joining organized Beatles fan clubs. Instead, they joined a few friends and did Beatles activities. These small groups of friends did the same things fan clubs had done in the past, but these groups had no newsletters, or even formal names.

Organized clubs were still around. As the word got out that Paul was at the Beverly Hills Hotel, members of the Boss Beatles Fan Club went there to meet him. Just as he did with Robyn and her friends, Paul sat on the bungalow steps with club members and other fans who showed up. Two girls, Mar Young and Fern Beckler, reported to Father Lennon's Many Children: "He was like everyone says. He is charming, witty, and very understanding." They also reported that Paul had a hairy belly button.

Unknown to all the fans who met Paul that day was that inside the hotel room was his companion for the weekend. He had just begun a romantic relationship with a photographer, Linda Eastman. Fans might not have been aware that Paul and Linda were having what they later referred to as their "dirty weekend," but Linda would soon be well known to every fan club member in America.

Yoko

Fans did not know about Linda, but they were starting to learn about John's new relationship with Japanese artist Yoko Ono. The news left them confused and angry. Rumors of John and his wife, Cynthia, divorcing, had been going around for years. At first, most fans believed the rumors of John leaving Cynthia for Yoko were unfounded. The Cyn Lennon Beatle Club reported in the May newsletter, "John and Cyn are not getting a divorce or splitting up! There is no truth to the rumor, so simply ignore it!"

By June, the newspapers reported that John had been seen around London with Yoko while his "attractive blonde wife" was on holiday. Shortly after that, fans read that John had declared his love for Yoko and planned to divorce Cynthia. At the time of the announcement, John and Yoko were putting on an art show, releasing 365 white balloons over London.

The first impression many had of Yoko was that she was crazy. In an interview in early summer, 1968 she said that she had given birth to a grapefruit. She had also made a film displaying 365 bare bottoms, and she frequently went on

John and his new girlfriend Yoko at an art installation. July 1, 1968.

stage and asked audience members to take scissors and cut off her clothes. She was very different from the sweetheart, Cynthia.

At first, club members took sides. Who caused the split? Was it John or Cynthia? Many fans felt that Cynthia was to blame. The Pottie Bird Beatle Club stated, "It takes two to make a marriage, and it takes two to break it. I don't blame John only. He wouldn't have looked twice at Yoko if he was happy with Cyn, right?"

The John Lennon Fan Club president was adamant that Cynthia was the guilty party. "No one can make up an awful, filthy adultery suit by themselves," she wrote in the *Norwegian Wood* newsletter. "It takes two to make a marriage and two to break one." One club member wrote to her advising her to stop believing that John was a knight in shining armor, and that she should accept that Cynthia was not the guilty one. This letter angered the officers so much that they kicked the author out of the fan club and returned her dues. The message was clear: to be in The John Lennon Fan Club, you must believe that John did nothing wrong.

Those who felt John was to blame sympathized with Cynthia and Julian. The Flying Cow, Ltd. stated, "All that's left is a broken home for Julian and sadness for Cyn." One of the United Beatles Fan Club members said, "I tend to dislike Yoko because I still feel best for Cyn and Julian." After receiving many hysterical letters from club members The Flying Cow, Ltd. tried to calm things, and get everyone back on the same page. "We have no right to judge John," the statement said. "We can disagree with his actions, some of which seem senseless. We have no right to put any blame on him or on Cynthia for what happened. Pray for John if you want, hate him if you want, but don't spread the hate."

There was a lot of hate going around. For the first time, the love and unity among Beatles fans seemed to be gone. Within their clubs, they shared their angry thoughts with others. "I have a very low opinion of Yoko Ono," stated one club member. "I don't think she really is a nice person. My opinion of John has lowered considerably by his going out with her."

Those were kind words compared to an editorial in the Father Lennon's Many Children newsletter. A John fan wrote it under the alias "Gripweed." She said she had always loved John and was not going to turn against him. Then she said, "I saw a picture of Miss Ono. She looks like Miss Hiroshima 1945, but I've stuck with John through thick and thin for four and a half years, and I'm not going to stop now!" The John Lennon Fan Club officers disliked Yoko so much they refused to print her name in the newsletter. They wrote, "At least he has not married that little animal yet." They felt that John's friends, including Paul, needed to talk John into ending the relationship because there was no way John could ever find happiness with Yoko.

Boss Beatles Fan Club President Cindi Gonzales had met Yoko while in London, and she was tired of letters blaming either John or Cynthia. "There is more to John than just his looks and his actions," she wrote in her newsletter. "Yes, John is human, he can make mistakes like anyone else, but why do they have to be so earth-shattering? People get divorced every day, but because he is a Beatle, it's headlines." Cindi believed the Lennon marriage breakup was an excellent opportunity to see who was a true Beatles fan. She took the opportunity of the upcoming divorce to "clean house" in her fan club. She asked all members to send in their old membership cards and a form stating that they wanted to remain in the Boss Beatles Fan Club, including the name of their favorite Beatle. Any member who did not return the form was removed from the club.

Some clubs chose to avoid the drama, and focus on The Beatles' music. Beatles (U.S.A.) Ltd.'s official statement read, "The Beatles have given us a lot of happiness, and the least we can wish them in return is a bit of peace in the private parts of their lives ... False rumors and silly gossip is not our concern at Beatles (U.S.A.) Ltd." Beatle Fans of the World, Unite! agreed, saying: "We prefer to keep our mouth closed concerning John's recent decisions. We can only hope and pray everything works out for the best."

John and Yoko's relationship brought an end to two major independent fan clubs. Kathy Burns had been president of The Cyn Lennon Beatle Club for three years, growing the club to 800 members. When John announced he was divorcing Cynthia, Kathy wasn't sure what to do. She could continue the club, but without Cynthia as a Beatle's wife, how much news would there be? The last thing she wanted to do was invade Cynthia's privacy, especially during such a difficult time. Kathy

5 ERRORS CONTEST

Take a peep at the Beatles- they are celebrating their latest release- Sgt. Pepper's Lonely Hearts Club Band at a party given by their manager Brian Epstein.
It's a real knockout!
But hey! What gives?
The top drawing is fine, but the bottom drawing contains five errors.
Can you spot them?
If you can, just draw a circle around each error with a pen or pencil, fill in the coupon below, tear out the page along the dotted line and mail the coupon to... 1313 Mockingbird Ln., USA

To each of the first five readers that can correctly identify all five errors correctly, wont' win anythin! Just the satisfaction of knowing that your love for The Beatles is so great, you were willing to tear out a page in this book!
Get those pencils and pens out and get busy!
Good luck, and remember, we're all winners when it comes to the Beatles!

RIGHT

- -

WRONG

5 ERRORS CONTEST JUL., 1967

NAME................................ MY AGE IS..........
STREET...
CITY................................ ZIP CODE..........
STATE.............................. ARE YOU A SUBSCRIBER?

MAIL TO " 5 ERRORS CONTEST" • DEAR BEATLE PEOPLE • 1313 MOCKINGBIRD LN. USA

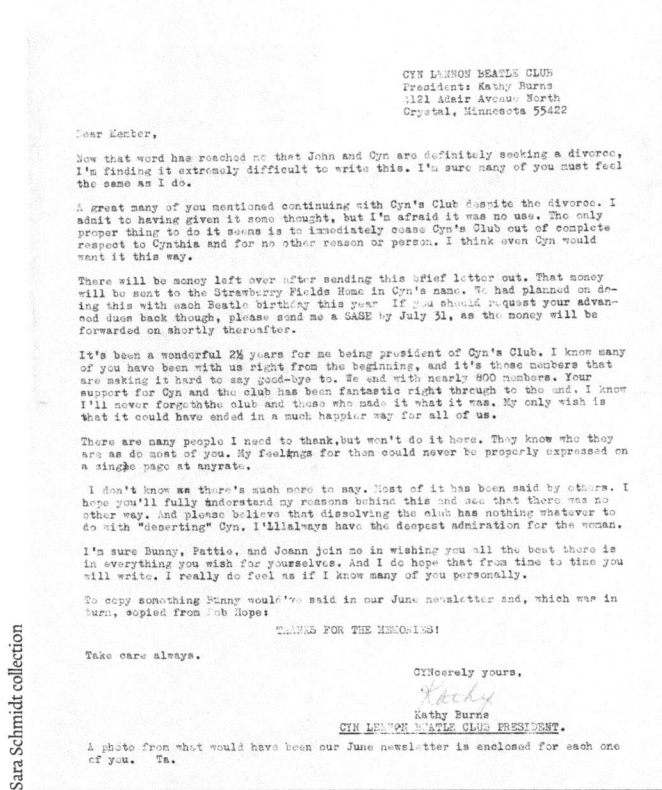

Cyn Lennon Beatle Club letter announcing the club is folding. June 1968.

decided the best thing was to disband the club. She sent each member a single page typed letter that explained, "The only proper thing to do it seems is to immediately cease Cyn's club out of complete respect for Cynthia and for no other reason or person. I think even Cyn would want it this way."

The former president of The John Lennon Fan Club, Judy Johnson, and Vice President of The Cyn Lennon Beatle Club, Bunny Racey, happened to be visiting Cynthia at her home the day she got the news. They told Kathy that Cynthia was disappointed that the club had ended. She felt that because she had lost her husband, everyone was turning against her. Though The Cyn Lennon Beatle Club was gone, the fans' love and support for Cynthia never went away.

Surprisingly the other club that closed was The John Lennon Fan Club. The club officers were still adamant that Cynthia was to blame for the split. The rug was pulled out from under them when President Vikki received a long-distance telephone call from a fellow club member. The member told her that the papers were reporting that Yoko was pregnant, and John intended to marry her as soon as their divorces were final. Vikki felt humiliated. She was sure club members across the country were laughing at her. In a long, dramatic letter she wrote, "I suddenly feel so empty and hurt, as if he were doing all this to me personally, to prove me as a complete ass and dunce for ever feeling he was worth all the pain, torment and tears." She believed everyone would be happy if the club ended, and she would leave still loving John.

The clubs may have ended for Kathy and Vikki, but it was not the end of their leadership roles in The Beatles fan club.

As they had in past summers, fans once again traveled to London during the summer of 1968 to see The Beatles in person. The four Beatles were busy in the studio, working on the songs that would be on the album *The Beatles* (the 'white album'). Fan club members wanted to see The Beatles so that they could give first-hand accounts of the boys' activities, and take exclusive photos to sell through the newsletters.

Boss Beatles Meet Paul

Cindi Gonzales and Lorelle "McCartney" were officers of the California-based Boss Beatles Fan Club. They took their trip to London in June, and were there for Paul's 26th birthday. They got a cake and wanted to deliver it to him themselves. With detective work they discovered Paul was going to be at a building on Waldron Street. Paul was shocked to see fans at the secret location. Cindi wrote about the experience in the July newsletter: "We handed Paul the cake first, and when he opened it, he said, 'I'm overwhelmed, girls.' He held it down for everyone to see." Paul was wearing red shoes and socks, striped pants, and a purple polka dot shirt. He thanked the girls and went inside the building. An hour later Paul appeared at the doorway and invited the American fans inside. Paul and a few other men were working on the Apple promotional film.

"I noticed our cake sitting on the table," Lorelle wrote. "Paul picked up a knife and cut the cake. He cut a piece for himself then told us to cut up the rest and pass it around." While Cindi and Lorelle were passing around the birthday cake, Paul was splicing the film together. After a while, John and Yoko came to see what Paul had done. They turned down Cindi when she offered them slices of birthday cake. As they watched the short film, John could not stop laughing whenever his friend, Magic Alex, came on the screen.

The couple left after watching it once, but Paul kept working on the project. At one point he accidentally broke the electronic table. While waiting for a new one, the fans had a chance to ask Paul some questions. Did he remember the bus ride in San Diego in 1965? And what about his upcoming trip to Los Angeles? They also asked him about a gift the fan club had sent him. Lorelle wrote, "I started by saying, 'Did you happen to get anything unusual in the mail around Valentine's Day?' And he said, 'Like what? I do get some unusual things.' And I said, 'Well, they

Paul McCartney at The Scaffold concert in London. May 31, 1968.

had hearts on them.' I was getting very nervous, so he said, 'Come on, you can tell me....' I casually said, 'like underwear?' He looked up so fast and questioned, 'Why? Did you send them?' I explained to him, and he said to the guy next to him, 'You heard that. Write it down in the books so we'll have something against her. Yes, I remember getting something like that.' The man next to him said, 'In other words, he isn't wearing them now.'"

The two girls had tickets to see John's play *In His Own Write*, and they asked Paul if he'd be there as well. He said he couldn't make it because he already had plans with Jane Asher. After spending three hours in the presence of Paul McCartney, it was time to leave. Cindi and Lorelle thanked him and went on their way, still shocked by their good luck.

Ida Lands a Job at Beatles (U.S.A.) Ltd.

As Cindi and Lorelle were flying home to the United States, more fans were flying into London, including Ida Langsam, her best friend, and her mother. As a present for Ida's high school graduation, her father sent mother and daughter on a three-week trip to Europe. "The only thing I really wanted to do was be in London," recalled Ida. "London was our first stop. We were there ten days, and nine of them were partially spent outside Paul McCartney's house, just standing there with the other fans." Every day about twenty fans stood outside the gates of

7 Cavendish Avenue, hoping to see Paul. Ida met boys and girls from all over the United States, Germany, France, Italy, and Sweden. Often Paul would take ten minutes to come outside to talk to the fans and sign autographs. He wasn't the only famous person the fans saw. Also coming in and out of the McCartney house was Paul's brother Mike McGear, John Lennon, Yoko Ono and her daughter Kyoko, as well as Vivian Stanshall from the Bonzo Dog Doo-Dah Band. The Beatles' road manager and friend, Mal Evans, went out of his way to talk to the fans and answer their questions about The Beatles.

Paul, with Ida Langsam in the background.

Ida's visit coincided with a busy time in Paul's life. In July 1968 Paul's long-term relationship with fiancée Jane Asher ended. Ida was about to see the aftermath of the breakup first hand. One afternoon, a big truck pulled into the driveway. Looking through a crack in the gate, she saw a dry cleaning truck dropping off many clothes. Not long afterward Jane Asher's mother arrived to retrieve her daughter's clothing. Early one morning, Ida and her friend rang the buzzer on Paul's gate. Paul's new girlfriend, Francie Schwartz, answered the door and informed the girls that Paul was sleeping. She also said that The Beatles' Apple Boutique was soon closing, so if they wanted to buy any souvenirs they had better get there quickly. The girls could not pass up the opportunity to purchase an item from a store owned by The Beatles. Ida bought some Apple pencils, a greeting card, and a vest with little mirrors on it.

The 17-year-old from New York had many great memories of her nine days on Cavendish Avenue. She was there the day before The Beatles would take part in the "Mad Day Out" photoshoot. She saw a large van with The Beatles' wardrobe for the shoot parked in the driveway. She watched all The Beatles arrive along with Yoko and Mal, and she spotted Paul, all decked out in a pink suit, greeting them. On another occasion, a group of girls decided to go over to the neighbor's house and peek over the wall at Paul, who was washing his car in front of his house. When he saw them, he playfully sprayed them with a garden hose. As the two friends waited outside Paul's house each day, Ida's mother went sightseeing and shopping in London. Occasionally she dropped off

Beatles Mad Day Out photo session. July 28, 1968.

lunch for the girls. During one of those lunch stops, Paul came to greet the fans. The group of girls suddenly became timid. Though they didn't talk to him, they did begin to giggle. "My mom marched straight through the crowd and up to Paul," Ida remembered. "She shook his hand and said, 'Now that I met you, I can go back to New York.'" Ida was embarrassed. She couldn't believe her mom would talk that way to Paul McCartney!

When the two Beatles friends got back home, Ida's friend wrote a letter to Mal Evans to thank him for his kindness toward them. He wrote back saying if the girls were ever in London again, they should give him a call. He included his phone number. Ida said, "We were so excited! We thought this is our ticket

LIFE magazine cover from the Mad Day Out photo session. July 28, 1968.

into The Beatles' inner circle." They decided to go to The Beatles fan club office in New York City to show them the letter. They showed it to director Sandi Morse, and she began to laugh. "They said he does that to everyone," Ida recalls. She remembers Sandi's explanation. "'He's hoping to, you know, score with you.' We had no idea that's what was going on." The naïve teenagers couldn't believe it, but Sandi said it was true. No one knows why Mal gave them his phone number, but Ida didn't try to find out. "There went our dream of being besties with The Beatles, but that was my intro to the fan club." Ida began volunteering at the club offices. She put together packages to be mailed to members, or she filed things away. Eventually, she would play a significant role in the fan club.

Fan Club Overhaul

During the summer of 1968, all members of Beatles (U.S.A.) Ltd. received an exclusive color Beatles poster. The poster's photo had been taken in the basement canteen of the EMI recording studios just before The Beatles' trip to India. Any members who renewed, or joined, the official club before July 31 would receive the poster.

Besides the poster, fan club members were allowed to purchase rare Beatles items directly from the club. New 8″ x 10″ black-and-white glossy pictures were now available. Fan club members in the U.K. had already been purchasing the photos (which they called "Superpix"), and now the American fans had the same opportunity. The first photo offer was four individual photos of John, Paul, George, and Ringo taken just before they left for India. The second offer was for ten photos taken during the *All You Need is Love* telecast the previous year, and the third offer was for two pictures of The Beatles from the *Hello Goodbye* film in 1967. Fan club members could purchase any of the photographs for 25 cents each, or five photos for $1. Fans could buy all the

Beatles (U.S.A.) Ltd. poster. 1968.

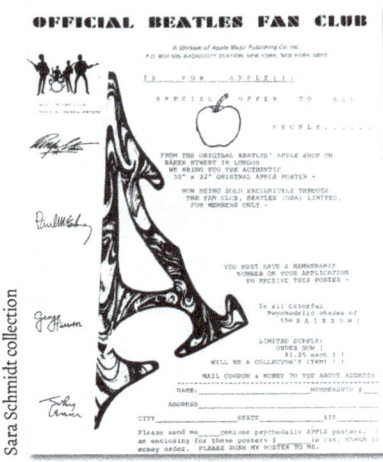

Beatles (U.S.A.) Ltd. "A is for Apple" order form (top) and the poster members would receive (above).

pictures for just $3. The club once again sold the individual photo albums from 1965. Members could buy the set for $1.25, or one for 35 cents, and non-members could buy the set for $2 or 50 each.

One of the most interesting items was the "A is for Apple" poster. This 22" x 30" poster was available only to members of the American fan club. It came from The Beatles' Apple Shop on Baker Street in London. The colorful, psychedelic poster sold for $1.25, and the fan club promised that it "will be a collector's item." Only a few members took advantage of this offer. The advertisement did not show the full poster, and it did not have a picture of The Beatles on it.

The summer brought a new director to Beatles (U.S.A.) Ltd., Sandi Morse. Sandi had been working with the club for quite some time, but her name did not start appearing on correspondence until the summer of 1968. No one remembers seeing the previous director, Fran Fiorino, at the offices. To most people she'd been a voice on the telephone. Suddenly Fran was gone, and Sandi had taken her place.

Sandi was a young, unmarried woman, and a Beatles fan, when she landed the job as the National Director of Beatles (U.S.A.) Ltd. Always full of energy, she had what it took to give the club the makeover it desperately needed. Sandi saw a club in shambles, but vowed to make the American fan club just as good as its British counterpart. Sandi regularly spoke to Freda Kelly, the National Director of The Official Beatles Fan Club in England. When Freda gave her advice Sandi took it to heart.

The other new name that appeared on fan club materials was Assistant Director, Nancy Applebaum. Nancy took care of photo and poster sales. Like Sandi, Nancy was a young, unmarried Beatles fan who was ready to help improve the fan club.

Summer Club Activities

Club members who weren't meeting one of The Beatles during the summer of 1968 were busy celebrating the band in other ways. The members of Father Lennon's Many Children had their first club meeting on Paul McCartney's birthday. They held the event in the rec room of President Barb Fenick's Minnesota home. The room

Sandi Morse and Rusty Rahn at Beatles (U.S.A.) Ltd. offices. 1968.

was decorated in Beatles posters and a large British flag. After helping Barb address, fold, staple, and stamp the club newsletters, the club enjoyed a blue iced birthday cake for Paul. In the afternoon the club members rode the rides at a local amusement park, and re-enacted scenes from *A Hard Day's Night* in a field. When they got back to Barb's house, one of the girls took out a guitar, and everyone gathered in a wooded area and sang Beatles songs. It was a great time, and, as Barb wrote, "It gave us all quite a feeling of closeness and deep realization of how important The Beatles have been in bringing so many people together."

The Boss Beatles Fan Club held a Beatles get-together in August. Though it was last-minute, thirty-five fans showed up. They had a good time looking at Beatles photographs and singing Beatles songs.

Fan Clubs Go to England

Several members of the George Harrison Fan Club got together in August for a trip to England. Their ultimate goal was to meet George and the other Beatles. The members who made the trip were president Pat Kinzer, Patricia Simmons, Joyce Kilbane, Nancy Scharfe, and Sandy Meckes.

Before leaving for England, Pat Kinzer sent a certified letter to George's home in Esher, informing him that she was coming to visit on August 5 at 2 PM. She made a list of questions to ask him, had a stack of items for him to autograph,

a camera with color film, and a few presents from other members. The five girls set off for London on August 1. Their first stop was Paul's house at 7 Cavendish Avenue. There they met up with former president of The John Lennon Fan Club, Judy Johnson, and club member Bunny Racey. The police were yelling at fans to keep them away from Paul's house, so the two Pats, Bunny, and Judy went to have lunch. While they were gone, Joyce, Nancy, and Sandy saw George leave Paul's house. In all the excitement, the pills Sandy took for rheumatoid arthritis fell out of her bag and scattered all over Paul's driveway, causing George to give her a strange look.

On the scheduled day, August 5, Sandy Meckes, Pat Kinzer, and Patricia Simmons ventured over to George's colorful house. After speaking to the housekeeper, Margaret, the girls waited at the end of the driveway. Patricia remembers, "We saw a car in the distance driving towards us, and Pat said, almost in a monotone, 'George's in that car.' I kept saying 'No, it couldn't be him,' but it was." As he drove by them, his car slowed. Pointing at the three girls, he looked directly at them and said, "Hey, aren't one of you....uh...." Then he pointed directly at Pat and said, "You!" Pat responded, "Yes, I have a fan club for you." To this, he said, "Yeah, that's right; you're Pat, aren't you?" Shocked that George Harrison knew her name, all she could say was, "Yes." Observing the exchange, Patricia remembered, "She reached in because he extended his hand to shake hands, and she reached so far into the car, she shook his elbow." Still in a daze, Sandy told him that she was the girl who had dropped the pills all over Paul's driveway.

George could not stay and talk to them because he was in a rush, but he made plans for them to return the next day at 1 PM. Once George left, Pat was overwhelmed. "I started to cry," she wrote in her trip diary. "I couldn't believe that the thing I've dreamed about and wished, hoped, and prayed for since January 1964 had finally come true!" The first order of business was to send telegrams to her parents and the fan club officers. The message was simple: Mission Accomplished!

The next day all five girls went to George's home promptly at 1 PM. There they were greeted by the housekeeper. She was expecting them, but George was not dressed yet. When he appeared at the door, he was wearing an orange shirt with striped pants, green striped socks, and gold shoes with big brass buckles. The girls were in such shock that they could not speak. Patricia recalls, "We could not believe he was standing in the doorway with this big smile on his face, and we were all nervous that nobody said anything for a minute." George broke the tension by asking if he should pose for photographs. They all began snapping pictures, including one special one Patricia took of George and the club's president.

The five girls lined up to get autographs. Patricia remembers, "Sandy and Nancy had brought an enormous pile of *Beatle Book Monthly* books for him to sign, and I wanted his autograph too. I had the Christmas issue of *Beatles Book Monthly*. When he looked at the picture, he said, 'Oh that must have been taken forty years ago.'"

Along with fan club prizes, the most important

George and Pat Kinzer. August 6, 1968.

item George signed was the revised George Harrison Fan Club Charter. Pat had typed up a new charter to replace the previous one George had only signed with his first name in 1966. She had brought along five copies for him to sign. She says, "Before he signed it, he actually read it and said, 'Why do you want to do this? You can be a member of Beatles (U.S.A.) Ltd., and they can do all the work.'" She assured George that she liked having an independent club and enjoyed doing all the work. George responded, "Okay, it's up to you. I'll sign these then, just wanted to be sure you don't take me to court."

The bewildered club president did not understand why George would say such a thing. She was his fan club president and would never dream of taking him to court. She gave George a copy to keep. Patricia said with a laugh, "I remember he was rolling up the paper and unrolling it. I'm sure he was thrilled. He was just so patient."

The fans played with his Siamese cats, talked about their British holiday, and discussed his favorite bands. He told them that Vanilla Fudge was not his "fave rave" and recommended a group from Woodstock, New York, called The Band. After nearly forty minutes George politely ended the visit. The girls had one more request. They wanted to take photos of the back of his house. George permitted this, and Joyce Kilbane noticed him watching them from the back window. They took pictures of the pool, and Sandy Meeks took a unique souvenir. "She had a little medicine container," Patricia said. "She took a sample of his pool. She said she had it in the refrigerator for a long time until it got too ripe, and her mom threw it out."

George told the girls that The Beatles would be recording at EMI Studios on Abbey Road in London the next day. They spent the entire night waiting outside the studio, and saw all four Beatles leave for home. They also spent some time with Mr. and Mrs. Harrison in Liverpool before heading back to the United States. They were armed with enough photos and memories to last a lifetime.

The First Beatles Convention

In late 1967 a few independent Beatles fan club officers talked on the telephone and had a fantastic idea. They could invite Beatles fan club members from all the United States clubs to one central location and have a big Beatles convention. Many of the girls had been pen pals for four years and wanted to meet each other in person. Jen Appel from Beatle Fans of the World, Unite! planned the gathering for August, 1968 in Chicago. As the time got closer, a communication problem caused the event to be moved from Chicago to Minneapolis. Kathy Burns and her friend, Mary, took over the planning and made proper arrangements through the Convention Bureau.

Flyer for the first Beatles convention in the U.S.A. August 1968.

Fans traveled from California, Maryland, Colorado, Ohio, Illinois, and Wisconsin for the first-ever Beatles Convention. Unofficially the fun began on Thursday, August 22, when some early arrivals met at Barb Fenick's house. They had a bonfire in her backyard, and roasted marshmallows, as they sang Beatles songs. The most exciting event was hearing two brand new Beatles songs, *Hey Jude* and *Revolution*. Hearing new Beatles songs was always exciting, but hearing them for the first time with other fans was unforgettable. In the English Bound Beatles Fan's Club newsletter, Jamie Sim wrote, "It was overwhelming to crowd around the transistor—nearly blowing our minds over the beauty of 'Hey Jude' and the excitement of 'Revolution.' We could hardly believe that they were real."

On Friday, August 23, all the convention-goers checked into the same hotel The Beatles had used in 1965: The Lemington Motor Inn. One room cost each fan $8.00 for the weekend. The girls had dinner together at the hotel and joined in a few activities, while getting to know each other better. A girl who called herself "Gripweed" brought a guitar and led the group in a Beatles sing-along. As the night went on, everyone crowded into one of the hotel rooms where they held a séance to try to talk to Brian Epstein. Kathy Burns remembers, "I'm not saying we did or didn't get to say hi to Eppie, but lots of girls scattered and screamed at one point, and we decided that was probably enough of that."

The next day, August 24, began with a meeting of all the independent fan clubs' officers. They discussed some rumors that their clubs might be forced to join Beatles (U.S.A.) Ltd. As a group they decided, if those rumors were true, they would stay united and independent. They all spent Saturday afternoon at the zoo riding the paddleboats.

The most significant event came that evening: the dress-up banquet at 7 PM in the hotel's banquet hall. Besides enjoying the turkey dinner, the girls talked, sang Beatles songs, put on hilarious skits, and got a sneak peek at the soon-to-be-released Beatles biography by Hunter Davies. The highlight of the banquet was the Beatle awards. Judy Johson and Shirley Poston tied for the Best Beatles Fan, Barb Fenick's club, Father Lennon's Many Children, won for the best Beatles fan club, and Susan "Richie" Lindgren was awarded Miss Congeniality.

On August 25, the final day included calling to London to see if they could get Paul McCartney on the line. They couldn't talk to him, but they did speak to Freda Kelly, the head of The Official Beatles Fan Club in the U.K. Freda was friendly and spoke to the girls for twenty minutes, but she had concerns about the convention. In a letter to Kathy she wrote: "There is just one snag! We, the fan club over here and also in America, cannot have anything to do with it, as the girl who is running it is not an official area secretary."

Even without the approval of the official fan club, the forty attending fans had a fantastic time. Afterward Jen wrote, "The convention was so much fun. I wish we could have them every weekend. Every person there was beautifully Beatle obsessed, and I love them all. My Beatle sisters: all for one and one for all!"

Summertime Fun On The East Coast

On the East Coast the activities for the members of chartered clubs went on with Beatles (U.S.A.) Ltd.'s blessing. Some girls held what they called "The First Annual Meeting of the Walrus Cornflake Sitting Society," and they made certificates for attendees. The fans sat around playing guitars and singing. Some members met in New York City's Central Park during the summer, and sat in the shade of a tree, while making music. Eventually, they'd row a boat on the lake, singing the whole time. By the end of the day, fans would inevitably jump into the water.

For the second year in a row, Beatles fans met at Shea Stadium on the anniversary of The Beatles concert in 1966. They stood in the parking lot displaying signs and playing games.

The M.B.E. (Members of The Beatles Empire) sponsored a big event, inviting all Beatles (U.S.A.) Ltd. members. The club posted an announcement in *The Beatle Bulletin* that they were having their very own *Magical Mystery Tour*. The organizer of this event was JoAnne McCormack, a.k.a "Johnny." She later recalled, "I was 18 at that time. I wasn't young. I was one of the old ones. I rented a school bus and printed out little tickets for the *Magical Mystery Tour*. We put signs all over the bus."

Proceeds from the tickets paid for the bus, and on September 15 at 10 AM, thirty Beatles fans took the mystery trip to Bear Mountain in upstate New York. Fans were dressed for the occasion. A few wore handmade *Sgt. Pepper* jackets, and others wore festive *Magical Mystery Tour* hats. Many brought Beatles signs and attached them to the bus.

Once the group arrived at Bear Mountain, they had a scavenger hunt and a three-legged race. The winners won Beatles photographs that came directly from Beatles (U.S.A.) Ltd. They had a picnic and sang Beatles songs. One of the fans did a Paul McCartney impression that was so good many believed Paul had recorded a message for them.

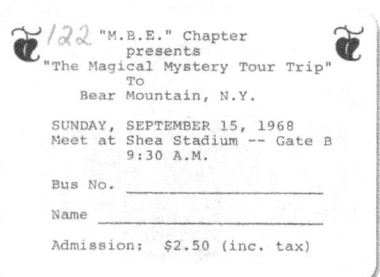

Front and back of the ticket for The Magical Mystery Tour Trip. September 15, 1968.

New York City area fan club members on the Magical Mystery Tour, September 15, 1968.

That autumn some girls who had been on that trip talked to the real Paul McCartney outside his London home. They told him that they had all gone on their very own *Magical Mystery Tour*. Paul seemed impressed by their story. The girls had already given photos from the trip to Nat Weiss at the Beatles (U.S.A.) Ltd. Headquarters in New York. Now they asked if Paul had seen the photographs. Much to their surprise, Paul said, "Yes. You were the girls in those pictures?"

Beatles (U.S.A.) Ltd. – Cease and Desist Orders

Beatles (U.S.A.) Ltd. had made considerable improvements. By the fall of 1968 dues were $2.50 a year. With the information in *Datebook* every month, new members were joining, and membership was back up. A new issue of *The Beatle Bulletin* went out, members could buy current photographs and an original Beatles postcard with faux autographs. Jock McLean noted, "The boys are extremely pleased with the club's progress lately!" However, one area was not improving: the chartered chapters of the fan club.

In 1968 many of the serious fans were happily involved in the independent clubs. Beatles (U.S.A.) Ltd. wanted those fans to join the official Beatles fan club, and end all independent fan clubs for good.

On August 21 Nat Weiss, The Beatles' lawyer in the United States, mailed out cease and desist letters to the 144 independent fan clubs in the United States. He sent the letter on Weiss Law Offices letterhead. Each fan club president received the same letter. The letter informed recipients that it had come to Weiss' attention that each of these fans was advertising a Beatles fan club without authority or permission. The message then targeted the fans' emotions, saying: "This is causing a great deal of confusion and embarrassment to The Beatles and their fan club." Weiss noted that it was his understanding that these independent clubs were selling Beatles photos and other items. He told each club president that she must cease and desist immediately. She had five days to respond, or "we shall have no alternative but to proceed in accordance with our clients' instructions."

The teenaged Beatles fan club presidents who received Nat Weiss's letter were intimidated. What did it mean? Was her little fan club illegal? Would The Beatles' lawyer take her to court? Was her club really embarrassing The Beatles? The last thing a fan wanted was to embarrass The Beatles.

LAW OFFICES
NATHAN M. WEISS
1501 BROADWAY
NEW YORK 36, N.Y.
OXFORD 5-2175

CABLE ADDRESS
NATWEISS NEW YORK

August 21, 1968

Mrs. Robin Gadbury
3719 Starr King Circle
Palo Alto, Calif. 94306

Dear Mrs. Gadbury,

This office represents the interests of John Lennon, Paul McCartney, Ringo Starr and George Harrison individually and collectively known as the Beatles.

It has come to our attention that you are advertising a Beatle fan club without authority or permission. This is causing a great deal of confusion and embarassment to both the Beatles and their affiliated fan club.

Please be advised that the only official fan club for the Beatles is Beatles (U.S.A.) Ltd. whose address is P.O. Box 505, Radio City Station, New York, New York.

It has also come to our attention that you are offering for sale pictures and other articles. According to our records and according to our clients, permission to manufacture and sell such products was never granted to you. If, in fact, you have received such permission, I would appreciate your forwarding me documentation of same. In the event you have not received such permission, demand is hereby made that you immediately cease and desist the manufacture and sale of these products.

I look forward to hearing from you within five days from your receipt of this letter. Failing same, we shall have no alternative but to proceed in accordance with our clients instructions.

Very truly yours,

Nathan M. Weiss

NMW:na

Cease and desist order from Nat Weiss. August 21, 1968.

Vincent Patanio collection

One club president, Robin Gadbury, ran Lennon Luvvers Limited. According to Robin, the club had begun as a chartered chapter, but the charter had been lost after changing hands several times. She responded to the letter, saying she did not advertise the club, nor did she sell photos. When she had learned of John's divorce, she'd calmed club members' anxieties with soothing words. Countless Lennon fans had written her thank you notes, saying that she had helped them see the news rationally. She explained, "I feel I was performing an essential service which could not have been performed by Beatles (U.S.A.) Ltd." She insisted that she had never done anything that would have caused embarrassment to John or the other Beatles.

The *Compleat Beatlemaniac* was an underground Beatles newspaper. The mystery editor spoke to Sandi Morse, who explained that The Beatles wanted all independent fan clubs and independent photo sales to end. "I am simply trying to do my job of carrying out the wishes of the boys," she said. "The Beatles feel this fan club is now so fantastic that there is no reason why there must be a million-odd independent clubs all over the U.S." The editor understood, but did not appreciate, Beatles (U.S.A.) Ltd.'s attempt to close the independent clubs. He wanted to know why they had to send a threatening letter. Sandi responded, "Of all the threatening we have done, we have never sued anybody. It is not our wish to sue a 16-year-old Beatles fan."

When writing to Beatles (U.S.A.) Ltd. supporters, Sandi referred to it as "the cleanup campaign of independent fan clubs." She wanted to recruit loyal Beatles (U.S.A.) Ltd. members to help her. "We have had plenty of trouble with them," she wrote. "I hope you will aid us in our endeavor to straighten these kids out who think they know what is better for The Beatles than The Beatles themselves."

Fan club employee Jock McLean felt that the independent fan clubs were giving the fans false information, which in return was making work harder for them at the official fan club because they were having to squash a lot of rumors. In an interview with *Datebook* Jock said, "I think a lot of independent fan clubs get their information second and third hand, so it becomes a bit distorted. I think there is a greater need for combining the independent fan clubs with the official club, consolidating them, so the club is centralized. This way, everyone would be in the mainstream of things. I know the boys feel this way too because they want to be assured that their fans are well informed as to what they are doing."

After hearing from various fan club presidents, Beatles (U.S.A.) Ltd. relented a little. Instead of dissolving the independent clubs, Sandi allowed them to join Beatles (U.S.A.) Ltd. and become chartered chapters. The catch was that they'd have to follow the rules to begin a chapter. Each club had to have at least twenty members, with dues paid to Beatles (U.S.A.) Ltd. Each chapter had to have a president, vice president, secretary, and treasurer. They were also expected to report news from Beatles (U.S.A.) Ltd., and they could not advertise the club in any publication or sell photographs through their club. They could charge dues to cover mailing costs, but they could not be more than $2 per member as

Letter sent to fan club members by 'The Beatles' explaining why they do not want independent clubs.

these dues would be in addition to the $2.50 to join Beatles (U.S.A.) Ltd. After they got the original cease and desist letter several clubs chose to end, including the Paul McCartney Fan Club, Around The Beatles, and Boss Beatles Fan Club. Cindi Gonzales wrote to Boss Beatles Fan Club members, "I've surrendered. I'm not a traitor, but I just couldn't see the sense of fighting anymore. I don't have the money, lawyers, or The Beatles as [Beatles (U.S.A.)] Ltd. does. Right away, I am fighting a losing battle. I still do not agree with [Beatles (U.S.A.)] Ltd. on a lot of things. This is why I am completely disbanding Boss Beatles. It has been a very heartbreaking decision to make because, after three years, this club has become a part of me, but it is my decision."

Other clubs decided to obey the official fan club's demands, and tried to become chapters. The Flying Cow, Ltd. told its members that they were joining forces with Beatles (U.S.A.) Ltd. to "establish the greatest and most organized club the U.S. had ever known." As for the independent clubs that did not want to go that route, they said, "There is no way anyone can fight [Beatles (U.S.A.)] Ltd. unless you'd like to take The Beatles to court."

Judy Vachon from The Pottie Bird Beatle Club tried to talk her club's members into joining Beatles (U.S.A.) Ltd. by convincing them they were changing from a rotten club into a great club. Judy spoke to Tony Barrow, Nat Weiss, and Sandi Morse. She claimed that they all had been unhappy with how Beatles (U.S.A.) Ltd. had been run up to then. Sandi promised from that point on, Beatles (U.S.A.) Ltd. members would receive the same items as the U.K. members, including the 1965 Christmas greeting. Judy encouraged members to pay their dues to Beatles (U.S.A.) Ltd. so that The Pottie Bird Beatle Club members could remain, but she knew not all fans would agree. "I feel now that this new policy is logical," she wrote. "If you 'fans' out there think of me as a traitor- tough! I would rather be one less thorn in The Beatles' side than being included under your definition of just what a fan is. Nat Weiss is The Beatles' American manager, so arguing with him is like trying to fight Brian Epstein. Would any of you do that?"

Kathie Bloesl had run the United Beatles Fan Club without any assistance for three years. She had a professional and successful Beatles fan club. However, after receiving the cease and desist letter, Kathie felt like she had no choice but to be part of the official club. One requirement was that she had to have four officers. She begged her members to help her, but they weren't interested. Kathie wrote in her last newsletter, "I feel so defeated. I asked you if you would like to be V.P., treasurer or secretary. You know what the majority said? No. Some said they are too busy. How can they be too busy? All they have to do is be an officer and help with suggestions."

The United Beatles Fan Club, along with many other independent clubs, had to end. They couldn't meet the requirements. By the end of the ordeal, only three clubs remained. One stayed independent, and the other two reluctantly became chapters.

George Harrison Fan Club vs. Beatles (U.S.A.) Ltd.

When Pat Kinzer came home from London, she had her own fan club charter signed by George Harrison. No other club in the world had the blessing from one of The Beatles. A few weeks after her return she received the cease and desist letter from Weiss. She felt confused. With her father's help, she wrote a letter to Mr. Weiss explaining that she would not end the George Harrison Fan Club. Pat had George's approval and did not have to do anything else. She sent a copy of the signed charter as proof. Pat did not hear back from Weiss but corresponded with Sandi. She wanted to stay independent. In late September, Pat got a letter from Jock McLean. Jock informed her that he personally spoke to George about her and her fan club, and George wanted her to join with Beatles (U.S.A.) Ltd. It would be a better way to serve him and his bandmates. Pat felt like she had no choice. "George said it, so I did it," she recalled. "I joined reluctantly. I insisted they call it The Official George Harrison Fan Club. The rest of the clubs couldn't put 'official' in front of them."

The Official George Harrison Fan Club was the last to ask its members to join Beatles (U.S.A.) Ltd. Pat may have given in, but she did not follow all the regulations. She did not force all her members to become part of the official club. While that was the expectation, it took only twenty members to start a chapter, and her club had over five hundred. She continued to sell copies of the photographs she, and other members, had taken of George. She kept reporting just as she always had. They could make her join, but she was not bowing down to them.

Beatles' Love Association vs. Beatles (U.S.A.) Ltd.

On the day The Beatles' airplane landed in New York City, Joanne Maggio started a Beatles Fan Club in Chicago. In 1968 this independent club was called Beatles' Love Association and had a monthly newsletter, *Luv n Stuff*. When she was contacted to cease and desist her club, she did not want to give it over to Beatles (U.S.A.) Ltd. Since Joanne knew that a battle against the official fan club would be a David vs. Goliath situation, she reached out for help.

The afternoon disc jockey at Chicago radio station WCFL was Jim Stagg. Jim had a positive reputation among Beatles fans. Unlike other radio personalities at the time, Jim did not use gimmicks or theatrics in his program. Instead, he kept the music at the forefront of what he did, which gained him respect with the maturing fans. He also wrote a column for the *Chicago Sun-Times* newspaper. He had been one of the reporters who traveled with The Beatles during the 1964 tour and interviewed them during the 1965 and 1966 tours. His support for The Beatles never wavered, and he was the best choice for Joanne to contact. In September, she sent Jim a letter which he reprinted in his newspaper column. In the letter she explained how she understood why Beatles (U.S.A.) Ltd. would want to eliminate Beatles clubs that were making money, but she did not understand why they'd come after the independent clubs that were not making a profit. She told Jim how important the independent clubs were for the fans, especially since The Beatles had stopped touring. Joanne feared that if the independent clubs ended, all of the fans would be lost. Jim told the readers of the *Chicago Sun-Times* that he'd placed several calls to the headquarters in New York City to help. He wrote, "We salute you and your members for all your hard work, loyalty and devotion to The Beatles."

By this time, Joanne had received a letter from Sandi Morse. Joanne told her club members about the "hopelessness conveyed through the letter." Included in the envelope was a letter from "The Beatles" stating their wishes for the end of independent clubs and instead having one "happy chapter family." Joanne suspected the letter to be a forgery, but at the same time wanted to follow The Beatles' wishes. Also concerning to Joanne was that the letter from Sandi included details that could only be known by reading *Luv n Stuff*. It bothered her that some unknown club member was not only speaking to Sandi about the newsletter, but also spreading outright lies about the club. It had taken Joanne five years of hard work and dedication to build her club to become a success, and for a spy to take it down with lies was something she did not want to happen.

Joanne wrote back to Sandi stating that she would like a copy of the information on becoming a chapter and would leave the decision up to the club members. In December 1968, Joanne made the decision to join Beatles (U.S.A.) Ltd. and become an official chapter. She felt like it was the right thing to do because The Beatles wanted one official club. In the end, fifty-eight members stayed and joined Beatles (USA) Ltd. and thirteen members left the club.

Joanne's outspokenness about the club made Sandi take notice of her. This most likely led to Joanne being asked to perform a leadership role in the official club in 1969.

FLMC vs. Beatles (U.S.A.) Ltd.

With Pat Kinzer and Joanne Maggio joining Beatles (U.S.A.) Ltd., there was only one independent club left, Father Lennon's Many Children. When Barb Fenick received Weiss' letter, she did something the others hadn't. She showed it to a lawyer. The lawyer explained that she was not breaking any laws by having an independent Beatles fan club. She did not have to close her club or join Beatles (U.S.A.) Ltd. if she did not want to. The 17-year-old could continue independently as she had for the past year. Unlike most others, Barb was not intimidated. She was mad, and she exchanged many letters with Sandi Morse. Sandi told her that they did not want her to give up her club; they just wanted her to join Beatles (U.S.A.) Ltd. as a chapter. Barb wrote to Sandi and told her that she was asking the members to decide what they wanted. She took a poll, and members mailed in their responses.

Sandi was livid! She wrote to Barb, "After reading your letter, I was completely shocked and appalled. First of all, I don't understand what is going on, but it seems your members do not understand that The Beatles don't want independent fan clubs. It was their suggestion that we 'close up shop' on independents and also independent photo selling. If you don't mind me saying so, the poll should never have been taken. You, as president and head of FLMC, should have conveyed to your members, and many of them are quite young and immature, I am sure, that they should not come first, but The Beatles should. How could your members feel that an independent club would be more personal? You say you can offer what Beatles (U.S.A.) Ltd. never can. I doubt that very much. Our business is to make sure that we please all Beatles and all Beatles fans. With all due respect to you, I think, and I'm sure that you'll agree that The Beatles know what's best for The Beatles. I cannot help but be aggravated, knowing that the faithful fans in the Father Lennon's Many Children club are not faithful fans at all, but just teenagers that are rebelling against what the boys really want. Only two independent fan clubs are left of the one hundred and forty-four I have written to that are being obstinate and stubborn. I know for a fact that The Beatles are becoming extremely annoyed with the ridiculous hassling and arguing back and forth. For the last and final time, I ask you as head of FLMC to abide by their wishes and once and for all, have your members of your club become a chapter of Beatles (U.S.A.) Ltd."

Of course, Barb strongly disagreed with Sandi. She might not know what was best for The Beatles, but she knew what was best for The Beatles' fans. Barb was insulted that Sandi called the members of FLMC 'young and immature.' In the end, Barb realized it was The Beatles that taught their fans to think for themselves and to stand up for what was right. She decided that joining Beatles (U.S.A.) Ltd. would make her a hypocrite. In the December 1968 newsletter she wrote: "FLMC remains independent! I could never be a loyal chapter. I believe in freedom and the unorthodox ways all of you are so used to from your unbiased president."

Barb cut all ties from Beatles (U.S.A.) Ltd. and was the only independent Beatles fan club in the United States. She never heard from Sandi, Nat Weiss, or any other Beatles representative again.

Area Secretaries

When The Official Beatles Fan Club moved to London in 1963, fans from various sections of Britain were assigned the job of area fan club secretaries. Club members contacted their area secretary with any Beatles questions they might have. This worked well for the official club, and five years later, Beatles (U.S.A.) Ltd. decided to use area secretaries. Each state would have one secretary, with larger states having two.

It was Sandi Morse's responsibility to find fans who would be area secretaries. She was looking for club members who were at least 17 years old, well organized, and had a typewriter.

The first area secretary was the former president of The Cyn Lennon Beatle Club, Kathy Burns. She got the job through the director of the U.K. club, Freda Kelly. Kathy had written to Freda, explaining that she no longer had a fan club to run. Freda wrote back, encouraging Kathy to work for Beatles (U.S.A.) Ltd. She wrote, "You could be a great help to them with your experience." Freda told her how kind Sandi and Nancy were, and wrote that Beatles (U.S.A.) Ltd. had been trying to improve. She explicitly told Sandi that Kathy would be an asset to Beatles (U.S.A.) Ltd. Kathy couldn't move to New York City to work for the fan club, so Sandi offered to make her area secretary for Minnesota. Kathy had been involved in The Beatles' fan community for over four years, and she knew plenty of former club members and pen pals who might also be interested in becoming area secretaries. One was Patricia Simmons in Ohio. Kathy and Patricia had been pen pals for a long time. She had been involved in various Beatles fan clubs but had never held a leadership position. Kathy gave Sandi Patricia's name. "Sandi must have sent me a letter asking me if I wanted to it. I said, 'Are you kidding? Of course, I wanted to do it!'" Patricia said. "But little did I know how much work it would be."

The area secretary for Louisiana, Richard Keen, got the job after typing a letter to Beatles (U.S.A.) Ltd. asking how he could get a copy of the 1967 Christmas message. They sent him a mimeographed information sheet about joining the fan club, but he was not interested. Richard just wanted the record. In another letter he asked about the record, but he received another copy of the flyer. He sent in his dues, along with a letter inquiring about the record.

After he had sent in his dues Sandi asked him to be the area secretary. She'd been impressed with his sensible, neatly typed letters. Richard eagerly accepted. Sandi said, "You are the only boy so far to be an area secretary for us, so I hope you won't feel funny." Richard was happy to have the job, but he did have one surprise. He was only 15 years old. Sandi had never asked his age and, due to his letters, assumed he was older. She got a little upset, and told him, "Do me a big favor and please, please don't tell the other area secretaries how old you are. As far as everyone else is concerned from now on, you're 17."

Being an area secretary was a big job, but well worth it. Area secretaries were always up to date on the latest Beatles' news. They also received complimentary copies of all the items that were sold through the club. This included the three tour programs, posters, photographs, and Christmas records.

Once a fan agreed to be an area secretary, he or she had to get a rubber stamp made with the secretary's name, address, state, and "Beatles (U.S.A.) Ltd." on it. Sandi sent a list of all the dues-paying fan club members in each secretary's state, suggesting that area secretaries put each member's name, address, and membership number on an index card, and file them alphabetically in a shoebox. The new area secretary had to send each member in their state a postcard introducing himself or herself, and including contact information. If a member had a question about The Beatles, he or she would write to their area secretary who would answer the questions. Sandi sent letters to the secretaries about once a week, so they were up to date on The Beatles' news. By the end of 1968, ten states and one city had secretaries: Maryland, Indiana, Louisiana, Vermont, Minnesota, California, New Hampshire, Michigan, Illinois, New York State, and New York City.

The New York Offices

While the area secretaries were busy getting things going in their home states, Beatles (U.S.A.) Ltd. employees were working hard at 1501 Broadway in New York City. Sacks of mail continued to pour into the office each day. Not only were fans joining the improved club, but there were thousands of photograph orders to be filled.

The workers dealt with more than just mail and money. Every Monday evening, Merle Frimark's task was to get the chart reports from *Billboard*, *Record World*, *Delight*, and *Cashbox* to see how any Beatles single was doing on the U.S. charts. She explained, "We had a Telex machine, and our Telex went right into the Apple Offices at Savile Row. Once I got the chart numbers, I would send a memo over the Telex machine and indicate what it was." Because of the time difference, the memo would get to London close to midnight. Sometimes one of The Beatles would be working at Apple when Merle's notices arrived. "One of the boys happened to be passing by the Telex machine," Merle said. "They sent me silly sayings back on the Telex. It was funny. The office was closed, but they were there and would jokingly Telex me back. That was a lot of fun."

The fan club offices were a fun place to be in 1968. As Arma Andon recalled, "We used to get high there and do silly stuff. One time we had a box of 45s, singles. It was a song by Cream called *I Feel Free*, and we were throwing them out of the fan club office window like Frisbees." Merle recalled another fun time: "The Beatles were releasing the song, *Back in the U.S.S.R.*, and it was shipped to us before it was released. When it came in, we played it right away. We were all dancing around the office. It was quite something."

Not many fans or outsiders knew where the fan club was, but occasionally Nat Weiss would meet someone and invite them up for a visit. Hash Howard was a musician and actor who had befriended Nat. He would stop by whenever he had the chance. "One of the young women who worked there gave me a box to look into," said Hash. "There were at least fifty or more rings, and she told me these were Ringo's rings. People had sent them to Ringo, and he got to see them, and then took whichever ones he felt were worth taking with him. I was offered my pick; they told me to take four. I chose four rings." Nat did not approve of the girls giving away gifts that were meant for The Beatles, but he turned a blind eye to this because he genuinely liked Hash.

One person who wanted to work for Nat Weiss was Lynne Volkman. Lynne was a regular at Mike Malkin's bar, where Nat often went. Lynne told Mike how much she wanted to work for Nat, so one night he took Lynne to Nat's table and introduced them. Though he was on the spot, Nat kindly gave her his business card and told her to call him. She made the phone call and came into his office. "My interview consisted of him playing the double white album before it came

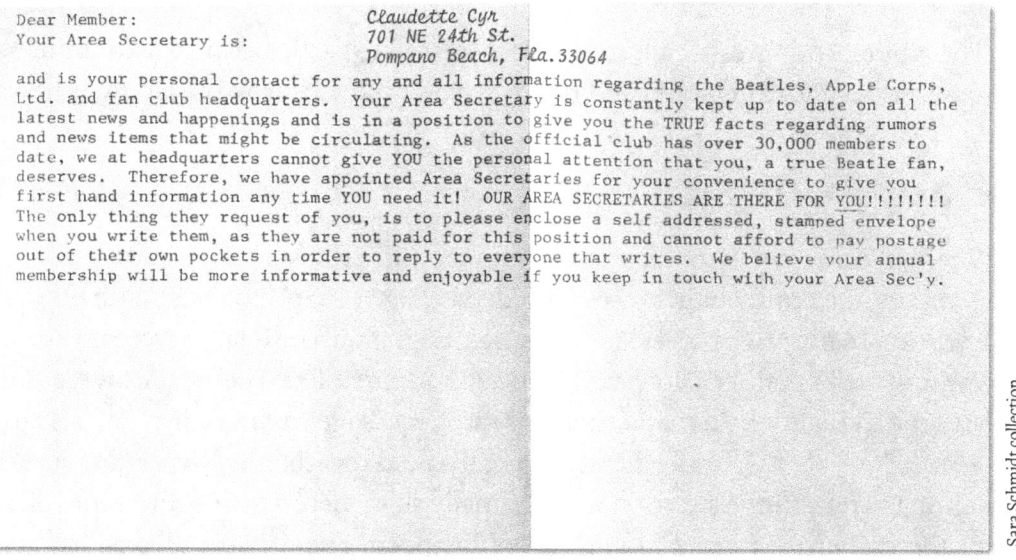

Notice about the area secretary for Florida. Late 1968.

out. He played the entire album, telling me stories, and in the end, he said, 'Do you know how to type?' I said, 'Yeah.' He goes, 'Okay. Start Monday.' My entire life changed at that moment."

The New Double Album

Not everyone had the privilege to hear the new Beatles album before it was released. Besides a few singles, the double album was the first new Beatles music in a full year. The album's official title was *The Beatles*. Fans were ready. As soon as it was released, radio stations began playing cuts. Newspapers covered the pandemonium, as a new wave of Beatlemania began. Radio station WPTR in upper New York State declared a Beatles war against competing stations. Every other song the station played was by The Beatles, mostly from the new album. Fan club members stayed glued to their transistors until they could get their hands on the album with the white cover. Once they got the two-record set, they were in for a surprise. The records included color photos of each Beatle and a large foldout poster of Beatles photos, some in color, and others in black-and-white. Fans promptly pinned these up in fan club offices, bedrooms, and dorms around the country. The other great surprise was the music. One reviewer said,

"The album itself is especially difficult to describe, partly because it contains 30 songs done in various styles and partly because the music on the album is new."

Happy Christmas

When it came time to record the annual Christmas message for fan club members, the boys couldn't record it together. Each Beatle was busy with his own activities. In hindsight it's evident this was a sign that The Beatles were no longer working well together. However, in 1968, it seemed like The Beatles were four busy individuals who'd made time to send a message to their fans. Each Beatle recorded his part separately, and it was all edited together by British disc jockey Kenny Everett. Ringo's section was a comedy skit where he used different voices for the various characters. John recited his poem about two balloons: *Jock and Yono*. The poem was full of wordplay similar to that in John's books. Paul sang an original song called *Happy Christmas*, accompanying himself on an acoustic guitar. George's portion was recorded in Nat Weiss' apartment in New York City. Arma Andon was in the room during the recording, and he remembers, "There were Jock, me, Nat, Mal, George, and Pattie. We arranged for Tiny Tim to come by Nat's to meet George. George and Tiny Tim sang on the Christmas record together." Tiny Tim can be heard playing the ukulele while singing *Nowhere Man*. Mal Evans also was included on the record wishing a Merry Christmas to children everywhere. Arma helped with some sound effects. "We opened the window because we wanted to get some sounds, traffic sounds like sirens or something as a little bit of background for the performance."

For the first time, the U.S. fan club received the Christmas message on a flexi disc instead of cardboard. American Corp pressed the two-sided disc. The Beatles' drawing for the disc's cover had been done by a fan club member from New Jersey, Patti Randall, who went by the nickname "Gripweed." It only appeared on the U.S. version. The 19-year-old had sent in her membership dues for 1969, and, as she told a newspaper: "I also included a few lines asking if they needed an artist and included a sketch I had made of Paul McCartney. They replied by asking me to do the label." It was an honor for a Beatles fan to draw a portrait of the band for the fan club, even though she was not paid. She took the job seriously. "I put six hours of work into the label they selected. I made four different labels," Pattie said.

The sleeve for the U.S. Christmas record was a modified version of the one U.K. fans had received in 1967. It had been designed by Ringo, John, and his young son, Julian. Most of the text from the U.K. release had been removed on the sleeve's back, and "The Beatles 1968 Christmas Record" was printed there.

The U.S. fans were finally getting the membership items they deserved; however, the independent clubs had to pay the ultimate price for it. No one was sure what 1969 would have in store for The Beatles fan club.

The Beatles' 1968 Christmas Record, front and back cover and flexi disc. Sara Schmidt collection

"Copyright 1968 -- Beatles (U.S.A.) Ltd."

In 1968 the Official Beatles Fan Club fan a contest to name Ringo's parrot, but never announced the winning name.

```
*****                NAME THE PARROT CONTEST                    *****
Ringo has a pet, as you can see from this adorable 8 x 10 black and white pic.
It is a colorful psychedelic parrot and we need a name for her.  To enter you
must be a member of our fan club.  If you are not yet a member, send your
$2.50 membership dues along with your entry.  On the outside
of the envelope PRINT in large letters "PARROT CONTEST".
Simply put the name of your choice for this adorable bird
on a slip of paper.  Be sure to put your name and address
on the same sheet and PRINT ALWAYS.  Also, if your member-
ship card is not included, your entry will automatically
be disqualified.  One name only is acceptable with each en-
try.  The winner of this contest will receive an English
copy of the brand new L.P. of the Beatles, not yet re-
leased in England.  HURRY, HURRY, HURRY!!!!!Contest ends
January 1st, 1969.

Hope to hear from you soon and 'til then,

                                   Good wishes to all,
                                   BEATLES (U.S.A.) LTD.


    Sandi                                                    Nancy Applebaum
```

Chapter 7 — Fan Facts and Fan Fiction

It was difficult for Beatles fans to keep up with all of the changes in their favorite four guys' lives. It was especially hard to tell fact from fiction. From concert rumors, new relationships, weddings, a new manager, and a wild story about the death of one of The Beatles, 1969 would become a crazy year for The Beatles and their fans.

Up On The Roof

Ever since The Beatles had stopped touring in 1966, there had been rumors of another live concert. Beatles fan club members never gave up hope. Almost three years later, in early 1969, petitions were still circulating in support of a show. Every time someone offered a million dollars for one Beatles performance, fans held their breath, hoping the boys would say yes. Fans gave up hope for a full tour, but still prayed for one big concert at a stadium.

Their prayers were almost answered. As 1969 opened The Beatles were making a documentary of themselves recording a new album called *Get Back*. They wanted to show themselves rehearsing and recording new songs, and end the film with a big performance. They considered various sites, including the Palladium and Roundhouse theaters in London, the Sahara Desert, the Pyramids of Giza, and the *Queen Elizabeth II* ocean liner. The most serious contender was a Roman amphitheater in Tunisia. The Beatles even sent someone to North Africa to check out the venue. Film director Michael Lindsay-Hogg remembers the plan for the film. "The Beatles were to start playing as the sun came up, and you'd see crowds flocking towards them through the day." But this never happened. As Apple executive Peter Brown put it, "We tried to arrange one last concert, but it was not practicable."

The Beatles perform on the roof of 3 Savile Row. January 30, 1969.

The rumors included the idea that fan club members from around the world would be randomly chosen to sit in the audience. Of course, none of those rumors panned out. In the end The Beatles decided to have what would prove to be their last concert on their own turf.

No one remembers who first thought of performing live on the Apple building's rooftop at 3 Savile Row. Some claim it was John, others say Ringo. Michael Lindsay-Hogg swears the idea was his. Regardless, on January 30, The

Beatles gave a live performance. Even then, it almost didn't happen. "George didn't want to do it," Lindsay-Hogg reported later. "Ringo started saying he didn't really see the point. Then John said, 'Oh fuck it – let's do it.'" On a cold, windy afternoon, The Beatles played a 42-minute set, featuring nine takes covering five songs. There was virtually no advance notice. The audience included The Beatles' inner circle, a few Apple employees, and people who worked down below on Savile Row.

Once the news of the rooftop concert spread to fans in the United States, they hoped this was the start of a wave of new Beatles performances. Maybe the boys would give another show in the States. *The Compleat Beatlemaniac* reported that promoter Sid Bernstein had upped his standing offer to four million dollars. He wanted The Beatles to perform live in New York, Chicago, Los Angeles, and Miami during the summer of 1969. Bernstein even traveled to London in February with the hope of convincing The Beatles in person. Ringo put rumors to rest when he told a reporter, "No more public shows – never. I suppose it's a bit nasty on the fans."

This wasn't what fans wanted to hear. "Oh, this is terrible," said 15-year-old Victoria Adrian. "I kept hoping they'd come back." To others it was disappointing, but not a shock. One fan, Florence Telders, said "It's awful news, but we knew it was coming. Nobody has seen them for years. But as long as they keep making records and films, it will be all right."

Nothing Is Beatleproof

On November 12, 1968, The Beatles' animated movie, *Yellow Submarine*, had its premiere in the United States. The film depicted the all-loving Beatles defeating the evil Blue Meanies. It was held at the six-hundred-and-two-seat theater at the Los Angeles County Museum of Art in California. Tickets were

The OBFC sold color Yellow Submarine *stationery through the club in 1969.*

Above: Yellow Submarine Benefit Première ticket.

The Blue Meanie costume was very popular for Halloween in October 1969.

$25. After the premiere, the film had a slow-release throughout North America. Most fans were able to see it in January, 1969.

Yellow Submarine was well received by the critics. They saw it as a cartoon for all ages that should not be missed. One reviewer said, "Beautiful, bright colors on huge theater screens in a beautiful turning on happy, loving celebration called *Yellow Submarine*." At a time when Walt Disney made the majority of popular animated movies, another reviewer said about the film, "It is as different from Disney cartoons as The Beatles differ from Mickey Mouse."

Reviewers' opinions weren't as important as those of the fans. One fan enjoyed the movie but had to watch it several times to understand it. The fans were no longer screaming during this Beatles movie. That wasn't the only difference. As one observer wrote, "There is definitely an enthusiastic audience in Boston. I saw several young men rapt in adulation. The strange thing is that they all wore their hair Beatle style, had on the same flared pants, wore no ties. Although there were eager young girls, I could see that this particular picture had more appeal for the male fans. There wasn't a shriek during the film."

Yellow Submarine 'Tri-Book' offer sheet included a three-ring binder, a standard size spiral notebook, and a small spiral notebook.

With the popularity of *Yellow Submarine* came a load of Beatles *Yellow Submarine* merchandise for fans to buy. Many of The Beatles fans in 1969 had been too young to buy earlier Beatles merchandise, but now they were happy to spend their money on *Yellow Submarine*-themed alarm clocks, watches, bicycles, Halloween costumes, lunch boxes, puzzles, banks, scrapbooks, and more. Beatles (U.S.A.) Ltd. jumped on this opportunity, offering *Yellow Submarine* stationery with matching envelopes so that pen pals could write to each other in style. The club also sold a set of *Yellow Submarine* school supplies. For $2.25 club members could purchase a three-piece set including the *Yellow Submarine* three-ring binder, a standard size spiral notebook, and a small spiral notebook. According to a club advertisement, "You're sure to be the envy of all those who do not belong to the club and cannot obtain these books."

The Fan Rumor Network

The underground Beatles newspaper *The Compleat Beatlemaniac* was getting tired of all the rumors; they wanted the truth. A tale by a teen writer using the alias "King Alfred" began one February day with a Chicago disc jockey's claim that George Harrison was soon coming to the Windy City.

"King Alfred" heard the claim, and not wanting to miss the chance to see George, the teen writer got on the telephone and began to figure out the scoop. First, he called Joanne Maggio, who was a chapter president in Chicago. She didn't know about George, but cautioned that the DJ who'd reported the rumor had a history of spreading false Beatles stories. Next, "King Alfred" called Vikki Paradiso, the Illinois area secretary, but there was no answer. He began to call newspapers, including the *News* and *The Tribune*, but they could offer no help. At offices at the fan club in New York City and Capitol Records in Los Angeles his queries didn't even get him return calls, but "King Alfred" did not give up.

He tried Pat Kinzer, president of The Official George Harrison Fan Club. She suggested calling George's sister, Louise Harrison Caldwell, and gave him her number. Louise had just moved to New York from Illinois. She said that as far as she knew, George was still in London with no plans of visiting the U.S.

After spending three hours, and a lot of money on long-distance phone calls, "King Alfred" realized he needed a system. The teen asked his fellow Beatles fans to help. "If we had a network of correspondents, we could count on not just during business hours, who could not only replay rumors but help check them, we might have something going," he wrote. But even if "King Alfred" had been able to get other fans to work together as a network, how could anyone ever get to the truth about all the rumors? It was an impossible task.

New Beatles Wives

Since September 1968, American Linda Eastman had been Paul McCartney's live-in girlfriend. That was a subject of gossip among Beatles fans on both sides of the Atlantic. According to one story, Linda had made a $5 bet with Nat Weiss that she was going to marry Paul one day. Fans took this to mean that she was with Paul for his fame rather than for love. But by early 1969, Linda had become a fixture on Paul's arm.

American and British pen pals shared stories of Linda calling the police and cussing at fans. American newspapers reported that Linda was a "gauche, abrasive woman, lacking in charm." Some said Paul's attitude toward fans had changed once Linda entered the picture. He was no longer friendly, or willing to chat and sign autographs. Instead, he was always yelling at the fans outside his front gate. Girls worldwide blamed Linda for this change in the Beatle, and they began to dislike Linda.

The British newspapers said Paul and Linda were heading down the aisle, but the couple refused to confirm or deny marriage rumors. One fan in New York claimed the pair had been married in early January, saying she knew one of the wedding guests. This rumor caused a minor panic among fans, but was quickly put to rest. The other story ended up being true: Linda was pregnant.

Linda's prediction of marrying Paul came true on March 12, 1969. That day, to the disappointment of fans around the world, Paul and Linda were married. Some fans were in tears. "I didn't think he would marry anyone. He didn't need to," one fan lamented.

Linda, Paul, and Heather. March 12, 1969.

Most girls were not upset that he had gotten married, but were curious about his new bride. As Paul and Linda traveled to New York City to start their honeymoon, area fan club members were anxious to see Paul. They were willing to give the new Mrs. McCartney a chance.

Things started well for the girls as they stood outside of Linda's apartment. From time to time, the newlyweds would come out to talk to them, sign autographs, and allow photos. The M.B.E. (Members of The Beatles Empire) president, Rita Angel, said, "Paul signed the Fool on the Hill picture I got from FLMC. I have it framed." Two girls, Carol and Mary Ann Laffin, gave the couple a crystal vase as a wedding gift, and Linda said they liked it. Carol pulled Linda aside and thanked her for making Paul happy. Later Linda came out alone and showed her wedding ring to the girls. It had not been sized yet, and was way too big for her finger. A photographer herself, Linda looked with interest at photographs fans had taken of Paul. Both Paul and Linda were friendly. Rita described one experience: "On March 30, he came home at midnight drunk! Linda had to hold him up. He was singing '*Hey Jude*' all off-key and staggering all over. All the time, he was friendly to us."

On the day Paul and Linda were married, police from Scotland Yard, along with a Golden Retriever named Yogi, raided George and Pattie's house, Kinfauns. Yogi led the police to a case that contained enough marijuana for 120 cigarettes. The police arrested the couple, took them to Esher jail, and released them after each had paid £480 for bail. This news was confusing to fan club members in the United States. Those in George's club questioned why he'd started smoking pot again.

George's mother, Louise, told club members, "George and Pattie do not smoke pot now and haven't since all the fuss years ago. The fact is that had a very small bit of it, but police made more of it." New York-based

Newlyweds Yoko and John. March 1969.

George girl Alfie asked Paul during his honeymoon trip how George was doing after the drug bust. Paul assured her that George would be all right, adding that he had been away from London, and wasn't sure what was up. Most concerning to fans were the rumors that the arrest would prevent George from coming to the United States. Everyone could only wait and see.

If that wasn't enough big news, on March 20, John and Yoko were married on the island of Gibraltar. Since John had already declared his plans to marry Yoko, the wedding did not shock fans. It was a happy time for the groom. "It is just great," John said on his wedding day. "It's been a fantastic buzz all morning." When the press reached out to ex-wife Cynthia, who fans continued to adore, she gave this dignified response, "The wedding comes as a surprise. Of course, I wish them much happiness." Fans in the U.K. showed their dislike for Yoko by calling her ugly. American fans, for the most part, did not understand Yoko's lifestyle choices and ignored her.

Allen Klein

At the start of 1969, John Lennon gave a shocking interview to Ray Coleman for *Disc and Music Echo* in England. In the interview, John stated, "We haven't got half the money people think we have. It's been pie-in-the-sky from the start. Apple's losing money every week because it needs close running by a big businessman. It doesn't need to make vast profits, but if it carries on like this, all of us will be broke in the next six months."

The quote came to fans in the United States through newspapers and fan club newsletters. Fans were surprised to hear that The Beatles did not have money and were going broke. They were unsure what this meant for Apple and, more importantly, for the band. One American who read the interview saw it as his opening to become The Beatles' manager. Allen Klein had a reputation in the music business for being aggressive and not holding back during negotiations. He had plenty of experience managing musicians; he'd managed Sam Cooke, The Rolling Stones, and numerous British Invasion groups. He had always dreamed of managing The Beatles, so he got on the first plane to London to meet with John and Yoko.

Meanwhile, George was trying to ease the fans' fears. "Apple has plenty of money – we all have," he said. "When John said we were losing money, he was talking about giving too much away to the wrong people. We have given too much to charity. We've just been too generous, and that's going to stop." It was true: Apple was losing money. In London, Apple employees and various hangers-on were robbing The Beatles. There was wasteful spending on alcohol, cigarettes, long-distance phone calls, and tabs at luxury restaurants. In addition to Apple's secretaries, guards, tea girls, and cooks, an entire homeless family, some Hells Angels, a man sitting on a file cabinet, and various hippies, all took advantage of The Beatles' hospitality without a second thought. In New York at Nat Weiss' office, and Beatles (U.S.A.) Ltd.'s offices in the Paramount Building, things were too laid back—not as bad as London, but alcohol and marijuana were prevalent among those seeking The Beatles' magic.

Allen Klein. 1969.

Klein had met John and Yoko a few months earlier during the Rolling Stones *Rock and Roll Circus* taping. John and Klein came from similar backgrounds, and could relate to one another. When meeting with the Lennons, Klein showed respect and interest in Yoko's art. Due to this, and reports of Klein's management skills, John asked Klein to be his personal manager. George and Ringo were soon on board. They wanted Klein to manage them personally, and to do it for The Beatles as well. Paul disagreed. He thought his in-laws, the Eastmans, should be leading the band.

But majority ruled, and on February 3, 1969, Allen Klein became The Beatles manager. In 1971 Klein told *Playboy*, "When I got to Apple, things were in shambles: The Beatles and Apple had nothing; they were broke. That's the situation I walked into. There was friction and misunderstanding, and nobody was doing anything about it. I know I get cast as a villain, but if you ask Ringo or George or John, they'll tell you I got them out of trouble, not into it."

Apple employees did not like Klein because he was very blunt and rough. He was a hardworking man who seemed to have The Beatles' best interest at heart, even at the expense of others. John had said, "Apple needs a new broom," and Klein was prepared to make a clean sweep. He dismissed staff and ended all lavish hospitality. He did this in London and New York City, firing employees, and eliminating excess spending.

HEY FAN CLUBBERS!

ART CONTEST WINNERS ANNOUNCED

Any groovy Cat or Kitten can enter this Way-Out contest! All you have to do draw or paint, any Beatle or group picture of the Beatles and send it in with a $1 entry fee and you could be a winner!

LOOK FOR DETAILS ABOUT THE NEXT CONTEST!

YOU COULD BE THE NEXT WINNER!
(IF SIMON DOESN'T ENTER)

**SIMON 6
SOMEWHERE, U.K.**

**SIMON 6
SOMEWHERE, U.K.**

**SIMON 6
SOMEWHERE, U.K.**

National fan club director of Beatles (U.S.A.) Ltd. Sandi Morse kept her job. As Arma recalled, "Sandi was wild, a real piece of work. She was the only one that survived Allen Klein's wrath. He kept her on." The Beatles fan club office moved from Nat Weiss' office to a building down the street at 1700 Broadway where Klein's office and company, ABKCO, were located.

Klein was not a fan club supporter. One employee, Laura Cohen, recalled, "Allen disliked the club. He said there was to be no advertising for the club. He eventually put an end to *The Beatles Book Monthly* being reproduced in *Datebook* magazine. I was asked to be interviewed on BBC radio about the fan club, but Klein would not allow it. I was able to talk about being a Beatles fan, but not about the club. There was a TV show in New York that wanted to do a show on fan clubs, but Allen [Klein] would not allow me to do it either." Thankfully, Klein had his hands full with The Beatles' finances, and his fan club changes did not immediately go into effect. The staff may not have liked Klein, but John, George, and Ringo were happy with the changes, and the money they were making. For the first time, the boys received bank statements, copies of bills, and an explanation of spending. John said, "Klein told me, George, and Ringo almost daily what he was going or trying to do to the point almost of boring us."

A Mystery Trip

Newspaper advertisement for Magical Mystery Tour.

One of the questions fan club members frequently asked was how they could see The Beatles' film *Magical Mystery Tour*. It had played on British television in December 1967, and was seen as a colossal failure—not much plot, and too psychedelic and "out there." American fans learned about the film from magazines, British pen pals, and the booklet that came with the *Magical Mystery Tour* LP. They wanted to see it themselves. It was rumored that a U.S. television network was negotiating to buy the rights, but they never reached an agreement.

Knowing what fans wanted, Arma Andon, Jock McLean, and Nat Weiss came up with a brilliant idea. "Nat talked to Paul, and we decided to tour the film like we would do a group," Arma said. "We'd play colleges. The only two people The Beatles trusted to take the film around was Jock and I. We went to different colleges and covered the nation in 18 months."

Beginning in January, 1969, the *Magical Mystery Tour* film started appearing on university campuses. From Berkeley to the University of Miami, the crazy sixty-minute Beatles film was well received. Typically, there were three showings in one day with each ticket costing $1.50. As Arma recalled, "*Magical Mystery Tour* was real money. We're talking suitcases full of cash. I got held up at gunpoint once in Terre Haute, and they took the money."

The audience wasn't just college students. Beatles fans flocked to it. As Patricia Simmons explained, "We were hyperventilating to see it!" The University of Toledo was having an arts weekend April 18-20. Events included a concert by the rock band Blood, Sweat & Tears, a concept art play, a ballet performance, and three showings of *Magical Mystery Tour*. When the area secretary for Ohio heard the news, she contacted the state's fans. "I looked up information on chartering a bus to take a bunch of us there. I looked in the *Yellow Pages* and got a bunch of members together. We filled the bus. We all split the cost, and it took us to that college, and we watched the *Magical Mystery Tour*."

Arma remembers meeting plenty of fan club members during the tour, and talking to them gave Jock an idea. As Arma recalled, "Those fans couldn't believe they were shaking hands with a guy who shook hands with The Beatles. Jock came up with the idea that we'd have a Q&A after we showed the film. Many people used to hang out for that. Jock came up with the format, and we used it the whole time."

College campuses in 1969 were not always about love and peace. While Jock and Arma were showing The Beatles' film, some campus protests over civil rights and the Vietnam War turned into riots. In one instance, the film could not be shown because the gymnasium where it was to be screened had been burnt down during a riot.

When Arma arrived in North Carolina to show the film at Duke University, he noticed everything in the town was boarded up. Crowds were protesting and state police were containing them. The committee that was showing the film wanted to cancel. They feared what might happen if they allowed people into the gymnasium. Though they'd sold plenty of tickets, they were not going to pay Arma if the film was canceled, and Arma refused to leave without being paid.

"I'll play it for no one," he said. "I'll run it for an hour. Give me my money. I don't care if anybody comes." The committee agreed and even allowed a few students inside. Seeing what was happening, more people started to arrive at the gymnasium doors. "The fucking riot stopped to go to the film!" Arma exclaimed. "They wanted to see it. We sold out the gymnasium! For an hour and a half, the campus was totally silent, totally chilled. This is what The Beatles brought to the table, okay? That superseded everything else. I remember telling John Lennon that story; he got a kick out of it."

The Official Beatles Fan Club

Beatles (U.S.A.) Ltd. continued improving the fan club in 1969. The first change in the New Year was to the club's name. The club became known as The Official Beatles Fan Club, [A Division of Apple Music Publishing Company]. As soon as the change was made members began referring to the club as "OBFC" in newsletters and correspondence.

With Allen Klein making cuts, the fan club staff was down to one director and one assistant director. Newlywed Sandi Morse remained director while the new assistant was a former fan club office receptionist, Merle Frimark. Merle recalled what it felt like to work for The Beatles, "I had to be professional. I was not there as a fan. Working there, we knew the size and scope of what was going on. But sitting in an office building in the heart of Times Square, there was nothing that said that."

Beatles (U.S.A.) Ltd. folded fan club card. 1969.

There was a new position held by Joanne Maggio. The title was The National Chapter Director. She was in charge of making sure all new fan club chapters met the requirements before issuing them their fan club charters. Without the charter, the fan club was not official and would have to close down. She also kept track of any special chapter events such as the party The M.B.E. (Members of The Beatles Empire) held on February 9 to celebrate The Beatles' fifth anniversary on *The Ed Sullivan Show*. She worked from her home in Chicago and was paid $25 a month to cover expenses.

Chapters weren't forming as quickly as The Official Beatles Fan Club hoped. Sandi wanted to have one chapter for each Beatle but was having trouble finding someone to start a Ringo chapter. It was not a lack of interest in the band, but a lack of money. Fans had to spend

Beatles (U.S.A.) Ltd. booklet and poster. 1969.

$2.50 to join The Official Beatles Fan Club and an additional $2.00 to join a chapter. Many members joined one chapter but did not have the funds to participate in any others. A few new chapters that were up and running in 1969 were Harrison-Lennon Followers, The Official Yoko Ono Chapter, PAJOGERI Chapter, Official Apple Chapter, The PAHN Shop, and Walrus Waves. Two fan clubs, The Beautiful Beatles and The Yellow Submarine Crew, were trying to recruit fans to join to get their official charters, but they couldn't find enough, and had to disband.

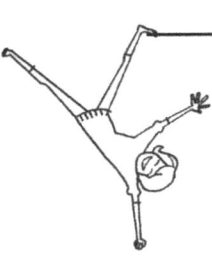

The 30,000 members of The Official Beatles Fan Club received some great items in 1969. For the first time, the cover of the annual book was in full color. Inside were two dozen brand new black-and-white photographs exclusively for the United States official Beatles fan club. During the summer, all current and new club members received a large poster of all four of The Beatles posing at John's new home, Tittenhurst Park. Unknown to anyone at the time, that photo session was The Beatles' last as a group. The poster was named "Revelation." It was an exclusive poster for club members and was only available between July and October. The back of the poster had a short newsletter and gave the names and home addresses of all the area secretaries.

The club offered more photos for sale, including some candid shots. New York City fan club member Kathy Dakis took the snapshots. Kathy was a fan who was often there whenever one of The Beatles came to New York City. She was not particularly close to any of the other club members, but she was friendly. She always had her camera, and her photographs were outstanding. The first of Kathy's photos the club offered was called "Groovy Couple," printed from a snapshot of George and his wife, Pattie. Kathy had taken it in November 1968. It was the first time one of The Beatles' wives appeared in a photograph sold by the club.

The response was overwhelmingly positive, and Beatles fans obviously wanted more wives and candid snapshots. This led to the use of three more of Kathy's photographs for the "Husband and Wife" special. This offering was a set of four postcard-sized color photos. They were the first color photos ever sold through the club, and they were one of the best selling items of that year.

The "Groovy Couple" photo, which was a fan-taken image of George and Pattie in New York, was so popular that postcards of all four couples were offered in 1969.

CHAPTER 7–FAN FACTS AND FAN FICTION

OFFICIAL BEATLES FAN CLUB
A Division of Apple Music Publishing Co. Inc.
P.O. BOX 505, RADIO CITY STATION, NEW YORK, NEW YORK 10019
(FORMERLY BEATLES (USA) LTD.)

<u>ATTENTION ALL BEATLE FANS WITH AN EYE FOR UNIQUELY STYLED PHOTOS!!</u>

"HUSBAND AND WIFE" SPECIAL...

IN GROOVY BEAUTIFUL <u>C O L O R</u> !!!!

We are now offering for the first time ever through the Official Beatles Fan Club, the most beautiful full colored photographs of the Beatles and their mates....

 George and Pattie Harrison
John and Yoko Lennon
Ringo and Maureen Starr
Paul and Linda McCartney

These fabulous 3½ x 5½ colored photos are all very recent and were taken by Miss Kathy Dakis, with the exception of one, the photo of John and Yoko, which was taken by an Apple photographer in Amsterdam. Kathy also took the photo of George and Pattie for our "Groovy Couple" Special!!

These four (4) pics are being sold as a SET <u>ONLY</u> for members <u>ONLY</u>! They are all candid shots and certainly will be an asset to your collection. REMEMBER, THEY ARE IN FULL GLORIOUS COLOR and are UNIQUELY DIFFERENT FROM ANY OTHER PHOTOS SOLD BY US BEFORE. We really promise you a definite surprise with these photographs and this set can be yours for the low, low price of $2.75 for the entire set of 4 pics...(These are not bound as regular pictures)......

TO: HUSBAND & WIFE SPECIAL   MY MEMBERSHIP # IS_____
OFFICIAL BEATLES FAN CLUB
PO Box 505; Radio City Station; New York, N.Y. 10019

I am herewith enclosing $2.75 for one (1) set of 4 pics of the fabulous Beatles and their wives. I am therefore enclosing $_____ for _____ (how many sets?) in cash, check or money order. Please rush my photos to me........

PLEASE SEND THE PHOTOS TO: NAME_____
ADDRESS_____CITY_____STATE_____ZIP

Sara Schmidt collection

Because The Official Beatles Fan Club was selling photographs, they had stringent rules about what fan club chapters could and could not sell. No chapter could sell any photos that came from a magazine. All images sold through a chapter had to be okayed by the area secretary. No fan club member could sell anything bearing the Beatles (U.S.A.) Ltd./OBFC copyright notice, including Christmas records, posters, and books. These items were not allowed to be listed in any chapter newsletter "Swap Shop" section. If a fan club member no longer wanted something she'd received through the fan club, she either gave it away for free, or traded with other fans.

Sadness touched The Official Beatles Fan Club in July 1969, when one of the club's members, 14-year-old Donna Travaligni, passed away from a severe kidney ailment. Knowing how much Donna loved The Beatles and their fan club, her mother traveled to New York City and donated her daughter's camera and typewriter in person at the fan club headquarters. Donna's death touched fans around the country. Gina Graff, area secretary in Philadelphia, took a collection from members, and donated it to the Kidney Foundation in Donna's memory and the name of The Beatles. The club was collecting funds for causes not so close to home as well. The area secretary for Alaska, Janet McNaughton, raised funds for the starving people in Biafra.

Area Secretaries

By the summer of 1969, every state had at least one area secretary. Members were reminded that they were representatives of The Official Beatles Fan Club, and their job was to help prevent rumors from spreading. The fans responded reasonably well to this change, and began addressing questions to the secretary for his or her state, instead of to national headquarters.

The first batch of area secretaries enjoyed their jobs and took their responsibilities very seriously. Anita Thornton got her position as area secretary for Oklahoma after writing to New York headquarters and volunteering for the task. "We had over five hundred fans in Oklahoma," she recalled. "They wanted to know what the boys were up to. They wanted to get autographed pictures. They were just hungry for any tidbit of information."

There were so many fan club members in Pennsylvania that the state had two area secretaries. Julie Alleva, who had the Pittsburgh area, remembered her time with the club fondly. "Once every month or so I got a big brown envelope in the mail from the main club that was full of letters from fans in my area for me to answer. I didn't mind because it was fun, and the fans were all really nice." Richard Keen, the area secretary for Louisiana, recalled how much money he had to spend to fill this volunteer position. "Being an area secretary involved quite a bit of work plus some money at our own expense. None of us were paid for our positions. It was just an honor to volunteer. I personally felt 'payment' when the club officially mailed out the summer poster to all members in America in which my name and address were listed on the back."

Printed 'autographed' photo sent to American Beatles fans who wrote to the club in the U.K.

Kathy Burns, previous president of The Cyn Lennon Beatle Club and area secretary for Minnesota, worked overtime helping Sandi find appropriate candidates for the job. She even asked Kathy to come to New York City and work for the fan club at their offices, but Kathy decided to stay where she was. One of the girls Kathy brought on was Joann Maloney from California. She had met Joann at The Beatles convention she had organized, knew that Joann loved John, and had received a letter from him. Joann would make a great area secretary for her state.

However, the mail Joann received wasn't just from teenage girls. "A substantial amount of mail I got was from young men in the military (Vietnam was ongoing). Most were seeking autographs of The Beatles or tour information. I did not have any direction regarding my response from The Official Beatles Fan Club, nor did they supply stationery or postage for me." Joann did her best to provide those serving in the military the latest news about the boys. Thousands of young men fighting in Vietnam were Beatles fans, and they often passed the letters around, happy for any morsel of information about their favorite group.

All of the area secretaries took their positions seriously and felt like they were doing something special to help The Beatles. Anita Thornton said, "The best part of being an area secretary was just knowing I was part of The Beatles organization, even in that very small way. I was still in high school, and it made me feel so important." Richard Keen was also proud of his job, "I felt honored to have my name listed on the back of the poster and in *Datebook* magazine. The worst part was not getting to see The Beatles. We were told that if they ever did come to our state, we would probably get to see them. But they never did."

For many years, Canada had been in limbo concerning The Official Beatles Fan Club. From 1966 to 1968 Canada bounced between The Official Beatles Fan Club in the U.K. and Beatles (U.S.A.) Ltd. During this time, there was one major fan club in Canada, The Beatles Canadian Enterprises. Joan Thompson ran it from her home in Scarborough, Ontario. When the shakedown of independent clubs occurred, Joan became the "National Secretary" for Canada.

Beatles Canadian Enterprises membership card. 1969.

Instead of having its own official Beatles fan club, and finding area secretaries for each Canadian province, the country got lumped in with the Beatles (U.S.A.) Ltd. One young girl was responsible for all the questions from the fans of her entire country. Joan continued to operate under the name "The Beatles Canadian Enterprises," and she sent a monthly newsletter to keep her country informed.

In 1969 she began looking for provincial area secretaries. Applications came in, and by the end of the year, Joan no longer had to carry the Canadian fan club's burden alone, because each province had its own secretary to help answer the fans' questions.

Waiting For The Beatles

The summer of 1969 was a busy one for The Beatles and their fans. John, Paul, George, and Ringo were back at work at EMI Studios in London. They'd put the *Get Back* album on hold and worked on a new album: *Abbey Road*. Meanwhile, fan clubs in the United States were organizing groups to spend two or three weeks in England. July and August were prime time for the fans to visit, and much to their shock, they were able to catch glimpses of all four Beatles darting in and out of EMI Studios on Abbey Road.

That summer, Barb Fenick changed the name of her independent fan club, Father Lennon's Many Children, to Beatles Rule. She had grown tired of explaining to people that the club was not just for John Lennon, but for all of The

Beatles. She also had been in the hospital with an extended illness and could not get any newsletters out for the first few months of the year. It was time for her independent club to get a fresh start. "The FLMC is dead," she wrote in the August newsletter. "Long live Beatles Rule, a new club conceived with free spirit and dedicated to the ones I love." The club had two hundred members, with most claiming Paul as their favorite. Because it was an independent club, photo sales were a hot commodity. Color photos sold for 35 cents each and black-and-whites were 20 cents each.

George running past fans at EMI Studios. July 1968.

That July, Barb, Susan "Richie" Lindgren, Sarah Nolte, and Jeri Glaeser came to London, representing Beatles Rule. Another Beatles Rule club member, Sue Bujnousky, came to London with her family at the same time. Also present that summer were Pat Kinzer, Patricia Simmons, and Lynn Berr from The Official George Harrison Fan Club. Other American fan club members present, including Becki Walgren, Fern Beckler, and Mar Young, wrote about their experiences in various fan club newsletters.

They spent a lot of time standing outside EMI Studios on Abbey Road behind the red barred fence. If they were fast enough, the girls could squeeze through the crowd and into the car park when one of The Beatles' cars drove in. "We saw all The Beatles arriving at EMI," recalled Patricia. "Normally they would just rush in and rush back out. They were not stopping to talk like they used to." The fans quickly figured out The Beatles' recording schedule, and what time to arrive each day. The girls were quite surprised when they first saw George Harrison. His hair had grown very long, and he tied it back with a ribbon. John and Yoko arrived every day in a white 'Rolls,' and would quickly dart inside the building. John tried to protect Yoko from the massive swarm of fans. She was tiny and pregnant, and he was scared she might get hurt. When they got to the top of the steps, John would occasionally do something funny, like yelling "Viva la France!" to a group of German fans.

Sometimes Paul would drive his Mini into the studio parking lot, and other times, he would walk from his home nearby. One day he was wearing a pink suit, and one of the American fans handed him three pink flowers that matched. All the fans crowded around him, snapping photos and asking questions until he safely made it to the top of the steps. Barb Fenick, who loved Paul the most, watched the entire thing in a daze. Sadly, Barb was unable to speak to Paul one-on-one during that summer.

Paul was very distant that summer. As Patricia remembers, "We saw Paul at EMI, and he was a real butthead because at that time fans were really cruel to Linda. They were writing all over the gates at Cavendish all these mean things about her. So, they lumped all the fans together. They'd arrive at EMI and would have the gates immediately closed so we couldn't get in the parking lot. He and Linda would get out of the car and flip us off. I thought, 'Hey! I didn't do anything! Don't lump me in with those other people!' but I could not open my mouth to say anything. I don't think it was a good time for any of them, but we were having fun with our friends."

Some of those fun times occurred outside the red gates of EMI after The Beatles went inside. Roadie Mal Evans or assistant Kevin Harrington would occasionally come out and talk to the fans. Other times the girls would entertain one another with funny impersonations or jokes. Memories were made for everyone present on Abbey Road that summer.

The Official Beatles Fan Club's assistant director in New York, Merle Frimark, was also in London in July, but she was not standing outside of the gates of EMI. She was inside of the studio with The Beatles, taking photographs the fan club would sell. Derek Taylor set things up for her, and she was ready to take pictures of The Beatles; however, her job was postponed when John and Yoko were hospitalized in Scotland after being injured in a car accident. While Merle waited for him to come back to London, she took advantage of the time to learn as much as she could from Derek. "Finally, Derek called me and said, 'You're going tomorrow.' I said, 'Okay, great.'" Merle recalled.

"So off I went to Abbey Road Studios, and they were putting some finishing touches on stuff, and I got some photos, and they were very, very nice." She took a variety of photographs of The Beatles while they were working at EMI. There are only a few pictures from the making of *Abbey Road*, and Merle was one of the only outsiders allowed in. Unknown to anyone on the outside, The Beatles were not on the best terms that summer. Merle said, "At the time there was no way of even having an inkling there were any problems within the band." However, when she looks back at her photographs years later, she notices something different. "I see distance. I see them all in different places, and they didn't seem to be communicating that well with each other. But I was there to do a job. When you are a young teenager, you're not privy to much. Looking back, though, the pictures certainly tell a story. You can see the distance. I didn't feel it, but I could see it. John had just gotten back from his accident. He had stitches under his chin. He had a beard. I bought him some white flowers, and he appreciated that." While she took photos of all The Beatles, The Official Beatles Fan Club in New York chose Merle's John Lennon photos to sell to the American fans. John had his full beard, white outfit, sandals, and love beads. He was sitting down, playing the guitar. According to the fan club's advertising, John posed for these photographs specifically for the American fans. They are fabulous, fantastic, and original. Three black-and-white 8" x 10" glossy photos were sold as "The John Bonus" for $1 each.

Fan club members who spent their time in London did not know what was happening inside the studio, so they broke off to do some sightseeing with a Beatles twist. Susan "Richie" Lindgren, Barb Fenick, and Jeri Glaeser went to Trafalgar Square one afternoon to attend an Indian religious festival. While they were there, they happened to see Pattie Boyd. The three American girls went to speak to her and asked her if she would like to

The Official Beatles Fan Club special photo offer for the 'John Luvers of America' along with the photos that could be purchased.

Maureen and Ringo at the reception for Give Peace a Chance. July 3, 1969.

purchase a Beatles Rule badge to "support her husband." Pattie told them that she did not have any money with her. The girls explained to her that it was just a joke, and Pattie took the button and pinned it right on her dress.

On August 3, Susan "Richie" Lindgren and Barb Fenick traveled to Surrey to find Ringo's house. When they got there, they discovered the gate was unlocked, so they walked up to the front door and knocked. Ringo's wife, Maureen, answered. She was wearing a bathrobe, and her short, blonde hair was wet from a fresh wash. They wished her a happy birthday and showed her the August 1969 issue of *The Beatles Book Monthly* that had her photo inside. When they asked about Ringo, his wife told them it was Sunday, his day off, but he'd be out of the bath in two hours. Two hours later, the two were knocking on the door once again. Ringo answered, wearing a bright pink bathrobe and sandals. Ringo thanked them for the gifts they had brought for him and Maureen. He told them that he and his wife were going into London to see Hank Snow at the Palladium that night to celebrate her birthday. They chatted with the drummer for about twenty minutes, then returned to London, where they immediately bought tickets to see Hank Snow. Ringo and Maureen looked surprised, but pleased, to see them that night.

On August 4, Pat Kinzer and Patricia Simmons found themselves back on familiar ground. The two girls and their friend, photographer Lynn Berr, had once again arranged to speak to George at his home, Kinfauns. When they first arrived, they saw George's chauffeur, Terry Doran, washing George's Mercedes. Lynn rang the bell, and the housekeeper answered. She told them that George was busy getting ready to go to work and could not speak to them. Pat explained that she was the president of his fan club in America, and that George was expecting her. The housekeeper left and returned to say that he would see them for a few minutes. When George came to the door, he was wearing flared blue jeans, a blue pinstriped shirt, a black jacket, and black shoes. "I knew he was in a rush, so I started to give him all the gifts and notes from various people," said Pat. One of the things she handed him was a letter from a club member named Pegi. In her letter Pegi asked George for permission to write a book about him and Pattie. Pat remembers, "He said she couldn't write a book about them because she didn't know that much about them. He said he couldn't even write a book about himself, let alone someone else try to do it." Besides that one upset, George was pleasant and signed whatever was given to him, including postcards, magazines, scraps of paper, and a birthday card that the president had designed herself. She made copies of this card and sent it to fan club members on their birthdays as a special greeting from George.

Photo of George taken by Lynn Berr when she, Pat Kinzer, and Patricia Simmons met him at Kinfauns.

The entire time Lynn was snapping photographs, and Patricia Simmons was also using a camera. As she explained, "I got a brainstorm to rent a movie camera. When we went to George's house, we talked to him for a little bit then I started filming him. I was trying to back up a little bit to get more of him in the film, and I almost fell backward in the rosebushes. I was mortified!"

George was in a rush and was unable to spend as much time with the girls as he had the previous year. "He apologized because he only had a few minutes," Patricia said. "George had to get to EMI. He was just very, very sweet and very, very nice. He signed autographs for us and let us take pictures. When he left for Abbey Road, we hightailed it back there because we knew they were recording."

Copy of the fan club birthday card autographed by George.

Sue Bujnousky was supposed to travel to Esher to find George's house with Barb and the other girls from Beatles Rule, but there was some miscommunication, and she ventured out alone on August 8. Like the girls four days earlier, the first thing Sue noticed when she arrived at Kinfauns was Terry Doran standing outside by the garage. She decided to talk to him. While they were talking, someone of Indian descent came and handed Terry something to give to George. While this was going on, Sue stepped back and got out of the way. Terry went inside the house with the package, and soon after, George came out to thank his friend. Sue stood in the shadows, silent. George noticed her and asked, "And what are you doing here?" Sue answered, "Oh, I'm just lurking about." George liked her answer, and allowed her to take his photo. He told her he had been re-mixing tapes for the new album. It was scorching hot that August afternoon, and Sue asked George for a glass of water. Much to her surprise, George said, "Sure. Come on in."

When they got to the kitchen, he gave her the choice of apple cider, orange soda, milk, or water. She said, "I'll take anything, as long as it's wet!" He got out a can of orange soda and began to struggle to get the lid off. Sue recalled, "It was really funny – there he was struggling with this can, and I'm just standing there next to him like I'd known him for years. He poured the soda into one of the tallest glasses I've ever seen. I thought I'd be scared silly, but I felt perfectly natural there. I couldn't believe he was so human and nice and natural."

The only Beatle they hadn't met was John. Many fans were intimidated by the Lennons and gave them their space that summer, but Barb and Sarah were brave and traveled to Weybridge to find Ringo's old house. They had learned that was where John and Yoko were temporarily staying. Once they found the place, they joined a few other fans in the driveway. After two hours in the hot sun, they decided to get a closer look. "We made it to the door, and brave Barb knocked very lightly on the door," Sarah Nolte wrote for the Beatles Rule newsletter. "Silence. We could hear people moving around. Suddenly the window above us opens, and a voice rings out, 'Piss off, will you?!!' Well, the tones could only have been those of John. I saw everyone in the driveway looking up. We started to walk back. When I turned around, I saw John knocking on the window, telling us to leave. We got out to the road and around the fence so John couldn't see us."

Third Rally At Shea

For the third time, New York area fan club members met outside of Shea Stadium for a Beatles Rally. As in previous years, fans made signs and sang Beatles songs. They also played Beatles songs on a tape recorder. Many of the fans wore hand-made Beatles clothes, including one fan, Evy Salas, who had her mother make a green and blue jacket that looked identical to the one Paul had worn during his visit to New York in May of 1968. Evy had also painted a beautiful painting of Paul playing the guitar. These fan club members wanted the baseball fans to know that Beatlemania was alive and well in 1969. For the first time, they bought tickets to the baseball game and took the rally indoors. Beatles fans sat in the stands with signs bearing slogans like: "Long Live Lennon," "Beatles Remain Supreme!," and "I Love Paul."

New York area Beatles fans gather at Shea Stadium to celebrate the third anniversary of The Beatles' last performance there. Fans painted posters, wore custom clothes, and sang songs from the stands during the ball game.

Abbey Road Album

It wasn't long before listeners could hear the album The Beatles had been working on. On October 3, 1969, much to fans and critics' delight, *Abbey Road* was released. The album was playing on turntables in college dorms, high schoolers' bedrooms, family living rooms, and FM radio stations. Some FM stations played the entire record. Everyone loved *Abbey Road*. "If anyone doubts The Beatles as musicians, *Abbey Road* should prove they are among the top musicians in the rock field as well as being the top vocalists," said one reviewer. No one could have guessed that the album was the last one the group would make together. The general feeling was that they were an even stronger band than they'd been on previous albums. "On *Abbey Road*, The Beatles are very together as a group. Yet each member is a distinct individual."

Newspaper advertisement for the new Beatles Abbey Road album, released October 3, 1969.

Fan club members were proud of the new album, and especially proud of George. Everyone celebrated with him when his song, *Something*, was released as a single. One Beatles Rule member wrote in the December newsletter, "The album is a beautiful piece of work, something a Beatle fan can say, 'Here, listen to this!' Some of the most beautiful guitar work I've ever heard is on the album, along with one of George's most beautiful songs."

Paul is Dead Rumors

Not long after the release of *Abbey Road*, the craziest Beatles rumor began to spread. Fans all over the country wanted to know if Paul McCartney was dead or alive. The same week *Abbey Road* arrived at record shops, the story appeared in a few university newspapers. According to the rumor Paul had died in an accident in 1966 and had been replaced by a look-alike.

On October 12, Detroit disc jockey Russell Gibb read one of the articles on the air, then spent two hours listing clues found in Beatles songs and album covers. The contention was that Paul had indeed died. Among the clues was the *Abbey Road* album cover depicting the band going to bury the barefoot Paul. Then there was the hand over Paul's head on the *Sgt. Pepper*'s cover: the Welsh sign of death. Paul wore a black carnation on his lapel on the *Magical Mystery Tour* LP's cover, and John's song *Glass Onion* said 'the walrus was Paul.' However, the most fascinating clue was when played backward on a turntable, it sounded as if *Revolution 9* from *The Beatles* (white album) had The Beatles saying, "Turn me on, dead man." When a clue wasn't there in the original article, Gibb would make one up right on the spot. He got help from a guy named Tom who called into the station.

The news spread from Detroit to the rest of the country through newspapers, television, and radio. These rumors put many Beatles fans in a tizzy. Fan club members were writing their area secretaries, demanding answers. Sympathy cards, flowers, and memorial gifts poured into the fan club office in New York City.

WMCA New York button given out during the Paul is Dead rumors. (Ted Amoruso collection)

Throughout the fall, Paul's supposed death was the hot topic among Beatles friends, giving fan clubs a reason to hold meetings. Fans would bring their albums and scour the covers for "Paul is dead" clues. They closely examined the poster from the double album, and gave careful scrutiny to the lyrics of all Beatles songs recorded after 1966.

Most of these fans did not believe the rumors, but they enjoyed the game of looking for clues. Many thought The Beatles had been preparing this as a publicity stunt, and tried to solve the mystery the boys had created for their fans. There were a few fans who believed Paul had died and been replaced. One New Jersey club circulated a petition they intended to send to Apple, demanding that Paul make a public appearance. One chapter president, Mary Donnelly, stated, "If he is dead, the American public should be told." She offered to interview the musician to determine if it was indeed him. The rumor's effects went far beyond the fan clubs. Two hundred college students gathered in Boston to discuss the topic, and almost twice as many gathered at Northeastern University for the same reason.

Mourning believers found themselves at odds with amused skeptics. This ripped the once-strong fabric connecting all Beatles fans. One Alabama fan, Ed, wrote to his area secretary, Bobby Hudgins, saying that he knew Paul had died. Ed listed the clues he felt proved it. Bobby wrote, telling Ed it was all made up, and he refuted some of the evidence. With Ed still unconvinced, Bobby tried to find a middle ground. He wrote "It is true, however, that when you play '*Revolution 9*' backward, the voice is saying 'Turn me on dead man'; it is probably some of John's foolishness. I think you know as well as I how crazy he can be at times."

Some clubs believed the hoax was annoying and a waste of time, a publicity stunt, unconnected to The Beatles. They thought U.S. radio stations were to blame. Barb Fenick from Beatles Rule wrote in the December 1969 newsletter, "The radio stations are using the airwaves with preknowledge that they were just playing with their eager listeners. I don't like to be played." She refused to report on the story or reprint any of the clues. She wrote, "I find it a sad state of affairs when supposedly intelligent college students take to playing records backward, upside down and inside out to 'prove' the death of the most talented and famous pop personality in this decade."

Pat Kinzer briefly reported on the story for The Official George Harrison Fan Club but wanted members to know she was not happy about the rumor. "This whole thing is getting on my nerves," she wrote in the *Harrison Herald*. "Every time you turn on the radio, they've got another rumor!"

No one was as annoyed as the national director of The Official Beatles Fan Club, Sandi Morse. Inundated with phone calls from newspapers, colleges, high schools, disc jockeys, and, of course, fans, Sandi couldn't attend to her work because the telephone wouldn't stop ringing. "They just keep calling in and calling in," Sandi told Howard Smith at WABC FM radio, "asking 'Is Paul dead?' 'Is Paul dead?' and I keep saying 'no, no, no!' There's so much controversy about it that I don't know how to handle it anymore."

Sandi's battle with the rumor began with a fan calling to ask if Paul was all right. Later callers asked if he'd died, and one fan claimed there'd been a look-alike contest to replace him. Paul had died two years prior, said the caller, and someone had taken his place. "I've seen Paul," Sandi told the caller. "I know he's alive."

Sandi began to laugh at this insane rumor, but three weeks later she was no longer laughing. She told one newspaper, "I'm flipping out with all these calls. My God, Paul is alive. We were just talking to him. He's such a groovy person, why are all these rumors going around?"

Sandi was accustomed to crazy Beatle rumors, but this one had gotten out of hand. Sandi thought she knew why The Beatles were always targeted. "They come out with such unusual albums with unusual lyrics and unusual jackets. In my opinion, everyone seems to copy them so that there is a bit of jealousy going on. They are so fantastic that everything they do, people have to read into it. They just can't accept it as it is."

The bottom line from The Beatles' headquarters was that Paul was alive and well. If fans wanted to believe Paul had died, they were free to do so, but it would not change reality. They could examine album covers and search for clues, but Paul remained alive.

Sandi was fed up with rumors. She had a message for club members: "They are the greatest musicians of today and should be left as that and not public figures because they have their own lives."

Sandi Goes to London

In the second week of December, Sandi traveled to London. When she went into the Apple offices on 3 Savile Row, she was treated as a vital Apple staff member. On December 8, Sandi saw a press screening of Ringo's movie with Peter Sellers, *The Magic Christian*. On the 15th, she went to the Lyceum Ballroom and saw The Plastic Ono Band with George in concert. She also attended a reception for the Apple group Badfinger. Paul had written their newly released song, *Come and Get It*.

According to Sandi, the highlight of her trip was when she met all four Beatles at the Apple offices. They discussed the U.S. fan club. Sandi wrote, "The Beatles were more than cooperative during our meeting and were more than interested in the great job the area secretaries are doing on behalf of the club." She may have met with all four Beatles together, but it's not likely. Paul had not been in the Apple offices for quite some time. Sandi could have spoken with John, George, or Ringo separately, however, because they would regularly come and go from the offices. It was essential to keep the image of The Beatles as friends. To avoid divisive issues Sandi told U.S. fans a white lie.

Area Secretaries' Apple Cubes

Sandi informed the area secretaries and chapter presidents that she'd brought back many fantastic items for the fans. One of these items was a surprise special

The "autographed" cube (mostly likely signed by Mal Evans or Neil Aspinall) sent exclusively to area secretaries and chapter presidents. December 1969.

Christmas gift. It was a small cardboard Apple Records cube. On three sides, there were images of a Granny Smith apple. One side was a full apple, the next had two bites taken out, and the third had the apple's core. The bottom had all four Beatles' autographs. The top of the cube said, "A Merry Christmas and Happy New Year From Apple." Sandi told the area secretaries in a letter included with the gift, "It was indeed a pleasure having them sign all of your Apple Box Christmas Cards."

The fifty-five area secretaries and chapter presidents loved the cube. One of them, Richard Keen, explained, "For Christmas, we were sent a special gift from The Beatles themselves: their autographs. This was our 'payment.'" Vikki Paradiso recalled, "The area secretaries got a special cardboard Apple Box signed by the boys (supposedly)." When Beatles autograph experts look at the signatures today, they believe that they are not the genuine autographs of John, Paul, George, or Ringo. Nonetheless, with so few of these cubes given out, the area secretary Apple Christmas Cube is still a highly collectible piece of Beatles memorabilia.

This Is To Wish You

As the decade ended, The Beatles had one last treat for their fan club members. As they had the previous year, each band member recorded his part of the traditional fan club Christmas record on his own time. Each section was recorded during the fall of 1969.

John and Yoko made their part on the grounds of their new home, Tittenhurst Park. Listeners can hear the autumn leaves crunch under their feet while they talk about peace. Much of what they recorded for the Christmas record was similar to the experimental LPs they had released earlier that year. However, this time they added a bit of humor, making it more enjoyable. Ringo recorded his bit at his home in Weybridge. He sang a song he had composed, and plugged *The Magic Christian*. George recorded his part inside the Apple offices in London. He only spoke one line, taking only six seconds. Richie Unterberger makes a good point in his book, *The Unreleased Beatles*, when he writes, "If he hadn't identified himself as George Harrison, some fans might have wondered if he was on the record at all." Paul recorded his section at his home on Cavendish Avenue in London. He sang a catchy McCartney original, accompanied on an acoustic guitar. It was called *This Is To Wish You*. Kenny Everett produced the record and included a snippet of The Beatles song *The End*.

For the only time, the U.K. and U.S. fan clubs received the same Christmas flexi in the same sleeve. The American club received a shipment of jackets directly from England. It stated the "Official Beatles Fan Club of Great Britain" on the back. The front cover was a psychedelic photograph Ringo had taken, and his four-year-old son Zak drew the picture on the back cover. The double-sided flexi disc did not come from England, but the United States. It had been pressed by Americom Corp. The record had a drawing of The Beatles on the front, once again designed by Patti "Gripweed" Randall. To get new members to join the club and get the album, Sandi wrote this in *Datebook*, "It is plastic, unbreakable and two-sided plus this collector's item has a groovy Beatles label."

Fan club members liked it. Barb Fenick wrote in the *Beatles Rule* newsletter, "I think my favorite parts were Mary's baby cry and Paul kind of talking to her. I also like Paul's fantastic sexy little song ... but then some people say I'm biased." Fan club members did not want to admit it, but the Christmas record showed that the boys were drifting apart. John was performing in concert with Yoko, not The Beatles. George played with another group for awhile, and temporarily quit the band. With each Beatle doing his own thing, the four of them could not find the time to record the Christmas message together. Fans were afraid that The Beatles were no longer friends. One fan, Richard Goldman, found the disc depressing and joyless. Later he reflected, "The 1969 [record] was sad because we knew 'the dream was over.' There are some cute, clever, and wonderful Beatle moments on there, but you could just sense they hated each other."

As the new decade opened fan club members were uncertain about what was in store for The Beatles. The fan base was not slowing down. More than

30,000 people were in The Official Beatles Fan Club, and new, younger members joined every day.

The Beatles' Happy Christmas 1969 fan club record, front and back cover and flexi disc.

Chapter 8 — The Autumn for Fan Clubs

The new decade started with great hope for The Beatles, but 1970 ended in despair and confusion.

The Official Beatles Fan Club Continues To Grow

As 1970 began, The Official Beatles Fan Club was in a good place. With well over 30,000 members, Sandi Morse continued as the club director. Her new assistant was Rusty Rahn. In her mid-20s, Rusty was a little older than the average fan, but she loved The Beatles and was a perfect addition to The Official Beatles Fan Club. Sandi and Rusty were a power team, striving to make the fan club the best. The power team also had a top-notch group of employees at the fan club office. Officers of the The M.B.E. (Members of The Beatles Empire), Laura Cohen, and Rita Angel were back working for the club, as was Ida Langsam, and two boys, Ivan Kral and Bruce. Their job was to open the letters, fulfill all of the orders, and stuff envelopes with fan club advertisements.

The Official Beatles Fan Club office was located at 1700 Broadway, in a suite one floor below Allen Klein's office. The first person people saw in the Apple suite was a receptionist behind a glass partition who buzzed in any guests. Straight ahead was an open area with desks for the Apple secretaries. The fan club office was located on the left, with a secretary outside the door. On one side was an empty office, and on the other was Apple promotion manager Pete Bennett's office.

As 1970 opened the fan club got a new logo: a drawing of The Beatles inside of an apple. It had been drawn by Patti "Gripweed" Randall, the same artist whose art had adorned the Christmas flexi discs. Now she had title of Official Beatle Fan Club Artist. Her new logo was on all 1970 membership cards.

Beatles 1970 fan club membership card front face and inside folded open. The new logo was designed by Beatles fan Patti 'Gripweed' Randall.

CHAPTER 8–THE AUTUMN FOR FAN CLUBS

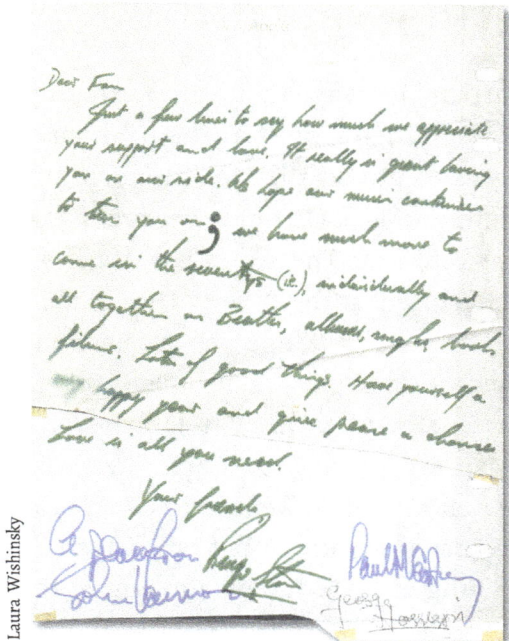

Sandi wrote in *Datebook*, "We felt it was time to get rid of the old Beatles image and try something up-to-date and groovy."

Along with the new membership card, fan club members also received the 1970 Official Beatles Fan Club book. The book had all the important events in The Beatles' story in chronological order and photographs. Sandi told club members, "The pictures are new and personally approved for our use by The Beatles themselves." Sandi had her choice of two Beatle letters thanking fans for support, one from Paul and the other from Ringo. The one supposedly written by Paul was her choice. Both of the signatures from these letters went inside the Beatles book for that year.

Above left: The original, autographed, draft letter for the 1970 Beatles Fan Club welcome letter.
Top: The 1970 Beatles Fan Club booklet. Bottom: The final letter sent to fan club members.

Ringo Starr in the United States

Ringo and Maureen (left) at the Los Angeles premiere after-party for The Magic Christian. *January 29, 1970.*

Ringo Starr and his wife, Maureen, flew to the United States in January 1970. Their primary purpose was to attend the U.S. premiere of Ringo's film, *The Magic Christian*. The premiere was at the Four Star Theatre in Los Angeles, with an after-party at the Beverly Hills Hotel. While in Los Angeles, Ringo was a guest on the TV show *Laugh-In*, and he made other appearances around town. On January 30, Ringo, Maureen, and U.S. Apple Records executive Ken Mansfield went to Las Vegas to see Elvis in concert. Ringo felt embarrassed when the King of Rock 'n' Roll announced to the audience that he was there, but that didn't stop the two musicians from chatting for two hours after the show.

Before heading back to London, the couple spent one day, February 2, in New York City. While there, Ringo made an unexpected appearance at *The Official Beatles Fan Club* office. Many fans questioned if the boys still cared about their fan club, so Ringo's visit spoke volumes. Barb Fenick wrote about it in the *Beatles Rule* newsletter, "This will dispel what some have said about the guys NEVER going up there."

Two of the most surprised fan club employees were Rita Angel and Laura Cohen. These two girls not only worked for the club but also ran The M.B.E. (Members of The Beatles Empire). "Ringo came into the office, and he was smoking a cigarette," Laura remembers. "He put the cigarette out on the floor. Rita made a circle around that cigarette butt and told no one to touch it." Fan club materials were stacked on the shelf. Ringo looked through them, then put them back where he'd found them. Rita scooped them up and held them because Ringo had touched them. Ringo was kind to everyone and showed a genuine interest in the club. Laura recalls, "Ringo was very sweet."

John Lennon's Haircut

While Ringo was in the United States, John Lennon was in Denmark with Yoko and her daughter, Kyoko. On a snowy day, the three got short haircuts so they could blend in with crowds. News of John's short hair caused controversy among media and fan club members. Many commentators wondered if a Beatle with short hair would start a new fashion trend. Fan club members found it confusing. "Hmp. He was proclaiming 'hair peace,' and now he gets it cut. Sort of hypocritical, don't you think?" one member

John and Yoko with their shocking new short haircuts.

of The Official Paul McCartney Chapter said. While in Los Angeles, Ringo was cornered by a reporter who asked about his bandmate's hair. "I've only seen photos of it. It's okay, I guess."

Illinois Fan Club Members Celebrate Six Years Of The Beatles

Until John got together with Yoko, Vikki Paradiso had been the president of The John Lennon Fan Club. She then became the area secretary for the state of Illinois, which had five hundred fan club members. Joanne Maggio had changed her Beatles' Love Association to The Official Paul McCartney Chapter. Since she was also located in Chicago, Joanne and Vikki paired up twice a year for a big Beatles fan gathering. On February 7, 1970, six years after The Beatles arrived in the United States, a meeting took place at the Executive House Hotel in Chicago.

Joanne Maggio and Vikki Paradiso at the fan club gathering to celebrate six years since The Beatles came to America.

Vikki and Joanne advertised that they would show The Beatles movie *Help!* They sold tickets, but failed to raise the necessary $450 they needed to show the film legally. Sandi Morse in New York tried her best to allow them to show any Beatles film to the fans, but she did not have any luck. Nonetheless, the meeting was set to start at 9 AM. By 8 AM, one hundred and fifty Beatles fans were trying to get inside the ballroom. Most were extremely disappointed by the film cancellation, and they wanted their money back.

About half of the fans stayed to see what would happen. The leaders tried to get a discussion going, but no one wanted to talk. One fan joked, "Let's have a John and Yoko party! Everyone strip!" This statement made everyone laugh. Vikki attempted a Beatles sing-along, but not even a chorus of *Yellow Submarine* could rouse the crowd. Joanne was disappointed by these attitudes. "These are Beatles fans?" She complained in The Official Paul McCartney Chapter newsletter, *Luv n Stuff*. "These were people celebrating the sixth anniversary of The Beatles landing in America? It was pitiful."

By noon, only fifty fans were left. Organizers sold photographs of The Beatles, but many of these were stolen by attendees. The remaining fans were given the opportunity to join The Official Beatles Fan Club's various chapters, and organizers raffled off a large Paul McCartney poster. They led fans in a Beatles trivia contest. Finally they brought out a cake to celebrate National Beatles Day, but Vikki did not feel like celebrating anything. She felt disappointed and discouraged. The area secretary decided to stop holding Beatles gatherings for members in Illinois. Joanne said she would continue to have them, but only for members of The Official Paul McCartney Chapter.

Older vs. Younger Members

Fan club members were aware of the friction with The Beatles, particularly between John and Paul. They blamed Allen Klein and John Eastman, though some put responsibility for the rift on Yoko and Linda. In early 1970 it was finally becoming clear that each Beatle had his individual projects, and the band was not recording together. Rumors of conflict between John and Paul put a dark cloud over the club, and soon their rifts spread to the club members.

Six years had passed since the start of the first Beatles fan club. Most of the original members were now between the ages of 19 and 23. Some were in college, others working full time. Some were already wives and mothers. Most had quit the fan clubs for more adult things, but plenty of first-wave fans remained active and involved in The Beatles fan world.

By 1970, a second wave of Beatles fans was joining the clubs. The Official Beatles Fan Club members' average age was 16, which meant she'd been only 10 when The Beatles first hit the scene. Most fans were females, but more boys were joining than ever before. Some boys were area secretaries and chapter presidents.

The original fans felt that the younger ones weren't capable of the same enthusiasm. These newcomers were too young to remember The Beatles on *The Ed Sullivan Show*, and they had never seen a Beatles concert. One first-wave fan club member explained in the *Luv n Stuff* newsletter, "They don't know. They can't feel what we do because they didn't live it. No matter how much they insist they understand, it's different."

Another issue was the attitude both groups had about The Beatles' wives. The older fans still loved Cynthia and Jane and disliked Yoko and Linda. Younger fans knew only Yoko and Linda and were willing to accept them. Joanne Maggio said, "Take Yoko. We in the old faction don't approve of her. But the 12-and-13-year-olds, they're all for her."

The younger fans did not like the know-it-all attitudes of many of their older counterparts. Younger fans had a lot of love for the band, but the older girls found much of their behavior to be childish. "They put Paul on a pedestal," said a first-wave member of The Official Paul McCartney Chapter. "They see him as pure and bubbly and innocent. They even call him 'Paulie.' God! He'd die if he heard that. They forget he is a grown man and can make mistakes, which he has." Some chapters stopped meeting because their meetings had become nonstop arguments. Naturally, several younger fans broke away from their original chapters and started their own.

New Fan Club Chapters

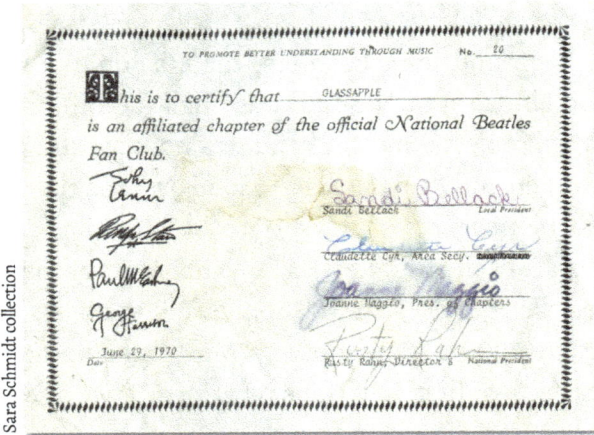

The Glassapple Chapter fan club charter and membership card. 1970.

One such club was The Glassapple Chapter out of Southern Florida run by 15-year-old Sandi Bellack. Sandi knew that many kids in her high school loved The Beatles, so she decided to start a fan club chapter. She recalled, "I would type newsletters on a typewriter and send them out. I did it totally because I enjoyed it." The boys and girls in her club were mostly local fans, and they held regular meetings. "We would have meetings, and we would show each other new pictures," Sandi recalled. "If someone had an eight-by-ten black-and-white picture of Paul McCartney and someone else liked it, they would trade. We would sing Beatles songs. We had one member that was a guitar player. She was a huge John Lennon fan and very funny. We would sit around in a circle, making jokes and singing. We all had a really good time."

Kum Back was one of the earliest bootleg Beatles albums available.

One of their exciting moments was meeting Andrea Dresner. In Miami in 1964, Andrea's father Buddy had been assigned to The Beatles' security guard detail. Buddy took them to his home to meet his family and eat a home-cooked meal. Sandi had set up an interview with Andrea that would appear in the newsletter. Sandi wanted to ask Andrea about the day The Beatles had visited her house.

"We went to the Dresners' house," Sandi said. "I saw George Harrison's shirt that he gave her. She also had two letters, one handwritten by Paul and the other from George. They thanked Buddy and said how it was great to meet his family."

Like many of the younger teenage fans, the members of The Glassapple Chapter were accepting of Yoko and Linda. At times, some of the girls were mad at Yoko for taking John away, but they would quickly change their mind, buy her album, and discuss how cool she looked. The younger people were such big fans of the guys that they were quick to accept the changing dynamic in their personal lives.

Another newly chartered club was Beatles International. In a reflection of the changing membership, a young man named Fred Arnold was the club's president. He ran the club entirely through the mail, sending out the newsletter *Revolution*. Unlike female-led clubs, Beatles International focused very little on The Beatles' personal lives and more on their music. The newsletter featured reviews of one of the newest trends among fans, bootleg records. These unauthorized Beatles recordings were pressed onto vinyl records and sold across the country in head shops and record stores' backrooms. The albums *Kum Back*, *A Studio Recording*, *I Dig a Pony*, and *Get Back* were analyzed and critiqued in the club's newsletters. *Kum Back* was deemed the best available of the known bootleg albums, and Fred offered to copy it onto cassette tape for any member willing to pay for postage. He wrote, "If you've got any or all of these LP's, keep them as they are collector's items."

Paul Splits from The Beatles

The Official Beatles Fan Club was shocked on April 10, 1970. Newspapers in England sported the headline announcing Paul had quit The Beatles. He had released a self-interview to the press meant to promote his upcoming solo album. In the interview, Paul stated that he did not see Lennon-McCartney as an active songwriting team. His reasons were their musical and business differences, and his feeling that he now had a better time with his family than with his bandmates.

Paul's statement caused a world of confusion. Had The Beatles broken up? Would they replace Paul? Could Paul make it without John? Would the fan club end? Rumors flew through American telephone lines, and everyone had an opinion. One 16-year-old believed it was right for Paul to leave. It would give him a chance to demonstrate his talents. A 17-year-old thought it was a good time for The Beatles to split because their music couldn't get any better. One teenager stated, "Nobody is ever bored with The Beatles. Paul is the best looking, and he will be very popular when he sings alone." Another fan thought The Beatles would perform well with a new bass player, but they would never be the same. Another 16-year-old fan did not believe that Paul was leaving the group. "The Beatles are not worn out. They are getting better and have a long way to go!"

No wonder fans felt confused by Paul's announcement. The Beatles themselves did not seem to understand it. George said that he thought The Beatles were separated, but not divorced. "Everyone this year is trying to do his individual album," he explained. "After that, I am ready to go back to work together again."

The other question was: who, if anyone, was to blame for the split? Many fans blamed Yoko. She had separated John from the other three. She also acted as if she was something more than a wife, and even part of the group. Others laid the blame on Linda for influencing Paul to be a family man instead of a band member. A few blamed John because he had been releasing solo songs for months. And the rest accused Allen Klein because The Beatles had seemed to be happy friends until he came along.

Overall, Paul's breakup announcement did not change anything with The Official Beatles Fan Club, or the individual clubs. Barb Fenick told everyone in the Beatles Rule fan club, "as far as this fan club is concerned apart or together Beatles Rules Forever! This is a fans' club if you give up only then will I." Pat Kinzer never considered her club for George to be a Beatles club in the first place, so the announcement didn't change her club either. "As far as the club is concerned, we will continue as we have over the past six years, to follow George with whatever he does. This club was never meant to be a Beatles fan club, only a club for George Harrison. We will not disband just because The Beatles themselves have."

The Official Beatles Fan Club printed a statement in the September issue of *Datebook*. Sandi Morse wrote that the club had no plans of disbanding, and that monthly membership had been increasing in 1970. "Everyone at Apple seems to feel that Paul's extracurricular activities will take him away from The Beatles temporarily, and no one seems concerned about The Beatles Empire falling," she wrote. She claimed that the press used what Paul had said in his self-interview to sell newspapers. "We have all the confidence in the world that all four Beatles have the insight to realize that the ultimate in creative ability is The Beatles as a group." Sandi's words put a lot of fan club members' minds at ease. The Beatles hadn't broken up, and Paul would eventually return and make more music with the group. They would just have to wait.

1700 BROADWAY, NEW YORK, N.Y. 10019   (212) 582-5533

April 9, 1970

TO: ALL AREA SECRETARIES AND CHAPTER PRESIDENTS

FROM: SANDI MORSE

During the past few days, the newspapers in New York have been implying that Paul McCartney is leaving the Beatles to do his own thing, and thereby splitting the Beatles as a group.

THIS IS NOT TRUE !!!!!

Paul has done his own album, with Linda, which will be released very soon on the Apple label. He has written, produced, sung, played all instruments, and designed the jacket for this album. This does not signify anything except that Paul has decided to do his own thing as John & Yoko did by forming "Bag Productions". It will not interfer with the Beatles as a group in any way whatsoever. I'm sure all you Paul fans will agree that this is a great opportunity to hear many McCartney original songs that might never have gotten on an album (as Paul has been writing continuously for the past couple of years), and he should have his own thing just as John has his Peace Movement and the Plastic Ono Band, Ringo is coming out with his own solo album as well as his acting career, and George has his Hare Krishna as well as becoming a producer.

Since we are affiliated with the top group in the world, we must realize that their talents lie in other fields as well as being the fabulous Beatles, and we must not only accept it, but be pleased and interested in everything they take upon themselves.

I am sure you all join me in wishing Paul success in this new endeavor, and as soon as we receive more information on his potential million seller album, we will be sure to forward it to you.

THIS IS VERY IMPORTANT - Michael Hargraves, President of the NEW DAY BEATLES CHAPTER has just recently advised us that his chapter is strictly for members residing in the JACKSONVILLE FLORIDA area only! Please specify this in all newsletters that you might send out as this will save Michael much time in so far that he will not have to write and explain this to members wishing to join his chapter.

PLEASE BE ADVISED THAT THE POTTIE BYRD CHAPTER (President who was Rosalie Wilson) is no longer affiliated with the Official Beatle Fan Club. Please make sure that this chapter is removed from ALL YOUR RECORDS! No-one is permitted to advertise this chapter as we now consider it to be independent! Thank you for your cooperation...

A letter sent to all area secretaries and chapter presidents denying the reports that Paul has quit The Beatles. April 9, 1970.

McCartney Album

Paul's announcement overshadowed his reason for making it: the release of his self-titled solo album *McCartney*. After recording *Abbey Road*, Paul fell into a deep depression. He stayed on his farm and drank whiskey while feeling uncertain about his future without The Beatles. With his wife's encouragement, Paul turned to what naturally made sense to him: recording music. He built a small studio in his London home and recorded fourteen songs. Paul wrote these songs and played all the instruments, with the only assistance coming from Linda singing harmony. The critics and fans praised the *McCartney* album calling it "the best one-man show going." The standout song was Paul's love song for Linda, *Maybe I'm Amazed*. It was the only song that wasn't recorded in Paul's home studio. Paul sneaked over to EMI Studios and used a pseudonym to record this fan favorite. No one loved the album as much as The Official Paul McCartney Chapter. They were thrilled to have Paul back in the spotlight, making great music, even without The Beatles. They especially enjoyed what a writer from the *San Francisco Examiner* said, "McCartney the vocalist gives us a quality never heard in his voice before, almost a sense of discovery, clarity, and brilliance." Some members felt Paul still needed his three bandmates. "The *McCartney* LP is a good one," a fan wrote. "But the magic is missing. Paul needs the electricity of the other Beatles to turn his great talent into sheer genius."

George Visits The Official Beatles Fan Club

On April 27, George Harrison and Derek Taylor arrived in New York City for a secret visit. George wanted to discover why the Apple recording artists he had produced weren't selling in the United States. Pattie did not accompany him because she was in Los Angeles working for a London art dealer. George took advantage of this trip to go on a shopping spree. He bought several shirts, a white denim outfit, and a pair of work boots. He also went to Manny's Music Store and rented a Fender Stratocaster.

The Official Beatles Fan Club got a shock on April 30. Sandi Morse was working at her desk when it happened. "Things were progressing as usual in the office," she said. "When all of a sudden, Derek and George walked in. At first, we didn't recognize George because his hair was long and tied in a ponytail." There he was standing inside the fan club office wearing faded denims, a dungaree jacket, yellow socks, and holding his shoes. Sandi offered him a seat, and for an hour, George sat and talked to Sandi and Rusty. Laura was in the office as well. She was very nervous around the Beatle and recalled that she had looked "gray." Because of this, Laura did not say a word the entire time. She just watched.

George asked how things were going at the fan club. They showed him the items fan club members received for

George Harrison photographed by Rusty Rahn in New York. May 1, 1970.

1970. George was impressed with the photographs in the fan club book. He liked the poster for the Radha Krishna Temple's Apple single *Govinda* and took some of these with him. He also asked if he could have some of the *Yellow Submarine* tri-books and stationery. Of course, the girls were more than happy to give him whatever he wanted. Sandi and Rusty told George that the fans wanted to buy new pictures of The Beatles, but there weren't any because new photographs had not been taken. George had a solution. He arranged for the girls to meet him in his hotel suite the following morning. Before being the assistant director of The Official Beatles Fan Club, Rusty Rahn had been a professional photographer. She could take photos of George to be sold exclusively to the American fan club members, while Sandi would ask George questions for her fan club column in *Datebook*.

"The next day bright and early, Rusty and I loaded down with posters, books, and other goodies readied ourselves for the big day with George Harrison," Sandi wrote. They were sworn to secrecy, and couldn't tell anyone that George was staying at the Pickwick Hotel. The suite had royal blue plush velvet carpet with stainless steel and glass furniture. George greeted his guests and offered them Coca-Colas. While Rusty snapped photos, George began talking about the fan club. Sandi wrote in *Datebook*, "He was very friendly, getting into conversation about the fan club and what we were currently offering and things to come."

During the shoot, George picked up the guitar he had rented and began singing *Who's Making Love With My Old Lady*, which made the two girls laugh. He then serenaded them with a performance of songs from *Abbey Road* as he set the bridge on the guitar. Over the next hour-and-a-half Rusty took seventy photographs of George, capturing him strumming, changing records, and clowning around. Sandi noticed he was not smiling for any of the photos and asked him about it. George answered, "You don't have to smile outwardly to be smiling inwardly. I'm always smiling."

The girls were sad when the session was over, but thrilled with their memory of spending time with George. "I fully say it was very enjoyable and worthwhile," Sandi concluded in her *Datebook* article. "The outcome was seventy of the most beautiful photos of George ever seen and an hour-and-a-half of the grooviest conversation ever had." They narrowed the photos down to the six best and offered them to American club members. These were sold as two sets of three, with each set costing $1.

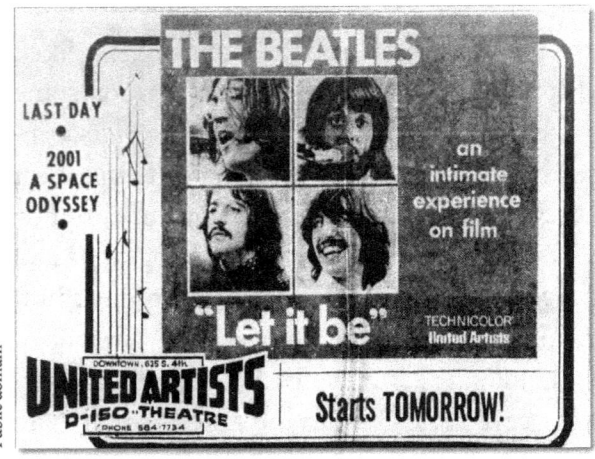

Newspaper advertisement for the Let It Be *movie. May 1970.*

Let It Be

Broken up or not The Beatles still had plenty to offer their fans. On May 13, the new film *Let It Be* premiered in the United States and Canada. This eighty-one minute documentary followed The Beatles through a recording session and finished with the January 1969 performance on the Apple building rooftop.

Many critics and fans alike found the film to be sorrowful and a shocking realization that The Beatles were over. "The first two-thirds of the film feels quite sad," wrote one of the critics. "The Beatles aren't lively. They're portrayed as humans who argue, talk, and play beautifully together." It was a stark contrast to the happy moptops in *A Hard Day's Night*, and it came as a shock to some fans.

Regardless of the sad feelings, fan club members went to see *Let It Be* on the big screen. California fans flocked to their theaters, which were sold out throughout the first week of the film's release, but the opposite happened in

Canada. As one Ottawa paper reported, "There was no line Friday night or all weekend and only a handful in the theater on Monday."

The days of fans screaming at a movie screen were gone, but not all fans were silent. When Yoko appeared on the screen, a loud hiss echoed through many U.S. theaters. Fan club members shared their thoughts on the film in club newsletters. Barb Fenick from Beatles Rule felt that the rooftop concert was outstanding and proved that The Beatles should be playing live again. George fan Jean Steinert only had eyes on one thing during the film. "George smiles so much it just makes you want to cry," she wrote. Jamie Sim spoke for most club members when she said, "The movie completely overwhelms me!" Overwhelmed or not, *Let It Be* was the must-see event for Beatles fans in 1970. As one critic wrote, "For die-hard Beatles' fans, the evening is well spent, if only because such evenings occur so infrequently and this may be the last time."

Changes in the OBFC

That summer was again a time of change in The Official Beatles Fan Club. At the beginning of July, Sandi was pregnant with her first child, and quit as director of the club. She wanted to be a stay-at-home mother. She gave birth to a premature son, Scott, on July 11. Before she left, she wrote in her last column for *Datebook*, "I am truly sorry to leave this position as I have very much enjoyed working with The Beatles and The Apple Corporation and, of course, all of you fans." Rusty Rahn was promoted from assistant director to director. Laura Cohen, an officer of The M.B.E. (Members of The Beatles Empire), and formerly of the New York office, became her assistant. "I was working as a clerk until I graduated high school in 1970," she recalled. "I was trained as a secretary and quickly moved up in the office. Sandi did not want me to use my real last name since I was Vice President of a chapter. I used the name 'Laura Cayne.'" Her

Rusty and Laura in the fan club office. August 1970.

responsibilities included answering letters from area secretaries, sending letters from fans to the correct area secretary, and writing a newsletter to the area secretaries about The Beatles news for them to pass onto their members.

At this point, Allen Klein stepped in and put an end to the fan club's connection to *Datebook*. *The Beatles Book Monthly* in England had ceased publication at the end of the previous year, so it was logical for the U.S. club to sever its ties with *Datebook*. Unfortunately, the magazine column had been essential in recruiting new members. Without it, membership began to decrease.

Beatles Rule Club Changes

Barb Fenick made changes to her club, Beatles Rule. The club had two hundred and fifty members, but only a quarter of them participated. The club had always been for the fans and not for The Beatles. Barb explained in the newsletter, "Beatles Rule as it is now is no longer serving the purpose I set out to achieve in '67 when I first began. The idea was to bring Beatle People together and to share with them all the enjoyment The Beatles gave me." Barb informed the members that if they wanted to remain in the club, they had to submit a drawing, poem, news report, or essay along with 50 cents for dues. Barb had no hard feelings toward fans who did not want to remain in the club. She offered to send a fan club membership list of those that focus on gossip and news, and a Beatles photograph, to anyone who sent her a self-addressed stamped envelope. When the dust settled, eighty members remained.

On May 22, some of those members gathered in Minneapolis for the second Beatles fan club convention. The main event was going to see *Let It Be* together at the movie theater, along with a discussion after the film. Once it got dark, the girls had a campout where they ate hamburgers and hot dogs along with roasted marshmallows. Of course, the evening would not have been complete without a Beatles sing-along with acoustic guitar. Illness and unforeseen circumstances kept many fans away, but attendees had a great time. Jamie Sim stated, "It was the most beautiful get together I've ever been to! There was a feeling of common emotions and desires. Everyone helped each other with a true spirit of brotherhood."

The Official Paul McCartney Chapter Changes

Sadly, that spirit was absent from The Official Paul McCartney Chapter. Ever since the fan club meeting in February the club's vibe had been negative, sparking rumors that the chapter was full of trouble. One of the club's most significant issues was photo sales. The club's vice president, Sue Romanelli, was in charge of filling all photo orders for Beatles group photos. Members complained that they had sent Sue the money but had not received their orders. Sue simply said she hadn't gotten the pictures developed. She was promptly let go from all of her duties. President Joanne Maggio informed her members, "Our club is getting a bad reputation because of her negligence. I'm waiting for her to return the negatives, money, and order forms so I can fill your orders."

Membership card for The Official Paul McCartney Chapter.

Joanne visited New York City for eight days, half of which she spent at The Official Beatles Fan Club office. Joanne met with Rusty Rahn and Laura Cayne to discuss the fan club. They gave Joanne a job with The Official Beatles Fan Club: National Chapter Director.

She tried to quit her presidency of The Official Paul McCartney Chapter. She didn't want the club to disband, explaining in the October newsletter, "I'll be having more responsibilities to the other chapters and area secretaries." Joanne's responsibility as the National Chapter Director was to examine every fan club chapter in the United States. Working from her home in Chicago, she assigned club charters and enforced active chapters' requirements. Despite her efforts, Joanne couldn't find an acceptable successor, so she continued as president of The Official Paul McCartney Chapter for the time being.

Visit to the Official Beatles Fan Club

Sandi Bellack visited Rusty Rahn and Laura Cayne at the fan club office at 1700 Broadway in New York City. August 1970.

Joanne wasn't the only fan club member who visited 1700 Broadway in New York City. While on vacation Sandi Bellack, president of The Glassapple Chapter, stopped by the fan club offices. She met Laura, who showed her around the headquarters. "I remember walking around, and there were pictures on the wall of The Beatles," she said. "We talked to Laura at her desk and took a few pictures with her. All the walls were covered with pictures of The Beatles."

Apple Juce

One summer day within The Beatles-covered walls of the fan club offices, Rusty approached fan club member and part-time worker Ida Langsam with a question. The area secretary of New York City, Ginny Murphy, had resigned from the position because she was going to college out of state. Rusty asked Ida if she was interested in filling the open position. Ida was thrilled and quickly accepted. She remembers, "I didn't want to use my name because I had this vision of fans being crazy like me. I was 18; I had my own phone, and I was listed in the telephone book. I didn't want to be under my name because I didn't want crazy fans calling my home." Ida decided to use her name in Hebrew, which is translated to Judith. She figured she'd go by Jude. "Rusty said 'no, no no, no, you can't be Jude because every Judith in the world is going by Jude.'" She'd chosen to call the New York area newsletter *Apple Juce*. "I explained the 'Ju' was going to stand for 'Jude.' We decided I would spell it 'Judee.' I told my best friend she could be my assistant area secretary, but she had to make a name that started with 'Ce' so we could be 'Apple Juce.' She picked Celine. We then needed last names. I had a crush on the actor Elliott Gould, so I became Judee Gould. My friend had a crush on comedian David Steinberg, and so she was Celine Steinberg." They decided to publish the newsletter four times a year. Ida was required to answer the letters from club members in the New York City area, which wasn't always easy. As she later recalled, "Some of their questions were stupid, like what color car does Pattie drive or what kind of toothpaste do they use. I don't know what kind of toothpaste they use, but if they wanted to know when the next record was coming out, I could answer that."

Mrs. Harrison's Death

Fan club members were grief-stricken when on July 7, George's mother, Louise Harrison, died of brain cancer at the age of 59. Mrs. Harrison had been a supporter of Beatles fan clubs around the globe. She wrote letters to fans and welcomed them into her home. The Official George Harrison Fan Club and its president, Pat Kinzer, felt the loss of Mrs. Harrison more than most. Pat said at the time, "I know we'll all miss Mrs. Harrison. She was a wonderful person and did more for George and his fans and his fan club than probably anyone else. She was a real friend to us all."

On July 11, The Official George Harrison Fan Club had a meeting. First, they had a picnic, and then the members gathered inside a gymnasium to watch the home movies Patricia Simmons had shot in London and Liverpool the previous summer. They watched a lively Mrs. Harrison blowing bubbles outside of her home. After watching the film, there was a surprise guest: Rusty Rahn, who had come to Pennsylvania from New York City to introduce herself to the George fans. The members were unaware of Mrs. Harrison's passing. Pat was too emotional and could not tell the members. That task was given to Rusty. The meeting ended on a sad note. The fan club's president wanted to do something to honor the life of Mrs. Louise Harrison. She decided The Official George Harrison Fan Club would hold a drive to raise money to donate to a cancer charity in Mrs. Harrison's name. Donations came pouring in, not just from members of George's club but from other clubs as well. Beatles fans around the country wanted to remember the one adult who supported and loved Beatles fans and the fan clubs.

Summer Trips to the U.K.

During the previous three summers Beatles fans had flocked to London with plans to meet the lads. The summer of 1970 was different. The Beatles were not recording. John was hidden somewhere in California doing some sort of therapy, and Paul was tucked away on his farm in Scotland with his family. George was in the middle of making his first solo album, and Ringo likewise was working on an album. Many fans decided to save their money for the next summer. A few decided to go to London anyhow.

Four members of Beatles Rule, including Kris Martell and Linda Reincke-Woods, went in July. By then, George had moved from his bungalow in Esher to a mansion in Henley-on-Thames named Friar Park. The girls decided to look at George's former home. They were surprised to find George and his driver, Terry Doran, moving boxes out of the bungalow. The girls reported, "George was so nice! He looked good, thinner, and his hair was very long and was tied back in a ponytail." He told them about his new album and allowed them to take photos and movies of him. After George left, they saw Mal Evans moving some boxes. Mal let them walk around the empty house. They spotted a large poster of George hanging in the garage and asked if they could have it. Mal said they couldn't take it because he wanted it.

The next place they found was Ringo's house. When they knocked on the front door, Maureen answered, seven months pregnant, in a bathrobe, and without make-up. One of the fans snapped her photo, and Maureen became angry and closed the door. The fans felt terrible about the situation and got her some carnations. They returned, and she smiled when they handed them to her. They saw the Starkey children, Zak and Jason, playing in the yard. Ringo and his driver, Alan, pulled up in the car. Ringo saw them and waved them away. They asked Alan about it, and he said, "He's always like that. He's a family man and wants to keep quiet."

They wanted to see Paul. Though they'd heard he did not wish to have visitors at his home on the farm, the girls pressed their luck, and flew to Scotland. They ventured into Campbeltown and walked for over three hours before they reached Paul's farm gates. They slowly walked onto his property only to find Paul himself standing in front of them in a maroon V-neck sweater, tan pants, and rubber boots. First, he informed the fans that he did not like people coming to his farm, but he accepted the gifts they'd brought for Paul's two daughters. His sheepdog, Martha, came out and jumped on one of the girls until Paul told his famous dog to stop. The former Beatle told them he was still writing songs, and he had no plans to return to London. The girls left feeling that Paul had been quiet and distant. He'd kept his head down the entire time. They did not understand what had happened to the cheerful man they loved.

The Beatles' hometown, Liverpool, had become a popular destination for American fans. At that time, there were no organized Beatles tours. The four fan club members from Beatles Rule arrived at Lime Street Station in August with only a map, addresses gleaned from club materials, and their determination to follow in The Beatles' footsteps. At the Cavern Club they explained to the owner that they'd came from the U.S.A. He gave them an exclusive tour.

One girl, Ginger Robinson, reported, "The Cavern extends under three warehouses. There's a large eating area upstairs. Downstairs is the stage. It's so small. Pictures of it make it look huge compared to its actual size." They went on a stroll down Penny Lane, stood at the gates of Strawberry Field, saw the childhood homes and schools of all four Beatles. They snapped photos of buildings, while ignoring the Scousers' looks. They were happy to see the city the way The Beatles had seen it.

Back in London, fans were confused by the moodiness of George and Ringo. Fans often spotted Ringo coming and going from the Apple offices. One fan said, "One minute, Ringo was pushing cameras away, and the next minute he's busy signing autographs galore." Fans hoped to catch him when he was in a pleasant

George walks by his fans as he gets into his Mercedes in the EMI car park. 1970.

mood. On most days, George visited EMI Studios. He was always in a good mood and, at times, would stand in the parking lot talking to fans for a half hour. However, George did not appreciate the fans who came on his property. That's when he got fed up, and sometimes said "rude" things to fans, demanding that they leave. When he treated one fan this way, she reported to The Official George Harrison Fan Club that she "was so mad at him, I bought a John and Yoko poster!"

Autumn at the Official Beatles Fan Club

Autumn of 1970 remained unusually quiet at The Official Beatles Fan Club Headquarters in New York City. Since The Beatles were not together, there were no new photos of them together. The club sold what was available: *Let It Be* items. A

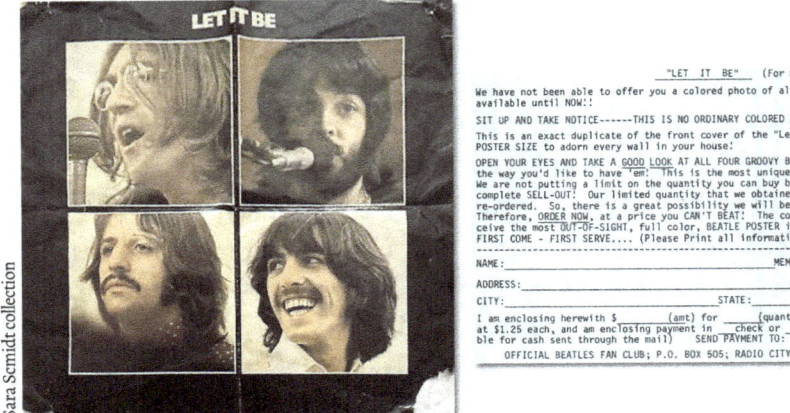

Let It Be *poster sold through the Official Beatles Fan Club. 1970.*

full-color poster of the album's front cover sold for $1.25. It was the same poster fans saw hanging in the windows of their local record shops. They also sold the *Let It Be* book for $3. It was full of color photographs and had only been available in the U.K. A set of six pictures taken from the film sold for $2. The club also went back into the files and offered collections of photos from *A Hard Day's Night* and *Help!* These all had "Copyright Official Beatles Fan Club 1970" printed at the bottom.

Fan club members were expecting a new Beatles poster by the end of the summer. Area secretaries spread the news that because the four guys were in different countries, the club in the U.K. was having a hard time getting current photos for the poster. When all was said and done, members did not receive a new poster. In November, Rusty Rahn sent a letter to each fan saying, "Since there are oh so many Beatles' posters available to the general public, we thought you might enjoy something a little different." What they got was a cube, similar to the one sent to area secretaries the previous Christmas. This one had color photos of the individual Beatles on the four sides and a big green apple on the top. There were pre-punched holes at the top so it could hang like a mobile.

Beatles Apple cube available through the fan club in the summer of 1970 (base shown at far right).

John's 30th Birthday

Meanwhile, in London, a group of Americans spent their days outside EMI Studios, where George was still working on his new album. John and Yoko had returned home, and fans couldn't wait to see them. They were in for a surprise on October 9, John's 30th birthday.

While fans were standing outside EMI, John and Yoko arrived. They smiled and waved while everyone wished John a Happy Birthday. When John stopped, one girl handed him an LP that was a birthday present. John jokingly said, "Oh, I sure hope it isn't *McCartney!*" Mal Evans came outside and gave each of the girls a slice of John's birthday cake. While they were eating cake, Ringo arrived. He was charming and stopped for photographs. Many fans had icing all over their cameras, and they noticed Ringo laughing about it.

When George arrived, he was carrying boxes and flowers. He gave the waiting fans a big smile. One of the girls said, "It was really super, all three of them in there together celebrating John's ancient age of 30."

Paul Records *Ram* in New York City

Things were not as happy for Paul in New York City. Along with Linda, Heather, and Mary, he arrived on October 8 to start recording the *Ram* album. It was a tough time for both Paul and Linda. Paul was still depressed and was drinking too much. He was trying to separate himself from The Beatles and their image, but couldn't figure out how to do it. Likewise, Linda was trying to find her place as a former Beatles' wife. Fans in England had mistreated her. She had been spat on, cursed at, robbed, and even injured slightly.

She hoped to avoid the same behavior from the fans in her own country.

The McCartney family arrives in New York City to begin the Ram *sessions. October 8, 1970.*

The fans in New York, of course, did not know about the McCartney family's struggles. All they knew was Beatle Paul was in New York City. They wanted to see him in person and hoped to talk to him. When the New York fans read in *Rolling Stone* that he was recording at Columbia Studios, they began spending time there, waiting to see him arrive and depart.

Their dreams of talking to happy Beatle Paul crumbled when they realized that this Beatle was ignoring them. Linda gave them icy stares. Paul didn't give any autographs, nor did he pose for pictures. He made it clear that he did not want anyone hanging around the studio when he arrived in the morning. He told the girls to get lost. Beatles fans are a determined bunch, and they continued to go to the studio every day.

One day they had a confrontation with Linda. It started when Paul and Linda rushed out of the building, and some of the fans followed them. One girl yelled out, "Paul, Linda, I just want to say 'Hello'!" Paul glanced at them and said, "Hello." Linda yelled back to them, "Hello! Now God damn it! Stop following us!" The fans crossed to the other side of the street and continued to walk. Linda stopped again and stared at the girls. One girl started to say they were just walking in the same direction, but Linda didn't want to hear it. "We're on a break. We're very tired from working." The girls asked, "Linda, why do you hate us so much?" Paul silently looked at his fans, and then they turned and walked away.

The next day the same girls were standing outside the studio when Paul and Linda came walking by arm-in-arm. They stopped, and Linda leaned close to the girls. "You're just like the rest of them," she declared. "A bunch of hypocrites." Then she and Paul walked inside. A few minutes later, Linda came back out alone. She told everyone that Paul didn't want them hanging outside the studio; it bothered him. The fans began to argue, wanting to know why Paul wasn't telling them himself. They mentioned that he'd never minded when the fans in England had hung around EMI. Linda said it was this way now with all the guys. She claimed, "Lennon doesn't care about his fans!" She then informed them they were no different from the British girls who had broken into their home or set their mail on fire. The girls all swore they were different and would never harm Paul or his property.

Linda wanted to know why they were always outside the studio. A few said to hang out with their friends. Others said because they love Paul. Linda did not like hearing them say that. She informed them that only she loved Paul so they couldn't love him. Then she said: "What is this – a fan club meeting?"

Linda had crossed a line. Most of the girls were fan club members, and the club was near and dear to them. The fan club girls let her have it. They began telling her how great Jane Asher was and how good Jane and Paul had been together. Linda had the last words: "You all hate me! You're bothering me! Go ahead. Stand out here. I don't care!"

Tensions remained high throughout the rest of the sessions. The fans did their best to avoid any more outbursts, and Linda tended to ignore them. On a good day, Paul might say a quick "hello" before getting into a cab. Assistant Director of The Official Beatles Fan Club Laura Cayne got to stand inside the studio and see Paul. "I was too scared to say that I was from the fan club," she recalled. "I wasn't sure how Paul would react."

Things weren't all doom and gloom for the McCartneys, as two fans, Jo Ann Di Filippe and Linda Rabe, discovered on Halloween. These two had spent some time waiting to see Paul outside of the studio the previous week.

On October 31, they were walking around the city, trying to discover where the McCartney family was staying. They noticed many children walking around in costumes, and the girls had fun handing out candy. They were on Fifth Avenue when they saw walking toward them two women and a man holding a baby. All were wearing yellow sheets and each had a different mask. The group neared the girls and made ghost noises with voices that sounded familiar. The girls played along and acted scared. The four ghosts closed in, making louder noises. The girls were convinced this was Paul and his family under the sheets. The group turned away, heading toward the Stanhope Hotel and saw an argyle sock, identical to the ones Linda always wore peeking out from below one sheet. They were right! Later, when a Halloween 1970 picture of Paul, Linda, Heather, and Mary appeared, sure enough, they were wearing yellow sheets and masks. They'd surely recognized Jo Ann and Linda, and decided to give the two fans a treat.

George Harrison The Musician

At the end of October, George was in New York City, having hand-carried the tapes of his upcoming album from London. The recordings were being pressed onto vinyl, and George wanted them to arrive safely. While they were being pressed, George and Pattie took a holiday trip to Jamaica and other warm-weather sites.

Ruben Betancourt was a young reporter in Fort Lauderdale, Florida. He had heard that George was there vacationing with his wife. Ruben contacted the

George and Pattie in New York to promote Badfinger, November 24, 1970.

area secretary for Florida, Claudette Cyr, to help track down George. Using her contacts Claudette learned he might be at the beach. Ruben and Claudette were driving there when they spotted George, Pattie, and two men walking through a parking lot. They couldn't believe it. When they approached George, he was happy to talk, saying he would soon be leaving for New York City. His new record was due to be released, and before that happened they'd come to Florida for some "rest and relaxation."

George was concerned that Ruben and Claudette would tell others where he was staying. He told them, "I am not famous anymore. I am not Beatle George anymore. If I wanted to hear screaming, I would play Shea Stadium, but I don't. I'm George Harrison, a musician. That's all." The two fans promised they would not tell anyone until after he had left. He signed autographs for both of them while Pattie, who looked stunning without any make-up, stood silently with a big smile on her face. Before he left, George mentioned how much he liked Florida and that he hoped to return soon. Not long after that, George returned to New York City to introduce the Apple-signed band Badfinger to the press. He then went back home to Friar Park.

John Lennon in New York City

The next Beatle to come to New York City was John. He and Yoko spent a lot of time at 1700 Broadway in Allen Klein's office, one floor above the fan club headquarters. The couple was unhappy with Klein's lack of decorations, and they hung some of The Beatles' gold records and other things on the walls.

The assistant director of the club, Laura Cayne, never knew when John was just one floor above her unless she got word from one of her friends who happened to be waiting in the lobby. She really wanted to see John. Later she recalled, "One day I said, 'That is it. I am going to just go up there and meet him.'" She got a tip from another employee about when John was going to be in the elevator. "I get the call, but we about missed the elevator," said Laura. "I got it to open, and there were John and Yoko in the back." Even though she was not a smoker, Laura told her co-worker, Pattie, who had already entered the elevator, that she wanted her to get some cigarettes, but since she was already there, she would go down with her. This was Laura's excuse to ride the elevator with John and Yoko. Laura and Pattie introduced themselves to the Lennons. Laura told them that they should stop by the fan club office sometime.

Much to Laura's surprise, they did just that. "A few days later, they came into the office, and John came up to my desk and asked me how he could help. I told John that the club had a membership drive. The area secretary that could recruit the most members would win a prize. I hoped he'd sign something." John ended up donating a T-shirt that he autographed for the winner.

All Things Must Pass

George's three-record set, *All Things Must Pass*, was released in time for Christmas, and the music blew away both fans and critics. Some, including a few fans, didn't expect much from George, but after listening to all six sides of his masterpiece, people understood. Many people felt *All Things Must Pass* was the best effort yet among the various Beatles' solo ventures. One Beatles Rule member, Jann Martin, was apprehensive, but she gave it a chance. Jann wrote, "I had to lay back and laugh because suddenly I knew George and why I loved him in the first place." She thought everyone should buy it because the songs were "good for the mind." Also, the album made for great decorating. "I must say my bedroom looks a lot better with the poster of George!"

All Things Must Pass album. 1970. (Eric Cash collection)

Many compared George's work with that of his bandmates. One critic wrote, "George did not set out on an ego trip à la McCartney's attempt to play all the instruments himself." Anita Thornton, the area secretary from Oklahoma, said the album proved that George didn't need the other three. One writer for The Official George Harrison Fan Club, going by the name "Sgt. Pepper" wrote,

"George's album is the rage of late '70 and will remain so in '71. To say it is absolutely fantastic seems so trite. One record is one thing, but coming out with three on your first try takes a lot of intestinal fortitude, even for a Beatle. But to pull it off, even to the point of being named one of the best albums of the year, well, that takes a hell of a lot of talent."

The Beatles Christmas Album

Traditionally, The Beatles had put out a Christmas record for fan club members at the end of each year. Now that the four were not together, members speculated on what that year's album would be like. Some thought each guy would record his message, and it would be edited together on one record. Others thought John, George, and Ringo might get together and record a message for the fans.

The front and back of the The Beatles Christmas Album. *December 1970.*

Even those in charge of the project didn't know. The director of The Official Beatles Fan Club in the U.K., Freda Kelly, came up with an ingenious idea. "I was at a meeting," she recalled, "I noted that people always wanted fan club records, so we decided, 'Well, why don't we just put the lot on an LP and give that as the final gift...'" It was a great plan with one problem. No one knew where the masters for the seven Christmas records were located. They used flexi-discs from Freda's collection to make the album.

The twelve-inch album was issued in the United States on the

Apple label on December 18, 1970. It was named *The Beatles Christmas Album*. It went out to all members of The Official Beatles Fan Club. The U.S. release had a silver-blue cover depicting The Beatles through the years.

Fan Club members were happy to receive the new album. As Wally Podrazik recalls, "That album was a godsend. For many of us, we could actually hear them for the first time." This album marked the first time American fans heard the 1964 and 1965 messages because they had never been released in the United States. In addition, the first three U.S. Christmas messages had come on cardboard postcards, making them difficult to play. *The Beatles Christmas Album* was a bright spot at the end of a gloomy year.

Paul Sues The Beatles

Unfortunately, that bright light went out on December 31 when Paul petitioned the High Court in London to end The Beatles' partnership. The writ stated that the relationship as The Beatles was to be dissolved.

This was the worst news any Beatles fan could hear. The Beatles broke up, and Paul was suing his friends, which seemed to mean they could never play together again. All hope was lost. Ohio area secretary Patricia Simmons wrote to the fans in her state, "Last April when Paul said he was splitting from the group, I wasn't sure if it was temporary or permanent, hope didn't seem all lost…" Rumors swirled that Eric Clapton or Klaus Voormann would replace Paul. Those who loved the band knew it wouldn't be the same without Paul. He was irreplaceable.

The club out of England quickly issued a statement saying, "Everything is running just as it always has at Apple, and the fan club has no intentions of disbanding." As 1971 opened, fans asked themselves, "How can we have a fan club for a band that is no longer together?"

Official Beatles Fan Club
A Division of Apple Music Inc.

For membership, send your $2.50 annual dues to THE OFFICIAL BEATLES FAN CLUB, P.O. Box 505, Radio City Station, New York, N.Y. 10019. If you wish information on how to start your own chapter, send a stamped self-addressed envelope to the same address, writing CHAPTER INFO on the outside, or a stamped self-addressed envelope writing PHOTOS AND SPECIALS INFO, if that is your interest.

DEAR BEATLE PEOPLE:

I would like to start off this newsletter by saying that I do hope you all had a very Merry Christmas and Happy New Year. I know I am a bit late with these wishes, but since we had no newsletter in the last issue please accept these wishes from all of us here at headquarters at this late date. As you can see from our new logo, we have changed our policy at headquarters by bringing the fan club to new heights and bringing you the "1970 BEATLES". We have received hundreds upon hundreds of letters saying how groovy the new X-Mas is and we are again proud that we could bring it to all of you. We are sorry that there was a delay in mailing the records out, but with all our fans eager to receive it, we truly did our best. We are now mailing out the 1970 OFFICIAL BEATLES FAN CLUB book to all new members and renewed members. We hope you dig it along with the groovy, out-of-sight new 1970 membership card and offers for great new pics, posters and goodies for the new year. We still have plenty of X-Mas records left and if you are not a member of the fan club, we ask that you mail in your annual $2.50 to us and we will send you your record, the new book and everything else you would be entitled to as a member.

BEATLE PICS: For the new year we now have in addition to our regulars Superpix, an additional six great new photos. They are numbered #19 through 24 . . . You can get all six of these new photos by ordering #25 on our photo list, which is a complete combination of numbers 19 through 24. You can also order #1 INDIA, #2 THE McCARTNEYS, #3 HELLO GOODBYE, #4 STRAWBERRY FIELDS — PENNY LANE, #5 RELAXATION TIME, #6 THE COMPOSERS, #7 GONE WITH THE WIND, #8 THE INVADERS, #9A PAUL, #9B PAUL, #10A JOHN, #10B JOHN, #11A GEORGE, #11B GEORGE, #12A RINGO, #12B RINGO, #13 REVOLUTION,, #14 THE FAB FOUR, #15 NEW TWO-SOME, #16 HEY JUDE, #17 GARDEN MEDITATION, #18 GROUP INSPIRATION as well as our PAUL SPECIAL and JOHN SPECIAL and brand new RINGO SPECIAL. We are also still selling our GROOVY COUPLE PIC, George and his wife Pattie. The APPLE POSTER is still going strong as well as our MAGICAL MYSTERY TOUR photo and the CONCERT BOOKS from 1964, 65 and 66. We are selling in addition to the above the 1969 BEATLES USA LTD. booklet, which we gave out to all members and the 1969 Spring "REVOLUTION" POSTER. Just send a self-addressed, stamped envelope to us at headquarters requesting "PHOTO INFO" and we will send you ALL the advertisements and coupons so that you can obtain these groovy photos. I suggest though that you order your photos NOW so you don't miss out on anything!! Photo info is sent upon request to members and non-members alike. Prices differ for members and non-members. We will soon be discontinuing the sale of photos to non-members as we feel that only fans who are members of the club should be entitled to these groovy we offer.

FAN CLUB NOTES: One thing that hasn't changed is that we have asked before and are still asking that you PLEASE PLEASE always place your membership number in the top left hand corner of your envelope when you write to the club. If you don't abide by our wishes we might not reply to your letter. We have over 40,000 fans and cannot stop and check to see if someone who writes has a membership number or not, so if you would like a reply, please help us here at headquarters by abiding by our policy and wishes. Many of you have either been putting your number inside or on the back of your envelope or omitting it altogether and we find it extremely difficult when sorting the mail. It is absolutely imperative that your membership number ALWAYS appears in the proper place!!

REMEMBER, we have an area secretary for the following states and if you live in any of these states please write to your area secretary instead of to headquarters. YOU WILL RECEIVE A MUCH MORE PROMPT REPLY. BE SURE TO SEND *ALL* PHOTO ORDERS TO HEADQUARTERS ONLY! Our Area Secretaries to help you are:

ALABAMA: Mr. Bobby Hudgins—3612 Kingshill Rd.; Birmingham 35223
ARIZONA: Patti Porcaro—939 E. Rose Lane; Phoenix 85014
CALIF. (NORTH): Joann Maloney—Freeborn Hall; Room 212; University of California; 2650 Durant Ave.; Berkeley, Calif. 94720
CALIF. (SOUTH): Patti O'Neil—5360 Oceanview Blvd.; La Canada 91011
CANADA: Joan Thompson—36 Scotia Avenue; Scarborough; Ontario; Canada
COLORADO: Eve Birgen—8031 Stuart Place; Westminster 80030
CONNECTICUT: Fran Tilewick—545 River Road; Hamden 06518

Newsletter sent to all members of The Official Beatles Fan Club informing them of what was available to purchase from the club. 1970.

Chapter 9 — Dear ~~Beatle~~ People

The first months of 1971 were difficult for Beatles fans. Paul's lawsuit was upsetting. When Ringo said Paul had acted like a spoiled child, it was hard to take. Ringo, the one band member who had remained neutral, now told a horrible story, under oath, of Paul shouting at him, and kicking Ringo out of his home. Weren't Paul and Ringo friends? It did not make sense to fans. One wrote in an essay, "Their break-up leaves you drained and disillusioned. It is a stark reminder of your own imperfections and those of the world."

Part one of John's two-part interview appeared in the Jan. 21, 1971 edition of Rolling Stone.

To add insult to injury, *Rolling Stone* magazine published a two-part interview with John titled *"Lennon Remembers."* In this candid interview, John's anger emerged. He spoke on shocking topics such as orgies while The Beatles were on tour, and his use of heroin and other drugs. He insulted not just Paul but also record producer George Martin. Fans hoped parts of the interview had been misquoted. They wanted John's stories to be outright lies. Those hopes were quashed when The Official Beatles Fan Club released a statement saying, "All the things John said were completely honest and quite truthful." The picture John painted of The Beatles in that interview ruined the image most fans had been holding onto for seven years.

It was all too much for some Beatlemaniacs. One fan, Iris, wrote to an advice column, saying, "I cannot accept the fact that The Beatles are over. I cannot understand John being so bitter as to say The Beatles were a myth and a phony image; that Paul treated him like a sideman." For other fans, the end of The Beatles brought on only deep sadness. These young adults had grown up with The Beatles. Through good times and bad The Beatles' records were always present. "The Beatles were a constant," Frank Barrows wrote, "Always good, always beautiful, always the same yet always different."

For the first time since 1964, when The Beatles had arrived, it was no longer "cool" to be known as a Beatles fan. Teenagers who still liked The Beatles were teased in high school. Some of their fellow students saw the group as childish and immature. Others were bullies who thought fans were babies who needed to grow up.

Iris wrote into a newspaper looking for advice, "Everybody's teasing me since The Beatles break-up," she lamented. "I was the leading Beatlemaniac and even reported on them in class. What am I to do? Break the albums and burn the posters?" The advice she got was to take down her posters and try listening to newer artists.

Tim Basgall, the area secretary for Kansas, was embarrassed. He didn't want his friends to know he was a Beatles fan. Worse, he was involved in their fan club. He'd even been hiding fan club materials, so his friends wouldn't give him a hard time.

The Official Beatles Fan Club

Membership may have been decreasing, but things were running as usual at The Official Beatles Fan Club. National Director Rusty Rahn and Assistant Director Laura Cayne still ran the club out of the 1700 Broadway office. They had each been assigned specific jobs, and things were running smoothly. The two girls spent their days sorting and typing incoming orders, processing new memberships, answering mail from fans and area secretaries, and keeping track of the inventory of items the club sold. The only other workers were part-time assistants, responsible for mailing out all memos and membership kits. These volunteers also filled photo orders and sent out membership cards. Joanne Maggio remained the National Chapter Director. She handled all questions and problems with current chapters, independent fan clubs, and prospective chapters.

Beatles fan club Director Rusty Rahn and Assistant Director Laura Cayne, 1971.

The beginning of the year was always busy. That's when new club membership cards and Beatles books had to be sent out to every current member. The 1971

Beatles fan club Director Rusty Rahn and Assistant Director Laura Cayne, in the trenches at the fan club offices. 1971.

membership card was not white; it was green as a Granny Smith apple. The book was the same bright color. Both items had Patti "Gripweed" Randall's drawing of the four Beatles inside of an apple. The book had photographs of The Beatles from 1963 to 1970. There was a photo of each Beatle with a short biography underneath. One thing club members asked for and received in the new book was a complete catalog of U.S. singles and albums.

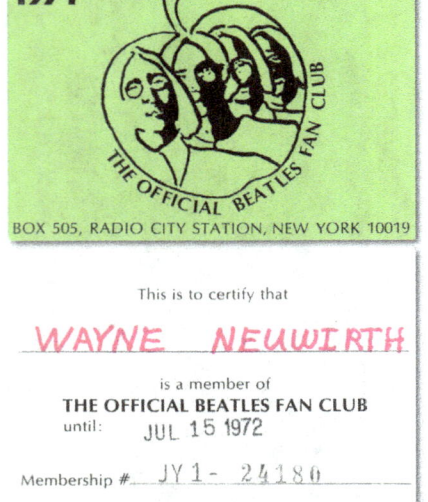

OFBC membership card. 1971 (front and back).
OFBC booklet. 1971 (cover shown).

Fan Club Chapters

Joanne Maggio took her position as the National Chapter Director seriously, and she informed the club presidents of the updated rules given to her by headquarters. All chapters should be thought of as mini fan clubs because they were a small representation of The Official Beatles Fan Club in New York City. The presidents needed to keep in mind that they were sanctioned by Apple and The Beatles, so they had to run professional chapters. "It is the responsibility of the president to maintain a decent chapter," Joanne wrote in a memo to the chapter officers. Newsletters were no longer allowed to be mailed out if they were handwritten with cross-outs, and had to be printed on heavy paper. All drawings had to have meaning. It was essential for presidents to tune in to current events, and not "linger in the Paulie stages of 1964 and 1965." Lastly, each president had to make sure the secretary for his or her state followed all proper procedures. With Joanne in charge of the fan club chapters, there was another push from the official club to stop the independent clubs. Instead of getting a letter from a lawyer, headquarters was going

CHAPTER 9–DEAR ~~BEATLE~~ PEOPLE

to pressure the independents to join. Any club member who knew of one of these clubs was supposed to turn in the club's name to Joanne. Once she contacted the president, if he or she still refused to join, Joanne was instructed to release the name and address to members. Their reason was "to keep you up to date on those people putting out 'news' which might not be to your liking."

The End of Beatles Rule

Among the names on Joanne's list were Beatles Rule and President Barb Fenick. Barb had been running the club independently since 1967 when she'd been 16 years old. After four years she made the difficult decision to end the club. "With the way things stand with The Beatles these days, there just doesn't seem much point to continue," she wrote in the last newsletter. The end of The Beatles wasn't the only thing that ended her club. Barb had become disillusioned with her fellow fans. In 1967, Beatles fans could do no wrong, and everyone treated one another as sisters. Four years later, Barb tried to keep sharing the love, joy, and happiness The Beatles had given her, but there was too much sadness among the fans.

Barb eventually found that joy again. Using the skills she learned as president of Father Lennon's Many Children, later renamed Beatles Rule, she started a new Beatles fan club in 1973 called The Write Thing. This club had thousands of members from around the world. Barb had one of the most respected Beatles publications of the 1970s and 1980s.

5 Bites of The Apple

Taking Beatles Rule's place as the independent fan club that didn't hold back was 5 Bites of the Apple. President Linda Reincke-Woods had been a Beatles Rule member and wrote about her adventures the previous summer when she had met Paul on his farm. She also documented her experiences with Linda McCartney. The New York-based club catered to older members, with the average age being 22. The club had a membership of 300 fans.

5 Bites of The Apple membership card, 1971.

When Linda got pressure from The Official Beatles Fan Club to join, she reluctantly gave in and got a charter, but she didn't follow all the rules. In one newsletter, she reported that Paul was in Los Angeles, mixing his new album. One of the members from the west coast got ahold of his pack of pot rolling papers called Monkberry Moon Delight. "When I printed the story in my newsletter, the OBFC warned me not to print stories like that. I was then summoned to come into the office for a chat with the director, Rusty. That's when I told her that the OBFC was basically wasting their time because The Beatles as a band were done."

Linda said in her club newsletter that there was a bad feeling in the air inside of club headquarters and that the office had became "an office filled with photos of The Beatles hung up on the dusty wall of memories." She strongly believed that the club would not last another year.

New Fan Club Chapters

Despite The Beatles' breakup, new fan club chapters were still being formed. One was the Sgt. Pepper's Chapter, run by a 16-year-old fan, Joan Alford. When a local children's program stopped playing re-runs of The Beatles' cartoons, Joan and her members sprang into action, writing letters of protest to the station. The program director contacted Joan and told her that he didn't realize there were still Beatles fans. The next week The Beatles' cartoons were back on the air. When asked why she was so passionate about her cause, Joan said, "I'm just striving to bring a little love and music into the dark corners where it's needed by way of a very deserving source: The Beatles."

Another new chapter started in Chicago. Its president, Sharon Uzarewicz, began the Let It Be Chapter. Dues were $2. Fans received a membership card and a plastic calendar photo cube with one black-and-white and four color photos of The Beatles. She wanted the fans to decide what would be in the club's newsletters because she wanted a club that reflected the modern-day Beatles fan. Sharon wrote, "It has been said that The Beatles are 'over,' or 'finished.' It was pure insanity to start a chapter in 1971. I read an article that stated, 'Anyone who has grown up with The Beatles will never get over them.' There's a feeling worth preserving. Let it be."

Fan Club Challenges

One of the biggest challenges in running a Beatles fan club chapter was picture sales. The Official Beatles Fan Club had some strict rules about photographs. Before a chapter could sell a picture, the National Chapter Director, Joanne Maggio had to have a copy of the photo. In return, she would send the officer in charge of photos a copyright card. The card guaranteed that the chapter had control over that particular photo, and no one else could sell it. The chapter could sell copies of the image only after it had gotten the card. If an officer saw a magazine photo she wanted to sell, she had to send Joanne the original magazine photo along with a photocopy of the page. Joanne would send the original back, and the officer then could have a negative made, then print and sell copies. Magazine photos did not get a copyright card. If a club disbanded, all of its copyrighted photos become available for other chapters to sell. The Official Beatles Fan Club repeatedly laid out these rules, but most clubs did not bother with the copyright card and just sold the photos without approval.

Mrs. Lennon's Apple Farm had shirts made with the name of the club, and a drawing of John and Yoko posed in an imitation of the "American Gothic" painting on the front. 1971.

The other big challenge for the fan club was the recruitment of new members. The Official Beatles Fan Club membership was down to less than 5,000 in the United States and Canada, so membership in the individual chapters was down as well.

Two employees of a New Jersey Sam Goody record store were not just Beatles fans, but also Beatles record collectors. They did not have access to one Beatles record. They discovered *The Beatles Christmas Album* was only available from The Official Beatles Fan Club. One of the boys went into 1700 Broadway and asked to buy the album. It was only available to current Beatles fan club members and not for purchase. He gave the secretary $5 and signed both him and his friend as members of the club. He walked out with two copies of *The Beatles Christmas Album*.

Typically, fans did not come in off the street to join the club. The consensus among the officers around the country was that the fans were out there somewhere. "I know a lot of the kids who think the world of The Beatles, only they don't know a club still exists," said Vickie Mikulis, president of the Apple Chapter. They brainstormed ideas on how to spread the word. Suggestions included club bumper stickers, putting club information in all pen pal correspondence, sending free newsletters to names found in friendship books, publishing the club's name and address in magazines, and changing the name. The general feeling was that more people would join if it were no longer called a 'fan club.' Rusty Rahn said they could not advertise because of issues with false advertising and misrepresentation. She told them the best way to promote was by word of mouth.

But one club in California had developed a great way to spread the word about their club. Mrs. Lennon's Apple Farm had shirts made with the name of the club, and a drawing of John and Yoko posed in an imitation of the *American Gothic* painting on the front. The shirts were unusual and eye-catching. People could come up to the wearer and learn about the club.

Beatles Movie Festivals popped up all across the U.S.A. featuring as many as three or four Beatles films shown one after the other.

Beatles at the Movies

Many movie theaters were offering a dream come true for fan club members who lived close to each other. "Beatles Movie Festivals" started, becoming moneymakers, especially in smaller cities in America. One Sunday, beginning at 6:30 pm the theater would show *A Hard Day's Night* followed by *Help!* and *Yellow Submarine*, then ending with *Let It Be*. Fans would spend over six hours together watching Beatles movies. Film clubs based in colleges and universities showed *Yellow Submarine*. Students studied the film for symbolism and the use of animation in telling a story. The Beatles' films were being taught in classes, and offered for students to see free of charge. Fans took the opportunity to see The Beatles movies with friends. Film clubs often paired a Beatles film with other music movies, such as The Rolling Stones' *Gimme Shelter* or the *Woodstock* documentary.

Fans could also watch the earlier Beatles films on television. In 1971 ABC stations aired *A Hard Day's Night* during primetime several times. Fans would call up their friends long-distance and experience the movie together over the phone. They would quote the lines and comment on the jokes. It was a fantastic way to temporarily forget that the band was no longer together.

The Grammy Awards

In March, Paul and Linda were in Los Angeles, California, mixing their new album. On a whim, they decided to attend the 13th Grammy Awards ceremony. Paul said, "We drove around the block a couple of times before we really decided to go in. It was just the two of us. No bodyguards, just the two of us. We eventually sort of drove in, got in the door, sort of leaped in there, and sat down in our seats at the back of the hall." The Beatles were nominated for five awards for *Let It Be*. They won the Grammy for Best Original Score. For the first time, The Grammys were broadcast on live television, and Beatles fans tuned in. Much to their shock, Paul and Linda accepted the award on behalf of the band. Paul and Linda came to the

Paul and Linda accepted a Grammy for Let It Be on behalf of the band at the Grammy Awards. March 15, 1971.

podium in sneakers. All Paul said was, "Thank you, Goodnight." As fans called each other buzzing about this, Los Angeles-area fans rushed to the Hollywood Palladium, hoping to see Paul and Linda as they left. The fans stood among the paparazzi with their Instamatic cameras in hand as Paul and Linda ran to their car in the parking lot. The fans couldn't control their screams, and before they knew it, he was gone. Everyone hoped his appearance was a positive move, aimed at reconciling with the other Beatles.

In another questionable act, Paul sent three photographs to The Official Beatles Fan Club to be printed and sold to fans. The pictures showed Paul hard at work on the album that would become *Ram*. Linda had taken them. Each photo was labeled at the bottom, "Official Beatles Fan Club – 1971 – Copyright McCartney Productions." At the time, it was unclear what McCartney Productions were, but most people assumed it was part of the fan club. These were the only new photos the official club offered in 1971.

John and Yoko in New York City

On June 2, John and Yoko came to New York City so Yoko could gain custody of her daughter, Kyoko. They did not keep their presence a secret. They were sighted on Broadway, and they appeared on WPLJ radio. By June 18, which happened to be Paul's birthday, fans had found John and Yoko at the Plaza Hotel. They noted the couple's daily trips to 1700 Broadway to see Allen Klein. One fan was 17-year-old Jude Stein, who was younger than most of her companions. She had only joined the waiting fans the previous fall when Paul had been at the Columbia recording studio. Many of the fans who stood with her were veterans of similar waits in London.

John and Yoko at the Apple offices for an interview. June 9, 1971.

Though she had been doing volunteer work on John and Yoko's immigration campaign, at times, Jude felt like the new kid on the block. She quickly learned the ropes. When John and Yoko left the hotel, Jude asked John a question. "I talked the way I would if I was joking with somebody," Jude recounted. "So, I said, 'John, what did you get Paul for his birthday?' He said, 'Nothin'! I got him nothin'!' and we laughed, and that was that."

Over at the Apple offices, a small group had gathered. Marie Lacey was in that group, and she knew John was inside because she had seen his chauffeur, Tom, go in. As John and Yoko walked out, the girls stood in shock, not moving or speaking. Yoko flashed the peace sign; John lit a cigarette. They walked to their limo, and the girls decided they would all wave as the car went by. Marie recalled, "We waved and much to our surprise, John perched up in his seat, turned himself completely towards us and with a big grin on his face, gave us the biggest wave you ever saw. Well, I nearly fell over. It was like 'wow, he really paid attention to us!'"

The next day the girls came with gifts for John and Yoko. When they left the Apple offices, the fans handed them flowers, an American flag pin (which John pinned on his jacket), a smile button, cologne, and perfume. The famous twosome got in their car but sat there for ten minutes. All the fans gathered around and watched as John looked at his gifts. One fan had a movie camera. John got in range of the lens and made funny faces. He signed ten autographs and passed them to Yoko so she could also sign. The signatures were dispersed among the gathered. As the car pulled away, everyone was amazed at John's kindness and generosity.

The Concert for Bangladesh

By mid-July, John and Yoko were back in London, but another Beatle soon arrived in New York City. A month earlier, George Harrison had been talking to his friend, Indian musician Ravi Shankar. Ravi told George that the people in his home country, Bangladesh, were suffering. Ravi wanted to do a benefit concert for Bangladesh. George knew that Ravi's performances did not draw huge crowds, but if he and other rock 'n' roll performers held a show, they could fill an auditorium, raising much more money. George started calling musicians. He booked August 1 at Madison Square Garden in New York City, and soon fans saw a blurb about the concert in the pop columns of their newspapers. Most thought it was a rumor. After all, how could anyone organize a major show in such a short period?

On the Tuesday before the concert at the ABKCO offices on the 41st floor of 1700 Broadway, George held a press conference. George and Ravi had microphones, and there was one for Ringo too. George explained: "He's in Spain finishing up a movie. But he will be at the concert." George touted his concert, telling reporters about all the performers who would be there to raise funds and focus attention on the starving refugee children from Bangladesh. The Apple offices had seldom seen this level of excitement. Fan club employees

George—white jacket on—at the Concert for Bangladesh, *Madison Square Garden. August 1, 1971.*

and volunteers could barely contain themselves. A Beatle was having a press conference just above them!

Tickets for both afternoon and evening concerts went on sale at the Madison Square Garden box office. Fans started lining up twelve hours before the office opened, ready to camp overnight. The ticket line was so long that it caused major traffic jams. In a fanzine a year later, Carol Applegate wrote, "I found myself sitting in line at Madison Square Garden, waiting for the tickets to go on sale. They put the tickets on sale ten hours early, and before I knew it, I had purchased tickets for both the evening and afternoon shows. I was in ecstasy!" Thomas Ednie also remembers the challenges of buying a ticket. "Standing in line was like being a sardine. We were almost crushed, as the crowd would lean forward. My friend got way ahead of me, so I threw him my wallet to pay for the tickets." Not everyone had to struggle to get tickets. Things were more manageable for some fan club members. "Chuck," area secretary for Michigan said, "The fan club offered the secretaries at least the possibility of obtaining tickets to the *Concert for Bangladesh* shows, but I didn't have the financial resources to take advantage of such an offer." Chuck wasn't the only area secretary who couldn't travel to New York for the concert, although some secretaries who lived a little closer went. Laura Cayne had asked Klein to let the area secretaries buy a block of tickets directly from the fan club office. She had mentioned this to them in their correspondence. Klein disliked the fan club, so he wouldn't allow this. Those who volunteered for the club, including the National Chapter Director Joanne Maggio, only learned that the block of tickets was not available after she had arrived in New York City for the concert. Fortunately she had a friend from her club who was able to obtain tickets for them both. Because they were Apple employees, Laura, Rusty, and their boyfriends each got third-row seats to the evening concert.

By August 1, forty thousand tickets had been sold. The majority of the concert-goers were in their early twenties. This concert marked the first time any Beatle had performed in the United States in five years, and for fans it was emotional, even if it was just half of the band. "It was my first time seeing George or Ringo in person. It meant the world to me because I wasn't allowed to see The Beatles in concert," said Jean Steinert, a member of The Official George Harrison Fan Club.

Besides George and Ringo, Leon Russell, Billy Preston, Jim Keltner, Eric Clapton, Klaus Voormann, Jesse Ed Davis, and Badfinger were all on stage. Bob Dylan surprised everyone by appearing, and he took the stage alone. A fan

George—jacket off—at the Concert for Bangladesh, *Madison Square Garden. August 1, 1971.*

named Susan wrote after the show, "George was wearing a white suit and looked nervous." After an excited crowd's long, loud, ovation George introduced Ravi Shankar and told the rock fans to listen to his Indian music. Everyone obeyed. Area secretary for Pittsburgh Julie Alleva explained what happened next: "Two large projection screens started to show a rather gruesome movie which showed all the people in East Pakistan suffering while the song "Bangla Desh" played through the PA system."

When the film ended and the stage lit up, the band launched into the song "Wah-Wah." Excitement ran through both shows. Carol Applegate wrote, "The atmosphere within the Garden was really a wonderful part of the concert. Everyone there seemed to appreciate everything, and it was beautiful!"

Beatlemania was in the hearts of the fans, yet this time everyone could hear the music. No one screamed during the songs. They saved their screams until after each song ended. George performed cuts from *All Things Must Pass*, as well as some of his Beatles numbers. Eric Clapton's reprise of his solo on "While My Guitar Gently Weeps" was a highlight for many. Julie Alleva caught something that only hardcore Beatles fans would notice. "During one of the fast numbers, George started doing a little of the 'Harrison shuffle,' which he was famous from the [A] *Hard Day's Night* days."

Bob Dylan's appearance was shocking because he had seldom performed live since his motorcycle accident five years earlier. He received a standing ovation before he sang a note. Another high point of the show was when Ringo was given the spotlight and sang his current hit single, "It Don't Come Easy." With amplifiers blocking their view, Laura and Rusty had to stand on their chairs in the third row to see Ringo. Carol said Ringo's performance was her favorite part. "He seemed to be in awe as to the ovation he received and his grin nearly stuck out part his face."

After two and a half hours, the *Concert for Bangladesh* was over. The fans were not ready for it to end. "When the show ended, the audience stood, clapped, whistled and stomped the floor shouting 'more!' This went on for twenty minutes," said Julie.

Fundraising for Bangladesh

The *Concert for Bangladesh* brought in $250,000. Organizers would eventually release an album and movie of the show, with proceeds going directly to the people of Bangladesh. George and Ravi set up a fund through UNICEF called "The George

Harrison – Ravi Shankar Special Emergency Relief Fun for Displaced People of Bangla Desh." Fan club members were encouraged to support the fund by buying George's single "Bangla Desh" and Ravi's single "Joi Bangla." The Official Paul McCartney Chapter, Beatles Kingdom, The Official John Lennon Chapter, The Orange Apple Jam Chapter, and The Glassapple Chapter specifically asked their members to send money directly to the fund in the name of The Official Beatles Fan Club. They suggested that donations be for the price the fan would have paid for a concert ticket. The Official George Harrison Fan Club reached out to the membership, "It is only right that we, George fans donate to this fund to help George support the cause he so deeply believes in," was written Pat Kinzer in the October issue of the *Harrison Herald* newsletter.

George Fans in England

One would have expected that the President of *The Official George Harrison Fan Club* would attend the *Concert for Bangladesh*, but President Pat Kinzer and area secretary for Ohio Patricia Simmons, had other plans. They had scheduled a three-week trip to London, Warrington, and Liverpool. "We found out George was going to do [The Concert for] Bangladesh," Patricia recalled. "We couldn't afford to knock off the plans because we had prepaid airfare." They were disappointed but determined to make the best out of it.

Before leaving, the two girls spent a couple of days in New York City, and visited the The Official Beatles Fan Club offices. With the concert

Pat Kinzer (left), "Sarg," and Patricia Simmons (right), Apple offices at 3 Savile Row, London. July 1971.

The reels of film that would eventually become The Beatles Anthology *and* Get Back *at the Apple Offices. London 1971.*

just a few days off, it was a busy place, and they got put to work. Pat remembered, "We had a really good time talking and laughing with Laura Cayne."

Once they arrived in the United Kingdom, their first stop was London, where they met the former area secretary of Delaware, Val Furbish. She had been living in London for several months. During that time, she got to know the night guard at the Apple building on Savile Row. He was a friendly older gentleman. Everyone called him "Sarg." One evening, after everyone had left for the night, Sarg took Patricia, Pat, and a few other fans on a tour of the Apple offices. Each Beatle had his own office. Ringo's had a big star on the door, and John's had a large photograph of him and Paul hanging over the fireplace. When they went into the kitchen, they spotted a common sight at any workplace. "There was a handwritten note by George that had something to do with food in the fridge being his. And to keep your mitts off it," laughed Patricia.

As they went upstairs, they found a room full of metal shelves holding stacked cans of film. Sarg said it was all the footage of the *Let It Be* sessions and other unseen Beatles footage. These films were used to make The Beatles' *Anthology* film in 1995 and the *Get Back* documentary in 2021.

The girls had a moment when temptation almost got the better of them. "There was a filing cabinet with all these drawers, "Patricia explained. "It was full of slides. They were all dusty and dumped in there. Sarg wasn't there. We could have taken them. But no, we couldn't steal from The Beatles. We couldn't do it."

The highlight on the tour was a place very few fans get to see, the location of The Beatles' final live performance: the rooftop of 3 Savile Row. It was getting dark when they got up there, so they didn't stay long. The girls thought it was cool just to be at such an important place in The Beatles' history.

The only Beatle they saw during the entire trip was Ringo. Because of all the turmoil, he was moody and wasn't talking to fans.

Pat and Patricia did not go to England just to see a Beatle. Over the previous year the fan club chapters in the United States had raised $315 for the cancer fund, and they wanted to present the money in Mrs. Harrison's name at the hospital that had treated her. On July 28, the two girls went to the hospital's radiotherapy unit, where Mrs. Harrison had gotten radiation for the brain tumor. They met four of her doctors, who treated the girls to a four-course meal. While they ate, they shared stories about Mrs. Harrison and her family. Pat then presented the doctors with the check from the fan club along with a plaque honoring the memory of Mrs. Louise Harrison.

It was important to her to go to the cemetery and pay her respects to Mrs. Harrison at her final resting place. Mr. Harrison had written out directions to the cemetery for her. Mrs. Harrison had been buried in an unmarked grave, so it was challenging to find the exact spot. The cemetery superintendent kindly supplied roses from the garden to be placed on her grave and helped the girls find where Mrs. Harrison had been buried. Pat took a few minutes to be alone and reflect. "It was an emotional moment, as I always felt very close to Mrs. Harrison, and her death affected me terribly."

The president of the Official George Harrison Fan Club never shared the location of Mrs. Harrison's grave with any members of the fan club. Out of respect for the Harrison family, she did not want Mrs. Harrison's grave to be turned into a Beatles tourist stop.

Dear ~~Beatle~~ People

It was apparent that The Beatles were no longer a band, but the four individual members put out new songs throughout 1971. Many of them had a Beatles sound. Fans still referred to John, Paul, George, or Ringo as "a Beatle." The Official Beatles Fan Club was still active around the globe.

In late August, things changed. Paul wrote a letter to The Official Beatles Fan Club members in England via Freda Kelly. He addressed the fans with "Dear People" instead of "Dear Beatle People," which had been the traditional greeting. He informed them that he had appreciated the support over the years, but it was time for him to withdraw from The Official Beatles Fan Club. He wrote, "I don't want to be involved with anything that continues the illusion that there is such a thing as The Beatles." Because he no longer was associated with The Beatles, Paul desired to focus on his family, privacy, and music. Strangely he signed the letter, "Paul, Child-Bride Linda, Boy Prodigy Heather, and Baby Mary." After sending out the message, the U.K. Club did as he asked, removing all news about Paul and his family from their newsletters.

In the United States, things were not so cut-and-dried. Paul hadn't sent a letter to New York City, and he had never specified whether his request was only to the British Club or all clubs. That left confusion about the club's direction. Joanne Maggio, president of the The Official Paul McCartney Chapter, was particularly confused. She was prepared to hand the club over to a fan in Brooklyn named Phyllis. Joanne wanted to focus her efforts on the official fan club. Then she heard about Paul's announcement, putting her club in limbo. "If OBFC remains for The Beatles, then the Paul chapter will have to either go independent or disband," she informed club members. They'd have to hope for the best while waiting on Allen Klein and Apple to tell them what to do. In the meantime, Joanne promised she'd "continue giving you what you deserve and try to maintain chapter relationships as if nothing were happening."

The Beatle rumor mill claimed Paul was starting a new band. Once that happened, McCartney Productions would start a club for the new group. Later in the fall, Paul and Linda announced the formation of their new band, Wings. A year later, The Wings Fun Club began. It became a well-received, well-run official club for Paul's fans.

The Apple Tree

The Official Beatles Fan Club decided that Paul was distancing himself not just from the British Club, but from all Beatles fan clubs. They took this as an opportunity to make changes. Without Paul's involvement and any new Beatles music, The Official Beatles Fan Club decided it was time for a significant overhaul. As Laura Cayne wrote to the area secretaries, "As you know, realistically, there is no longer a group called The Beatles, although we hate to say so." She explained that the fan club was going to be updated to go in a new direction. The Official Beatles Fan Club was going to be called The Apple Tree, sponsored by Apple Records. It represented all recording artists on the Apple label, including John Ono Lennon, Yoko Ono Lennon, George Harrison, Ringo Starr, Paul and Linda McCartney, Badfinger, Mary Hopkin, and any other recording artists on the Apple recording label. The purpose was to bring news and photos on those in the organization.

It was evident that The Apple Tree had found a loophole to keep Paul in the fan club. Since his records were still on the Apple label, he was included along with the other former Beatles. The term "fan club" was missing from all the new information. This was not a mistake. "We feel leaving out the words 'fan club' will be extremely advantageous," explained Laura.

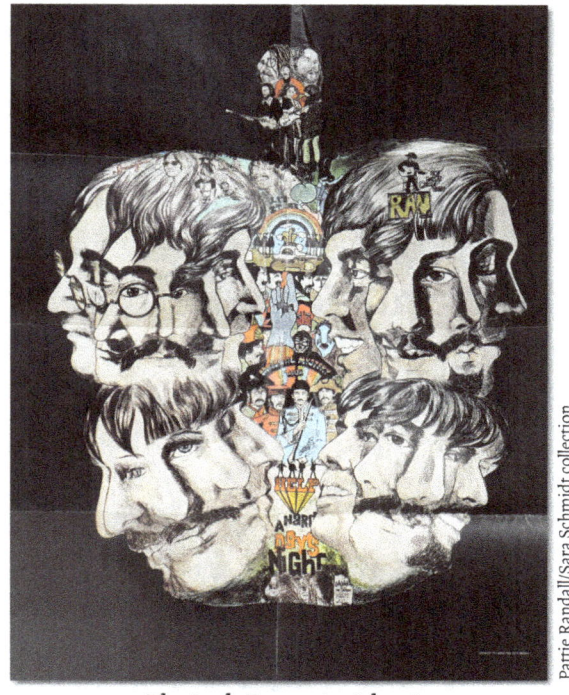

The Apple Tree poster (above) and envelope (top). 1971.

Any chapter that used the name "Beatles" in the title had to change the name. Any reference to The Beatles had to be eliminated. Laura gave the chapters a few suggestions. "I foresee no major problem as 'Beatles' can easily be replaced by 'Apple,' such as 'Apple International' or 'Apple Kingdom.'" All changes in names had to be sent to Joanne Maggio for approval. Once new names were approved, a new charter would be issued. Area secretaries were told to order a new rubber stamp that said "The Apple Tree." Until the new stamp arrived, they were to draw a line through 'OBFC' and write 'The Apple Tree' above it on all envelopes.

At the end of September, club members received the summer fan club item: a poster of all the Apple artists within the shape of an apple. In the accompanying bulletin Rusty wrote, "We feel we have surpassed everything else we have sent out to date. This magnificent masterpiece was done by Patti "Gripweed" Randall. I hope you all love it as much as we do." The drawing became the new logo for The Apple Tree. The bulletin informed the general membership about the change to The Apple Tree. Rusty reassured everyone that The Apple Tree would still offer the latest photos and news on John, Paul, George, and Ringo.

The changes to the club went into effect on October 1. At the same time Rusty quietly quit her job as National Director and moved to Florida. Laura was promoted to be the new National Director of The Apple Tree. Although there was no formal announcement, The Official Beatles Fan Club artist, Patti "Gripweed" Randall, became Assistant Director. The club continued to offer the same Beatles items for the remainder of the year. After the new year, new things would be available from The Apple Tree.

John and Yoko Return to the United States

In August, John and Yoko returned to New York City. Though no one knew it at the time, this was a permanent move. John would never return to his homeland. The couple settled into the St. Regis Hotel, and fans soon learned where they were staying. John and Yoko would leave the hotel and go to Allen Klein's office. The fans would see the couple leave the hotel and get into their waiting car. While John

John and Yoko return to the U.S. August 1971.

and Yoko were held up in heavy Manhattan traffic, the fans rushed on foot to the Apple offices, beating them every time.

Jude Stein explained, "It got to be a running joke with them. He thought he'd beat us there, but he never did, and he'd let us know. 'Do you guys have wings?' 'Are you flying?' he'd ask. We'd be there, leaning on the big potted plants outside of the office, like we'd been there for hours. We'd just play along with him." The more the fans treated John as if he wasn't anybody special, the more likely he would stop and talk to them. One of the girls always kept her voice and face deadpan, and John ate it up. Another fan, a hippie girl who went by the name Sagittarius, caught John's attention. As Jude recalled, "She was a very sweet, nice person and she looked like she just came home from Woodstock. She'd wear these long flowing skirts, and we'd all be in jeans and T-shirts. John got a kick out of her. He would look at her and say, 'Oh! What do we have here?'"

One day the girls decided to do something silly. As John and Yoko were getting into their car, the fans bowed down and as if they were in the movie *Help!* yelling," Oh, Kaili!" Everyone started to laugh, especially John, who was giggling like a child. He looked at them and, while still laughing, said, "Get up, you fools!"

The photo John requested of Laura Cayne wearing a "YOKO ONO" T-shirt. 1971.

John and Yoko were very busy that autumn. They were in court, still trying to get custody of Yoko's daughter, Kyoko, in meetings with their immigration lawyer, Leon Wildes, promoting John's new album, *Imagine*, on television and radio, and putting on a major art show in Syracuse, New York. John still took the time to visit the fan club office now and then. John knew Laura by name, and would ask her questions about the changes to the club. One day a photographer approached Laura with a request. "For Yoko's birthday, John wanted to make a photo album of everyone Yoko had ever met wearing a white 'Yoko Ono' T-shirt." The photographer took a photo of Laura wearing the shirt, and gave it to John. She wasn't sure if her photo made the album, but liked the idea of being a part of the gift.

On November 1, John and Yoko moved out of the hotel and into an apartment on Bank Street. Laura was asked to help with the move. "May Pang worked in the New York office for Allen Klein. One day she asked me to go with her to help pack up John and Yoko's things. I had a date with the man that would later be my husband, so I told her, 'I am not interested in John's underwear. If he is not going to be there, then I don't want to go.'" The fans quickly found the location of John and Yoko's new apartment. John asked them to keep this information to themselves. He wanted some privacy. The fans did as John asked. People knew they had moved, but their address never appeared in any fan newsletters.

Blindman

Allen Klein's company, ABKCO Films, co-produced a movie called *Blindman*. It was a western, and Ringo played the part of an outlaw named Candy, who was in love with the rancher's daughter. His character gets killed by the movie's main character, a blind cowboy with a seeing-eye horse. Viewers were warned that the film would be graphically violent.

The film wasn't released in the United States until 1972, but on October 26, 1971, there was a special showing of *Blindman* in New York City. All of the area Apple employees, including those who worked at The Apple Tree, were allowed to attend. Also present were George Harrison, Leon Russell, Mal Evans, Neil Aspinall, Ian Macmillan, and the *Blindman* himself, Tony Anthony.

Laura, her boyfriend, and two other friends were sitting in the front row when they were told they should move and sit on the floor. The front row seats were reserved for "older people." Laura recalls, "My future husband and I were leaning against a door when all of a sudden the door flew open and my future husband fell right to the floor. George Harrison opened the door, and he asked, 'Is this the place?'" The "older people" were George and his crew. While he was in New York appearing on *The Dick Cavett Show*, George visited the fan club. He came to speak to Rusty, but she longer worked there. Laura was the only person he found. She and George talked for about five minutes.

Christmas 1971

To the disappointment of many, at the end of 1971, The Apple Tree did not send out anything for Christmas. Earlier in the year there had been talk of a Christmas surprise calendar, but members did not even receive a bulletin. Several chapters sent out unique things for the holidays. The Official George Harrison Fan Club published a more extensive newsletter than usual called *The George Gernal*. Pat Kinzer had been sending these newsletters at the end of every year, but the 1971 *George Gernal* was more: a combination of her usual newsletter along with poems, articles, lyrics, a timeline, and photos. The John Lennon Chapter sent members a pocket calendar for 1972 with a new picture of John and Yoko on the front.

John and Yoko 1972 pocket calendar front (top) and back side (above).

The year ended with John and Yoko's Christmas message for peace. They released the song, and plastered billboards worldwide, saying: "War is Over (If You Want It)." If only that slogan had worked for The Apple Tree and its chapters in 1972.

1972

1972 was supposed to be the year The Apple Tree took off. There were plans to sell new photos and the 1972 book and membership card. The book had to have the approval of everyone pictured inside. When Paul McCartney saw the book, he wanted some changes. As Laura Cayne recalled, "He crossed out Heather as his step-daughter and put 'adopted daughter.' He crossed out the end where it said 'to be continued' and a few other things. Allen Klein would not allow the book to be sent out to members."

There wasn't a need to make new books or even membership cards for The Apple Tree. Not long after the start of the new year, Laura was called into Allen Klein's office. Lying on Klein's desk was the December 1971 issue of The Official George Harrison Fan Club newsletter, *The George Gernal*. An unhappy Klein demanded to know who Pat Kinzer was. He informed Laura that George had gotten a copy of the newsletter and was livid over it. George called it garbage and disclaimed not just his own chapter but the entire fan club. The angry George called the London Apple offices, who then contacted Klein in New York to express how mad George was about the newsletter and the fan club. No one told Pat exactly what the problem was.

Laura Cayne on the phone at the OBFC office in New York City.

This behavior wasn't anything new. Freda Kelly, the director of the British fan club, told Patricia Simmons that in the 11 years of the club, at some point each of The Beatles had been very moody about the club, and had wanted to end it. Soon the Beatle would change his mind and be supportive again. But now things were different.

One of the things Laura initially did not understand was how George got a copy of *The George Gernal*. "One of the big rules for the fan club was not to send their newsletters to England," she recalled. "The Official George Harrison Fan Club sent one to England and George didn't like something in it. Klein didn't ever like the fan club to begin with, so when he heard about the newsletter, he put an end to the fan club." Pat had a good reason for sending the newsletter to England. George's sister, Louise Harrison Caldwell, was going through a divorce, and Pat had learned that Louise had moved in with her brother. She had been sending a copy of the newsletter to Louise since 1966, so she sent the most recent issue to Friar Park. She did not know that Louise had not moved and was living in New York. Instead, the newsletter landed in the hands of a moody George.

George's anger over the newsletter resulted in a meeting at the Apple offices in London. In attendance were George, Ringo, Freda, and a member of the Apple staff. The newsletter was not discussed; instead, the initial conversation was about the expense of changing the name of the club to The Apple Tree. Freda made an unexpected announcement. After eleven years with the club, she was resigning. Freda was a Beatles fan and was not interested in the other Apple artists. More importantly, she was expecting her second child, and it would be too difficult for her to run the club with two young children.

On hearing the news, George and Ringo decided to end The Official Beatles Fan Club. Freda had been with them from the very beginning of The Beatles. They loved her and considered her part of The Beatles' family. The Beatles were over as a band, and without Freda running things in England, the fan club needed to end as well. In talking to the media, Ringo announced, "We don't want to keep The Beatles myth going since we are no longer together."

Part-time worker Ida Langsam, also known as Judee Gould, was stuffing envelopes in the mailroom when Laura came in and told her George Harrison did not want the club anymore. On January 19, Laura sent a letter to the area secretaries and chapter presidents saying that with The Beatles no longer together, Apple's management no longer wanted an active fan club. She told them that all clubs in the U.S. and U.K. were immediately dissolved. The letter also stated, "What pulled the trigger was one of our FINEST chapters sent out a newsletter, which did not agree with either John, George or Ringo. They all feel that they do not want news, such as this newsletter contained, being sent out."

Freda Kelly talks on the telephone at the U.K. Fan Club headquarters in Liverpool, England.

The area secretaries were shocked and angry at this news. Patricia Simmons said at the time, "I feel like the last three years I spent as area secretary were all a waste and feel like taking my pile of letters and dropping them over their heads." Likewise, Laura was also devastated. "Once I got the news, I cried and cried. I talked on the phone with Freda for two hours."

Fan club secretaries called each other, Laura, and Freda, trying to figure out what happened. Laura did not share the name of the club that caused the original problem, but she did tell callers it was George who was angry. Patricia wrote to fans in Ohio, "It hardly seems fair to disband the entire club because of one chapter's newsletter. Can't it be gone over with George pointing out exactly what he didn't like about it and what changes he'd want and let it go?" Betty Heiser, the president of The Orange Apple Jam Chapter, informed her members that it was George who wanted the club closed. She said he "let loose with his famous Harrison temper."

The truth was revealed when Pat received a mimeographed letter sent to all members of The Official Paul McCartney Fan Club dated January 24. The letter informed her that it was her club and newsletter that had angered George. President of The Official Paul McCartney Fan Club, Joanne, did not know that Pat had not been told it was her newsletter that caused the issues, and was unhappy with the way the situation was handled. Understandably, Pat felt terrible. "Upset was not a strong enough word to describe my feelings. Betrayed, insulted, humiliated, spit on, trashed, and furious are appropriate words." She sent her members an emotional letter. She told them what had happened and the dissolution of The Official Beatles Fan Club, and the The Official George Harrison Fan Club. She was angry at George for claiming his ignorance of the club as he disowned it. Pat told the members that George was not the nice guy everyone once thought he was. She wanted them to remember what he had done.

In her search for answers, Pat wrote letters to anyone who might help her discover the truth. She heard back from Freda, who explained to Pat that she had resigned from the club due to her pregnancy. She told her that the fan club was going to end anyhow. "I know that your newsletter did cause a lot of trouble, but please don't think it was you who caused the closure of the club." George's father also wrote back to her and said that George was not mad about her newsletter specifically but with the fan club in general. George felt like fans were being misled by false information printed in club materials.

No one was ever told precisely what in *The George Gernal* made George so mad. During a phone call with Patricia at the time, Laura said that she had read through *The George Gernal*, and all the news was accurate, and she did not understand what caused him so much disturbance. Today Laura and Pat both think his anger stemmed from a reprint of an article from the *Daily Mirror*

Apple

January 1972

Dear Fans;

As you are all well aware, The Beatles are no longer recording as a group. Since it was the intention of the club when it was formed that it be a Beatle Fan Club, the management of Apple, at this time, feel it is unfair to keep the club active on this basis.

At some later date, if it is possible to form a different kind of club, we hope you might be interested enough to join.

Thank you for your support and hope that you will enjoy the items sent and continue to enjoy the music put out by John, George, Ringo and Paul.

Best wishes,

Rusty Rahn

Rusty Rahn

Laura Cayne

Laura Cayne

Judee

JUDEE GOULD
N. Y. C. Area Secretary
THE APPLE TREE
67-15 102 Street
Rego Park, N. Y. 11375

~~Enc.~~

Sara Schmidt collection

Notice to all Beatles fan club members, dated January 1972 on Apple letterhead, informing them of the closure of The Beatles Official Fan Club.

where Pattie stated that she and George would consider adoption. George was unhappy about the interview and did not want the story to be shared in a newsletter.

Ida remembers hearing that George Harrison was bothered by fans wanting to know where his mother was buried, and that is why he wanted the club closed. A rumor had been going around in England that American fan club members were conducting tours of Mrs. Harrison's grave site. This rumor was, of course, the farthest thing from the truth. The only members of the fan club who had visited Mrs. Harrison's grave were the two from the Official George Harrison Fan Club. They went with Mr. Harrison's permission and did not give tours. They went to pay their respects to their friend.

Apple Records Inc. refund check in the amount of 75 cents. January 21, 1972.

Most fan club members weren't angry with Pat. They didn't blame her for the club's break-up. They knew that in the big picture, it was not her fault at all. The Beatles themselves had broken up as a group, and there was no longer a need for an official fan club. The club was on its last leg as it entered 1972 and most likely would not have made it through another year.

Even though the club was dissolved, there were still some loose ends. All 4,200 members needed to be notified and refunds had to be issued. "I typed out all the checks for the refunds," recalled Laura. "Depending on how many of the three items given a fan received, they would get either a 75 cents or a $1.25 refund."

Most fans had received the 1970 release of *The Beatles Christmas Album*, fan club book for 1971, and The Apple Tree poster, so they received a check for 75 cents. Members who had joined in 1971 did not receive the Christmas album, so they received the $1.25 refund. The checks were mailed from Apple Records Inc. Many fans chose to keep this check rather than cash it; it was a new item for their

Beatles collection. These uncashed checks created an accounting nightmare. In her letter to members, Laura kept things open, writing, "At some later date, if it is possible to form a different type of club, we hope you might be interested enough to join." That was never meant to be. The United States never had an official fan club for The Beatles again.

When the time came to pack up the fan club office, everyone took things. Ida grabbed a few items before they went in the trash. "I was able to take some odds and ends out of the office," said Laura. "I got a broken Grammy award. It was missing the plate that said it was given to The Beatles."

The area secretaries and chapter presidents also needed to tie up loose ends. All money collected for the Bangladesh fund had to be turned in, and remaining photos and stationery had to be sold. Patricia Simmons went ahead with the fan gathering she had planned for January 29 for fans in Ohio. She had a taping session in her home. Since 1964 Patricia had been tape recording The Beatles on radio and television. Many fans had received cassette tape recorders for Christmas and asked her to make copies of her materials. Instead of doing it for each fan, she invited them over. "I decided I may as well play the tapes for everyone, fan club members, pen pals, and friends all at once," she said.

Each of the twenty-two chapters had to make its own decision. With The Official Beatles Fan Club gone, there was no barrier to forming independent clubs. With George's feelings clear, Pat immediately closed The George Harrison Fan Club. Betty Heiser at The Orange Apple Jam Chapter felt the same way. "George has made it quite clear that he does not want a fan club. This club was started for George, and so that leaves me in a curious position. So partially because of George's wishes, partly because of lack of time and partly because of money, I'm folding Orange Apple Jam. I just couldn't keep it up knowing that George wants no part of it. I hope you all understand," she wrote in her last newsletter.

Once the fan club office closed, the office at 1700 Broadway became the headquarters for John and Yoko.

A few clubs decided to continue as independents. Those clubs included 5 Bites of the Apple, Dig It (which became With a Little Help From My Friends), Harrison Organization (which became the Harrison Alliance), and McCartney Ltd. Many of these clubs were successful and lasted into the 1980s. *The Harrison Alliance* lasted until after George's death in 2001.

Once the fan club office inside 1700 Broadway had been cleaned out, the National Headquarters for John and Yoko moved in. The group's purpose was to help John and Yoko fight their immigration battles to stay in the United States. Ida Langsam, the New York-area secretary known as "Judee Gould," began working for the National Headquarters. She brought the shoebox full of index cards with the names of former New York-area fan club members. Those were the people who they contacted to sign the petition to keep John and Yoko in the U.S.A. Ida was paid to stuff envelopes and file the petitions. They stayed there until the day John, George, and Ringo fired Allen Klein. Since Klein did not want anything about The Beatles in his office, everyone that worked there was thrown out.

Lasting Friendships

The Official Beatles Fan Club in the United States made a significant impact on thousands of members. Friendships lasting over fifty years started in the club. It was also a springboard to bigger and better career opportunities. Hundreds of people involved in the club began careers in the music industry, journalism, and writing. Many area secretaries and chapter presidents landed their first jobs with skills they'd learned working for the club.

The Official Beatles Fan Club may have ended in 1972, but the gathering of Beatles fans has never ceased. In the 21st century, Beatles fans still meet at conventions and festivals. As was true in 1964, the fans still sing Beatles' songs, trade photographs, and discuss their music. The Beatles still help people form lasting friendships, and their message of peace and love will never end.

Bibliography

Adams, Marjory. "Beatles' shiny 'Yellow Submarine' Mad Vehicle." *The Boston Globe*, November 20, 1968.

Akron Wilson, Karyn. "They Didn't Seem to Hurry to Seek Safety." *Beacon Journal*, August 15, 1966.

Allen, Kathy. "Letters to the Editor." *The Ottawa Journal*, December 24, 1965.

Alleva, Julie. Telephone correspondence with the author. November 19, 2019.

Alterman, Loraine. "Detroit's Beatle Club Has Indian 'Daughter.'" *Detroit Free Press*, January 7, 1966.

Anderson, Fred. "Beatle Bobbies Bubble." *Fort Lauderdale News*, January 14, 1965.

Andon, Arma. Telephone correspondence with the author. September 25, 2018.

AP. "Beatles Fan Club On Its Last Stanza." *Trenton Evening Times*, February 9, 1972.

AP. "George Harrison Thinks Beatles Will Reunite." April 29, 1970.

AP. "Lennon Claims Beatles on Brink of Bankruptcy." *The Los Angeles Times*, January 18, 1969.

Appel, Jennifer. E-mail message to the author. October 29, 2017.

Applegate, Carol. "Witness to Bangla Desh." *Independent Free Apple*, April 1972.

Bastone, William (editor). "Backstage Rider Hall of Fame." The Smoking Gun, August 13, 2010. http://www.thesmokinggun.com/backstage/hall-fame/beatles

"Beatle Fan Club and How It Grew." *Nevada State Journal*, April 21, 1964.

"Beatle Fans Nearly Wreck Coliseum." *The Los Angeles Times*, June 7, 1964.

Beatles Booster. "From Maplewood." *Newark Star Ledger*, September 12, 1965.

"Beatles' Club to Perform." *Waukesha Daily Freeman*, January 21, 1965.

"Beatles For the Fans." *Liverpool Echo*, December 17, 1966.

"Beatles Forever, Palladium Never." *The News-Palladium*, February 8, 1966.

Beatles, The. *The Beatles Anthology*. San Francisco: Chronicle Books, 2000.

"Beatles Zap Fans, $1000 Grand." *Michigan Daily*, March 28, 1969.

"Beatles Zap USA Ltd." *Rolling Stone*, February 10, 1968.

Beaver, Lotebel. "Mansfield Girl Describes Show." *News Journal*, August 25, 1965.

Bellack, Sandi. Telephone correspondence with the author. August 22, 2018.

Belmer, Scott ("Belmo"). *The Beatles Invade Cincinnati: 1964 & 1966*. Ft. Mitchell, KY: Belmo Publishing, 2014.

Bender, Elaine McAfee. Telephone correspondence with the author. August 3, 2017.

Berghofer, Dolores. "Beatle Fans Rally to Right Tilted Haloes of Rock Idols." *Arcadia Tribune*, August 14, 1966.

Berman, Garry. *"We're Going to See the Beatles!": An Oral History of Beatlemania as Told by the Fans Who Were There*. Santa Monica, California: Santa Monica Press LLC, 2008.

Betancourt, Ruben. "George Harrison Stops to Chat." *Fort Lauderdale News*, November 21, 1970.

"Big Beatles Rally Here." *The Times*, August 7, 1964.

Bledsoe, Barbara. "It's Ringo for President." *Kingsport Times News*, August 1, 1964.

Boone, Pat. Interview by Gary James. Classic Bands. http://www.classicbands.com/PatBooneInterview.html

Brandel, Laurie. "Dream Job at the Beatles HQ." *Datebook* magazine, Summer 1965.

Brigham, Maurie. "Letters From Times Readers." *The Times*, August 15, 1964.

Burns, Kathy. *The Guitar's All Right as a Hobby, John*. Lexington, Kentucky, 2014.

Campbell, Tom. "Rebirth of Paul McCartney." *San Francisco Examiner*, April 18, 1970.

Canadian Press. "Beatle Fans From Afar in Toronto." *Montreal Gazette*, August 21, 1965.

Cantor, George. "Tom Clay, Disc Jockey in Exile." *Detroit Free Press*, April 25, 1965.

Caserta, Jeannette. "Celebrating Anniversary." The Beatles Wives and Girls. August 23, 2018. https://johnandcynthialennon.blogspot.com/2018/08/celebrating-anniversary.html?m=0

Cash, Rosanne. E-mail message to the author. October 12, 2017.

Champlin, Charles. "Rich Beatles Don't Need the Misery." *The Des Moines Register*, January 8, 1967.

Chatterly, Claire. "*Disc* Prize Winner in USA Finds Beatles Fab Most." *Disc* magazine, August 22, 1964.

Cockram, Mary. E-mail message to the author. November 25, 2017.

Crawford, Bill. *The Lawton Constitution*, August 24, 1966.

Crichton, Patti. Online message to the author. January 21, 2019.

Crowley, John F. "The Presentation." The Canteen, 2004. http://www.thecanteen.com/mark.html

Crowley, Mike. "Teen Fans Give Views About Paul Leaving The Beatles." *Courier-Post*, April 11, 1970.

Daley, Frank. "At the Movies." *The Ottawa Journal*, May 19, 1970.

Deutsch, Linda. "She's the Top Beatle Fan." *Asbury Park Press*, February 4, 1966.

Dimaggio, Joanne. E-mail to the author. March 20, 2022.

Dugas, Sandra. "Beatles Impressive to Jackson Teener." *Clarion-Ledger*, August 23, 1965.

Dusty. "Rubber Sole: Nothing on a Shoe." *Daily World*, January 11, 1966.

Ednie, Thomas. Online message to the author. April 23, 2020.

Edwards, Marti. Interview with the author. Rosemont, Illinois, August 12, 2017.

Edwards, Warren. "Clinton Teenagers Back Beatles Ban." *Clarion-Ledger*, August 9, 1966.

Eichelbaum, Stanley. "Ringo, the Film Star in Beverly Hills." *San Francisco Examiner*, January 29, 1970.

Elias, Dee. *Confessions of a Beatlemaniac!!* Santa Barbara, California, 2014.

Elias, Dee. Online message to the author. June 12, 2017.

Ellis, Geoffrey. *I Should Have Known Better: A Life in Pop Management: The Beatles, Brian Epstein and Elton John*. London, England: Thorogood Publishing, 2004. Kindle.

Esper, George. "Oh, Gosh, Gee Whiz!" *The Indianapolis News*, May 5, 1965.

"Fan Club Boss Jody Books a Beatle Date." *The Gazette*, September 5, 1964.

"Fan Club Reports." *The Independent Record*, August 29, 1965.

"Fan Clubs." *The Compleat Beatlemaniac*, November 18, 1968.

Feder, Robert. "Feder Flashback: WLS Meets The Beatles." Robert Feder. January 22, 2014. https://www.robertfeder.com/2014/01/22/feder-flashback-wls-meets-the-beatles/

Flairive, Frank. "Beatles Wild Greeting." *San Francisco Chronicle*, August 19, 1964.

Flanagan, Barbara. "Five South Side Girls Pledge Allegiance to Beatles." *Star-Tribune*, April 1, 1965.

Flans, Robyn. Online message to the author. May 10, 2019.

Flynn, Angela. "Meeting the Beatles." *Hour Detroit*, September 4, 2014. www.hourdetroit.com/Hour-Detroit/September-2014/Meeting-the-Beatles

Gallo, Patti. Interview with the author. Rosemont, Illinois, August 12, 2018.

Geiger, Eric. "Hair-Cut Creates Big Furor." *The Indianapolis Star*, March 21, 1965.

"George, but No Ringo." *Daily News*, July 28, 1971.

gigi shapiro. "Lynn2" YouTube video, 2:50, November 25, 2013. https://www.youtube.com/watch?v=TmhtreSlCFI&t=53s

Gilbert, Eugene. "Time is Catching Up With The Beatles." *Arkansas Democrat*, September 5, 1965.

"Girls Visit Beatles." *The Times*, September 3, 1964.

Gleason, Ralph. "Beatles Last Visit?" *San Francisco Chronicle*, September 1, 1965.

Goldman, Richard. Online message to the author. November 6, 2018.

Gunderson, Chuck. *Some Fun Tonight! The Backstage Story of How the Beatles Rocked America: The Historic Tours of 1964 to 1966*: San Diego, California: Gunderson Media, 2014.

Harris, Suzanne. "Long Hair Set Screams for 'Help!' and Beatles." *St. Petersburg Independent*, August 20, 1965.

"Healing Buddha." The Official Hash Howard Tribute Site. www.hashhoward.com. October 25, 2015.

Healy, Leslie. Telephone correspondence with the author. January 27, 2018.

Hedlund, Marilou. "Teens Plot and Plan to Meet The Beatles." *Chicago Tribune*, August 28, 1964.

Hemmingsen, Piers. *The Beatles in Canada: The Origins of Beatlemania!* Toronto, Ontario: Hemmingsen Publishing, 2016.

Hernandez, Yolanda. "Sharing a Coke and a Smile with The Beatles." *Elegant Island Living*, April 10, 2014. http://www.elegantislandliving.net/ssi-archives/sharing-a-coke-and-a-smile-with-the-fab-four/

Hill, Judi. "Eeeeeee, Aaaaaah, Oh, Paul!... 270 Go to Beatleland." *Democrat and Chronicle*, August 18, 1966.

"Hip, Hippie, Hooray!" *The Press-Tribune*, September 14, 1967.

Hirschhorn, Paul. "On the Arts." *The News-Herald*, November 14, 1969.

Hiss, Anthony. "A Report from Hiram." *The New Yorker*, August 15, 1964.

Holt, Karen. "Another Beatle Fan Club Needed in This Community." *The Independent Record*, January 14, 1966.

Howard, Lisa. "The New York Underground Fans." Meet The Beatles For Real. June 1, 2010. www.meetthebeatlesforreal.com/2010/06/this-blog-as-often-focused-on-wonderful.html

Hull, Dave. *Hullabaloo! The Life and (Mis)Adventures of L.A. Radio Legend Dave Hull*. Redondo Beach, California: Final Word Press, 2013. Kindle.

Hurwitz, Matt. "The Beatles' Christmas Records: A Feat of Fan Appreciation and Devotion." *Variety*, December 14, 2017. www.variety.com/2017/music/news/beatles-christmas-records-box-set-120263584

Jaacks, Jo Ann. Online message to the author. March 23, 2018.

Jarvis, Jack. "Beatles Show Puckish Humor at Interview." *Seattle Post-Intelligencer*, August 22, 1964.

"John and Paul on the Tonight Show." *TeenSet* magazine, August 1968.

Johnson, Jared. "George's LP Tops Beatles Solo." *The Atlanta Constitution*, January 10, 1971.

Johnson, Judy. Letter to the author. January 1, 2018.

Johnston, Chuck. E-mail message. December 3, 2017.

Jones, Katie. Online message to the author. January 21, 2019.

"July 7, 1964." *Santa Ana: The Orange County Register*, February 6, 1984.

Kaiser, Kathleen. Telephone correspondence with the author. December 29, 2017.

Kamm, Val. "Confessions of a Beatlemaniac." *Michigan History*, May-June 2013.

Kandalis, Jo. "We Met and Protected the Beatles. You Can Too." Charlton Publications, Summer 1965.

Keen, Richard. E-mail message to the author. November 17, 2017.

"Keep Jackson Beatleful is Youth's New Slogan." *The Clarion-Ledger*, October 17, 1965.

Kelley, Larry. "Take the Artful Case of Gripweed." *Trenton Evening Times*, January 17, 1969.

Kendall, Brian. *Our Hearts Went Boom: The Beatles' Invasion of Canada*. Toronto, Ontario: Viking, 1997.

"Kids Doubt Beatles Want Legal Leaves." *Orlando Sentinel*, August 5, 1967.

King Alfred. "Loose Rumors Call for New Strategy." *The Compleat Beatlemaniac*, March 10, 1969.

Kotal, Kent. "The Friday Flash." Forgotten Hits. September 14, 2012. http://forgottenhits60s.blogspot.com/2012/09/the-friday-flash-getting-jump-on.html

Kottke, Lee. "Loyal Beatle Fans Still Want to Hold Their Hands, Yeah, Yeah." *Star-Tribune*, February 8, 1966.

Kras, Phil. "The New Beatles Album: The Continuing Story of Ringo Raccoon." *The Concordiensis*, November 22, 1968.

LaMastra, Felice. "Firsthand Account of The Beatles Junior Press conference." Interview by Jay Spangler. The Beatles Ultimate Experience. http://www.beatlesinterviews.org/db1966.beatles.junior2.html

Langsam, Ida. Telephone correspondence with the author. July 20, 2017.

Lee, T.J. "Voice of the People." *Clarion-Ledger*, August 9, 1966.

Lewisohn, Mark. Interview with Carol Condit. March 28, 2007.

Lewisohn, Mark. Interview with Jenny Condit. March 25, 2007.

Lewisohn, Mark. Interview with Karen Cammarato, April 27, 2007.

Liscio, Sherry. E-mail message to the author. December 10, 2013.

Liss, Sharon. "Beatleite." *Philadelphia Daily News*, August 27, 1966.

"'Lucy' or LSD? Or Maybe Both." *The News Journal*, September 1, 1967.

Lundy, Walker. "Nick in Jam with Granddaughter, Wigs Up." *The Tampa Tribune*, August 14, 1964.

Maher, Jack. "Beatles Bug as They Control Air." *Billboard*, February 29, 1964.

Maloney, Joann. E-mail message to the author. March 12, 2018.

Mancuso, Pat. *Do You Want to Know a Secret?: The Story of the Official George Harrison Fan Club*. West Conshohocken, Pennsylvania: Infinity Publishing, 2005.

Mancuso, Pat. Fan Club Panel at the Fest for Beatle Fans, August 11, 2018.

Mannweiler, David. "Beatles 'Let it Be' Letdown on Purpose?" *The Indianapolis News*, May 15, 1970.

"Mansfield Girl Describes Show by The Beatles." *The News Journal*, August 25, 1965.

Marcos Alexandre de Silva. "Ringo Interview-San Francisco." YouTube video, 3:57, June 13, 2014. https://www.youtube.com/watch?v=2TUIT5O-zPI

Marji. "Newshounds Get Out Own Beatle Bulletin." *Hartford Courant*, February 27, 1965.

Martin, Bill. Online message to the author. January 22, 2019.

Matheson, Judy. Online message to the author. December 14, 2018.

McCall, Walter. "Geared Up for Beatles Show." *Windsor Star*, August 18, 1965.

McCormack, JoAnne. Telephone correspondence with the author. March 12, 2018.

Mellons, Cathi. "She Likes Ringo." *Kingsport Times-News*, August 28, 1964.

Merryfield, Mary. "Our Teens Get The Message From Song Lyrics." *Chicago Tribune*, September 17, 1967.

Milne, Jude. Telephone correspondence with the author. April 26, 2020.

Moran, Victoria. Telephone correspondence with the author. December 9, 2017.

Morse, Sandi. "An Interview With Jock McLean." *Datebook* magazine, April 1969.

Morse, Sandi. "Beatles News." *Datebook* magazine, March 1970.

Morse, Sandi. "Beatles News." *Datebook* magazine, September 1970.

"Mpls Not Rushing for Beatles Tix." *Variety*, May 26, 1965.

Mullin, Barry. "Just a Hard Day's Night." *Calgary Herald*, August 20, 1964.

"No Cries for 'Help' as Beatle Movie Opens." *Red Bank Register*, August 24, 1965.

Norman, Philip. *Shout! The Beatles in Their Generation*. New York City: Fireside, 1981.

Onion, Mary. Telephone correspondence with the author. April 28, 2015.

Paradiso, Vikki. E-mail message to the author. November 15, 2017.

Parker, Bonnie and Smith, Monica. "Beatles Reward Portland Fans for Good Behavior." *Seattle Daily Times*, August 24, 1965.

Parmenter, Tom. "Ringo's New Bands Say Phones Ringing Here." *Chicago American*, February 11, 1965.

Pauley, Gay. "Jane Asher Won't Discuss Romance." *Lubbock Avalanche-Journal*, February 24, 1967.

Pavia, Joe. Interview with Trudy Medcalf. "Station to Station." Podcast audio. March 18, 2017. https://www.listennotes.com/podcasts/station-to-station/episode-15-trudy-medcalf-rsC4PkOFfUX/

Pearson, Michael and Aldus, Matt. Interview with Merle Frimark, Beatles City. Podcast audio. December 30, 2018.

Phillips, Walt. "Beatles Fan Club Here." *Greenfield Recorder-Gazette*, November 4, 1965.

Piano, Evelyn. "Sound Track." *Fitchburg Sentinel*, June 1, 1967.

Pierce, Jeanne. "Says No to Ringo." *Kingsport Times-News*, August 5, 1964.

Pinder, Rodney. "Ringo Starr, Wife Return Home, They Don't Like Spicy Food." *Standard-Speaker*, March 2, 1968.

"Playback from Teen Readers." *Evening Star*, February 20, 1965.

"Police Tell of Ejecting Girls at Beatles' Motel." *Star Tribune*, August 25, 1965.

Rainer, Pat. Telephone correspondence with the author. October 8, 2018.

Ramsburg, Jim. E-mail message to the author. September 5, 2017.

Regan, Simon. "I Lived With The Beatles at Their Guru's Retreat." *The Californian*, May 18, 1968.

Reice, Sylvie. "Screaming Girls Turn Into Ladies at Press Conference with Beatles." *Daily Press*, September 11, 1966.

Robb, Inez. "'Ringo for President' Bandwagon Now Rolling Along in San Francisco." *The Cedar Rapids Gazette*, July 14, 1964.

"Rock of Gibraltar Setting for Lennon-Yoko Ono Vows." *The Daily Oklahoman*, March 21, 1969.

Rodriguez, Robert. Interview with Deb Gendler. "Something About The Beatles." Podcast audio. September 17, 2017.

Runtagh, Jordan. "Beatles Famous Rooftop Concert: 15 Things You Didn't Know." *Rolling Stone*. January 29, 2014. https://www.rollingstone.com/music/music-news/beatles-famous-rooftop-concert-15-things-you-didnt-know-58342/

Runtagh, Jordan. "Beatles' Rare Fan Club Christmas Records: A Complete Guide." *Rolling Stone*. December 15, 2017. https://www.rollingstone.com/music/music-lists/beatles-rare-fan-club-christmas-records-a-complete-guide-120854/pantomime-everywhere-its-christmas-1966-121505/

Russo, Joanne. Telephone correspondence with the author. August 4, 2017.

Roumell, Stephanie. "One Year Later, It's a Beatle-In at Shea." *The New York Times*, August 24, 1967.

Schall, Vickie. Online message to the author. November 6, 2018.

Shulte, Ellen. "Students Have a Brush with Beatle Cover Art." *The Los Angeles Times*, August 19, 1967.

Schultz, Terri. "Old Beatles Never Die; They Just —." *Chicago Tribune*, March 12, 1970.

Silive, Annalise K. "A 50-Year Friendship That Started With a Letter." *Staten Islander*, December 16, 2015. www.silive.com/news/2015/12/staten_islander_invites_pen_pa.html

Simmons, Pat. Telephone correspondence with the author. November 16, 2017.

Sky, Susan. "My Beatles Memories." Heritage Auctions Catalogue. October 11, 2010.

Smith, Howard and Brookstein, Ezra. *The Smith Tapes: Lost Interviews with Rock Stars & Icons 1969-1972*. New York City: Princeton Architectural Press, 2015. Kindle.

Smith, Ron. "'Sgt. Pepper' Will Turn You On." *Kokomo Tribune*, August 26, 1967.

Snapp, Carrie Mae. Telephone correspondence with the author. December 29, 2017.

Somach, Denny. *Ticket to Ride*. New York City: William Morrow & Co, 1989.

Soocher, Stan. *Baby You're a Rich Man: Suing The Beatles for Fun and Profit*. Lebanon, New Hampshire: University Press of New England, 2015. Kindle.

Sounes, Howard. "Only Linda Knew How to Save Him." *The Daily Mail*, August 17, 2010.

Spangler, Jay. "Beatles Interview: Carroll James, Washington Coliseum 2/11/1964." The Beatles Ultimate Experience, 1997. http://www.beatlesinterviews.org/db1964.0211cj.beatles.html

Spinetti, Victor. *Up Front...: His Strictly Confidential Autobiography*. London: Portico, 2015.

Stagg, Jim. "Mama Cass In Las Vegas." *Chicago Sun Times*, September 1968.

Steinert, Jean. Online message to the author. April 22, 2020.

Stover, Janis. Email message to the author. July 6, 2014.

Susan. "Musicians Laud Album By Beatles." *The Evening Sun*, July 3, 1967.

Susan. "Speaking of the Beatles." *The Evening Sun*, September 21, 1966.

Symon, John. "Don't Worry, John Lennon, Trenton's Fans are Loyal." *Trenton Evening Times*, August 14, 1966.

Syse, Glenna. "Beatles a Hit." *Chicago Sun-Times*, August 21, 1965.

"Teen Girls Throng Home to Meet Beatle's Sister." *The Indianapolis News*, May 31, 1965.

Thornton, Anita. Online message to the author. September 30, 2017.

"To Tell the Truth." To Tell the Truth: Head of Beatles' Fan Club, Bat expert; PANEL: Sally Ann Howes (June 29, 1964), YouTube video, 25:56, October 28, 2016. https://www.youtube.com/watch?v=xLrTWYDZJys

Towne, Jacqueline and Hand, Michael. "Tacoma Girls Meet Beatles: Wonderful." *The News Tribune*, August 22, 1964.

"True Beatle fan" [unknown letter writer]. "Beatles' New York Show Impressed Fan." *Wilkes-Barre Times Leader*, August 19, 1965.

Unterberger, Richie. *The Unreleased Beatles*. San Francisco, California: Bookbay, 2014.

UPI. "Beatles' Boy Warns Dallas." *The Times*, September 15, 1964.

UPI. "Beatles Breaking Up Due to the Tax Man." *Press-Telegram*, January 23, 1967.

UPI. "Beatles Fans Splash in Civic Center Pond." *Redlands Daily Facts*, August 11, 1964.

UPI. "Their Fans Conclude Beatles Breaking Up." *The Indianapolis Star*, November 10, 1966.

UPI. "Won't Tear Down Hilton: S.F. Beatle Fans Pledge Order." *Press-Telegram*, August 15, 1964.

"Views." *The Kansas City Times*, October 8, 1964.

Visco, Frank. E-mail message to the author. August 31, 2017.

Voltz, Jeanne. "They Leave a Broken Heart." *The Herald Examiner*, August 25, 1964.

"WASI Beatles Boosters." *Cashbox*, February 8, 1964.

"We Loved Them Yeah Yeah Yeah: When the Beatles Came to Town." *Deseret News*, February 7, 1994.

"Weeping Girls Mourn Beatle Paul McCartney's Marriage." *The News Leader*, March 12, 1969.

Whitaker, Robert. 2016 Interview by Tony Barrell. Accessed October 2, 2018. https://www.tonybarrell.com/guys-and-dolls/

Williams, Pam. Online message to the author. July 19, 2015.

Wishinsky, Laura. Telephone correspondence with the author. April 30, 2017.

Woods, Linda. Interview by the author. New York City, April 6, 2019.

"Yeah, Yeah, Who?" *The Evening Sun*, March 11, 1966

Fan Club Newsletters:
5 Bites of the Apple (1971-1972)
Apple Juce (1970-1972)
Apple Seed (1971-1972)
ASCP Newsletter (1971)
Beatles Boosters (1964-1965)
Beatles Fans of the World, Unite! (1967-1968)
The Boss Beatles (1966-1968)
The Bugle (1967-1968)
Cyn Lennon Beatle Fan Club (1966-1968)
English Bound Beatles Fans (1968-1969)
Father Lennon's Many Children/Beatles Rule (1968-1971)
The Flying Cow (1968)
The Glass Apple Gazette (1970-1971)
The Harrison Herald/The George Gernal (1966-1972)
The Harrison Hugger (1967)
Kingdom Beat (1971-1972)
Lennon Lyrics/Norwegian Wood (1967-1968)
Louise Harrison Caldwell Fan Club (1965-1966)
Luv n Stuff (1967-1971)
Mrs. Lennon's Apple Farm (1971-72)
Newslennon (1968 - 1972)
Orange Apple Jam (1971-1972)
Paul McCartney Fan Club (1966-1968)
Paulie Press News (1968)
Pottie Birds Beatles (1968 - 1970)
Revolution (1970)
Simmons' B.S. Sheet (1970-1972)
Starr Times (1969-1970)
Trails of George and John (1969-1971)
The Tripper/The Natch (1966-1968)

Scan For Quote Index

Official Beatles Fan Club photos 1968-1971

Number from OBFC order forms	OBFC order form name	OBFC order form description	Year or years photo was available for purchase	Photo
No number	*Magical Mystery Tour*	8 x 10 glossy of the Beatles in the Magical Mystery Tour	1968-1970	
No number	autograph bonus	glossy photo officially autographed by the Beatles	1968	
1	Latest pics! (later called "India pics!")	Special photos taken just before the Beatles visit to India. Set consists of four individual photos of the Beatles.	1968 - 1970	
1	Latest pics! (later called "India pics!")		1968 - 1970	

1	Latest pics! (later called "India pics!")		1968 - 1970	
1	Latest pics! (later called "India pics!")		1968 -1970	
2	Our World	The entire set consists of 10 group shots of the Beatles. These pics were taken when The Beatles sang "All You Need Is Love" on the recent 'Our World' television special.	1968 (only)	
2	Our World		1968	

2	Our World		1968	
2	Our World		1968	
2	Our World		1968	
2	Our World		1968	
2	Our World		1968	
2	Our World		1968	

2	Our World		1968	
3	Our World		1968	
2	Our World		1968	
3	Hello Goodbye	We bring you two exciting pics of The Beatles as they appeared on the recent 'Ed Sullivan Show' singing "Hello Goodbye."	1968 - 1970	
3	Hello Goodbye		1968 -1970	

4	Beatles photo albums	We made up individual photo albums of each Beatle. There is one book devoted to Ringo, one to Paul, one to George, and one to John. Each book consists of collections of 7 pages of 8 x 10 photos.	1968 (originally sold in 1965) not available after 1968	THE JOHN LENNON PHOTO ALBUM
4	Beatles photo albums			THE PAUL McCARTNEY PHOTO ALBUM
4	Beatles photo albums			THE GEORGE HARRISON PHOTO ALBUM
4	Beatles photo albums			THE RINGO STARR PHOTO ALBUM

5	Special combination	You can order 15 assorted group shots that will include photos from 1, 2, 3	1968 (only)	
6	The Composers	A serious shot of Paul and John together after writing Revolution	1968-1970	
7	Gone with the Wind	All 4 out on a wind-blown venture	1968-1970	
8	The Invaders	All 4 in the weirdest get-up imaginable	1968-1970	
9 a	Paul	A great individual shot of Paul bound in chains without his shirt	1968-1970	

9 b	Paul	A super shot of Paul with his sheepdog, Martha	1968-1970	
10 a	John	An individual pic of John as you never saw him before. We call it "John. At his best."	1968 – 1970	
10 b	John	A close up of John wearing his crash helmet	1968 – 1970	
11 a	George	A look at George in a natural pose	1968 – 1970	
11 b	George	A lovable close-up, which is indescribable	1968 – 1970	

12 a	Ringo	A cute pic of Ringo with a parrot on his shoulder	1968 – 1970	
no number	Paul luvers of America	2 black and white 8 x 10 photos of Paul without his shirt	1969-1970	
no number	Paul luvers of America		1969-1970	
no number	John luvers of America	3 never before seen photos of John recording at EMI	1969	
no number	John luvers of America		1969	

no number	John luvers of America		1969	
no number	George Special	6 photos of George taken in a hotel room	1970	
no number	George Special		1970	
no number	George Special		1970	
no number	George Special		1970	

no number	George Special		1970	
no number	George Special`		1970	
1	India pics	same photos as 1 above		
2	The McCartneys	3 beautiful photos of Paul and Linda McCartney. These photos were taken in England, and we know you'll love them.	1970	
2	The McCartneys		1970	
2	The McCartneys		1970	

3	Hello Goodbye	Same 2 photos as 3 above		
4	Strawberry Fields/ Penny Lane	We bring you 7 super exciting photos from the promo films for Strawberry Fields and Penny Lane	These were first offered in 1967 and then again in 1969	
4	Strawberry Fields/ Penny Lane		1969-1970	
4	Strawberry Fields/ Penny Lane		1969-1970	
4	Strawberry Fields/ Penny Lane		1969-1970	
4	Strawberry Fields/ Penny Lane		1969-1970	
4	Strawberry Fields/ Penny Lane		1969-1970	

5	Relaxation Time	Ringo, Paul, and Paul's dog Martha outside in Paul's sun dome	1969-1970	
6	The Composers	same photo as #6 above		
7	Gone with the Wind	same photo as #7 above		
8	The Invaders	same photo as #8 above		
9a	Paul	same photo as #9a above		
9b	Paul	same photo as #9b above		
10a	John	same photo as #10a above		
10b	John	same photo as #10b above		
11a	George	same photo as #11a above		
11b	George	same photo as #11b above		
12a	Ringo	same photo as #12a above		
12b	Ringo	same photo as #12b above		
13	Revolution	Fabulous photo of all 4 Beatles. Taken from their film clip "Revolution" to coincide with the record.	1969-1970	

14	The Fab Four	John	1969-1970	
14	The Fab Four (5 pics)	Paul both serious and wearing a beautiful smile	1969-1970	
14	The Fab Four	George with windblown shoulder-length hair	1969-1970	
14	The Fab Four	Ringo more handsome than you ever have seen him look	1969-1970	
14 a	The Fab Four	Group shot	1969-1970	

15	New Two Some	Jackie Lomax and George Harrison	1969-1970	
16	Hey Jude	McCartney profile taken during Hey Jude	1969-1970	
17	Garden Meditation	The Beatles in one of their more serious moments taken in 1968	1970	
18	Group Inspiration	A group pic for a true Beatle fan. You'll flip over the pic of the creative quartet. Taken 1969	1970	
19	Come Together	This exciting group shot taken in the backyard of John's new home shows just how together the number one superstars of the '70s really are.	1970	

20	Oh Darling	Is much befitting Paul in this dreamy, romantic close-up Superpix that will steal the heart of any Beatle fan	1970	
21	Because	He's John Lennon, that's why! Because his expression makes you wonder what he'll be up to next, we off this new Superpix	1970	
22	I want you	There won't be a shadow of a doubt in your mind when you see this Superpix of Ringo's new image. "The Starr"	1970	
23	For You Blues	A smashing shot of George that gives off energy, gives off love, gives off light, and is guaranteed to provide an instant remedy for your blues	1970	

24	Dig It	And dig it you will when you get your hands on this great group picture taken in the alcoves of John's new house near Ascot	1970	
25	Super special	Get the newest photos #19-24 for $2		
26	Let it Be	Six Great shots from the film Let it Be	1970	
26	Let it Be		1970	
26	Let it Be		1970	

26	Let it Be		1970	
26	Let it Be		1970	
26	Let it Be	Six great shots from the film Let it Be	1970	
27	A Hard Day's Night	Four shots from the 1964 film	1970	
27	A Hard Day's Night		1970	

27	A Hard Day's Night		1970	
27	A Hard Day's Night		1970	
28	Help!	4 shots from the slopes of Austria to the sands of the Bahamas	1970	
28	Help!		1970	

28	Help!		1970	
28	Help!		1970	
29	The Early Sixties	Four Group photos of the early Beatles	1970	
29	The Early Sixties		1970	
29	The Early Sixties		1970	

29	The Early Sixties		1970	
no number	Ringo luvers of America	3 of the clearest, finest, most recent photos and completely different photo you have ever seen of Ringo	1970	
no number	Ringo luvers of America	Shades of the Magic Christian	1970	
no number	Ringo luvers of America		1970	
no number	John Special	taken onstage at the Toronto Festival	1970	

no number	John Special	taken at his home in Ascot	1970	
no number	John Special	Taken at his home in Ascot	1970	
No number	Paul in the studio		1971	
No number	Paul in the studio		1971	
No number	Paul in the Studio		1971	

The Official Beatles Fan Club Checklist

1964 Beatles (USA) Ltd. Membership kit items

- ☐ Beatles (USA) Ltd. membership card
- ☐ The Beatle Bulletin (A Hard Day's Night script)
- ☐ Beatles (USA) Ltd. book (1964 tour book)
- ☐ Tri-fold "Season's Greetings" record (postcard)
- ☐ Beatles fact sheet (mail away to receive)

1964 Fan Club items available to purchase

- ☐ Four 8 x 10 glossy photographs of each individual Beatle
- ☐ Fifteen 8 x 10 glossy photographs of The Beatles
- ☐ Seven 8 x 10 glossy photographs of The Beatles in A Hard Day's Night

1965 Beatles (USA) Ltd. Membership kit items

- ☐ The 1965 Beatle Bulletin (with one "Beatles Roulette" included)
- ☐ Beatles (USA) Ltd. book (1965 tour book)
- ☐ Christmas card

Brian Epstein Fan Club membership kit (free to any Beatles (USA) Ltd. member in 1965)

- ☐ Brian Epstein Fan Club membership card
- ☐ 8 x 10 glossy photograph of Brian Epstein
- ☐ Brian Epstein fact sheet
- ☐ 3 x 5 photo of Brian Epstein (mail away to receive)

1965 Fan Club items available to purchase

- ☐ Beatles photo albums (1 for each individual Beatle)
- ☐ Beatles Roulette – (1 pen and ink sketch of each Beatle by William Fogé)
- ☐ Beatles (USA) Ltd. book (1965 tour book)

1966 Beatles (USA) Ltd. Membership kit item

- ☐ The 1966 Beatle Bulletin
- ☐ 1966 Christmas record (postcard)

1966 Fan Club items available to purchase

- ☐ Help! hardback book
- ☐ Beatles (USA) Ltd. book (1966 tour book)

1967 Beatles (USA) Ltd. Membership kit items

- ☐ Sgt. Pepper poster (with The Beatles Bulletin on the back)
- ☐ 1967 Christmas record (postcard)

1967 Fan Club items available to purchase

- ☐ Seven 8 x 10 glossy photographs of The Beatles during the filming of "Strawberry Fields Forever / Penny Lane"
- ☐ Five 8 x 10 glossy photographs of The Beatles while recording "All You Need is Love"

1968 Official Beatles Fan Club Membership kit items

- [ ] Beatles Poster "India." (the image on this poster is flipped due to the use of a slide. The US poster does not have the Beatles Fan Club logo on the poster and has The Beatles Bulletin on the back)
- [ ] The Beatles Bulletin (dated September 1968)
- [ ] Christmas flexi-disc

1968 Fan Club items available to purchase

- [ ] 8 x 10 glossy "autographed" photograph of The Beatles before leaving for India
- [ ] 8 x 10 photograph of the Beatles from the film Magical Mystery Tour
- [ ] Four 8 x 10 individual photographs of each Beatle before leaving for India
- [ ] Ten 8 x 10 photographs of the group recording "All You Need is Love"
- [ ] Two 8 x 10 photographs of The Beatles from "Hello Goodbye"
- [ ] Three 8 x 10 photographs of The Beatles during the Mad Day Out
- [ ] Two 8 x 10 photographs of John during the Mad Day Out
- [ ] Two 8 x 10 photos of George during the Mad Day Out
- [ ] Two 8 x 10 photos of Paul during the Mad Day Out
- [ ] Two photos of Ringo from the Mad Day Out
- [ ] 30 x 22 "A is for Apple" poster
- [ ] The Beatles by Hunter Davies with an 18 x 30 color poster of the book's jacket

1969 Official Beatles Fan Club Membership kit items

- [ ] Official Beatles Fan Club 1969 Membership Card
- [ ] Beatles poster "Revelation" with Beatles Bulletin on the back (the image on this poster is flipped due to the use of slides)
- [ ] Welcome letter
- [ ] 1969 Beatles Book (color photo from the Mad Day Out on the cover)
- [ ] 1969 Christmas flexi-disc

1969 Fan Club items available to purchase

- [ ] "Groovy Couple" 8 x 10 photograph of George and Pattie
- [ ] "John Luvers of America" three 8 x 10 photographs of John during the recording of Abbey Road
- [ ] "The 2nd John Special" – three 8 x 10 photographs of John
- [ ] Four 8 x 10 photographs of The Beatles during the Mad Day Out
- [ ] "Paulie Luvvers of America" - two 8 x 10 photographs of Paul in chains during the Mad Day Out
- [ ] Ten 8 x 10 photographs of The Beatles making "Strawberry Fields Forever"/"Penny Lane"
- [ ] 8 x 10 photograph of The Beatles during the filming of "Revolution"
- [ ] Five 8 x 10 photographs of each Beatles and one group shot of the last photoshoot
- [ ] 8 x 10 photograph of Paul, Ringo, and Martha during the Mad Day Out
- [ ] 8 x 10 photograph of George and Jackie Lomax
- [ ] 8 x 10 photograph of Paul during the recording of "Hey Jude"

(cont'd)

☐ "Husbands and Wives Special" – Four color postcards of each Beatle with his wife

☐ 17 x 22 Beatles poster – "Something"/"Come Together"
(only 500 of these posters were sold)

- [ ] Eighteen different styles of Yellow Submarine stationery and envelopes
- [ ] Six 14 ½ x 10 ¼ color Yellow Submarine postcards
- [ ] Four Beatles Yellow Submarine bookmarks (one of each Beatle)
- [ ] Yellow Submarine Tri-books (1 ½ inch ring binder, 10 ½ x 8 inch fifty sheet composition book, and 7 ¾ x 5 inch 60 sheet notebook)

1970 Official Beatles Fan Club Membership kit items

- [ ] Official Beatles Fan Club 1970 membership card
- [ ] Welcome letter
- [ ] 1970 Beatles Book (has a photo from 1969 on the cover)
- [ ] Apple photo cube
- [ ] Beatles Christmas LP

1970 Fan Club items available to purchase

- ☐ Six 8 x 10 photographs from the film Let it Be
- ☐ Four 8 x 10 photographs from the film A Hard Day's Night
- ☐ Four 8 x 10 photographs from the film Help!
- ☐ Five 8 x 10 photographs of early Beatles
- ☐ Six 8 x 10 photographs of George taken in May of 1970
- ☐ "Ringo luvvers of America" - three 8 x 10 photographs of Ringo in the film The Magic Christian
- ☐ "The McCartneys" - two 8 x 10 photographs of Paul and Linda
- ☐ Three 8 x 10 photographs of The Beatles (Mad Day Out, Sailing of the Fritz & Last Photo Shoot)
- ☐ Four 8 x 10 photographs of the individual Beatles
- ☐ 8 x 10 photograph of The Beatles at Tittenhurst
- ☐ "John Special" - three 8 x 10 photographs of John with a beard
- ☐ 24 x 24 poster of Let it Be
- ☐ Let it Be book that came with the UK release of the album
- ☐ Beatles (USA) Ltd books (tour books for 1964, 1965, 1966)

1971 Official Beatles Fan Club/Apple Tree Membership kit items

- ☐ 1971 Official Beatles Fan Club membership card
- ☐ 1971 Beatles Book (Apple green cover)
- ☐ Apple Tree poster

1971 Fan Club items available for purchase

- ☐ Three 8 x 10 photographs of Paul in the studio taken by Linda

www.ingramcontent.com/pod-product-compliance
Lightning Source LLC
Chambersburg PA
CBHW081739100526
44592CB00015B/2233